THE MEANING OF MEANING

C. K. Ogden, 1889-1957, was educated at Magdalene College, Cambridge. In 1909 he began work on a study of International Commuication and the influence of language on thought. He visited schools and universities throughtout Europe, in India, and in the United States to study language-teaching methods. Dr. Ogden then organized the Orthological Institute. He was inventor of the Basic English system, an 850-word vocabulary designed to be an international language. In addition to books written in collaboration with I. A. Richards, Dr. Ogden is the author of *The Meaning of Psychology* (1926), *System of Basic English* (1934), *General Basic English Dictionary* (1942), and other books.

I. A. Richards was born in 1893 in Sandbach, Cheshire, England, and was educated at Clifton College in Bristol and at Magdalene College, Cambridge. In 1922 he became lecturer in English and Moral Sciences at Cambridge, and four years later was made a Fellow of Magdalene College. During this period he collaborated with C. K. Ogden on *Foundations of Aesthetics* (1921) and *The Meaning of Meaning* (1923). His later works include *Principles of Literary Criticism* (1925), *Practical Criticism* (1929; Harvest Book 16, 1956), *Coleridge on Imagination* (1935), *The Philosophy of Rhetoric* (1936), *How to Read a Page* (1942), *Speculative Instruments* (1955). In recent years he has published two volumes of verse, *Goodbye Earth and Other Poems* (1958) and *The Screens and Other Poems* (1960), and a verse play, *Tomorrow Morning, Faustus!* (1962). The National Institute of Arts and Letters awarded him the Loines Award for Poetry in 1962. He is now University Professor at Harvard University.

The Meaning of Meaning

A STUDY OF THE INFLUENCE OF LANGUAGE UPON THOUGHT AND OF THE SCIENCE OF SYMBOLISM

by

C. K. Ogden & I. A. Richards

WITH SUPPLEMENTARY ESSAYS BY

B. Malinowski *Ph.D., D.Sc.* and F. G. Crookshank *M.D., F.R.C.P.*

A Harvest/HBJ Book
Harcourt Brace Jovanovich
New York and London

ISBN 0-15-658446-8

NOP

FIRST PUBLISHED IN 1923

PREFACE

To the First Edition

THE following pages, some of which were written as long ago as 1910, have appeared for the most part in periodical form during 1920-22, and arise out of an attempt to deal directly with difficulties raised by the influence of Language upon Thought.

It is claimed that in the science of Symbolism,[1] the study of that influence, a new avenue of approach to traditional problems hitherto regarded as reserved for the philosopher and the metaphysician, has been found. And further that such an investigation of these problems is in accordance with the methods of the special sciences whose contributions have enabled the new study to be

[1] The word Symbolism has certain historical associations through the various dictionary meanings of 'symbol,' which are worth noting. In addition to its constant underlying sense of a sign or token (something 'put together') the term has already enjoyed two distinct *floruits*. The first, traceable to Cyprian, applies to the Creed regarded as the 'sign' of a Christian as distinguished from a heathen, as when Henry VIII talks about "the three Creeds or Symbols." A mythological perversion of the derivation (1450-1550, *Myrr. our Ladye* III, 312) states that "Thys crede ys called *Simbolum*, that ys to say a gatherynge of morselles, for eche of the xii. apostles put therto a morsel." Other historical details will be found in Schlesinger's *Geschichte des Symbols* (1923).

Secondly, there is the widespread use of the adjective Symbolist in the nineties to characterize those French poets who were in revolt against all forms of literal and descriptive writing, and who attached symbolic or esoteric meanings to particular objects, words and sounds. Similarly, art critics loosely refer to painters whose object is 'suggestion' rather than 'representation' or 'construction,' as symbolists.

In the following pages, however, a standpoint is indicated from which both these vague captions can be allotted their place in the system of signs and symbols; and stress is laid upon those aspects of symbolism whose neglect has given rise to so many false problems, both in æsthetics and in philosophy.

differentiated from vaguer speculations with which it might appear to be associated.

Amongst grammarians in particular a sense of uneasiness has prevailed. It has been felt that the study of language as hitherto conducted by traditional methods has failed to face fundamental issues in spite of its central position as regards all human intercourse. Efforts to make good the omission have been frequent throughout the present century, but volumes by painstaking philologists bearing such titles as *The Philosophy of Language*, *Principes de Linguistique Théorique* and *Voraussetzungen zur Grundlegung einer Kritik der allgemeinen Grammatik und Sprachphilosophie* have, as a rule, been devoid of fruitful suggestion. They have neither discovered the essential problems nor, with few exceptions, such as Bréal's *Semantics*, opened up interesting though subordinate fields of investigation. "Breadth of vision is not conspicuous in modern linguistics," says so well-informed an authority as Jespersen in his latest work; and he attributes this narrow outlook to "the fact that linguists have neglected all problems connected with the valuation of language." Unfortunately, Jespersen's own recommendations for a normative approach, the three questions which he urges philologists to consider—

> What is the criterion by which one word or one form should be preferred to another?
>
> Are the changes that we see gradually taking place in languages to be considered as on the whole beneficial, or the opposite?
>
> Would it be possible to construct an international language?—

hardly touch the central problem of meaning, or the relations of thought and language; nor can they be profitably discussed by philologists without a thorough examination of this neglected preliminary. And, as we shall see in our ninth chapter, philosophers and psychologists, who are often supposed to be occupied with such researches, have done regrettably little to help them.

There are some who find difficulty in considering any matter unless they can recognize it as belonging to what is called 'a subject' and who recognize a subject as something in which, somewhere at least, Professors give instruction and perhaps Examinations are undergone. These need only be reminded that at one time there were no subjects and until recently only five. But the discomfort experienced in entering the less familiar fields of inquiry is genuine. In more frequented topics the main roads, whether in the right places or not, are well marked, the mental traveller is fairly well assured of arriving at some well-known spot, whether worth visiting or not, and will usually find himself in respectable and accredited company. But with a new or border-line subject he is required to be more self-dependent; to decide for himself where the greater interest and importance lies and as to the results to be expected. He is in the position of a prospector. If the venture here recorded should be found to assist any others in the study of symbols, the authors will consider it justified. Needless to say they believe it to be of greater importance than this.

In order at least not to fail in the more modest aim of calling attention to a neglected group of problems, they have added as an Appendix a number of selected passages indicative of the main features of similar undertakings by other writers in the past.

Of their own contributions towards the foundations of a science of Symbolism the following seem to them to have most value:

(1) An account of *interpretation* in causal terms by which the treatment of language as a system of signs becomes capable of results, among which may be noticed the beginning of a division between what cannot be intelligibly talked of and what can.

(2) A division of the functions of language into two groups, the symbolic and the emotive. Many notorious controversies in the sciences it is believed can be shown to derive from confusion between these functions, the same words being used at once to make statements and to excite attitudes. No escape from the fictitious differences so produced is possible without an understanding of the language functions. With this understanding it is believed that such controversies as those between Vitalism and Mechanism, Materialism and Idealism, Religion and Science, etc., would lapse, and further the conditions would be restored under which a general revival of poetry would be possible.

(3) A dissection and ventilation of 'meaning' the centre of obscurantism both in the theory of knowledge and in all discussion.

(4) An examination of what are confusedly known as 'verbal questions.' Nothing is commoner in discussion than to hear some point of difference described as purely or largely 'verbal.' Sometimes the disputants are using the same words for different things, sometimes different words for the same things. So far as either is the case a freely mobilizable technique of definition meets the difficulty. But frequently the disputants are using the same (or different) words for nothing, and here greater modesty due to a livelier realization of the language situation is recommendable.

Hitherto no science has been able to deal directly with the issue, since what is fundamentally involved is the theory of Signs in general and their interpretation. The subject is one peculiarly suitable for collaboration, and in this way only is there reasonable hope of bringing to a practical issue an undertaking which has been abandoned in despair by so many enterprising but isolated inquirers, and of dispelling the suspicion of eccentricity which the subject has so often evoked. Historical research shows that since the lost work of Antisthenes and Plato's *Cratylus* there have been seven chief methods of attack—the Grammatical (Aristotle, Dionysius Thrax), the Metaphysical (The Nominalists, Meinong), the Philological (Horne Tooke, Max Müller), the Psychological (Locke, Stout), the Logical (Leibnitz, Russell) the Sociological (Steinthal, Wundt) and the Terminological (Baldwin, Husserl). From all these, as well as such independent studies as those of Lady Welby, Marty, and C. S. Peirce, from Mauthner's *Kritic der Sprache*, Erdmann's *Die Bedeutung des Wortes*, and Taine's *De l'Intelligence*, the writers have derived instruction and occasionally amusement.

To Dr Malinowski the authors owe a very special debt. His return to England as their work was passing through the press enabled them to enjoy the advantage of his many years of reflection as a field-worker in Ethnology on the peculiarly difficult border-lands of linguistics and psychology. His unique combination of practical experience with a thorough grasp of theoretical principles renders his agreement on so many of the more heterodox conclusions here reached particularly encouraging. The contribution from his pen dealing with the study of primitive languages, which appears as a Supplement, will, the writers feel sure, be of value not only to ethnologists but to all who take a living interest in words and their ways.

The practical importance of a science of Symbolism even in its present undeveloped form needs little emphasis. All the more elaborate forms of social and intellectual life are affected by changes in our attitude towards, and our use of, words. How words work is commonly regarded as a purely theoretical matter, of little interest to practical persons. It is true that the investigation must at times touch upon somewhat abstruse questions, but its disregard by practical persons is nevertheless short-sighted. The view that language works well enough as it is, can only be held by those who use it merely in such affairs as could be conducted without it—the business of the paper-boy or the butcher, for instance, where all that needs to be referred to can equally well be pointed at. None but those who shut their eyes to the hasty re-adaptation to totally new circumstances which the human race has during the last century been blindly endeavouring to achieve, can pretend that there is no need to examine critically the most important of all the instruments of civilization. New millions of participants in the control of general affairs must now attempt to form personal opinions upon matters which were once left to a few. At the same time the complexity of these matters has immensely increased. The old view that the only access to a subject is through prolonged study of it, has, if it be true, consequences for the immediate future which have not yet been faced. The alternative is to raise the level of communication through a direct study of its conditions, its dangers and its difficulties. The practical side of this undertaking is, if communication be taken in its widest sense, Education.

Convinced as they are of the urgency of a stricter examination of language from a point of view which is at present receiving no attention, the authors have preferred to publish this essay in its present form rather than to wait, perhaps indefinitely, until, in lives otherwise sufficiently occupied, enough moments of leisure had accumulated for it to be rewritten in a more complete and more systematized form. They are, they believe, better aware of its failings than most critics will suppose, and especially of those due to the peculiar difficulties which a fundamental criticism of language inevitably raises for the expositors thereof.

For two reasons the moment seems to have arrived when an effort to draw attention to Meaning may meet with support. In the first place there is a growing readiness amongst psychologists to admit the importance of the problem. "If the discovery of the psychological nature of Meaning were completely successful," writes Professor Pear (*Remembering and Forgetting*, 1923,

p. 59), "it might put an end to psychology altogether." Secondly, the realization that men of learning and sincerity are lamentably at the mercy of forms of speech cannot long be delayed, when we find for instance Lord Hugh Cecil concluding a reasoned statement of his attitude to Divorce with the words "The one thing, as it seems to me, that Christians are bound, as Christians, to resist, is any *proposal to call* that marriage which, according to the revelation of Christ, is adultery" (*The Times*, Jan. 2, 1923). The italics are ours.

It is inevitable in such a work that emphasis should be laid on what to some may appear to be obvious, and on the other hand that terms should be employed which will render portions of the inquiry less easy than others, owing to the alteration of the angle from which the subject is to be viewed. At the same time it is hoped that even those who have no previous acquaintance with the topics covered may, with a little patience, be able to follow the whole discussion, condensed though it has occasionally been in order to keep the exposition within reasonable compass. A full list of Contents, designed to be read as part of the book, has therefore been provided.

A Summary, a few Appendices on special problems, and many Cross-references have been added for the benefit of readers who have not the opportunity of devoting equal attention to every part of the field, or who desire to pursue the study further.

C. K. O.
I. A. R.

MAGDALENE COLLEGE,
CAMBRIDGE,
January 1923.

PREFACE

To the Second Edition

The peculiar reception of the First Edition of the present work by persons of the most diverse predilections, the fact that within two years of its publication it was officially used in a number of Universities, including Columbia, and in particular the marked interest which it excited in America, led the authors to meet, in New York, in the Spring of 1926, for purposes of discussion and revision. As a result it has been possible to take into account the requirements of a wider audience than that to which the book was primarily addressed. Not only have some local allusions been modified but various improvements in emphasis and structure will, it is hoped, have lightened the task of the reader.

At the same time no change in the positions maintained has been found necessary. The authors, however, have not been idle, and some reference to the supplementary works for which they have been responsible may not be out of place. *Principles of Literary Criticism* (I. A. R.) endeavours to provide for the emotive function of language the same critical foundation as is here attempted for the symbolic. *Word Magic* (C. K. O.) will present the historical and philological apparatus by the aid of which alone can current linguistic habits be explained—and it has been possible to reduce the inordinate length of an original Chapter II in view of this independent study. A general introduction to the psychological problems of language study will be found in *The Meaning of Psychology* (C. K. O.) while *Science and Poetry* (I. A. R.) discusses the place and future of literature in our civilization.

But these additions still leave much of the new ground opened by *The Meaning of Meaning* to be explored. Chief among these desiderata are the development of an educational technique whereby both the child and the adult may be assisted to a better use of language, the investigation of the general principles of notation with its bearing on the problem of a universal scientific language, and the analytical task of discovering a grammar by means of which translation from one symbol-system to another could be controlled. These are projects which demand an Institute of Linguistic Research with headquarters in Geneva, New York, and Peking.

CAMBRIDGE,
June, 1926.

C. K. O.
I. A. R.

PREFACE

To the Third Edition

THE demand for a Third Edition affords us an opportunity of correcting a number of minor errors and discrepancies. Of the desiderata to which reference is made above, the second and the third have been the object of attention in *Basic English* (C. K. O.), a system of English adapted to the requirements of a Universal Language, and described in Vols. IX and X of *Psyche* (1928-30); with the first, *Practical Criticism* (I. A. R.), an educational application of Chapter X, is concerned, and the experience gained by its author as Visiting Professor at Peking (1929-30) makes the need for further work upon all these questions appear still more urgent.

CAMBRIDGE,
January, 1930.

C. K. O.
I. A. R.

PREFACE

To the Fourth Edition

In this edition we have removed a few inconsistencies and obscurities noted during a correspondence with Dr. Ishibashi who has translated the work into Japanese (1936).

Since the appearance of the Third Edition, *Bentham's Theory of Fictions* (C. K. O.) has focussed attention on a neglected contribution to the subject which is of more than historical interest. *Mencius on the Mind* (I. A. R.) examines the difficulties which beset the translator and explores the technique of multiple definition, which is further elucidated in *Basic Rules of Reason* (I. A. R.). *Coleridge on Imagination* (I. A. R.) offers a new estimate of Coleridge's theory in the light of a more adequate evaluation of emotive language. *Opposition* (C. K. O.) is an analysis of an aspect of definition which is of particular importance for linguistic simplification.

Cambridge,
May, 1936.

C. K. O.
I. A. R.

PREFACE

To the Eighth Edition

The curiosity aroused by references to this work in a number of popular applications of the principles of linguistic therapy here advocated, and by the widespread adoption of Basic English as an educational method, has necessitated further printings. In the four latest editions we have made a few further changes, and have expanded certain parts of Chapters II and X in separate publications —*Psyche*, Vols. XVI-XVIII (C. K. O.), and *Interpretation in Teaching* and *How to Read a Page* (I. A. R.).

Cambridge,
May, 1946.

C. K. O.
I. A. R.

CONTENTS

Chapter IV

SIGNS IN PERCEPTION

Chapter V

THE CANONS OF SYMBOLISM

Chapter VI

DEFINITION

Chapter VII

THE MEANING OF BEAUTY

Chapter VIII

THE MEANING OF PHILOSOPHERS

Chapter IX

THE MEANING OF MEANING

Chapter X

SYMBOL SITUATIONS

SUPPLEMENTS

THE MEANING OF MEANING

"*All life comes back to the question of our speech—the medium through which we communicate.*" —HENRY JAMES.

"*Error is never so difficult to be destroyed as when it has its root in Language.*" —BENTHAM.

"*We have to make use of language, which is made up necessarily of preconceived ideas. Such ideas unconsciously held are the most dangerous of all.*" —POINCARÉ.

"*By the grammatical structure of a group of languages everything runs smoothly for one kind of philosophical system, whereas the way is as it were barred for certain other possibilities.*" —NIETZSCHE.

"*An Englishman, a Frenchman, a German, and an Italian cannot by any means bring themselves to think quite alike, at least on subjects that involve any depth of sentiment: they have not the verbal means.*" —Prof. J. S. MACKENZIE.

"*In Primitive Thought the name and object named are associated in such wise that the one is regarded as a part of the other. The imperfect separation of words from things characterizes Greek speculation in general.*" —HERBERT SPENCER.

"*The tendency has always been strong to believe that whatever receives a name must be an entity or being, having an independent existence of its own: and if no real entity answering to the name could be found, men did not for that reason suppose that none existed, but imagined that it was something peculiarly abstruse and mysterious, too high to be an object of sense.*" —J. S. MILL.

"*Nothing is more usual than for philosophers to encroach on the province of grammarians, and to engage in disputes of words, while they imagine they are handling controversies of the deepest importance and concern.*" —HUME.

"*Men content themselves with the same words as other people use, as if the very sound necessarily carried the same meaning.*" —LOCKE.

"*A verbal discussion may be important or unimportant, but it is at least desirable to know that it is verbal.*" —Sir G. CORNEWALL LEWIS.

"*Scientific controversies constantly resolve themselves into differences about the meaning of words.*" —Prof. A. SCHUSTER.

CHAPTER I

THOUGHTS, WORDS AND THINGS

Let us get nearer to the fire, so that we can see what we are saying.
—*The Bubis of Fernando Po.*

THE influence of Language upon Thought has attracted the attention of the wise and foolish alike, since Lao Tse came long ago to the conclusion—

"He who knows does not speak, he who speaks does not know."

Sometimes, in fact, the wise have in this field proved themselves the most foolish. Was it not the great Bentley, Master of Trinity College, Cambridge, Archdeacon of Bristol, and holder of two other livings besides, who declared: "We are sure, from the names of persons and places mentioned in Scripture before the Deluge, not to insist upon other arguments, that Hebrew was the primitive language of mankind"? On the opposite page are collected other remarks on the subject of language and its Meaning, and whether wise or foolish, they at least raise questions to which, sooner or later, an answer is desirable. In recent years, indeed, the existence and importance of this problem of Meaning have been generally admitted, but by some sad chance those who have attempted a solution have too often been forced to relinquish their ambition—whether through old age, like Leibnitz, or penury, like C. S. Peirce, or both. Even the methods by which it is to be attacked have remained in doubt. Each science has tended to delegate the unpleasant task to another. With the errors and omissions of metaphysicians we shall be much concerned in the sequel, and philologists must bear their share of the guilt. Yet it is a philologist who, of recent years, has, perhaps, realized most clearly the necessity of a broader treatment.

"Throughout the whole history of the human race," wrote the late Dr Postgate, "there have been no questions which have caused more heart-searchings, tumults, and devastation than questions of the correspondence of words to facts. The mere mention of such words as 'religion,' 'patriotism,' and 'property' is sufficient to demonstrate this truth. Now, it is the investigation of the nature of the correspondence between word and fact, to use these terms in the widest sense, which is the proper and the highest problem of the science of meaning. That every living word is rooted in facts of our mental consciousness and history it would be impossible to gainsay; but it is a very different matter to determine what these facts may be. The primitive conception is undoubtedly that the name is indicative, or descriptive, of the thing. From which it would follow at once that from the presence of the name you could argue to the existence of the thing. This is the simple conception of the savage."

In thus stressing the need for a clear analysis of the relation between words and facts as the essential of a theory of Meaning, Dr Postgate himself was fully aware that at some point the philosophical and psychological aspects of that theory cannot be avoided. When he wrote (1896), the hope was not unreasonable that the science of Semantics would do something to bridge the gulf. But, although M. Bréal's researches drew attention to a number of fascinating phenomena in the history of language, and awakened a fresh interest in the educational possibilities of etymology, the net result was disappointing. That such disappointment was inevitable may be seen, if we consider the attitude to language implied by such a passage as the following. The use of words as though their meaning were fixed, the constant resort to loose metaphor, the hypostatization of leading terms, all indicate an unsuitable attitude in which to approach the question.

"Substantives are signs attached to things: they contain exactly that amount of truth which can be contained by a name, an amount which is of necessity small in proportion to the reality of the object. That which is most adequate to its object is the abstract noun, since it represents a simple operation of the mind. When I use the two words *compressibility, immortality,* all that is to be found in the idea is to be found also in the word. But if I take a real entity, an object existing in nature, it will be impossible for language to introduce into the word all the ideas which this entity or object awakens in the mind. Language is therefore compelled to choose. Out of all the ideas it can choose one only; it thus creates a name which is not long in becoming a mere sign.

For this name to be accepted it must, no doubt, originally possess some true and striking characteristic on one side or another; it must satisfy the minds of those to whom it is first submitted. But this condition is imperative only at the outset. Once accepted, it rids itself rapidly of its etymological signification; otherwise this signification might become an embarrassment. Many objects are inaccurately named, whether through the ignorance of the original authors, or by some intervening change which disturbs the harmony between the sign and the thing signified. Nevertheless, words answer the same purpose as though they were of faultless accuracy. No one dreams of revising them. They are accepted by a tacit consent of which we are not even conscious" (Bréal's *Semantics*, pp. 171-2).

What exactly is to be made of substantives which "contain" truth, "that amount of truth which can be contained by a name"? How can "all that is found in the idea be also found in the word"? The conception of language as "compelled to choose an idea," and thereby creating "a name, which is not long in becoming a sign," is an odd one; while 'accuracy' and 'harmony' are sadly in need of elucidation when applied to naming and to the relation between sign and thing signified respectively. This is not mere captious criticism. The locutions objected to conceal the very facts which the science of language is concerned to elucidate. The real task before that science cannot be successfully attempted without a far more critical consciousness of the dangers of such loose verbiage. It is impossible to handle a scientific matter in such metaphorical terms, and the training of philologists has not, as a rule, been such as to increase their command of analytic and abstract language. The logician would be far better equipped in this respect were it not that his command of language tends to conceal from him what he is talking about and renders him prone to accept purely linguistic constructions, which serve well enough for his special purposes, as ultimates.

How great is the tyranny of language over those who propose to inquire into its workings is well shown in the speculations of the late F. de Saussure, a writer regarded by perhaps a majority of French and Swiss students as having for the first time placed linguistic upon a scientific basis. This author begins by inquiring, "What is the object at once integral and concrete of linguistic?" He does not ask whether it has one, he obeys blindly the primitive impulse to infer from a word some object for which it stands, and sets out determined to find it. But, he continues, speech (*le langage*), though concrete enough, as a set of events is not integral. Its sounds imply movements of speech, and both, as instruments of thought, imply ideas. Ideas, he adds, have a social as well as an individual side, and at each instant language implies both an established system and an evolution. "Thus, from whatever side we approach the question, we nowhere find the integral object of linguistic." De Saussure does not pause at this point to ask himself what he is looking for, or whether there is any reason why there should be such a thing. He proceeds instead in a fashion familiar in the beginnings of all sciences, and concocts a suitable object—'*la langue*,' the language, as opposed to speech.

"What is *la langue?* For us, it is not to be confounded with speech (*le langage*); it is only a determinate part of this, an essential part, it is true. It is at once a social product of the faculty, of speech, and a collection of necessary conventions adopted by the social body to allow the exercise of this faculty by individuals. . . . It is a whole in itself and a principle of classification. As soon as we give it the first place among the facts of speech we introduce a natural order in a whole which does not lend itself to any other classification." *La langue* is further "the sum of the verbal images stored up in all the individuals, a treasure deposited by the practice of speaking in the members of a given community; a grammatical system, virtually existing in each brain, or more exactly in the brains of a body of individuals; for *la langue* is not complete in any one of them, it exists in perfection only in the mass."[1]

Such an elaborate construction as *la langue* might, no doubt, be arrived at by some Method of Intensive Distraction analogous to that with which Dr Whitehead's name is associated, but as a guiding principle for a young science it is fantastic. Moreover, the same device of inventing verbal entities outside the range of possible investigation proved fatal to the theory of signs which followed.[2]

[1] *Cours de Linguistique Générale*, pp. 23-31.

[2] A sign for de Saussure is twofold, made up of a concept (signifié) and an acoustic image (signifiant), both psychical entities. Without the concept, he says, the acoustic image would not be a sign (p. 100). The disadvantage of this account is, as we shall see, that the process of interpretation is included by definition in the sign!

De Saussure actually prided himself upon having "defined things and not words." The definitions thus established "have nothing to fear," he writes, "from certain ambiguous terms which do not coincide in one language and another. Thus in German *Sprache* means '*langue*' and '*langage*.' . . . In Latin *sermo* rather signifies *langage et parole* while *lingua* designates '*la langue*,' and so on. No word corresponds exactly to any of the notions made precise above; this is why every definition made apropos of a word is idle; it is a bad method, to start from words to define things" (*ibid.*, p. 32). The view of definition here adopted implies, as will be shown later, remarkable ignorance of the normal procedure—the substitution, namely, of better understood for obscure symbols. Another specimen of this naivety is found in the rejection of the term 'symbol' to designate the linguistic sign (p. 103). "The symbol has the character of never being quite arbitrary. It

As a philologist with an inordinate respect for linguistic convention, de Saussure could not bear to tamper with what he imagined to be a fixed meaning, a part of *la langue*. This scrupulous regard for fictitious 'accepted' uses of words is a frequent trait in philologists. Its roots go down very deep into human nature, as we shall see in the two chapters which follow. It is especially regrettable that a technical equipment, otherwise excellent, should have been so weak at this point, for the initial recognition of a general science of signs, 'semiology,' of which linguistic would be a branch, and the most important branch, was a very notable attempt in the right direction. Unfortunately this theory of signs, by neglecting entirely the things for which signs stand, was from the beginning cut off from any contact with scientific methods of verification. De Saussure, however, does not appear to have pursued the matter far enough for this defect to become obvious. The same neglect also renders the more recent treatise of Professor Delacroix, *Le Langage et la Pensée*, ineffective as a study of the influence of language upon thought.

Philosophers and philologists alike have failed in their attempts. There remains a third group of inquirers with an interest in linguistic theory, the ethnologists, many of whom have come to their subject after a preliminary training in psychology. An adequate account of primitive peoples is impossible without an insight into the essentials of their languages, which cannot be gained through a mere transfer of current Indo-European grammatical distinctions, a procedure only too often positively misleading. In the circumstances, each field investigator might be supposed to reconstruct the grammar of a primitive tongue from his own observations of the behaviour of a speaker in a given situation. Unfortunately this is rarely done,

is not empty; there is the rudiment of a natural tie between the signifying and the signified. The symbol for justice, the scales, could not be replaced by something else at random, a carriage for instance."

since the difficulties are very great; and perhaps owing to accidents of psychological terminology, the worker tends to neglect the concrete environment of the speaker and to consider only the 'ideas' which are regarded as 'expressed.' Thus Dr Boas, the most suggestive and influential of the group of ethnologists which is dealing with the vast subject-matter provided by the American-Indian languages, formulates as the three points to be considered in the objective discussion of languages—

> First, the constituent phonetic elements of the language;
>
> Second, the groups of ideas expressed by phonetic groups;
>
> Third, the method of combining and modifying phonetic groups.

"All speech," says Dr Boas explicitly, "is intended to serve for the communication of ideas." Ideas, however, are only remotely accessible to outside inquirers, and we need a theory which connects words with things through the ideas, if any, which they symbolize. We require, that is to say, separate analyses of the relations of words to ideas and of ideas to things. Further, much language, especially primitive language, is not primarily concerned with ideas at all, unless under 'ideas' are included emotions and attitudes—a procedure which would involve terminological inconveniences. The omission of all separate treatment of the ways in which speech, besides conveying ideas, also expresses attitudes, desires and intentions,[1] is another point at which the work of this active school is at present defective.

[1] Not that definitions are lacking which include more than ideas. Thus in one of the ablest and most interesting of modern linguistic studies, that of E. Sapir, Chief of the Anthropological Section, Geological Survey of Canada, an ethnologist closely connected with the American school, language is defined as "a purely human and non-instinctive method of communicating ideas, emotions and desires by means of a system of voluntarily produced symbols" (*Language*, 1922, p. 7). But so little is the emotive element considered that in a discussion of grammatical form, as shown by the great variation of word-order in Latin, we find it stated that the change from 'hominem femina videt'

In yet another respect all these specialists fail to realize the deficiencies of current linguistic theory. Preoccupied as they are—ethnologists with recording the details of fast vanishing languages; philologists with an elaborate technique of phonetic laws and principles of derivation; philosophers with 'philosophy'—all have overlooked the pressing need for a better understanding of what actually occurs in discussion. The analysis of the process of communication is partly psychological, and psychology has now reached a stage at which this part may be successfully undertaken. Until this had happened the science of Symbolism necessarily remained in abeyance, but there is no longer any excuse for vague talk about Meaning, and ignorance of the ways in which words deceive us.

Throughout the Western world it is agreed that people must meet frequently, and that it is not only agreeable to talk, but that it is a matter of common courtesy to say something even when there is hardly anything to say. "Every civilized man," continues the late Professor Mahaffy, to whose *Principles of the Art of Conversation* we owe this observation, "feels, or ought to feel, this duty; it is the universal accomplishment which all must practise"; those who fail are punished by the dislike or neglect of society.

There is no doubt an Art in saying something when

to 'videt femina hominem' makes "little or no difference beyond, *possibly*, a rhetorical or a *stylistic* one" (p. 65). The italics are ours; and the same writer sums up his discussion of the complex symbol 'The farmer kills the duckling,' with the remark: "In this short sentence of five words there are expressed thirteen distinct concepts" (p. 93). As will be noted at a later stage, the use of the term 'concept' is particularly unfortunate in such an analysis, and a vocabulary so infested with current metaphysical confusions leads unavoidably to incompleteness of treatment.

By being forced to include under 'concepts' both 'concrete concepts'—material objects, and 'Pure relational concepts' (abstract ways of referring), Sapir is unable in this work—which was unfortunately never followed by his projected volume on Linguistics—to make even the distinctions which are essential inside symbolic language (cf. Chapter V., p. 101 *infra*); and when we come to deal with translation (Chapter X., p. 228) we shall find that this vocabulary has proved equally unserviceable to him.

there is nothing to be said, but it is equally certain that there is an Art no less important of saying clearly what one wishes to say when there is an abundance of material; and conversation will seldom attain even the level of an intellectual pastime if adequate methods of Interpretation are not also available.

Symbolism is the study of the part played in human affairs by language and symbols of all kinds, and especially of their influence on Thought. It singles out for special inquiry the ways in which symbols help us and hinder us in reflecting on things.

Symbols direct and organize, record and communicate. In stating what they direct and organize, record and communicate we have to distinguish as always between Thoughts and Things.[1] It is Thought (or, as we shall usually say, *reference*) which is directed and organized, and it is also Thought which is recorded and communicated. But just as we say that the gardener mows the lawn when we know that it is the lawn-mower which actually does the cutting, so, though we know that the direct relation of symbols is with thought, we also say that symbols record events and communicate facts.

By leaving out essential elements in the language situation we easily raise problems and difficulties which vanish when the whole transaction is considered in greater detail. Words, as every one now knows, 'mean' nothing by themselves, although the belief

[1] The word 'thing' is unsuitable for the analysis here undertaken, because in popular usage it is restricted to material substances—a fact which has led philosophers to favour the terms 'entity,' 'ens' or 'object' as the general name for whatever is. It has seemed desirable, therefore, to introduce a technical term to stand for whatever we may be thinking of or referring to. 'Object,' though this is its original use, has had an unfortunate history. The word 'referent,' therefore, has been adopted, though its etymological form is open to question when considered in relation to other participial derivatives, such as agent or reagent. But even in Latin the present participle occasionally (e.g. *vehens* in equo) admitted of variation in use; and in English an analogy with substantives, such as 'reagent,' 'extent,' and 'incident' may be urged. Thus the fact that 'referent' in what follows stands for a thing and not an active person, should cause no confusion.

that they did, as we shall see in the next chapter, was once equally universal. It is only when a thinker makes use of them that they stand for anything, or, in one sense, have 'meaning.' They are instruments. But besides this referential use which for all reflective, intellectual use of language should be paramount, words have other functions which may be grouped together as emotive. These can best be examined when the framework of the problem of strict statement and intellectual communication has been set up. The importance of the emotive aspects of language is not thereby minimized, and anyone chiefly concerned with popular or primitive speech might well be led to reverse this order of approach. Many difficulties, indeed, arising through the behaviour of words in discussion, even amongst scientists, force us at an early stage to take into account these 'non-symbolic' influences. But for the analysis of the senses of 'meaning' with which we are here chiefly concerned, it is desirable to begin with the relations of thoughts, words and things as they are found in cases of reflective speech uncomplicated by emotional, diplomatic, or other disturbances; and with regard to these, the indirectness of the relations between words and things is the feature which first deserves attention.

This may be simply illustrated by a diagram, in which the three factors involved whenever any statement is made, or understood, are placed at the corners of the triangle, the relations which hold between them being represented by the sides. The point just made can be restated by saying that in this respect the base of the triangle is quite different in composition from either of the other sides.

Between a thought and a symbol causal relations hold. When we speak, the symbolism we employ is caused partly by the reference we are making and partly by social and psychological factors—the purpose for which we are making the reference, the proposed effect of our symbols on other persons, and our own attitude. When we hear what is said, the symbols both cause us to perform an act of reference and to assume an attitude which will, according to circumstances, be more or less similar to the act and the attitude of the speaker.

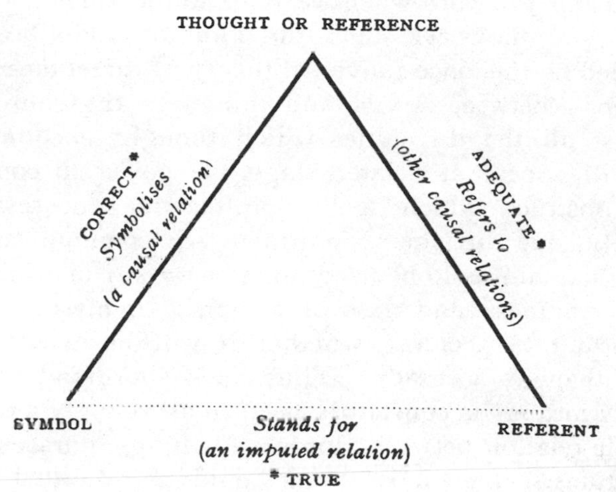

Between the Thought and the Referent there is also a relation ; more or less direct (as when we think about or attend to a coloured surface we see), or indirect (as when we 'think of' or 'refer to' Napoleon), in which case there may be a very long chain of sign-situations intervening between the act and its referent : word—historian—contemporary record—eye-witness—referent (Napoleon).

Between the symbol and the referent there is no relevant relation other than the indirect one, which consists in its being used by someone to stand for a referent. Symbol and Referent, that is to say, are not connected directly (and when, for grammatical reasons, we imply such a relation, it will merely be an imputed,[1]

* Cf. Chapter V., pp. 101-2.
[1] See Chapter VI., p. 116.

as opposed to a real, relation) but only indirectly round the two sides of the triangle.[1]

It may appear unnecessary to insist that there is no direct connection between say 'dog,' the word, and certain common objects in our streets, and that the only connection which holds is that which consists in our using the word when we refer to the animal. We shall find, however, that the kind of simplification typified by this once universal theory of direct meaning relations between words and things is the source of almost all the difficulties which thought encounters. As will appear at a later stage, the power to confuse and obstruct, which such simplifications possess, is largely due to the conditions of communication. Language if it is to be used must be a *ready* instrument. The handiness and ease of a phrase is always more important in deciding whether it will be extensively used than its accuracy. Thus such shorthand as the word 'means' is constantly used so as to imply a direct simple relation between words and things, phrases and situations. If such relations could be admitted then there would of course be no problem as to the nature

[1] An exceptional case occurs when the symbol used is more or less directly like the referent for which it is used, as for instance, it may be when it is an onomatopœic word, or an image, or a gesture, or a drawing. In this case the triangle is completed; its base is supplied, and a great simplification of the problem involved appears to result. For this reason many attempts have been made to reduce the normal language situation to this possibly more primitive form. Its greater completeness does no doubt account for the immense superiority in efficiency of gesture languages, within their appropriate field, to other languages not supportable by gesture within *their* fields. Hence we know far more perfectly what has occurred if a scene is well re-enacted than if it be merely described. But in the normal situation we have to recognize that our triangle is without its base, that between Symbol and Referent no direct relation holds; and, further, that it is through this lack that most of the problems of language arise. Simulative and non-simulative languages are entirely distinct in principle. Standing for and representing are different relations. It is, however, convenient to speak at times as though there were some direct relation holding between Symbol and Referent. We then say, on the analogy of the lawn-mower, that a Symbol refers to a Referent. Provided that the telescopic nature of the phrase is not forgotten, confusion need not arise. In Supplement I., Part V. *infra*, Dr Malinowski gives a valuable account of the development of the speech situation in relation to the above diagram.

of Meaning, and the vast majority of those who have been concerned with it would have been right in their refusal to discuss it. But too many interesting developments have been occurring in the sciences, through the rejection of everyday symbolizations and the endeavour to replace them by more accurate accounts, for any naïve theory that 'meaning' is just 'meaning' to be popular at the moment. As a rule new facts in startling disagreement with accepted explanations of other facts are required before such critical analyses of what are generally regarded as simple satisfactory notions are undertaken. This has been the case with the recent revolutions in physics. But in addition great reluctance to postulate anything *sui generis* and of necessity undetectable [1] was needed before the simple natural notion of simultaneity, for instance, as a two-termed relation came to be questioned. Yet to such questionings the theory of Relativity was due. The same two motives, new discrepant facts, and distaste for the use of obscure kinds of entities in eking out explanations, have led to disturbances in psychology, though here the required restatements have not yet been provided. No Copernican revolution has yet occurred, although several are due if psychology is to be brought into line with its fellow sciences.

It is noteworthy, however, that recent stirrings in psychology have been mainly if not altogether concerned with feeling and volition. The popular success of Psycho-analysis has tended to divert attention from the older problem of thinking. Yet in so far as progress here has consequences for all the other sciences and for the whole technique of investigation in psychology itself, this central problem of knowing or of 'meaning' is perhaps better worth scrutiny and more likely to promote fresh orientations than any other that can be suggested. As the Behaviorists have also very

[1] Places and instants are very typical entities of verbal origin.

properly pointed out, this question is closely connected with the use of words.

But the approach to Meaning, far more than the approach to such problems as those of physics, requires a thorough-going investigation of language. Every great advance in physics has been at the expense of some generally accepted piece of metaphysical explanation which had enshrined itself in a convenient, universally practised, symbolic shorthand. But the confusion and obstruction due to such shorthand expressions and to the naïve theories they protect and keep alive, is greater in psychology, and especially in the theory of knowledge, than elsewhere; because no problem is so infected with so-called metaphysical difficulties—due here, as always, to an approach to a question through symbols without an initial investigation of their functions.

We have now to consider more closely what the causes and effects of symbols are.[1] Whatever may be the services, other than conservative and retentive, of symbolization, all experience shows that there are also disservices. The grosser forms of verbal confusion have long been recognized; but less attention has been paid to those that are more subtle and more frequent. In the following chapters many examples of these will be given, chosen in great part from philosophical fields, for it is here that such confusions become, with the passage of time, most apparent. The root of the trouble will be traced to the superstition that words are in some way parts of things or always imply things corresponding to them, historical instances of this still potent

[1] Whether symbols in some form or other are necessary to thought itself is a difficult problem, and is discussed in *The Meaning of Psychology* (Chapter XIII.) as well as in Chapter X. of the present work. But certainly the recording and the communication of thought (telepathy apart) require symbols. It seems that thought, so far as it is transitive and not in the form of an internal dialogue, can dispense with symbols, and that they only appear when thought takes on this monologue form. In the normal case the actual development of thought is very closely bound up with the symbolization which accompanies it.

instinctive belief being given from many sources. The fundamental and most prolific fallacy is, in other words, that the base of the triangle given above is filled in.

The completeness of any reference varies; it is more or less close and clear, it 'grasps' its object in greater or less degree. Such symbolization as accompanies it—images of all sorts, words, sentences whole and in pieces—is in no very close observable connection with the variation in the perfection of the reference. Since, then, in any discussion we cannot immediately settle from the nature of a person's remarks what his opinion is, we need some technique to keep the parties to an argument in contact and to clear up misunderstandings—or, in other words, a Theory of Definition. Such a technique can only be provided by a theory of knowing, or of reference, which will avoid, as current theories do not, the attribution to the knower of powers which it may be pleasant for him to suppose himself to possess, but which are not open to the only kind of investigation hitherto profitably pursued, the kind generally known as scientific investigation.

Normally, whenever we hear anything said we spring spontaneously to an immediate conclusion, namely, that the speaker is referring to what we should be referring to were we speaking the words ourselves. In some cases this interpretation may be correct; this will prove to be what he has referred to. But in most discussions which attempt greater subtleties than could be handled in a gesture language this will not be so. To suppose otherwise is to neglect our subsidiary gesture languages, whose accuracy within their own limited provinces is far higher than that yet reached by any system of spoken or written symbols, with the exception of the quite special and peculiar case of mathematical, scientific and musical notations. Words, whenever they cannot directly ally themselves with and support themselves upon gestures, are at present a very imperfect means of communication. Even for private thinking thought is often ready to advance, and only held back by the treachery of its natural symbolism; and for conversational purposes the latitude acquired constantly shows itself to all those who make any serious attempts to compare opinions.

We have not here in view the more familiar ways in which words may be used to deceive. In a later chapter, when the function of language as an instrument for the *promotion of purposes* rather than as a means of *symbolizing references* is fully discussed, we shall see how the intention of the speaker may complicate the situation. But the *honnête homme* may be unprepared for the lengths to which verbal ingenuity can be carried. At all times these possibilities have been exploited to the full by interpreters of Holy Writ who desire to enjoy the best of both worlds. Here, for example, is a specimen of the exegetic of the late Dr Lyman Abbott, pastor, publicist, and editor, which, through the efforts of Mr Upton Sinclair, has now become classic. Does Christianity condemn the methods of twentieth-century finance? Doubtless there are some awkward words in the Gospels, but a little 'interpretation' is all that is necessary.

"Jesus did not say 'Lay not up for yourselves treasures upon earth.' He said 'Lay not up for yourselves treasures upon earth *where moth and rust doth corrupt and where thieves break through and steal*.' And no sensible American does. Moth and rust do not get at Mr Rockefeller's oil wells, and thieves do not often break through and steal a railway. What Jesus condemned was hoarding wealth."

Each investment, therefore, every worldly acquisition, according to one of the leading divines of the New World, may be judged on its merits. There is no hard and fast rule. When moth and rust have been eliminated by science the Christian investor will presumably have no problem, but in the meantime it would seem that Camphorated Oil fulfils most nearly the synoptic requirements. Burglars are not partial to it; it is anathema to moth; and the risk of rust is completely obviated.

Another variety of verbal ingenuity closely allied to this, is the deliberate use of symbols to misdirect the listener. Apologies for such a practice in the case of the madman from whom we desire to conceal the whereabouts of his razor are well known, but a wider justification has also been attempted. In the Christian era we hear of "falsifications of documents, inventions of legends, and forgeries of every description which made the Catholic Church a veritable seat of lying.'[1] A play upon words in which one sense is taken by the speaker and another sense intended by him for the hearer was permitted.[2] Indeed, three sorts of equivocations were distinguished by Alfonso de Liguori, who was beatified in the nineteenth century, which might be used with good reason;[3] a good reason being "any honest object, such as keeping our goods, spiritual or temporal."[4] In the twentieth century the intensification of militant nationalism has added further 'good reason'; for the military code includes all transactions with hostile nations or individuals as part of the process of keeping spiritual and temporal goods. In war-time words become a normal part of the mechanism of deceit, and the ethics of the situation have been aptly summed up by Lord Wolseley: "We will keep hammering along with the conviction that 'honesty is the best policy,' and that truth always wins in the long run. These pretty sentences do well for a child's copy-book, but the man who acts upon them in war had better sheathe his sword for ever."[5]

[1] Westermarck, *The Origin and Development of Moral Ideas*, Vol. II., p. 100.
[2] Alagona, *Compendium Manualis D. Navarri* XII., 88. p. 94.
[3] Alfonso di Liguori, *Theologia Moralis*, III., 151, Vol. I., p. 249.
[4] Meyrick, *Moral and Devotional Theology of the Church of Rome*, Vol. I., p 3. Cf. further Westermarck, *loc. cit.*
[5] *Soldier's Pocket Book for Field Service*, p. 69.

The Greeks, as we shall see, were in many ways not far from the attitude of primitive man towards words. And it is not surprising to read that after the Peloponnesian war the verbal machinery of peace had got completely out of gear, and, says Thucydides, could not be brought back into use—"The meaning of words had no longer the same relation to things, but was changed by men as they thought proper." The Greeks were powerless to cope with such a situation. We in our wisdom seem to have created institutions which render us more powerless still.[1]

On a less gigantic scale the technique of deliberate misdirection can profitably be studied with a view to corrective measures. In accounting for Newman's *Grammar of Assent* Dr E. A. Abbott had occasion to describe the process of 'lubrication,' the art of greasing the descent from the premises to the conclusion, which his namesake cited above so aptly employs. In order to lubricate well, various qualifications are necessary :

"First a nice discrimination of words, enabling you to form, easily and naturally, a great number of finely graduated propositions, shading away, as it were, from the assertion 'x is white' to the assertion 'x is black.' Secondly an inward and absolute contempt for logic and for words. . . . And what are words but toys and sweetmeats for grown-up babies who call themselves men ?"[2]

But even where the actual referents are not in doubt, it is perhaps hardly realized how widespread is the

[1] As the late C. E. Montague (*Disenchantment, p.* 101) well put it, "the only new thing about deception in war is modern man's more perfect means for its practice. The thing has become, in his hand, a trumpet more efficacious than Gideon's own. . . . To match the Lewis gun with which he now fires his solids, he has to his hand the newspaper Press, to let fly at the enemy's head the thing which is not." But this was a temporary use of the modern technique of misdirection, and with the return of peace the habit is lost ? Not so, says Mr Montague. "Any weapon you use in a war leaves some bill to be settled in peace, and the Propaganda arm has its cost like another." The return of the exploiters of the verbal machine to their civil posts is a return in triumph, and its effects will be felt for many years in all countries where the power of the word amongst the masses remains paramount.

[2] *Philomythus*, p. 214.

habit of using the power of words not only for *bona fide* communications, but also as a method of misdirection; and in the world as it is to-day the naïve interpreter is likely on many occasions to be seriously misled if the existence of this unpleasing trait—equally prevalent amongst the classes and the masses without distinction of race, creed, sex, or colour—is overlooked.

Throughout this work, however, we are treating of *bona fide* communication only, except in so far as we shall find it necessary in Chapter IX. to discuss that derivate use of Meaning to which misdirection gives rise. For the rest, the verbal treachery with which we are concerned is only that involved by the use of symbols as such. As we proceed to examine the conditions of communication we shall see why any symbolic apparatus which is in general use is liable to incompleteness and defect.

But if our linguistic outfit is treacherous, it nevertheless is indispensable, nor would another complete outfit necessarily improve matters, even if it were ten times as complete. It is not always new words that are needed, but a means of controlling them as symbols, a means of readily discovering to what in the world on any occasion they are used to refer, and this is what an adequate theory of definition should provide.

But a theory of Definition must follow, not precede, a theory of Signs, and it is little realized how large a place is taken both in abstract thought and in practical affairs by sign-situations. But if an account of sign-situations is to be scientific it must take its observations from the most suitable instances, and must not derive its general principles from an exceptional case. The person actually interpreting a sign is not well placed for observing what is happening. We should develop our theory of signs from observations of other people, and only admit evidence drawn from introspection when we know how to appraise it. The adoption of the other method, on the ground that all our knowledge of others is inferred from knowledge of our own states, can only lead to the *impasse* of solipsism from which modern speculation has yet to recoil. Those who allow beyond question that there are people like themselves also interpreting signs and open to study should not find it difficult to admit that their observation of the behaviour of others may provide at least a framework within which their own introspection, that special and deceptive case, may be fitted. That this is the practice of all the sciences need hardly be pointed out. Any sensible doctor when stricken by disease distrusts his own introspective diagnosis and calls in a colleague.

There are, indeed, good reasons why what is happening in ourselves should be partially hidden from us, and we are generally better judges of what other people are doing than of what we are doing ourselves. Before we looked carefully into other people's heads it was commonly believed that an entity called the soul resided therein, just as children commonly believe that there is a little man inside the skull who looks out at the eyes, the windows of the soul, and listens at the ears. The child has the strongest introspective evidence for this belief, which, but for scalpels and microscopes, it would be difficult to disturb. The tacitly solipsistic presumption that this naïve approach is in some way a necessity of method disqualifies the majority of philosophical and psychological discussions of Interpretation. If we restrict the subject-matter of the inquiry to 'ideas' and words, *i.e.*, to the left side of our triangle, and omit all frank recognition of the world outside us, we inevitably introduce confusion on such subjects as knowledge in perception, verification and Meaning itself.[1]

1 This tendency is particularly noticeable in such works as Baldwin's elaborate treatise on *Thoughts and Things*, where a psychological apparatus of 'controls' and 'contents' is hard to reconcile with the subsequent claim to discuss communication. The twist given to grammatical analysis by Aristotle's similar neglect of Reference is dealt with in Appendix A.

If we stand in the neighbourhood of a cross road and observe a pedestrian confronted by a notice *To Grantchester* displayed on a post, we commonly distinguish three important factors in the situation. There is, we are sure, (1) a Sign which (2) refers to a Place and (3) is being interpreted by a person. All situations in which Signs are considered are similar to this. A doctor noting that his patient has a temperature and so forth is said to diagnose his disease as influenza. If we talk like this we do not make it clear that signs are here also involved. Even when we speak of symptoms we often do not think of these as closely related to other groups of signs. But if we say that the doctor interprets the temperature, etc., as a Sign of influenza, we are at any rate on the way to an inquiry as to whether there is anything in common between the manner in which the pedestrian treated the object at the cross road and that in which the doctor treated his thermometer and the flushed countenance.

On close examination it will be found that very many situations which we do not ordinarily regard as Sign-situations are essentially of the same nature. The chemist dips litmus paper in his test-tube, and interprets the sign red or the sign blue as meaning acid or base. A Hebrew prophet notes a small black cloud, and remarks "We shall have rain." Lessing scrutinizes the Laocoön, and concludes that the features of Laocoōn *père* are in repose. A New Zealand school-girl looks at certain letters on a page in her *Historical Manual for the use of Lower Grades* and knows that Queen Anne is dead.

The method which recognizes the common feature of sign-interpretation[1] has its dangers, but opens the

[1] In all these cases a sign has been interpreted rightly or wrongly, *i.e.*, something has been not only experienced or enjoyed, but understood as referring to something else. Anything which can be experienced can also be thus understood, *i.e.*, can also be a sign ; and it is important to remember that interpretation, or what happens to (or in the mind of) an Interpreter is quite distinct both from the sign and from that for which the sign stands or to which it refers. If then

way to a fresh treatment of many widely different topics.

As an instance of an occasion in which the theory of signs is of special use, the subject dealt with in our fourth chapter may be cited. If we realize that in *all* perception, as distinguished from mere awareness, sign-situations are involved, we shall have a new method of approaching problems where a verbal deadlock seems to have arisen. Whenever we 'perceive' what we name 'a chair,' we are interpreting a certain group of data (modifications of the sense-organs), and treating them as signs of a referent. Similarly, even before the interpretation of a word, there is the almost automatic interpretation of a group of successive noises or letters as a word. And in addition to the external world we can also explore with a new technique the sign-situations involved by mental events, the 'goings on' or processes of interpretation themselves. We need neither confine ourselves to arbitrary generalizations from introspection after the manner of classical psychology, nor deny the existence of images and other 'mental' occurrences to their signs with the extreme Behaviorists.[1] The Double language hypothesis, which is suggested by the theory of signs and supported by linguistic analysis, would absolve Dr Watson and his followers

we speak of the meaning of a sign we must not, as philosophers, psychologists and logicians are wont to do, confuse the (imputed) relation between a sign and that to which it refers, either with the referent (what is referred to) or with the process of interpretation (the 'goings on' in the mind of the interpreter). It is this sort of confusion which has made so much previous work on the subject of signs and their meaning unfruitful. In particular, by using the same term 'meaning' *both* for the 'Goings on' inside their heads (the images, associations, etc., which enabled them to interpret signs) and for the Referents (the things to which the signs refer) philosophers have been forced to locate Grantchester, Influenza, Queen Anne, and indeed the whole Universe equally inside their heads—or, if alarmed by the prospect of cerebral congestion, at least 'in their minds' in such wise that all these objects become conveniently 'mental.' Great care, therefore, is required in the use of the term 'meaning,' since its associations are dangerous.

[1] That the mind-body problem is due to a duplication of symbolic machinery is maintained in Chapter IV., p. 81. Cf. also *The Meaning of Psychology*, by C. K. Ogden (1926), Chapter II., where this view is supported with reference to contemporary authorities who hold it.

from the logical necessity of affecting general anæsthesia. Images, etc., are often most useful signs of our present and future behaviour—notably in the modern interpretation of dreams.[1] An improved Behaviorism will have much to say concerning the chaotic attempts at symbolic interpretation and construction by which Psycho-analysts discredit their valuable labours.

The problems which arise in connection with any 'sign-situation' are of the same general form. The relations between the elements concerned are no doubt different, but they are of the same sort. A thorough classification of these problems in one field, such as the field of symbols, may be expected, therefore, to throw light upon analogous problems in fields at first sight of a very different order.

When we consider the various kinds of Sign-situations instanced above, we find that those signs which men use to communicate one with another and as instruments of thought, occupy a peculiar place. It is convenient to group these under a distinctive name; and for words, arrangements of words, images, gestures, and such representations as drawings or mimetic sounds we use the term *symbols*. The influence of Symbols upon human life and thought in numberless unexpected ways has never been fully recognized, and to this chapter of history we now proceed.

[1] In the terminology of the present work, many of the analyst's 'symbols' are, of course, signs only; they are not used for purposes of communication. But in the literature of psycho-analysis there is much valuable insistence on the need of wider forms of interpretation, especially in relation to emotional overcharge. Cf., e.g., the late Dr Jelliffe's "The Symbol as an Energy Condenser" (*Journal of Nervous and Mental Diseases*, December 1919), though the metaphor, like many other psycho-analytic locutions, must not be stretched too far in view of what has been said above and of what is to follow (cf. pages 102–3 and 200 *infra*).

CHAPTER II

THE POWER OF WORDS

Le mot, qu'on le sache, est un être vivant . . . le mot est le verbe, et le verbe est Dieu.—*Victor Hugo*.

Athenians! I observe that in all respects you are deeply reverential towards the Gods.—*Paul of Tarsus*.

He who shall duly consider these matters will find that there is a certain bewitchery or fascination in words, which makes them operate with a force beyond what we can naturally give account of.—*South*.

FROM the earliest times the Symbols which men have used to aid the process of thinking and to record their achievements have been a continuous source of wonder and illusion. The whole human race has been so impressed by the properties of words as instruments for the control of objects, that in every age it has attributed to them occult powers. Between the attitude of the early Egyptian and that of the modern poet, there would appear at first sight to be but little difference. "All words are spiritual," says Walt Whitman, "nothing is more spiritual than words. Whence are they? Along how many thousands and tens of thousands of years have they come?" Unless we fully realize the profound influence of superstitions concerning words, we shall not understand the fixity of certain widespread linguistic habits which still vitiate even the most careful thinking.

With the majority, and in matters of ordinary discussion, the influence of this legacy is all-pervasive, in language no less than in other spheres. "If we could open the heads and read the thoughts of two men of the same generation and country, but at the opposite ends of the intellectual scale, we should probably find their minds as different as if the two belonged to different species. . . . Superstitions survive because, while they shock the views of enlightened members of the community, they are still in harmony with the thoughts and feelings of others, who, though they are drilled by their betters into an appearance of civilization, remain barbarians or savages at heart."[1]

Most educated people are quite unconscious of the extent to which these relics survive at their doors, still less do they realize how their own behaviour is moulded by the unseen hand of the past. "Only those whose studies have led them to investigate the subject," adds Dr Frazer, "are aware of the depth to which the ground beneath our feet is thus, as it were, honeycombed by unseen forces."

The surface of society, like that of the sea, may, the anthropologist admits, be in perpetual motion, but its depths, like the depths of the ocean, remain almost unmoved. Only by plunging daily into those depths can we come in contact with our fellow-men; only—in the particular case of language—by forgoing the advantages of this or that special scientific symbol system, by drinking of the same unpurified stream, can we share in the life of the community. If the clouds of accumulated verbal tradition burst above us in the open—in the effort to communicate, in the attempt at interpretation—few have, as yet, evolved even the rudiments of a defence.

The power of words is the most conservative force in our life. Only yesterday did students of anthropology begin to admit the existence of those ineluctable verbal coils by which so much of our thought is encompassed. "The common inherited scheme of conception which is all around us, and comes to us as naturally and unobjectionably as our native air, is none

[1] J. G. Frazer, *Psyche's Task*, p. 169.

the less imposed upon us, and limits our intellectual movements in countless ways—all the more surely and irresistibly because, being inherent in the very language we must use to express the simplest meaning, it is adopted and assimilated before we can so much as begin to think for ourselves at all."[1] And from the structure of our language we can hardly even think of escaping. Tens of thousands of years have elapsed since we shed our tails, but we are still communicating with a medium developed to meet the needs of arboreal man. And as the sounds and marks of language bear witness to its primeval origins, so the associations of those sounds and marks, and the habits of thought which have grown up with their use and with the structures imposed on them by our first parents, are found to bear witness to an equally significant continuity.

We may smile at the linguistic illusions of primitive man, but may we forget that the verbal machinery on which we so readily rely, and with which our metaphysicians still profess to probe the Nature of Existence, was set up by him, and may be responsible for other illusions hardly less gross and not more easily eradicable? It may suffice at this point to recall the prevalence of sacred or secret vocabularies, and of forbidden words of every sort. Almost any European country can still furnish examples of the tale in which a name (Tom-Tit-Tot, Vargaluska, Rumpelstiltskin, Finnur, Zi) has to be discovered before some prince can be wedded, or some ogre frustrated.[2] And on the contextual account of reference which is the outcome of modern developments of associationism, with its immense stress on the part played by language in memory and imagination, it is clear that in the days before psychological analysis was possible the evidence for a special world of words

[1] F. M. Cornford, *From Religion to Philosophy*, p. 45.

[2] J. A. Macculloch, *The Childhood of Fiction*, pp. 26-30, is the last to collect the references to these, and to relate them, as did Mr Clodd in his *Tom-Tit-Tot*, to the general practice of Verbal Magic.

of power, for *nomina* as *numina*, must have appeared overwhelming.

In ancient Egypt precautions were taken to prevent the extinction of the eighth or Name-soul, and to cause its continuance along with the names of the Gods.[1] In the Pyramid texts we find mentioned a God called Khern, *i.e.*, Word: the Word having a personality like that of a human being. The Creation of the world was due to the interpretation in words by Thoth of the will of the deity. The greater part of mankind must once have believed the name to be that integral part of a man identified with the soul, or to be so important a portion of him that it might be substituted for the whole, as employers speak of factory 'hands.' In *Revelation* we read "There were killed in the earthquake names of men seven thousand," and again in the letter to the Church of Sardis, "Thou hast a few names in Sardis which did not defile their garments." The beast coming up out of the sea has upon his head "names of blasphemy." Blasphemy itself is just such an instance; for the god is supposed to be personally offended by the desecration of his name: and even in the reign of Henry VIII. a boy was put to death by burning because of some idle words he had chanced to hear respecting the sacrament which he ignorantly repeated.[2]

"Why askest thou after my name, seeing it is secret" (or 'ineffable' with Prof. G. F. Moore), says the angel of the Lord to Manoah in the book of *Judges*. Nearly all primitive peoples show great dislike to their names being mentioned; when a New Zealand chief was called Wai, which means water, a new name had to be given to water; and in Frazer's *Golden Bough* numerous examples of word taboos are collected to show the universality of the attitude. Not only chiefs but gods, and moreover the priest in whom gods were

[1] Budge, *The Book of the Dead*, pp. lxxxvi-xc.
[2] Pike, *History of Crime in England*, Vol. II., p. 56.

supposed to dwell (a belief which induced the Cantonese to apply the term 'god-boxes' to such favoured personages), are amongst the victims of this logophobia. We know how Herodotus (II. 132, 171) refuses to mention the name of Osiris. The true and great name of Allah is a secret name,[1] and similarly with the gods of Brahmanism[2] and the real name of Confucius.[3] Orthodox Jews apparently avoid the name Jahweh altogether.[4] We may compare 'Thank Goodness' 'Morbleu'—and the majority of euphemisms. Among the Hindus if one child has been lost, it is customary to call the next by some opprobrious name. A male child is called Kuriya, or Dunghill—the spirit of course knows folk as their names and will overlook the worthless. Similarly, God knows each man by his name—"and the Lord said unto Moses 'Thou hast found grace in my sight and I know thee by thy name.'" Every ancient Egyptian had two names—one for the world, and another by which he was known to the supernal powers. The Abyssinian Christian's second name, given at baptism, is never to be divulged. The guardian deity of Rome had an incommunicable name, and in parts of ancient Greece the holy names of the gods to ensure against profanation were engraved on lead tablets and sunk in the sea.

Children are often similarly anxious to conceal their names; and just as children always demand what the name of a thing is (never if it has a name) and regard that name as a valuable acquisition, so we know that the stars all have names. "He telleth the number of the stars and calleth them all by their names." Here we may note the delightful proverb which might appear on the title-page of every work dealing with Symbolism: "The Divine is rightly so called."

[1] Sell, *The Faith of Islam*, p. 185.

[2] Hopkins, *Religions of India*, p. 184.

[3] Friend, *Folk-Lore Record*, IV., p. 76.

[4] Herzog-Plitt, *Real-Encyclopädie*, VI., p. 501. Hence the name Adonai, read instead of the ineffable Name; from which, by insertion of the vowels of Adonai in the tetragrammaton, we got Jehovah.

In some ways the twentieth century suffers more grievously than any previous age from the ravages of such verbal superstitions. Owing, however, to developments in the methods of communication, and the creation of many special symbolic systems, the form of the disease has altered considerably; and, apart from the peculiar survival of religious apologetic, now takes more insidious forms than of yore. Influences making for its wide diffusion are the baffling complexity of the symbolic apparatus now at our disposal; the possession by journalists and men of letters of an immense semi-technical vocabulary and their lack of opportunity, or unwillingness, to inquire into its proper use; the success of analytic thinkers in fields bordering on mathematics, where the divorce between symbol and reality is most pronounced and the tendency to hypostatization most alluring; the extension of a knowledge of the cruder forms of symbolic convention (the three R's), combined with a widening of the gulf between the public and the scientific thought of the age; and finally the exploitation, for political and commercial purposes, of the printing press by the dissemination and reiteration of *clichés*.

The persistence of the primitive linguistic outlook not only throughout the whole religious world, but in the work of the profoundest thinkers, is indeed one of the most curious features of modern thought. The philosophy of the nineteenth century was dominated by an idealist tradition in which the elaboration of monstrous symbolic machinery (the Hegelian Dialectic[1] provides a striking example) was substituted for direct research, and occupied the centre of attention. The twentieth opened with a subtle analysis of the mysteries of mathematics on the basis of a 'Platonism' even

[1] Jowett in comparing the Dialectic of Hegel with that of Plato remarks: "Perhaps there is no greater defect in Hegel's system than the want of a sound theory of language."—*The Dialogues of Plato*, Vol. IV., p. 420.

more pronounced than that of certain Critical Realists of 1921.[1] Thus we read :—

"Whatever may be an object of thought, or may occur in any true or false proposition, or can be accounted as *one*, I call a *term*. . . . A man, a moment, a number, a class, a relation, a chimera, or anything else that can be mentioned is sure to be a term; and to deny that such and such a thing is a term must always be false. . . . A term is possessed of all the properties commonly assigned to substances or substantives. . . . Every term is immutable and indestructible. What a term is it is, and no change can be conceived in it which would not destroy its identity and make it another term. . . . Among terms it is possible to distinguish two kinds, which I shall call respectively *things* and *concepts*." [2]

With the aid of this strange verbal rapier many palpable hits were claimed. Thus the theory of "adjectives or attributes or ideal things in some way less substantial, less self subsistent, less self identical, than true substantives, appears to be wholly erroneous";[3] whole philosophical systems were excluded, for "the admission (involved in the *mention* of a man and a chimera) of many terms destroys monism"; [4] and a modern Platonism reconstructed, whereby a world of certain of the 'things' 'mentioned' by means of 'terms the world of universals, was rehabilitated. Here the reason builds a habitation, "or rather finds a habitation eternally standing, where our ideals are fully satisfied and our best hopes are not thwarted. It is only when we thoroughly understand the entire independence of ourselves, which belongs to this world that reason finds, that we can adequately realize the profound importance of its beauty."[5] For here everything is "unchangeable, rigid, exact, delightful to the mathematician, the logician, the builder of metaphysical systems, and all who love perfection more than life." This world was commended to the working man, in contrast to the

1 Cf. Chapter VIII., pp. 164 ff.
2 B. Russell, *The Principles of Mathematics* (1903), Vol. I., pp. 43-44.
3 *Ibid.*, p. 46.
4 *Ibid.*, p. 44.
5 *Mysticism and Logic* (1918), p. 69.

world of existence which is "fleeting, vague, without sharp boundaries, without any clear plan or arrangement though it "contains all thoughts and feelings." Both worlds are equally there, equally worth contemplation, and "according to our temperaments, we shall prefer the contemplation of the one or of the other."[1]

It is regrettable that modern Platonists so seldom follow Plato in his attempts at a scientific study of Symbolism, but it is interesting to note that they recognize the kinship of their theory with Greek speculation, for both have their origin in the same linguistic habits. The ingenuity of the modern logician tends to conceal the verbal foundations of his structure, but in Greek philosophy these foundations are clearly revealed. The earlier writers are full of the relics of primitive word-magic. To classify things is to name them, and for magic the name of a thing or group of things is its soul; to know their names is to have power over their souls. Nothing, whether human or superhuman, is beyond the power of words. Language itself is a duplicate, a shadow-soul, of the whole structure of reality. Hence the doctrine of the *Logos*, variously conceived as this supreme reality, the divine soul-substance, as the 'Meaning' or reason of everything, and as the 'Meaning' or essence of a name.[2]

The Greeks were clearly assisted in their acceptance of an Otherworld of Being by the legacy of religious material which earlier philosophers incorporated in their respective systems. The nature of things, their *physis*, was regarded, *e.g.*, by Thales, as supersensible, a stuff of that attenuated sort which has always been attributed to souls and ghosts; differing from body

[1] B. Russell, *The Problems of Philosophy*, Home University Library, p. 156. That portions of this world, which Mr Russell would probably recognize to-day as having a purely linguistic basis, still adhere to the cosmos envisaged in his *Analysis of Mind*. 1921, is suggested at p. 54 *infra*. His latest admissions are to be found on page 688 of *The Philosophy of Bertrand Russell* (1944) and page 34 of *Polemic* 2 (1946).

[2] Cornford, *op. cit.*, *From Religion to Philosophy*, pp. 141, 186, 248.

only in being intangible and invisible. Consequently the World of Being, in which bogus entities reside, had at first that minimum of materiality without which nothing could be conceived. But as logic developed and the power of words attracted more attention, this materiality was gradually lost, until in the *Symposium*, 211, and the *Phaedo*, 80, Plato has evolved a realm of pure ideality, also described as *physis*, in which these name-souls dwell, pure, divine, immortal, intelligible, uniform, indissoluble and unchangeable.

This development has been shown to be due largely to the influence of Pythagoreanism and the intervening stages are of peculiar interest for the history of Symbols. It was Heracleitus who first appealed to words as embodying the nature of things, and his influence on Plato is manifest in the *Cratylus*. Heracleitus saw in language the most constant thing in a world of ceaseless change, an expression of that common wisdom which is in all men; and for him the structure of human speech reflects the structure of the world. It is an embodiment of that structure—"the *Logos* is contained and in it, as one meaning may be contained in many outwardly different symbols."[1]

The Pythagoreans on the other hand were chiefly puzzled by number symbols. "Since everything appeared to be modelled in its entire character on numbers," says Aristotle,[2] "and numbers to be the ultimate things in the whole universe, they became convinced that the elements of numbers are the elements of everything." In fact, in its final stages, Pythagoreanism passed from a doctrine of the world as a procession of numbers out of the One, to the construction of everything out of Number-souls, each claiming an immortal and separate existence.[3]

[1] Cornford, *op. cit.*, p. 192.

[2] *Metaphysics*, A. 5; trans. A. E. Taylor.

[3] A record of Pythagoreanism and arithmosophy generally is provided by Dr R. Allendy in *Le Symbolisme des Nombres, Essai d'Arithmosophie*, 1921. The author's object has been "to examine some

Parmenides, who followed, was occupied with the functions of negative symbols. If 'Cold' only means the same as 'not hot,' and 'dark' the same as 'not light,' how can we talk about absences of things? "Two bodies there are," he says, "which mortals have decided to name, one of which they ought not to name, and that is where they have gone wrong." They have given names to things which simply are not, to the not-things (μὴ ἐόν). But in addition to the problem of Negative Facts, which involved Plato in the first serious examination of the relations of thought and language (*Sophist*, 261), Parmenides handed on to Plato his own Orphic conundra about the One and the Many, which also have their roots in language. So that, quite apart from the difficulties raised by his Ideal World where the Name-souls dwelt, and its relations with the world of mud and blood (to which entities on æsthetic grounds he hesitated to allow 'ideas,' much as theologians debated the existence of souls in darkies), Plato had every reason to be occupied by linguistic theory.

It is, therefore, all the more unfortunate that the dialogue, *The Cratylus*, in which his views on language are set forth, should have been so neglected in modern times. Plato's theory of Ideas or Name-souls was accepted from the Pythagoreans; but as a scientist he was constantly approaching the problem of names and their meaning as one of the most difficult inquiries which could be encountered. His analysis, in an age when comparative philology, grammar, and psychology were all unknown, is a remarkable achievement, but he fails to distinguish consistently between symbols and the thought symbolized.

aspects of the numerical key under which the religious and occult philosophy of all times and of all schools has veiled its teachings. . . . From this standpoint the study of Numbers should constitute the foundation of all Occultism, of all Theosophy." In the preposterous medley which results, the curious will find ample evidence that numerical magic has been hardly less prevalent than the magic of words.

The main tradition of Greek speculation remained faithful to the verbal approach. There are two ways, wrote Dr Whewell, of comprehending nature, "the one by examining the words only and the thoughts which they call up; the other by attending to the facts and things which bring these notions into being. . . . The Greeks followed the former, the *verbal* or *notional* course, and failed." And again, "The propensity to seek for principles in the common usages of language may be discovered at a very early period. . . . In Aristotle we have the consummation of this mode of speculation."[1] It has been generally accepted since the time of Trendelenburg[2] that the Categories, and similar distinctions which play a large part in Aristotle's system, cannot be studied apart from the peculiarities of the Greek language. "Aristotle," says Gomperz, "often suffers himself to be led by the forms of language, not always from inability to free himself from those bonds, but at least as often because the demands of dialectic will not allow him to quit his arena. . . . Thus a distinction is drawn between knowledge in general and the particular sciences, based solely on the fact that the objects of the latter are included in their names. . . . His classification of the categories is frequently governed by considerations of linguistic expediency, a circumstance which, it must be allowed (*sic*), ought to have restrained him from applying it to ontological purposes."[3]

The practice of dialectical disputation in Aristotle's time was based on the notion of a definite simple meaning for every term, as we see from the Scholia of Ammonius to the *De Interpretatione*. Thus the ques-

[1] *History of the Inductive Sciences*, I., pp. 27, 29.

[2] *Kategorienlehre*, p. 209, where it is contended that linguistic considerations "guided, but did not decide" the classification. Already in the first century A.D. various peripatetic eclectics had maintained that the categories were entirely concerned with words, though as Dr P. Rotta suggests (*La Filosofia del Linguaggio nella Patristica e nella Scholastica*, p. 56), this is, perhaps, rather from the angle of the nominalist-realist controversy.

[3] T. Gomperz, *Greek Thinkers*, IV., pp. 40-41.

tioner asked, "Is Rhetoric estimable?"; and in one form of the game, at any rate, the respondent was expected to answer simply Yes or No. Certain words were regarded as equivocal, chiefly as a result of studying their 'contraries,' in the current vocabulary. Aristotle enumerates various rules with regard to equivocation and other devices conceived with the object of driving an opponent into some form of verbal inconsistency, in his *Topics*.

Mauthner, after a detailed argument to show that the Aristotelian docrines of the Negative and the Categories "made the extant forms of speech the objects of a superstitious cult, as though they had been actual deities," remarks that "Aristotle is dead because he was, more than perhaps any other notable writer in the whole history of Philosophy, superstitiously devoted to words. Even in his logic he is absolutely dependent on the accidents of language, on the accidents of his mother-tongue. His superstitious reverence for words was never out of season."[1] And again:—

> "For full two thousand years human thought has lain under the influence of this man's catchwords, an influence which has been wholly pernicious in its results. There is no parallel instance of the enduring potency of a system of words."[2]

It is curious that in the *De Interpretatione* Aristotle puts forward views which are hard to reconcile with such a verbal approach. He there insists that words are signs primarily of mental affections, and only secondarily of the things of which these are likenesses.[3]

[1] Mauthner, *Aristotle*, English Translation, pp. 84, 103-4. Cf. the same author's *Kritik der Sprache*, Vol. III., p. 4, "If Aristotle had spoken Chinese or Dacotan, he would have had to adopt an entirely different Logic, or at any rate an entirely different theory of Categories."

[2] *Ibid.*, p. 19. See also Appendix A for a discussion of the influence of Aristotle on Grammar.

[3] *De Interpretatione*, 16, a. 3. It is worth noting that Andronicus of Rhodes, who edited the first complete edition of Aristotle's works when the Library of Theophrastus was brought to Rome from Athens as part of Sulla's loot, marked this treatise as spurious. Maier's arguments in its favour have, however, persuaded scholars to accept it as Aristotelian.

And he elaborates a theory of the proposition which, though incomplete and a source of endless confusion, yet indicates a far more critical attitude to language than his logical apparatus as a whole would suggest. For here Aristotle finds no difficulty in settling the main question raised by Plato in the *Cratylus*. All significant speech, he says, is significant by convention only, and not by nature or as a natural instrument—thereby neglecting Plato's acute observations as to the part played by onomatopœia in verbal origins. In the *De Interpretatione* various branches of significant speech are deliberately excluded, and we are there invited to consider only that variety known as *enunciative*, which, as declaring truth or falsehood, is all that belongs to Logic; other modes of speech, the precative, imperative, interrogative, etc., being more naturally regarded as part of Rhetoric or Poetic.[1]

That verbal superstition would play a large part in Greek philosophy might have been expected from the evidence of Greek literature as a whole; and Farrar finds it necessary to suppose that Æschylus and Sophocles, for example, must have believed in Onomancy, which, as we shall see, is always bound up with primitive word-magic. Even the practical Romans, as he goes on to show, were the victims of such beliefs; and would all have echoed the language of Ausonius:—

> Nam divinare est nomen componere, quod sit Fortunæ,
> morum, vel necis indicium.

[1] In the *Poetics* (1456 b. Margoliouth, p. 198) Aristotle again alludes to "the operations of which Speech is the instrument, of which the Divisions are demonstration and refutation, the arousing of emotions, such as pity, fear, anger, etc., exaggeration and depreciation." In commenting on the enunciative or 'apophantic' use of language (*D. I.* 17 a. 2), Ammonius refers to a passage in one of the lost works of Theophrastus, where 'apophantic' language, which is concerned with things, is distinguished from other varieties of language, which are concerned with the effect on the hearer and vary with the individuals addressed. These different kinds of propositions, five in number according to the later Peripatetics, were further elaborated by the Stoics. Cf. Prantl (*Geschichle der Logik*, Vol. I., p. 441), Steinthal (*Geschichte der Sprachwissenschaft bei den Griechen und Römern*, Vol. I., p. 317), H. Maier, *Psychologie des Emotionalen Denkens*, pp. 9-10.

In their levies, Cicero informs us, they took care "to enrol first such names as Victor, and Felix, and Faustus, and Secundus; and were anxious to head the roll of the census with a word of such happy augury as Salvius Valerius. Cæsar gave a command in Spain to an obscure Scipio simply for the sake of the omen which his name involved. Scipio upbraids his mutinous soldiers with having followed an Atrius Umber, a 'dux abominandi nominis,' being, as De Quincey calls him, a 'pleonasm of darkness.' The Emperor Severus consoled himself for the immoralities of his Empress Julia, because she bore the same name as the profligate daughter of Augustus";[1] just as Adrian VI., when he became Pope, was persuaded by his Cardinals not to retain his own name, on the ground that all Popes who had done so had died in the first year of their reign.[2]

When we reflect on the influences which might have concentrated the attention of Græco-Roman thinkers on linguistic problems, it is at first sight surprising that many of those whose constructions were so largely verbal were also in certain respects fully aware of the misleading character of their medium. The appeal of the Heracliteans to language as evidence for the doctrine of Change was, as we know from the *Cratylus*, vigorously opposed by the Parmenidean logicians, as well as by believers in the Ideas. And an equal readiness to admit that the presuppositions of Language have to be combated was manifested by Plotinus. Language, in the Neo-Platonic view, "can only be made to express the nature of the soul by constraining it to purposes for which most men never even think of employing it"; moreover, "the soul cannot be described at all except by phrases which would be nonsensical if applied to body or its qualities, or to determinations of particular bodies."[3]

[1] F. W. Farrar, *Language and Languages*, pp. 235-6.
[2] Mervoyer, *Etude sur l'association des idées*, p. 376.
[3] Whittaker, *The Neo-Platonists*, p. 42.

The rejection of misleading forms of language was carried still further by Buddhist writers in their treatment of the 'soul.' Whether it was called *satta* (being), *attā* (self), *jiva* (living principle), or *puggăla* (person) did not matter :

> "For these are merely names, expressions, turns of speech, designations in common use in the world. Of these he who has won truth makes use indeed, but he is not led astray by them."[1]

The Buddhists, whose attitude towards language was exceptional, were quite ready to make use of customary phrases for popular exposition, but it is not clear whether any more subtle approach to fictional problems had been developed.[2]

But though all the post-Aristotelian schools, and particularly the Stoics, whose view of language had considerable influence on Roman jurists,[3] devoted some attention to linguistic theory, nowhere in ancient times do we find evidence of these admissions leading to a study of symbols such as Plato and Aristotle seemed at times to be approaching. As we shall see, this was owing to the lack of any attempt to deal with signs as such, and so to understand the functions of words in relation to the more general sign-situations on which all thought depends. Yet just before the critical spirit was finally stamped out by Christianity, notable discussions had taken place in the Græco-Roman world, and the central problem was being examined with an acuity which might have led to really scientific developments. The religious leaders were aware of the danger,

[1] Digha N. I. 263 ; cf. C. A. F. Rhys Davids, *Buddhist Psychology*, p. 32.

[2] For an elaborate study of Eastern schools of thought and their behaviour with words, see *op. cit.*, *Word Magic*, by C. K. Ogden.

[3] Lersch, *Die Sprachphilosophie der Alten*, Vol. III., pp. 184-6. Aelius Gallus is cited for the definition of flumen as " aquam ipsam, quæ fluit " ; and, according to Gellius, Antistius Labeo was profoundly interested in Grammar and Dialectic, " Latinarumque vocum origines rationesque percalluerat, eaque præcipue scientia ad enodandos plerosque iuris laqueos utebatur."

and there is even a passage in St Gregory of Nazianzus, where trouble is complained of, since "the Sexti and Pyrrhoneans and the spirit of contradiction were perniciously intruded into our churches like some evil and malignant plague."[1] In fact the whole theory of signs was examined both by Aenesidemus, the reviver of Pyrrhonism in Alexandria, and by a Greek doctor named Sextus between 100 and 250 A.D. The analysis offered is more fundamental than anything which made its appearance until the nineteenth century.[2]

This brief survey of the Græco-Roman approach to language must suffice to represent pre-scientific speculation upon the subject. Moreover, it has had a greater influence on modern European thought than the even more luxuriant growth of oriental theories. The atmosphere of verbalism in which most Indian philosophy developed seems to have been even more dense than that of the scholastics or of the Greek dialecticians. In this respect the Mīmāṁsā-Nyāya controversy, the Yoga philosophy, the Vijñānavāda categories, the Prābhākara Mīmāmsakas[3] are hardly less remarkable than the doctrine of the Sacred Word AUM and the verbal ecstasies of the Sufi mystics,[4] a part of whose technique was revived by Dr Coué.

The history of spells, verbal magic and verbal medicine, whether as practised by the Trobriand magician,[5] by the Egyptian priest of the Pyramid texts, or by the modern metaphysician, is a subject in

[1] Cf. N. Maccoll, *The Greek Sceptics* (p. 108), where it is noted that thirteen centuries later, when authority was once again challenged, the remains of these thinkers at once attracted attention. Foucher wrote a history of the New Academy and Sorbière translated the Hypotheses of Sextus.

[2] See R. D. Hicks, *Stoic and Epicurean*, p. 390 ff., on Aenesidemus; and *infra*, Appendix C.

[3] Keith, *Indian Logic*, Chapter V.; Dasgupta, *History of Indian Philosophy*, Vol. I., pp. 148-9, 345-54; Rama Prasad, *Self-culture or the Yoga of Patañjali*, pp. 88, 148, 152, 156, 215; Vedānta Sūtras, *Sacred Books of the East*, Vol. XLVIII., p. 148.

[4] *The Science of the Sacred Word* (translated by Bhagavan Das); R. A. Nicholson, *Studies in Islamic Mysticism*, pp. 6-9.

[5] Malinowski, *Argonauts of the Western Pacific*, pp. 408-10.

itself and is dealt with at length in *Word Magic*, which is designed as an expansion of the present chapter.

The extent to which primitive attitudes towards words are still exploited by the astute is fully revealed only when the achievements of some cynical rhetorician are accorded the limelight of the law courts, or when some particularly glaring absurdity is substituted for the more patient methods of suggestion favoured by repetitive journalism. But these same attitudes are universal in childhood, and are so strengthened by the prevailing verbalism that even the most accurate scientific training has often done little to render the adult less subservient to his medium. Indeed, as we have seen, the ablest logicians are precisely those who are led to evolve the most fantastic systems by the aid of their verbal technique. The modern logician may, in time to come, be regarded as the true mystic, when the rational basis of the world in which he believes is scientifically examined.

Turning then to the more emotional aspects of modern thought, we shall not be surprised to find a veritable orgy of verbomania. The process whereby the purely verbal systems so characteristic of pistic speculation have attained such formidable dimensions, has recently been examined by Rignano.[1] Attributes found by experience to be contradictory are gradually dematerialized, and in their place are put "verbal envelopes, void of all intelligible content, so as to eliminate the reciprocal contradiction and inhibition to which these attributes would inevitably give rise if they were allowed to furnish matter for the imagination in however small a degree"; and parallel with this dematerialization, a formidable dialectic edifice such as that of scholasticism is constructed, with the object of convincing human reason of the absence of logical inconsistency in the greatest of absurdities.[2]

[1] *The Psychology of Reasoning*, Chap. XI., on Metaphysical Reasoning.
[2] Cf. Guignebert, "Le dogme de la Trinité," *Scientia*, Nos. 32, 33, 37 (1919-14).

In this way the idea of Divinity, for example, has been slowly reduced to a "conglomerate of attributes, purely, or almost purely verbal." So that finally, as William James puts it, "the ensemble of the metaphysical attributes imagined by the theologian" (God being *First Cause*, possesses an existence *a se;* he is *necessary* and *absolute*, *absolutely unlimited*, *infinitely perfect;* he is *One* and *only*, *Spiritual*, *metaphysically simple*, *immutable*, *eternal*, *omnipotent*, *omniscient*, *omnipresent*, etc.) "is but a shuffling and matching of pedantic dictionary adjectives. One feels that in the theologians' hands they are only a set of titles obtained by a mechanical manipulation of synonyms; verbality has stepped into the place of vision, professionalism into that of life."[1]

Similarly, in reasoning commonly spoken of as metaphysical, language has chiefly the function of furnishing "a stable verbal support, so that inexact, nebulous, and fluctuating concepts may be recalled to the mind whenever required, without any prejudice to the elasticity of the concepts"; for which purpose the phraseology adopted is "as vaporous and mysterious as possible. Hence the so-called terms 'written in profundity,' referred to by Ribot, and dear to all metaphysicians, just because they are so admirably suited both to contain everything that it is desired to have them include, and to conceal the contradictions and absurdities of the doctrines based on the concepts in question. . . . The function of the verbal symbol is therefore to keep inconsistent attributes forcibly united, though all of them could not possibly be present to the mind at the same moment just because they inhibit each other; it being important that the metaphysician should have them at his disposal in order to deduce from the concept, from their aggregate, sometimes one set of conclusions and some-

[1] W. James, *The Varieties of Religious Experience*, pp. 439-46.

times another, according to the presentation of reality desired."

Ultimately the word completely takes the place of the thought—Denn eben wo Begriffe fehlen, da stellt ein Wort zur rechten Zeit sich ein, as Mephistopheles remarked. And Rignano aptly likens the process to the shedding of the *carapace* by a crustacean. "Without this verbal carapace the disappearance of all intellectual content would involve the disappearance of all trace of the past existence of such content. But the carapace preserves something which, just because it proves the past existence of a concept which formerly had a real life, may quite well be taken for one still existing. So that this something, although devoid of all intellectual content, always constitutes a valuable point of attachment and support for the corresponding emotion, which is so intense that it does not perceive that the cherished resemblances no longer clothe the beloved object."[1]

But the carapace, the verbal husk, is not merely a valedictory *point d'appui*; it also has a certain bombic capacity, an 'affective resonance' which enables the manipulator of symbols such as the Absolute to assure himself that his labours are not altogether vain. "When language is once grown familiar," says Berkeley, "the hearing of the sounds or sight of the characters is often immediately attended with those passions which at first were wont to be produced by the intervention of ideas that are now quite omitted."[2] From the symbolic use of words we thus pass to the emotive; and with regard to words so used, as in poetry, Ribot has well remarked that "they no longer act as signs but as sounds; they are musical notations at the service of an emotional psychology."[3] So that though at this extreme limit "metaphysical reasoning

[1] Rignano, *op. cit.*, Chap. XI.

[2] *Treatise*, Introduction, § 20.

[3] *La Logique des Sentiments*, p. 187. Cf. Erdmann, *op. cit.*, p. 120, where the methods of kindling "das Strohfeuer einer wohlfeilen und gedankenlosen Begeisterung" are considered.

may be intellectually quite incomprehensible; though, that is to say, it may actually become 'vocem proferre et nihil concipere,' it acquires by way of compensation," as Rignano says, "*an* emotive signification which is peculiar to it, *i.e.*, it is transformed into a kind of musical language stimulative of sentiments and emotions." Its success is due entirely to the harmonious series of emotional echoes with which the naïve mind responds—*et reboat regio cita barbara bombum.*

In practical affairs these influences are no less potent and far more disastrous. We need only instance the contention of the late Dr. Crookshank, supported by an abundance of detailed evidence, that "under the influence of certain schools of thought, and certain habits of expression, we have become accustomed to speak and write as if a disease were a natural object"; that these disastrous verbal habits must be resisted, for "no great advance is probable in the domain of Medicine until the belief in the real existence of diseases is abandoned"; and that the linguistic problem must be faced at once, for "no measure of useful agreement will be achieved unless we are first in accord concerning the principles of method and thought."[1] Coming from one with thirty years' experience of the healing art, so striking a confirmation of the views we have been advancing cannot be lightly rejected; and on another page Dr Crookshank himself gives further reasons for considering that its rejection could only be based on a failure to appreciate the facts.[2]

Until recent times it is only here and there that efforts have been made to penetrate the mystery by a direct attack on the essential problem. In the fourteenth century we have the Nominalist analysis of William of Occam, in the seventeenth the work of Bacon and Hobbes. The discussion rises to an apex with the

[1] *Influenza*, 1922, pp. 12, 61, 512.
[2] *Infra*, Supplement II., pp. 344-5.

Third Book of Locke's *Essay* and the interest of Leibnitz in a Philosophical Language—a *Characteristica Universalis.* Berkeley and Condillac kept the issue alive, and with Horne Tooke and his followers we reach the nineteenth-century movement, in which the work of Bentham, Taine, and Mauthner was especially significant.[1]

With the disappointing achievements of Comparative Philology, on which public interest was long centred through the efforts of Steinthal, Max Müller, and others, we need not here concern ourselves; the *Philological* and *Sociological* approaches still, in fact, leave the field-worker without guidance. To the chaos of the *Grammarians* we address ourselves in Appendix A; and in Appendix D, in addition to the summary of the work of C. S. Peirce, will be found examples of what has been achieved by others who have looked to *Logic* for a solution, as well as by those who appear to have relied mainly upon *Terminology.* With contemporary writers who have made use of the two remaining avenues (of the seven chief methods of approach) the *Metaphysicians* and the *Psychologists*, we shall be frequently occupied in our remaining chapters. For the rest, an endeavour has been made to give credit where credit is due—from Anselm's *De Grammatico*, through Delgarno (1661), Wilkins (1668), Freke (1693), to Silberer (1917) and Cassirer's *Philosophie der symbolischen Formen* (1923)—in the survey of man's progress towards verbal independence which has been appearing intermittently in *Psyche* since 1927.[2]

As a result of all these efforts a Science of Symbolism has become possible, but it is necessary constantly to bear in mind the special forms in which the Power of Words may make itself felt in modern times.

[1] For a detailed discussion of the linguistic achievements of Bacon, Hobbes, and Berkeley, see *Psyche*, 1934, pp. 9-87. The fundamental but neglected contribution of Jeremy Bentham, which so remarkably anticipates contemporary developments, has been dealt with in C. K. Ogden's *Bentham's Theory of Fictions* (International Library of Psychology), 1932.

[2] See especially Vol. XVIII (1946), where the nucleus of a posthumous treatise on "Word Magic" may at last be taking shape.

> "Who hath not owned, with rapture-smitten frame
> The power of grace, the magic of a name?"

asked the simple poet a century ago;[1] and to-day: "All sounds," says Yeats, "evoke indefinable and yet precise emotions . . . or, as I prefer to think, call down among us certain disembodied powers whose footsteps over our hearts we call emotions."

Ancient beliefs may be dead, but the instinct, or the hope, is strong:—

> "I do believe,
> Though I have found them not, that there may be
> Words which are things."[2]

That which we call a rose, we flatter ourselves, "by any other name would smell as sweet." But followers of the late M. Coué should hesitate to regale themselves with a rose named The Squashed Skunk. "When I partake," says Bergson, "of a dish that is supposed to be exquisite, the name which it bears suggestive of the approval given to it comes between my sensation and consciousness; I may believe that the flavour pleases me when a slight effort of attention would prove the contrary."[3]

And words may come between us and our objects in countless subtle ways, if we do not realize the nature of their power. In logic, as we have seen, they lead to the creation of bogus entities, the universals, properties and so forth, of which we shall have more to say in the sequel. By concentrating attention on themselves, words encourage the futile study of forms which has done so much to discredit Grammar; by the excitement which they provoke through their emotive force, discussion is for the most part rendered sterile; by the various types of Verbomania and Graphomania, the satisfaction of naming is realized, and the sense of personal power factitiously enhanced.

[1] Campbell, *The Pleasures of Hope.*
[2] Byron, *Childe Harold.*
[3] *Time and Free-Will*, p. 131.

It is not surprising that a consideration of the ways in which Language has been made to serve mankind in the past should frequently lead to a sceptical reaction. As an able but little-known writer has remarked :—

> "Suppose someone to assert : *The gostak distims the doshes.* You do not know what this means ; nor do I. But if we assume that it is English, we know that *the doshes are distimmed by the gostak.* We know too that *one distimmer of doshes is a gostak.* If, moreover, the *doshes* are *galloons*, we know that *some galloons are distimmed by the gostak.* And so we may go on, and so we often do go on."

And again, for what do the words we use in everyday life stand? "We do not often have occasion to speak, as of an indivisible whole, of the group of phenomena involved or connected in the transit of a negro over a rail-fence with a melon under his arm while the moon is just passing behind a cloud. But if this collocation of phenomena were of frequent occurrence, and if we did have occasion to speak of it often, and if its happening were likely to affect the money market, we should have some name as 'wousin,' to denote it by. People would in time be disputing whether the existence of a wousin involved necessarily a rail-fence, and whether the term could be applied when a white man was similarly related to a stone wall."[1]

That it is "all a matter of words," or that "we can never get anywhere—you put it one way and I put it another, and how can we ever know that we are talking

[1] A. Ingraham, *Swain School Lectures* (1903), pp. 121-182, on "Nine Uses of Language." The nine uses are given as follows :

(i) to dissipate superfluous and obstructive nerve-force.
(ii) for the direction of motion in others, both men and animals.
(iii) for the communication of ideas.
(iv) as a means of expression.
(v) for purposes of record.
(vi) to set matter in motion (magic).
(vii) as an instrument of thinking.
(viii) to give delight merely as sound.
(ix) to provide an occupation for philologists.

about the same thing?" are conclusions to which the study of verbal difficulties not infrequently leads those who are confronted by them for the first time. But a thorough understanding of the ways in which these difficulties arise—the two cases just quoted are good specimens—gives no ground for linguistic nihilism.

The best means of escape from such scepticism as well as from the hypnotic influences which we have been considering, lies in a clear realization of the way in which symbols come to exercise such power, and of the various senses in which they are said to have Meaning. As an essential preliminary we are confronted by the need for an account of the simplest kind of Sign-situation, which will enable us to understand how we come to 'know' or 'think' at all.

The contextual theory of Signs to which, then, we first proceed, will be found to throw light on the primitive idea that Words and Things are related by some magic bond; for it is actually through their occurrence together with things, their linkage with them in a 'context' that Symbols come to play that important part in our life which has rendered them not only a legitimate object of wonder but the source of all our power over the external world.

CHAPTER III

SIGN-SITUATIONS

> Studium linguarum in universis, in ipsis primordiis triste est et ingratum; sed primis difficultatibus labore improbo et ardore nobili perruptis, postea cumulatissime beamur.—*Valcknaer.*

MEANING, that pivotal term of every theory of language, cannot be treated without a satisfactory theory of signs. With some of its senses (in which 'my meaning' = 'what I am thinking of') the question to be answered is, in brief, "What happens when we judge, or believe, or think of something: of what kind of entities does the something consist: and how is it related to the mental event which is our judging, our believing, our thinking?" The traditional approach to this question has been through introspection and through the logical analysis of Judgment, with the result that all the many answers which have been given from this angle will be found, in contrast to that which is outlined below, to be variants of one opinion. They agree, that is, in holding that, when we think of anything, we have to it (or sometimes to something else) a relation of a quite unique kind. In other words thinking is regarded as an unparalleled happening. Thus the problems of symbolization and reference come to be discussed in isolation as though there were no allied fields of inquiry.

This assumption of the uniqueness of the relation between the mind and its objects is the central tenet in views which otherwise have no point of agreement. Thus it is plausibly held by some that when we are believing (say) that we are alive, we are in a direct relation of a unique kind to an entity which is neither in time nor in space, to be called the proposition 'that we are alive.' Others pretend that there is nothing of this sort, but that instead we are then related by a multiple relation, again of an unique kind, with a variety of entities—among which are (perhaps) we ourselves and certainly something to be called a 'concept' (or 'universal' or 'property'), namely aliveness or being alive. On both views the uniqueness in kind of the relation between a thought as a mental event and the things, whatever they may be, which the thought is 'of,' is too obvious to be questioned.

As a representative of the realist school which claims to have assimilated the modern scientific outlook, we may cite Keynes, who adopted the view that philosophically we must start from various classes of things with which we have direct acquaintance. "The most important classes of things with which we have direct acquaintance are our own sensations, which we may be said to *experience*, the ideas and meanings, about which we have thoughts and which we may be said to *understand*, and facts or characteristics or relations of sense data or meanings, which we may be said to *perceive*. . . . The objects of knowledge and belief—as opposed to the objects of direct acquaintance which I term sensations, meanings, and perceptions—I shall term *propositions*." As an example of direct knowledge we are told that from acquaintance with a sensation of yellow "I can pass directly to a knowledge of the proposition 'I have a sensation of yellow.'"[1] Lest it should be supposed that this odd, but very prevalent, doctrine is peculiar to a school, we may refer to the justification of *das Urteil*, "spaceless, timeless and impersonal," the specific object of logical inquiry, elaborated by Lipps;[2]

[1] *A Treatise on Probability* (1921), pp. 12-13.

[2] *Psychologische Untersuchungen*, Vol. II., section 1, "Zur 'Psychologie' und 'Philosophie,'" pp. 4-10.

to the similar doctrine which vitiates so much of Husserl's analysis of language;[1] and to the still more extraordinary phantasies of van Ginneken, a subtle linguistic psychologist who, influenced doubtless by Meinong as well as by Theology, advances the same view as a theory of 'adhesion.' No account of thinking in terms of verbal images and representations of things is, according to this author, sufficient. "We find ourselves confronted by a new force: something non-sensible, transcendental . . . by means of which we understand and know in a new manner, and a more perfect one than we could through our animal nature. We . . . adhere to the present reality, to that which is really and actually there . . . and also to the possible, the *essence*."[2] It is plain that on any such view a scientific account of thinking is ruled out from the very beginning.

"What happens when we think?" is a question which should be of interest to every thinker. The triteness of the answer "When we think, we think," offered by such views may help to explain the smallness of the interest which is shown. In the following pages an attempt is made to outline an account of thinking in purely causal terms, without any introduction of unique relations invented *ad hoc*. It is with this end in view, the provision of a natural as opposed to an artificial theory of thinking, that we begin with the consideration of signs.

Throughout almost all our life we are treating things as signs. All experience, using the word in the widest possible sense, is either enjoyed or interpreted (*i.e.*, treated as a sign) or both, and very little of it escapes some degree of interpretation. An account of the process of Interpretation is thus the key to the understanding of the Sign-situation, and therefore the be-

[1] See Appendix D, where Mr Russell's similar (1903) view will also be found.

[2] *Principles de Linguistique Psychologique*, pp. 52, 55, 68-9.

ginning of wisdom. It is astonishing that although the need for such an account has long been a commonplace in psychology, those concerned with the criticism and organization of our knowledge have with few exceptions entirely ignored the consequences of its neglect.

Attempts to provide this account have been given in many different vocabularies. The doctrines of the associationists,[1] of apperception,[2] of suggestion,[3] have led up to restatements in terms of process rather than of content: 'instinctive sequences'[4] taking the place of 'mental chemistry,' with advantage but without essential change in the views maintained. The most recent form in which the account appears is that adopted by Semon, the novelty of whose vocabulary seems to have attracted attention once more to considerations which were no doubt too familiar to be thought of any importance.

These otherwise valuable methods of approach tend to separate the treatment of fundamental laws of mental process from that of sign-interpretation, which is unfortunate for psychology. They have led not only to the discussion in isolation of problems essentially the same, but also to a failure to realize the extent of the ground already covered by earlier thinkers.

Since the formulation has always been given in causal terms, it will be convenient to use that terminology. Its use is indeed almost unavoidable in the interests of intelligibility, and *need* not be misleading if the correct expansion is remembered. Thus in this preliminary account we are merely using causal language as an expository convenience for the sake of its brevity and its verbs. The fuller statement which follows avoids all mention of causes, effects, and dependence,

[1] D. Hartley, *Observations on Man*, Prop. X.
[2] G. C. Lange, *Apperception*, Part I, §§ 1, 2.
[3] I. Miller, *The Psychology of Thinking*, p. 154.
[4] C. Lloyd Morgan, *Instinct and Experience*, p. 194.

and deals merely with observable correlations or contextual uniformities among events.

The effects upon the organism due to any sign, which may be any stimulus from without, or any process taking place within, depend upon the past history of the organism, both generally and in a more precise fashion. In a sense, no doubt, the whole past history is relevant: but there will be some among the past events in that history which more directly determine the nature of the present agitation than others. Thus when we strike a match, the movements we make and the sound of the scrape are present stimuli. But the excitation which results is different from what it would be had we never struck matches before. Past strikings have left, in our organization, engrams,[1] residual traces, which help to determine what the mental process will be. For instance, this mental process is among other things an awareness that we are striking a *match*. Apart from the effects of similar previous situations we should have no such awareness. Suppose further that the awareness is accompanied by an expectation of a flame. This expectation again will be due to the effects of situations in which the striking of a match has been followed by a flame. The expectation is the excitation of part of an engram complex, which is called up by a stimulus (the scrape) similar to a part only of the original stimulus-situation.

A further example will serve to make this clearer. The most celebrated of all caterpillars, whose history is in part recorded in the late Professor Lloyd Morgan's *Habit and Instinct*, p. 41, was striped yellow and black and was seized by one of the professor's chickens. Being offensive in taste to the chicken he was rejected. Thenceforth the chicken refrained from seizing similar caterpillars. Why? Because the sight of such a cater-

[1] Semon's terminology: *Die Mneme*, particularly Part II. (English translation, p. 138 ff.). For a critique of Semon's theory, see *op. cit.*, *Principles of Literary Criticism*, Chapter XIV., and *op. cit.*, *The Meaning of Psychology*, Chapter IV.

pillar, a part that is of the whole sight-seize-taste context of the original experience, now excites the chicken in a way sufficiently[1] like that in which the whole context did, for the seizing at least not to occur, whether the tasting (in images) does or not.

This simple case is typical of all interpretation, the peculiarity of interpretation being that when a context has affected us in the past the recurrence of merely a part of the context will cause us to react in the way in which we reacted before.[2] A sign is always a stimulus similar to some part of an original stimulus and sufficient to call up the engram[3] formed by that stimulus.

An engram is the residual trace of an adaptation[4] made by the organism to a stimulus. The mental process[5] due to the calling up of an engram is a similar adaptation: so far as it is cognitive, what it is adapted to is its referent, and is what the sign which excites it stands for or signifies.

The term 'adapted,' though convenient, requires expansion if this account is to be made clear—and to this expansion the remainder of the present chapter is devoted. Returning to our instance, we will suppose that the match ignites and that we have been expecting a flame. In this case the flame is what we

[1] The degree of likeness necessary is a matter of dispute. Yellow and black thus becomes a *sign* for offensiveness in taste.

[2] To use the terminology of the Gestalt school, when a 'gestalt' or 'configuration' has been formed, a system that has been disturbed will tend towards the 'end-state' determined by former occurrences. This view and terminology are discussed in *op. cit., The Meaning of Psychology*, pp. 108-11, and 114-15 where a paragraph will be found in which six different phrases could all be replaced by the word *gestalt*, if desired (though the paragraph seems clearer as it is).

[3] If the reader is doubtful about engrams he may read "to call up an excitation similar to that caused by the original stimulus."

[4] This is not necessarily a right or appropriate adaptation. We are here only considering adaptation so far as it is cognitive, and may disregard the affective-volitional character of the process.

[5] The account here given may be read as neutral in regard to psychoneural parallelism, interaction, and double aspect hypotheses, since the problem of the relation of mind and body is—in so far as it is not itself a phantom problem — a later one. Cf. Chapter IV., p. 81, and *op. cit., The Meaning of Psychology*, Chapter II.

are adapted to. More fully, the mental process which is the expectation is similar to processes which have been caused by flames in the past, and further it is 'directed to' the future. If we can discover what this 'directed to' stands for we shall have filled in the chief part of our account of interpretation.

Besides being 'directed to' the future our expectation is also 'directed to' flame. But here 'directed to' stands for nothing more than 'similar *to what has been caused by*.' A thought is directed to flame when it is similar in certain respects to thoughts which have been caused by flame. As has been pointed out above, we must not allow the defects of causal language either to mislead us here or alternatively to make us abandon the method of approach so indicated. We shall find, if we improve this language, both that this kind of substitute for 'directed to' loses its strangeness, and also that the same kind of substitution will meet the case of 'direction to the future' and will in fact explain the 'direction' or *reference* of thinking processes in general.

The unpurified notion of cause is especially misleading in this connection since it has led even the hardiest thinkers[1] to shrink from the identification of

[1] Exceptions such as Mr E. B. Holt and Mr Russell, who have independently adopted causal theories of reference, have not succeeded in giving precision to this view. The former, who holds (*The Freudian Wish*, p. 168) that in behaviour there is "a genuine objective reference to the environment," yet continues—"Even when one is conscious of things that are not there, as in hallucination, one's body is adjusted to them as if they were there," or again (p. 202), "Why does a boy go fishing? . . . Because the behaviour of the growing organism is so far integrated as to respond specifically to such an environmental object as fish in the pond. . . . The boy's thought (content) is the fish." It will be seen that the contextual theory of reference outlined in the present chapter provides an account of specific response which applies, as Mr Holt's does not, to erroneous and to truly adapted behaviour alike. Mr Russell, on the other hand, who, like Mr Holt, has now abandoned the theory of direct knowledge relations between minds and things, obscures the formulation of the causal account in his *Analysis of Mind* by introducing considerations which arise from a quite incompatible treatment. "It is a very singular thing," he says (p. 235), "that meaning which is single should generate objective reference, which is dual, namely, true and false." When we come to the analysis of complex references we shall see how this anomaly disappears. The supposed distinction between 'meaning' in this sense and objective reference is one merely of degree of complexity accentuated by symbolic

'thinking of' with 'being caused by.' The suggestion that to say 'I am thinking of A' is the same thing as to say 'My thought is being caused by A,' will shock every right-minded person; and yet when for 'caused' we substitute an expanded account, this strange suggestion will be found to be the solution.

A Cause indeed, in the sense of a something which forces another something called an effect to occur, is so obvious a phantom that it has been rejected even by metaphysicians. The current scientific account, on the other hand, which reduces causation to correlation, is awkward for purposes of exposition, since in the absence of a 'conjugating' vocabulary constant periphrasis is unavoidable. If we recognize, however, as the basis of this account the fact that experience has the character of recurrence, that is, comes to us in more or less uniform contexts, we have in this all that is required for the theory of signs and all that the old theory of causes was entitled to maintain. Some of these contexts are temporally and spatially closer than others: the contexts investigated by physics for instance narrow themselves down until differential equations are invoked; those which psychology has hitherto succeeded in detecting are wide, the uniformly linked events being often far apart in time. Interpretation, however, is only possible thanks to these recurrent contexts, a statement which is very generally admitted

conventions. It will be further noticed that Mr Russell's causal account of meaning, especially pp. 197 ff. and 231 ff., differs from that developed here in the importance assigned to images, meaning or reference being defined either through the similarity of images to what they mean or through their 'causal efficacy,' the 'appropriateness' of their effects. The chief objections to this view are the obscurity of 'appropriateness,' the variation of 'causal efficacy' with identity of meaning, and the complexities which result in connection with the problem of Truth. Professor Eaton in his *Symbolism and Truth* (1925), p. 23, adopts a view somewhat similar to that of Mr Russell: "The simplest solution for the purposes of the theory of knowledge is to accept as unique a *meaning activity*. . . . Towards every object certain activities are appropriate." The contention of the present chapter, on the other hand, is that it is possible and profitable to go behind this 'appropriateness.'

Mr. Russell's less accessible exposition (*The Dial*, August, 1926, pp. 117-119) admits that images should not be introduced to explain meaning.

but which if examined will be found to be far more fundamental than has been supposed. To say, indeed, that anything is an interpretation is to say that it is a member of a psychological context of a certain kind. An interpretation is itself a recurrence.

A concrete illustration may be considered at this point. There is a well-known dog in most books upon animal behaviour which, on hearing the dinner-bell, runs, even from parts of the house quite out of reach of scents and savours, into the dining-room, so as to be well placed, should any kind thoughts towards him arise in the diners. Such a dog *interprets* the sound of the gong as a sign. How does this happen? We shall all agree about the answer; that it is through the dog's past experience. In this experience there have been so to speak recurrent clumps of events, and one such clump has been made up roughly as follows: Gong, savoury odour, longing contemplation of consumption of viands by diners, donations, gratification. Such a clump recurring from time to time we shall call an *external* context. Now on a particular occasion the gong is heard out of reach of savours. But thanks to past experience of gong-sounds together with savours in the interpretative dog, this present gong-sound gets into a peculiar relation to past gongs and savours, longings, etc., so that he acts in the sagacious manner described, and is in evidence at the meal. Now this set of mental events—his present hearing of the gong, his past hearings of similar sounds, his past savourings together with gongs, etc., and also his present mental process owing to which he runs into the dining-room—such a set we shall call *psychological* context. A context of this sort may plainly recur as regards its more general features. It is also clear that the members of it may be indefinitely numerous and may be widely separated in time, and that it is through this separateness in time that such a psychological context is able to link together external contexts, the recurrent clumps of experiences of the gong-savour kind above mentioned. In a similar fashion all learning by experience will illustrate the point that to be an act of interpretation is merely to be a peculiar[1] member of a psychological context of a certain kind; a psychological context being a recurrent set of mental events peculiarly related to one another so as to recur, as regards their main features, with partial uniformity.

Little hesitation will be felt in granting that without such recurrence or partial uniformity no prediction, no inference, no recognition, no inductive generalization, no knowledge or probable opinion as to what is not immediately given, would be possible. What is more difficult to realize is that this is so only because these processes, recognitions, inferences or thinkings are members of certain recurrent psychological contexts. To say that I recognize something before me as a strawberry and expect it to be luscious, is to say that a present process in me belongs to a determinative psychological context together with certain past processes (past perceptions and consumptions of strawberries). These psychological contexts recur whenever we recognize or infer. Usually they link up with (or form wider contexts with) external[2] contexts in a peculiar fashion.[3] When they do not, we are said to have been mistaken.

The simplest terminology in which this kind of linkage can be stated is that of signs. Behind all interpretation we have the fact that when part of an external context recurs in experience this part is, through its linkage with a member of some psychological context (*i.e.*, of a causally connected group of mental events often widely separated in time) sometimes a sign of the rest of the external context.

Two points require elucidation if this outline is to

[1] A further analysis of the peculiarity appears in Appendix B.

[2] If we never discussed psychology 'external' might be read as 'physical.'

[3] Cf. p. 62 *infra*, and Appendix B.

be filled in. The first concerns Contexts;[1] the second the sense in which they are Uniform.

(1) *A context is a set of entities (things or events) related in a certain way; these entities have each a character such that other sets of entities occur having the same characters and related by the same relation; and these occur 'nearly uniformly.'* In our instance of the match-scrape event and the flame event the uniting relation evidently includes proximity in time and space—a scrape in America and a flame in China would not constitute such a context—but it is important to realize that no restriction need be initially imposed as to the kind of relation which may occur as the uniting relation in a context, since which relations actually occur will be discovered only by experience. Contexts, moreover, may have any number of members; dual contexts containing only two members seem to be rare, though for purposes of exposition it is convenient to suppose them to occur. The constitutive characters involved present a certain difficulty. In our instance of the match-scrape event and the flame event they may be written 'being a scrape' and 'being a flame,' but these are plainly shorthand names for very elaborate sets of properties. It is not all scrapes from which we expect flames, and we would be surprised if our match flamed like magnesium ribbon.

[1] Throughout the present volume the term context is used in the strictly technical sense defined below, which differs from the ordinary use. A literary context is a group of words, incidents, ideas, etc., which on a given occasion accompanies or surrounds whatever is said to have the context, whereas a determinative context is a group of this kind which both recurs and is such that one at least of its members is determined, given the others. A somewhat similar but vaguer use appears to have been adopted by Professor Baldwin (*Thought and Things*, Vol. I., p. 48), though it becomes clear as his exposition proceeds (cf. also Appendix D) that the resemblance is illusory, since, *e.g.*, an image (Vol. I., p. 81) can be "convertible into a context," and we read of "the development within a content itself of the enlarged context of predicated and implicated meanings." (Vol. II., p. 246.) Such uses have more in common with that of Professor Titchener, who after the second passage which we quote in Chapter VIII., says, "I understand by context simply the mental process or complex of mental processes which accrues to the original idea through the situation in which the organism finds itself."

(2) The difficulty here suggested in choosing constitutive characters is connected with the problem 'In what sense do contexts occur *nearly uniformly?*' It is plain that if sufficiently general characters are taken and sufficiently general uniting relations, contexts not 'nearly' but perfectly uniform can easily be found. For instance, the context constituted by two entities having each the character of 'being an event' and related by the relation of 'succession.'[1] On the other hand if we make the constitutive characters and uniting relation too specific, recurrence becomes uncertain. For this reason our account has to be in terms of probability. In our instance, to say that the context of which 'scrape' and 'flame' are constitutive characters recurs (or is a context) is to say:—

either that whenever there is a scrape there will probably be a flame having the required relation to the scrape;

or that whenever there is a flame there was probably a scrape having the converse relation to the flame;

or both these statements.

In the first case the context is said to be determinative in respect of the character flame; in the second in respect of the character scrape; in the third in respect of both characters.

A dual context is here taken for the sake of simplicity, a fact which tends to make the account appear artificial. Multiple contexts of three or more terms involve no further problems. They must be determinative in respect of one constitutive character, and may be so in respect of any number.

In this account we have carefully avoided all mention

[1] It should be noted that it is not necessary for the characters in respect of which a sign is interpreted to be 'given,' *i.e.*, for us to know that they belong to it. This circumstance is of importance in considering the processes of interpretation by which we arrive at knowledge of other entities than sensations. It should be further observed that a constitutive character may be of the form 'being either A or B or C, etc.'

of images—those revivals or copies of sensory experience which figure so prominently in most accounts of thinking. There are good reasons why attempts to build a theory of interpretation upon images must be hazardous. One of these is the grave doubt whether in some minds they ever occur or ever have occurred. Another is that in very many interpretations where words play no recognizable part, introspection, unless excessively subtle and therefore of doubtful value as evidence, fails to show that imagery is present. A third and stronger reason is that images seem to a great extent to be mental luxuries. Before the appearance of an image, say, of an afanc, something can be observed to occur which is often misleadingly described as 'an intention of imagining' an afanc. But that this is not *merely* an intention becomes plain upon reflection. When we speak of an intention in this way we are speaking of affective-volitional characters, those, roughly speaking, on account of which a state of mind changes from a relatively inchoate to a relatively organized and articulate condition. An intention by itself is as impossible as an excitement. There has to be something which is excited, and there has to be something for the intention to belong to. Now what is this in such cases as we are examining?

Whatever it is it has that peculiar character of being directed towards one thing rather than another, which we here call reference. This reference may be uncertain and vague, but seems to be the same in kind as that which occurs in more articulate and clear-cut cases of thinking, where symbols in the form of images or words have been provided. In the initial stages of such references it is hard to suppose that images are playing any essential part. Any image which does arise is at once accepted or rejected as it accords or disaccords with the reference, and this accordance is not a question of matching between images or of similarity in any intrinsic characters. If images of any sort are involved in these states of beginning to think of things, it is certain that they are not always involved *qua* images, *i.e.*, as copying or representing the things to which the reference points, but in a looser capacity as mere signs and not in their capacity as mimetic or simulative signs.

Indeed, it may be questioned whether mimetic imagery is not really a late, sporadic product in mental development. We are so accustomed to beginning psychology with images that we tend to think that minds must have begun with them too. But there is no good reason to suppose that the mind could not work equally well without them. They have certain oddly limited uses as economizing effort in certain restricted fields. The artist, the chess-player, the mathematician find them convenient. But these are hardly primitive mental occupations. Hunger rarely excites taste images, the salivary flow occurs without them. Route-finding in pathless wilds or Metropolitan suburbs is best done by sense of direction and perception alone. On the whole, a mimetic sign is not the kind of thing that a primitive mind would be able to make much use of. Other signs would serve equally well for most purposes, and the few advantages of images would be more than counterbalanced by 'the risk of danger' to which their users expose themselves. An inaccurate or irrelevant image is worse than no image at all. Such arguments as there are in favour of images as very primitive and fundamental products, the argument from dreams, for example, or the alleged prevalence of images among children and primitive peoples, are obviously difficult to estimate. Imagery may be prevalent without necessarily serving any important function; in day-dreaming, for instance, the gratifications which it affords are no proof that the references concerned could not occur without it. Similarly those who naturally produce exhaustive images of their breakfast-table can often know all about it without a glimmer of an image, unless too much indulgence in images has impaired their natural ability.

For these reasons, any theory of interpretation which can refrain from making images a corner-stone has clear advantages over those which cannot. It is mainly on this point that the view here developed differs from Mr Russell's account[1] of meaning, which should, however, be consulted by those who desire a more simple discussion of the part played by Mnemonic causation in knowledge than our brief outline provides.

Suppose now that we have struck our match and have expected a flame. We need some means of deciding whether our expectation has been true or false. Actually we look to see whether there was a flame or not, but the question we have to answer is, how do we pick out, amongst all the other possible events which we might have selected, this particular flame as the event on which the truth or falsity of our expectation depended.[2] We pick it out by means of certain external contexts to which it belongs: namely, it is that event, if any, which completes the context whose other member in this case is the scrape, and thus comes to be linked to the expectation through the psychological context made up of that expectation and past experiences of scrapes and flames.

If now there be an event which completes the external context in question, the reference is *true* and the event is its referent. If there be no such event, the reference is *false*, and the expectation is disappointed.

The above account covers beliefs of the form 'a flame will follow this scrape' prompted by a present

[1] See *The Analysis of Mind*, especially pp. 207-210. One point in this treatment is of extreme importance. "Generality and particularity," according to Mr Russell, "are a matter of degree" (p. 209). For a causal theory of reference no other conclusion appears possible. Absolute particulars and absolute universals ought therefore to be out of court and beneath discussion.

[2] A more formal and elaborate account of this crucial step in the theory of interpretation will be found in Appendix B, to which those who appreciate the complexity of the subject are directed.

sensation. Instead of a present sensation a belief may itself be a sign for a further belief which will then be an interpretation of this belief. The only cases of this which appear to occur are introspective beliefs of the form 'I believe that I am believing, etc.' which may, it is important to recognize, be false as often as, or more often than, other beliefs. As a rule a belief not prompted by a sensation requires a number of beliefs simultaneous or successive for its signs. The beliefs, 'There will be a flame' and 'I am in a powder factory,' will, for most believers, be signs together interpreted by the belief 'The end is at hand.' Such is one of the psychological contexts determinative in respect of the character of this last belief.[1] Whether the belief in question is true or not will depend upon whether there is or is not some entity forming together with the referents of the two sign beliefs, in virtue of its characters and their characters and a multiple relation, a context determinative in respect of their characters. In other words—upon whether the place does blow up.

In this way the account given can be extended to all cases of particular expectations. Further, since the uniting relations of contexts are not restricted to successions it will also apply to all cases of inference or interpretation from particular to particular. The next step, therefore, is to inquire what kind of account can be given of general references.

The abstract language which it is necessary to employ raises certain difficulties. In a later chapter arguments will be brought in favour of regarding such apparent symbols as 'character,' 'relation,' 'property,'

[1] The additional assumption required here is that the effects of a belief are often similar, in respect of derivative beliefs, to the effects of the verifying sensation. Few people will deny that the belief that an unseen man in a bush is shooting at me will have effects (in respect of such derivative beliefs as that it would be better for me to be elsewhere) similar to those which would be occasioned by the sight of the man so shooting. Such contexts, in which a belief in the occurrence of A and A's occurrence itself are alternative signs for interpretations the same in these respects, are as well established as any in psychology.

'concept,' etc., as standing for nothing beyond (indirectly) the individuals to which the alleged character would be applicable. The most important of these arguments is the natural incredibility of there being such universal denizens of a world of being. As we shall see, these apparent symbols are indispensable as machinery, and thus for some purposes such credulity is harmless. But for other purposes these baseless (or purely symbolically based) beliefs are dangerous impediments. Thus a chief source of opposition to an extension of the account here outlined to general references, is phantom difficulties deriving from faith in this other world.

Such references may be formulated in a variety of ways:—'All S is P' and '$(x): \phi(x) \supset \psi(x)$' are favourites. What we have to discover is what happens when we have a belief which can be symbolized in these ways. Let us take as an instance the belief 'All match-scrapes are followed by flames.' There is good reason to suppose that such beliefs are a later psychological development than beliefs of the form which we have been considering. It is plausible to suppose that some animals and infants have particular expectations but not any general beliefs. General beliefs, it is said, arise by reflection upon particular beliefs. Thus we may expect to find that general beliefs arise in some way out of particular beliefs. But the generality and particularity to be attributed to simple or primordial references are certainly not those which logical formulation endeavours to introduce. Nor should it be supposed that genetically a stage or era of particular reference precedes general thinking. It is rather the case that in all thought processes two tendencies are present, one towards greater definiteness or precision, the other towards wider scope and range. It is the conditions under which this second tendency takes effect that we are here considering.

Following this clue let us try to set down some of the

conditions under which a general belief might develop from such particular references as we have been considering. To begin with we may suppose

(1) that a number of true and verified interpretations of match-scrapes have occurred in the same organism, and
(2) that no interpretation which has been shown to be false, by the absence in the related sensation of the expected flame character, is concerned in the genesis of the general belief.

The second of these conditions is plainly more important than the first. We often seem to pass to general beliefs from single experiences and not to require a plurality, but (exceptionally powerful thinkers apart) we do not base general beliefs upon directly contradictory evidence. We may therefore retain the second condition, but must revise the first. In some cases, no doubt, repeated verified expectations do condition the general expectation, but they condition its degree rather than its reference. On the other hand some experience of repetition would seem to be required. A primordial mind's first thought could hardly be a general thought in the sense here considered. It seems justifiable to assume that some series of similar verified interpretations should be included in the context of a general belief, though how closely this need be connected with the particular interpretation which is being generalized must at present be left uncertain.

Another condition which can only be put rather vaguely concerns the inclusiveness of a general reference. The togetherness involved in such a reference does not seem to require any properties in a 'mind' beyond those already assumed and stated, but the inclusiveness might be thought to raise an additional problem. The kind of experience required, however, is not difficult to discover. On many occasions so far as the verifying stimuli are concerned it is indifferent whether we think of all of a given set of objects or of each of them in turn. The child who finds all his fingers sticky might equally well have found each of them sticky. On other occasions his smallest fingers will not need to be washed. Thus the difference between inclusive and non-inclusive sets of objects as referents, the difference between 'some' and 'all' references, will early develop appropriate signs. Individuals can be found who throughout their lives 'think' of these differences by means of such images, *i.e.*, use such images as adjunct-signs in their interpretations. In other cases no such imagery nor even the use of the words 'all' or 'some,' or any equivalents, is discoverable. Yet even in these cases some lingering trace of the engraphic action due to situations of this sort may reasonably be supposed as conditioning interpretations which 'employ these notions.' In attempting therefore to set out the kind of psychological context of which a general reference consists, terms representing them would require inclusion.

Such in very tentative outline is the account which the causal theory of reference would give of general beliefs. The detailed investigation of such contexts is a task to which sooner or later psychology must address itself, but the methods required are of a kind for which the science has only recently begun to seek. Much may be expected when the theory of the conditioned reflex, due to Pavlov, has been further developed.[1]

It remains to discuss in what sense, if any, a false belief, particular or general, has a referent. From the definitions given it will be plain that the sense in which a false belief may be said to have a referent must be quite other than that in which a true belief has a referent. Thus the arguments now to be given for a more extended use of the term in no way affect what has been said; and it will also be purely as a matter

[1] For an account of this method and its applications see *op. cit.*, *The Meaning of Psychology*, Chapter IV.

of convenience that we shall use the term in connection with false beliefs.

In the first place it is clear that true and false references alike agree in a respect in which processes such as sensing, breathing, contracting muscles, secreting, desiring, etc., do not agree with them. It is convenient to have a term, such as reference, to stand for this respect in which they agree. The term 'belief' which might at first appear most suitable is less convenient, both because of its association with doctrines such as those above discussed which postulate an unique relation 'thinking of,' and because it is becoming more and more often used with special reference to the affective-volitional characters of the process. A second and stronger reason derives from what may be called the analysis of references. If we compare, say, the references symbolized by 'There will be a flash soon,' and 'There will be a noise soon,' it is at least plausible to suppose that they are compounds containing some similar and some dissimilar parts. The parts symbolized by 'flash' and 'noise' we may suppose to be dissimilar, and the remaining parts to be similar in the two cases. The question then arises: "What are these parts from which it would seem references can be compounded?"

The answer which we shall give will be that they are themselves references, that every compound reference is composed wholly of simple references united in such a way as will give the required structure to the compound reference they compose. But in attempting to carry out this analysis a special difficulty has to be guarded against. We must not suppose that the structure of the symbol by which we symbolize the reference to be analysed does in any regular fashion reflect its structure. Thus in speaking of the parts symbolized by 'flash' and 'noise' above we are running a risk. Illegitimate analyses of symbols are the source of nearly all the difficulties in these subjects.

Another point which must first be made clear concerns the sense in whch references may be compounded. To speak of a reference is to speak of the contexts psychological and external by which a sign is linked to its referent. Thus a discussion of the compounding of references is a discussion of the relations of contexts to one another.

What are usually called the 'logical forms' of propositions, and what we may call the forms of references, are, for the view here maintained, forms or structures of the determinative contexts of interpretations. They are at present approached by logicians mainly through the study of symbolic procedure. A more direct approach appears however to be possible, though, as yet, difficult. Thus the remaining portions of the complete contextual theory of reference, namely the accounts of references of the forms 'p or q,' 'p and q,' 'not p,' and of the difference between 'all S' and 'some S,' regarded as concerned with the interweaving of contexts, are, if still conjectural, plainly not beyond conjecture.

With this proviso, we may resume the consideration of the referents of false and of the analysis of compound beliefs.

We have seen that true and false beliefs are members of the same kinds of psychological contexts, and that they differ only in respect of external contexts.[1] Let

[1] A complex of things as united in a context may be called a 'fact.' There need be no harm in this, but as a rule the verbal habits thus incited overpower the sense of actuality even in the best philosophers. Out of facts spring 'negative facts'; 'that no flame occurs' becomes a negative fact with which our expectation fails to *correspond* when we are in error. It is then natural to suppose that there are two modes of reference, towards a fact for a true reference, away from it for a false. In this way the theory of reference can be made very complicated and difficult, as for instance by Mr Russell in his *Analysis of Mind*, pp. 271-78. As regards negative facts, Mr Russell has allowed his earlier theories to remain undisturbed by his recent study of Meaning. The general question of 'negative facts' is discussed in Appendix E; and we shall find, when we come to distinguish the various senses of meaning, that to raise the question of the correspondence of belief with fact is for a causal theory of reference to attempt to solve the problem twice over. When the problem of reference is settled that of truth is found to be solved as well.

us consider this difference again, taking for the sake of simplicity the case of particular beliefs. Suppose that of two possible beliefs, 'There will be something green here in a moment,' 'There will be something red here in a moment,' the first is true and the second false. But the second, if it can be regarded, as having contained or included the belief, 'There will be something here in a moment,' will have included a belief which is true and similar to a belief included in the first belief. Reverting now to our definition of a context let us see in what sense this belief is included and how it can be true.

In such a case the external context may consist of two entities, say *s* (a sign) and *g* (something green), having the characters *S*, *G*, and related by space and time relations which may be taken together. But it is clear that both *s* and *g* will have other characters besides *S* and *G*. For instance, *s* has succeeded other entities and may be interpreted in respect of this character as well as in respect of *S*, so[1] interpreted it gives rise to the belief, 'There will be something here in a moment'; interpreted also in the further respect of *S* it gives rise to the complex belief, 'There will be something green here in a moment,' or to the complex belief, 'There will be something red here in a moment,' true and false interpretation of *s* in this further respect as the case may be. In either case, however, the contained belief, 'There will be something here in a moment,' will be true if there is something (say *g*) which forms with *s*, in virtue of *s*'s character of being a successor (or other temporal characters) and *g*'s temporal characters, a context determinative of this character of *s*. Thanks to the generality of these characters such contexts never fail to recur, a fact which accounts for the ease with which true predictions of this unspecific kind can be made.

[1] Whether this is a sufficient character for the interpretation need not be considered in this brief outline of the theory.

It appears then that a belief may contain other less specific beliefs, and that a compound definite belief is composed of simpler, less specific beliefs, united by such relations as will yield the required structure.[1]

One objection to such a view derives from language. It is usual to restrict the term belief to such processes as are naturally symbolized by propositions and further to those among such processes as have certain affective-volitional characters in addition to their characters as cognitions. The simple references which would be required if the analysis suggested were adopted would rarely lend themselves to propositional formulation and would be lacking as a rule in accompanying belief, feelings and promptings to action. Thus the terms 'idea' and 'conception' would often be more suitable for such processes. To extend a metaphor which is becoming familiar, these might be regarded as 'electronic' references. But the ideas or conception with which we are here concerned would have to be clearly distinguished from the 'concepts' of those metaphysicians who believe in a world of universals. We shall deal at greater length with the question in Chapter V.

Let us consider the idea or conception of green. It arises in the reader in this case through the occurrence of the word 'green.' On many occasions this word has been accompanied by presentations of green things. Thus the occurrence of the word causes in him a certain process which we may call the idea of green. But this process is not the idea of any one green thing; such an idea would be more complex and would require a sign (or symbol in this case) with further characters for him to interpret—only so will his idea be specific.

[1] The important and intricate problems raised by these relations are to be approached in the same fashion as the problem of the generality of references, which is in fact an instance. The great question 'What is logical form?' left at present to logicians whose only method is the superstitious rite 'direct inspection,' must in time be made amenable to investigation.

The psychological context to which it belongs is not of a form to link any one green thing with the sign rather than any other. If now we write instead, 'a green thing,' the same process occurs—unless the reader is a logician or philosopher with special theories (*i.e.*, peculiar linguistic contexts). In both cases the idea can be said to be 'of' any sensation similar to certain sensations which have accompanied in the past the occurrence of the sensation taken as a sign. Compare now the indefinite belief symbolized by 'There are green things.' Here any one of the same set of sensations that the idea was said to be 'of' will verify the belief. For if there be one or more entities similar to certain entities which are members of its psychological context, it will be true; otherwise it will be false. We may therefore extend the term 'referent' to cover these entities, if there be any such, without the usage leading to confusion.

It will be noticed that strictly simple indefinite beliefs (illustrated by, 'There are green things' as opposed to 'There are green things now') only require for their truth a condition which is present among their psychological contexts. This happy state of things has its parallel in the fact that strictly simple ideas raise no problem as to whether they are ideas 'of' anything or not. But complex ideas, such as glass mountains, phœnixes, round squares, and virtuous triangles may be made to bristle with such problems. The distinction between an idea and a belief is, however, one of degree, although through symbolic conventions it can sometimes appear insuperable.

We can now define the usage of the term 'referent' for false beliefs. All beliefs whether true or false are theoretically analysable into compounds whose constituents are simple references, either definite or indefinite, united by the relations which give its 'logical form' to the reference.

Definite simple references are not very common.

Sometimes when we say 'this!' 'there!' 'now!' we seem to have them. But usually, even when our reference is such that it can have but one referent, it can be analysed. Even references for which we use simple symbols (names), *e.g.*, Dostoevski, are perhaps always compound, distinct contexts being involved severally determinative of distinct characters of the referent.[1] What is more important is to understand the peculiar dispersion which occurs in false reference. Illustrations perhaps make this clearer than do arguments.

Thus, if we say, 'This is a book' and are in error, our reference will be composed of a simple indefinite reference to any book, another to anything now, another to anything which may be here, and so on. These constituents will all be true, but the whole reference to this book which they together make up (by cancelling out, as it were, all but the one referent which can be a book and here and now) will be false, if we are in error and what is there is actually a box or something which fails to complete the three contexts, book, here, and now. To take a slightly more intricate case, a golfer may exclaim, "Nicely over!" and it may be obvious to the onlooker that his reference is to a divot and its flight, to his stroke, to a bunker, and to a ball. Yet the ball remains stationary, and these constituent or component references, each adequate in itself, are combined in his complex reference otherwise than are their separate referents in actual fact. There is clearly no case for a non-occurrent flight of a golf-ball as an object of his belief; though he may have been referring to the feel of his stroke, or to an image of a travelling ball. In these last cases we should have to suppose him to be shortening his own interpretative chain instead of breaking loose and venturing a step too far

[1] This sentence like all sentences containing words such as 'character,' is redundant and should rather read . . . "distinct contexts being involved severally, indefinitely, determinative of the referent." But this pruning of its redundancies would lead to failure in its communicative function. Cf. p. 96 *infra*.

by what may be called saltatory interpretation. His language (cf. also Canon IV., page 103 *infra*) does not bind us to either alternative. Thus we see in outline how compound false beliefs may be analysed.

The referent of a compound false belief will be the set of the scattered referents of the true simple beliefs which it contains. We shall, in what follows, speak of beliefs, and interpretations, whether true or false, and of ideas, as references, implying that in the senses above defined they have referents.

We thus see how the contextual theory of reference can be extended to cover all beliefs, ideas, conceptions and 'thinkings of.' The details of its application to special cases remain to be worked out. Logicians will no doubt be able to propound many puzzles,[1] the solving of which will provide healthy exercise for psychologists. The general hypothesis that thinking or reference is reducible to causal relations ought however to commend itself more and more to those who take up (at least sometimes) a scientific attitude to the world. Subject to the proviso that some satisfactory account of probability can be given, 'meaning' in the sense of reference becomes according to this theory a matter open to experimental methods.

A satisfactory account of probability, however, though very desirable, does not seem likely to be forthcoming by current methods. Evidently a change of attack is required. The late Lord Keynes' *Treatise* starting as it does with an unanalysable logical relation, called probability, which holds between equally mysterious and unapproachable entities, called propositions, is too mediæval in its outlook to be fruitful; and it remains to be seen whether scientists will be able to profit by Reichenbach's more empirical *Wahrscheinlichkeitslehre*.

It seems possible on the contextual theory of refer-

[1] As, for instance, whether in the example taken above, if one or both of the sign beliefs were false, and yet the room we were in did blow up through other causes, our belief could be true? This problem is easily solved if we notice that although the belief symbolized in the speaker would be false, a belief incited in a hearer might be true.

ence to suggest an expansion of this kind of obscure shorthand and so come nearer the formulation of the yet undiscovered central question of probability. What are talked about by logicians as propositions are, according to this theory, relational characters of acts of referring—those relational characters for which the term 'references' is used. Thus to believe, or entertain, or think of, a proposition, is on this view simply to refer, and the proposition as a separate entity is to be regarded as nothing but a linguistic fiction foisted upon us by the utraquistic subterfuge.[1] Two 'thinkings of' the same 'proposition' are two thinkings with the same reference, the same relational property, namely 'being contextually linked in the same way with the same referent.' It will be noted that on this account of propositions the logical relations of propositions to one another must be dealt with far less summarily and formally than has hitherto been the case.

With propositions so understood there occurs a sense in which a single proposition by itself without relation to other propositions, can intelligibly be said to be probable. Probability here has still a relational aspect, and it is only because propositions (*i.e.*, references) are relational that they can be said to be probable. This very fundamental sense is that in which the uniformity of the context upon which the truth of a reference depends is probable.

We have seen that by taking very general constitutive characters and uniting relation, we obtain contexts of the highest probability. Similarly by taking too specific characters and relation the probability of the context dwindles until we should no longer call it a context. In this way, whether a context is probable can be seen to be a question about the degree of generality of its constitutive characters and uniting relation; about the number of its members, the other contexts to which they belong and so on . . . a question

[1] Cf. Chapter VI., p. 134.

not about one feature of the context but about many. We can always for instance raise the probability of a context by adding suitable members. But this last though a natural remark suffers from the linguistic redundance to which the difficulties of the problem are chiefly due. 'Probability' in the fundamental sense in which a context is probable is a shorthand symbol for all those of its features upon which the degree of its uniformity depends.

In considering conscious and critical processes of interpretation we must not fail to realize that all such activity, *e.g.*, of the kind discussed in the theory of induction, rests upon 'instinctive' interpretations. If we recognize how essential 'instinctive' interpretation is throughout, we shall be able to pursue our investigations undisturbed by the doubts of causal purists or the delay of the mathematicians in bringing their differential equations into action. For the working of a differential equation itself, that most rational process of interpretation, will break down unless many 'instinctive' interpretations, which are not at present capable of any mathematical treatment, are successfully performed.

It is sometimes very easy by experimental methods to discover what a thought process is referring to. If for instance we ask a subject to 'think of' magenta we shall, by showing various colours to him, as often as not find that he is thinking of some other colour. It is this kind of consideraton which makes the phrase 'adapted to' so convenient an equivalent for 'referring to,' and if we bear in mind that 'being adapted to' something is only a shorthand symbol for being linked with it in the manner described, through external and psychological contexts, we may be able to use the term without its purposive and biological associations leading to misunderstanding.

We have still to give an account of misinterpretation, and to explain how unfounded beliefs can arise. To begin with the first, a person is often said to have introduced *irrelevant*, or to have omitted relevant, considerations or notions when he has misinterpreted some sign. The notion of relevance is of great importance in the theory of meaning. A consideration (notion, idea) or an experience, we shall say, is *relevant* to an interpretation when it forms part of the psychological context which links other contexts together in the peculiar fashion in which interpretation so links them.[1] An irrelevant consideration is a non-linking member of a psychological context. The fact that 'baseless' convictions occur might be thought to be an objection to the view of thinking here maintained. The explanation is however to be found in the fact that mental processes are not determined purely psychologically but, for example, by blood pressure also. If our interpretation depended only upon purely psychological contexts it might be that we should always be justified in our beliefs, true or false. We misinterpret typically when we are asleep or tired. Misinterpretaton therefore is due to interference with psychological contexts, to 'mistakes.' Whether an interpretation is true or false on the other hand does not depend only upon psychological contexts—unless we are discussing psychology. We may have had every reason to expect a flame when we struck our match, but this, alas! will not have made the flame certain to occur. That depends upon a physical not a psychological context.

[1] Other psychological linkings of external contexts are not essentially different from interpretation, but we are only here concerned with the cognitive aspect of mental process. The same sense of relevance would be appropriate in discussing conation. The context method of analysis is capable of throwing much light upon the problems of desire and motive.

CHAPTER IV

SIGNS IN PERCEPTION

La Nature est un temple où de vivants piliers
Laissent parfois sortir de confuses paroles ;
L'homme y passe à travers des forêts de symboles
Qui l'observent avec des regards familiers.—
Baudelaire.

THOUGH with the growth of knowledge we have become much less certain than our ancestors about what chairs and tables are, physicists and philosophers have not yet succeeded in putting the question entirely beyond discussion. Every one agrees that chairs and tables are perfectly good things—they are there and can be touched—but all competent to form an opinion are equally agreed that whatever we see is certainly not them. What shall we do about it?

Why scientists and others are now agreed that what we see is not chairs and tables will be at once obvious if we consider what we do see when we look at such objects. On the other hand, the accounts given of what we do see have not taken the matter further, owing to bad habits, which we form in tender years, of misnaming things which interest us. The following, for example, is a common method of procedure illustrating the way in which these habits arise :—

"I remember on one occasion wanting the word for Table. There were five or six boys standing round, and, tapping the table with my forefinger, I asked, 'What is this?' One boy said it was a *dodela*, another that it was an *etanda*, a third stated that it was *bokali*, a fourth that it was *elamba*, and the fifth said it was *meza*. These various words we wrote in our note-book, and congratulated ourselves that we were working among a people who possessed so rich a language that they had five words for one article."[1]

The assumption of the reverend gentleman is that, having asked a definite question, he was entitled to a definite answer. Very little study of what he actually saw or tapped might have saved him the trouble of discovering at a later stage that "one lad had thought we wanted the word for tapping; another understood we were seeking the word for the material of which the table was made; another had an idea that we required the word for hardness; another thought we wished for a name for that which covered the table; and the last, not being able, perhaps, to think of anything else gave us the word *meza*, table—the very word we were seeking."

A similar discovery awaits the experts, and it may not be inapposite to indicate the main features of this imminent advance in knowledge. It is at first sight surprising that modern investigators should have been so long in taking up the analysis of sign-situations as begun by Aenesidemus and Occam. But their uneasiness in matters which they supposed to fall within the domain of 'the metaphysicians,' seems to have been sufficient to inhibit their curiosity as to the principles of interpretation involved at every stage of their work. Moreover, so long as controversy with specialists in other fields was avoided, a great deal could be achieved without the realization that perception can only be treated scientifically when its character as a sign-situation is analysed.

The isolated utterance of Helmholtz is therefore all the more significant, for not only was Helmholtz one of the profoundest scientific thinkers of modern times,

[1] *Among Congo Cannibals*, by J. H. Weeks, p. 51.

but, as we know from his correspondence, he took throughout his life a lively interest in philosophic controversies. In 1856 we even find him referring to the problem of the way in which we pass from simple sensations to judgments of perception as one to which no modern philosopher had devoted serious attention. He was much influenced by Kant, who, in spite of his disconcerting technique, seems constantly on the verge of approaching the central issues of interpretation, and who has been claimed as the most convinced Nominalist of modern times:[1] but there is nothing particularly Kantian about the theory of signs which can be found in various parts of Helmholtz' writings.[2] Our knowledge, he contended, takes the form of signs, and those signs we interpret as signifying the unknown relation of things in the external world. The sensations which lie at the basis of all perceptions are subjective signs of external objects.[3] The qualities of sensations are not the qualities of objects. Signs are not pictures of reality.

"A sign need have no kind of similarity whatever with what it signifies. The relation consists simply in the fact that the same object acting under similar circumstances arouses the same sign, so that different signs correspond always to different sensations."[4]

In discussing the way in which we interpret sensations in terms of an external world, Helmholtz has occasion to point out that the multiplicity of the optical signs which we use is such that we need not be surprised at the variety and complexity of the news which they give us. The elementary signs of language are only 26 letters. If out of these 26 letters we can get the whole of literature and science, the 250,000 optic nerve fibres can be relied on for an even richer and more finely graded knowledge.

[1] H. Wolff, *Neue Kritik der reinen Vernunft*, p. 17.
[2] Collated by Kühtmann, *op. cit.*, p. 66.
[3] *Vorträge und Reden*, I., 393.
[4] *Die Tatsachen in der Wahrnehmung*, p. 39.

What do we see when we look at a table? First and foremost, a lighted region containing some air, lit by rays coming partly from the direction of the table, partly from other sources; then the further boundaries of this region, surfaces of objects, including part of the surface of the table. If now we point at what we see and name it *This*, we are in danger, if our attention is concentrated on the table, of saying: This is a Table. So that we must be careful. And where is colour according to this scheme? Somewhere in the eye, as anyone who cares to strike his eye will discover.

What we have described is not the Table, though part of what we have described is part of the table. Anything which we say under these circumstances which involves the Table must also involve *Interpretation*. We interpret a sign, some part of what is given,[1] as signifying something other than itself, in this case the table.

But this is not the whole of the story, and here it seems possible to say something quite new. It would be strange to suggest that we see anything which is not in front of the eye, or which does not, like a *musca volitans*, throw images on the retina. Thus purists will have to maintain that we never see colours. Yet it is colours and such directly apprehended entities that are the initial signs on which all interpretation, all inference, all knowledge is based. And what is it that by interpretation we come to know? It is what is present—a whole which, as we learn in course of time, is com-

[1] It has long been recognized that there is something amiss with the term Datum. The 'given' is often of all things the most difficult to accept.

(i) A thing can be a 'Datum,' given in the sense that it is what is actually *present* with all its characters, whether we know what they are or not, and whether we cognize it rightly or not.

(ii) In a narrower sense, only those entities which are directly apprehended, *i.e.*, are actually modifications of our sense-organs, are said to be given—the '*Datum datissimum*'; and their alleged possessor, or remote cause, the tables, atoms, etc., is only a datum as being present, or part of which is present in sense (i).

Thus a datum, in sense (i), can be said to have 'an appearance' which is a datum in sense (ii). A 'total visible cone' is a datum in sense (i), and 'something elliptical' a datum in sense (ii).

posed of the lighted region, the air, etc., to which we allude above, but in which we only distinguish these namable components after a long process of interpretation conducted on experimental methods—"The infant learns first, etc., etc."

What then is this direct apprehending to which so important a rôle is assigned? The correct answer is usually rejected without hesitation, so contrary is it to some of our favourite verbal habits. To be directly apprehended is to cause certain happenings in the nerves, as to which at present neurologists go no further than to assert that they occur. Thus what is directly apprehended is a modification of a sense organ, and its apprehension is a further modification of the nervous system, about which we may expect information at some future date.[1]

But this is mere materialism? Suitably misunderstood, it is. In itself, however, it is no more than a highly probable step in the most plausible systematic account of 'knowing' which can be given. On all other accounts yet suggested, at least one indefinable idea has at some point to be introduced, at least one ultimately and irredeemably mysterious extra entity has to be postulated—some relation of 'immediate knowing' and further inexplicables in its train. Meanwhile it is generally granted that much is known. There are the sciences; and it is here urged that we already have the material for an account of knowing itself—provided, that is, certain symbolic entanglements are first penetrated or swept aside.

[1] As a direct objection to this it is often argued that a 'sense-datum' seems very unlike a modification of the retina, but so is passing through a station in an express very unlike what the station-master sees. Here there is only one event, the passage of the train; but the signs are very different. Similarly with the 'sense-datum.' We should expect the greatest difference between the *references* involved—the referents being the same—since one, direct apprehension, is as simple as possible, a first order reference, and the other, reference to a sense organ modification, is immensely complicated and arrived at only after a long chain of interpretations. It is another order of reference. This all-important problem of orders or levels of references and of signs is further discussed in the following chapter (pp. 93-4).

The chief of these rest upon misunderstanding as to the nature of statement. To make a statement is to symbolize a reference. What a reference is we have seen in the preceding chapter. However much we may try, we cannot go beyond reference in the way of knowledge. True reference is reference to a set of referents as they hang together. False reference is reference to them as being in some other arrangement than that in which they actually hang together. The advance in knowledge is the increase in our power of referring to referents as they actually hang together. This is all we can do. By no manner of make-believe can we discover the *what* of referents. We can only discover the *how*. This is, of course, old and familiar doctrine but it needs to be reaffirmed whenever the metaphysician intervenes, whether he comes as a *materialist*, spiritualist, dualist, realist or with any other answer to an impossible question. Unfortunately in our present ignorance of the mechanism of language, he has a good opportunity of setting up apparently impenetrable barriers. The only way by which these may be avoided is to set out from the known facts as to how we acquire knowledge. Then with an account of interpretation, such as that which is here sketched, the way is open to the systematization of all that is known and further of all that will ever come to be known.[1]

To resume our outline sketch of a systematic account of perception. Directly apprehended retinal modifications such as colours, are therefore *initial* signs of 'objects' and 'events' (or however we agree to symbolize

[1] A certain sense of chill or disappointment is not uncommon in those who entertain such a view for the first time. The renunciations which seem to be involved by the restriction of knowledge to reference, diminish, however, when due attention is paid to those other 'non-symbolic' uses of language which are discussed in Chapter X. It has often been said that Metaphysics is a hybrid of science and poetry. It has many of the marks of the hybrid; it is sterile, for example. The proper separation of these ill-assorted mates is one of the most important consequences of the investigation into symbolism.

referents); characters of things which we discover by interpretation, such as shapes of cones or tables, are signs of second or third order respectively. On the other hand shapes of initial signs, *e.g.* retinal modifications, are first order signs.

Place a new nickel florin on the palm of the hand with the arm extended horizontally, and note that a truthful person would describe its shape as elliptical. Now look at it vertically from above and agree that it is round. Is the florin circular or elliptical? What an insoluble problem!

If we say that it is the *surface* of the florin which is *given* us in both cases, then it seems to be both circular and elliptical. Which is absurd—since we 'know,' and every physicist stoutly maintains,[1] that it has not measurably changed, and is actually circular. We have, therefore, the option on the one hand of opining with the Metaphysicians that the Universe is very paradoxical, with the polite Essayists that it is very odd, or with the Bishops that it is very wonderful; or, on the other, of saying that it is not the surface which is given in either sense.

Anyone who watched our procedure with the florin, if appealed to for assistance at this point, would say that what was present in each case was a whole containing as parts, cones[2] whose apices are in the eye, and whose bases are the limits of our vision, or, where objects such as florins are about, their surfaces. Here there are two cones with the circular surface of the florin for base. In the first case the cone is elliptical

[1] As Rougier says (*Paralogismes*, p. 408), the theory of primary and secondary qualities, which seemed to have been disposed of by Berkeley's arguments, is once more receiving serious attention. "Nous n'avons aucun motif sérieux pour penser que les sensations de forme géométrique ne soient pas objectives." But it is hardly sufficient to dismiss the matter with the remark that the paradox of the bent stick, "n'existe que pour celui qui ne connaît pas les lois de la réfraction de la lumière." Apart from an adequate Theory of Signs the laws of refraction make a poor show against the ingenuity of the ontologist.

[2] The word 'cone' is used here merely to fill in a linguistic gap and by metaphor. It is shorthand for 'region intervening between surface and retina,' which in most cases is conical or pyramidal in shape.

in cross-section, and the surface of the florin is an oblique section ; in the second case the cone is circular, and the surface of the florin a cross-section, also circular. What here is taken as the apparent shape of the florin is most plausibly said to be the cross-section of the cone. This is the sign which we interpret as the surface, and in no case is that surface a 'datum datissimum'—directly given. This simple application of the Theory of Signs frees us from the paradox, the oddness, and the wonder, restores our faith in the physicist, and enables us to get on with our business, viz., a proper account of perception of the Nature of Things.

The method by which this ancient scandal is removed may be applied with equal success to all the other 'fundamental problems.' Whenever the ingenious mind discovers a self-contradiction ("This same florin that I see is both round and elliptical," or "This same stick which I see in the water is both straight and bent") bad symbolization is indicated, and we must expand the peccant symbol[1] until we discover the ambiguous sign-situation which caused the trouble. We then note this ambiguity, and improve our symbolism so as to avoid the nonsense to which we shall otherwise be led. Thus in the case of the florin we say : "The base of this cone that is my sign is oblique and circular, and is the surface of the florin that I see ; but a normal section of this cone is elliptical. I can equally be said to see the florin or to see any section of the cone, but no one of these is directly *given*. Even the whole cone of which they are parts is picked out from the wider cone which includes besides the florin cone the cones of all that I am seeing, the total *datum* which is my field of view."

This selection of partial cones out of the total cone

[1] In the case of the florin, to " This cone that I see, whose base is the florin, is both round and elliptical." Here the sign, namely, the cone, may be interpreted as signifying either an elliptical cross-section, *i.e.*, normal section, or a circular oblique section.

which is the visual field is, in normal circumstances, effected without mistake. It might, in fact, never have been suspected that even here interpretation is at work, were it not for the case of 'double images.' For each eye there is a separate total cone, but we learn normally to identify certain partial cones within these as having the same base. If the retinal correspondence through which we do this is upset (as when we push the eyeball a little, or look past a near at a distant object) we fail to make the right identification, and say we see two florins (double-images). Here once again we let our language trick us. What is present is, as always in binocular vision, two cones with a common base. Thanks to the retinal shift, the normal, automatic method of identification breaks down, and we 'see' one florin *as though it were* in two places; we interpret two cones with a common base as though they were cones with separate bases. Reflection and refraction—the whole of the theory of vision is full of such 'puzzles,' to be solved by the above Theory of Signs.[1]

Through this Theory of Signs then we can not only remove the standard pre-scientific paradoxes, but provide a new basis for Physics. It is commonly assumed that contrasted with what we see are the things we imagine, which are in some sense unreal. This distinction between Vision and Imagination is misleading, and of those things which we rightly claim to see the parts we do not see are as real as those we do. The

[1] In connection with sign-situations, a few words are required with regard to the most resolute attempt to deal with data in terms of signs since Reid's *Inquiry*—that developed at p. 24 ff. of Professor John Laird's *Studies in Realism*. "The visual sense-datum," says Professor Laird, "is as much a *sign* as a *fact*, and it is always apprehended so." He goes on to state that we always perceive *Significance* (the relation in virtue of which a sign signifies), we always perceive sign-facts, not data devoid of significance. Thus, when he adds that "meaning is directly perceptible just like colour or sound," if we understand 'meaning' in the sense of 'significance,' this assertion is not so paradoxical as it would be if 'meaning' were confused with 'what is meant.' Cf. Hoernlé, *Mind*, 1907, p. 86—"I regard the consciousness of meaning as primary and fundamental, and the distinction between sign and meaning as a product of reflection." What kind of 'meaning' this is may perhaps be gathered from Chapter VIII.

other side of the moon, which we never see, is as real as the side which vision perceives. The atoms, whose paths are photographed, the electrons which we do not 'see', are, if this interpretative effort of the physicist be sustained, as real as the signs given to perception from which he starts. When we look at our chairs and tables we 'see' a datum datissimum, then cones, then surfaces, chair, legs-seat-back, wood, bamboo, fibres, cells, molecules, atoms, electrons . . . the many senses of 'see' proceeding in an ordered hierarchy as the sign-situations change. And as the point of view, interest, scientific technique or purpose of investigation alters, so will the levels represented by these references change in their turn.

CHAPTER V

THE CANONS OF SYMBOLISM

> A happy nomenclature has sometimes been more powerful than rigorous logic in allowing a new train of thought to be quickly and generally accepted.—
> *Prof. A. Schuster.*

> For the rest I should not be displeased, sir, did you enter a little farther into the details of the turns of mind which appear marvellous in the use of the particles.—*Leibnitz.*

At the basis of all communication are certain postulates or pre-requisites — regulative presumptions without which no system of symbols, no science, not even logic, could develop. Their neglect by logicians is not surprising, since it has hitherto been nobody's business to discuss them. Logic, which may be regarded as the science of the systematization of symbols, has been preoccupied either with judgments which are psychological, or with 'propositions,' which were treated as objects of thought, distinct from symbols and not psychological. Modern mathematicians, who have done so much for the formal development of symbolic method, either tacitly assume these Canons, or when confronted by difficulties due to their neglect, introduce additional *ad hoc* complexities [1] into their systems. Actually they are as essential to all discourse as chemistry to physiology, dynamics to ballistics, or psychology to æsthetics. In any logic which is not purely formal, in the sense of being

[1] For instance, the Theory of Types—to deal with Epimenides and the alleged mendacity of Cretans; or Subsistence Theories in the interpretation of "Phœnixes exist."

devoted to some elaboration of the possibilities of symbol-manipulation,[1] the study of these Canons is a first essential, and their strict observance would render otiose whole tracts of the traditional treatment.

It will be convenient to state some of these Canons in terms of Symbols and Referents. The triangle of Reference given on p. 11 should be consulted. The First Canon of Symbolism, the Canon of Singularity, is as follows :—

I.—*One Symbol stands for one and only one Referent.*

This one referent may be, and in most cases is, complex. 'All Mongolian Imbeciles,' for instance, is a symbol which has one referent. Similarly (x or y) has one referent. The symbols of mathematics, however, are peculiar in that they are symbols either of other symbols or of operations with symbols. This peculiarity is what is often expressed by saying that pure mathematics is abstract, or formal, or that it does not mention anything at all. Symbols may contain necessary parts, *e.g.*, the negative, and words like 'the' and 'which,' which themselves have no specific referents. The study of such non-symbolic *structural* elements of symbols is the business of grammar.

These indications of structure appear in ordinary language in a bewildering variety of forms. The inflexions, the conjunctions, distributives, auxiliary verbs, some of the prepositions, the main use of the copula, etc., all have this function. In mathematics, owing to the simplicity of its outlook, these structural elements are reduced to the minimum ; otherwise such symbols for counting operations as two and three, or such symbols of symbols as algebraic expressions could never be handled systematically. Recent views on mathematics show a refreshing reaction from the logical mysticism or

[1] In *op. cit., Symbolism and Truth* (pp. 92 and 224 ff.) Professor R. M. Eaton deals interestingly with the rules of a logical syntax from a semi-orthodox standpoint.

arithmosophy of Frege, Couturat and others, prevalent at the beginning of the century. It is clearly felt that an account which does not invoke supersensible entities must be given of what mathematicians do.

Some, like Wittgenstein, have been able to persuade themselves that "The propositions of mathematics are equations, and therefore pseudo-propositions," and that "the method by which mathematics arrives at its equations is the method of substitution. For equations express the substitutability of two expressions, and we proceed from a number of equations to new equations, replacing expressions by others in accordance with the equations."[1] Such a view can be presented without the background and curtain of mysticism which this author introduces. Those parts of mathematics, the Theory of Sets of Points, for instance, which do not seem to be merely concerned with equations then remain to be accounted for.

Others maintain with Rignano[2] that mathematics throughout is merely the performance of imagined physical experiments, recorded and represented in symbols. This amplification of the view of James Mill[3] and Taine, though it fits some parts of mathematics well enough, is less plausible for others. As Rignano develops it, too little importance is assigned to symbols; hightly systematized sets of symbols such as those of mathematics are something more than a mere means of representing our mental performances. They become, as it were capable of performing on their own account. They become thinking machines which, suitably manipu-

[1] *Tractatus Logico-Philosophicus*, 6.2 and 6.24.

[2] *The Psychology of Reasoning*, Chapters VII. and VIII.

[3] *The Analysis of the Human Mind*, Vol. II., p. 9. "Numbers therefore, are not names of objects. They are names of a certain process; the process of addition. . . . One is the name of this once performed, or of the aggregation begun; two, the name of it once more performed." Mill *fils* in his editorial notes on this passage holds that "numbers *are*, in the strictest propriety, names of objects. *Two* is surely a name of the things which *are* two, two fingers, etc. The process of adding one to one which forms two is connoted, not denoted, by the name two." An obscure remark, since this is not even J. S. Mill's ordinary use of 'connote.'

lated, yield results which cannot be foreseen by any process of imagining physical experiments.

A third school would present mathematics not as a thinking machine, but as a set of directions for the use of such a machine, the machine in question being the mind. For this school mathematics would contain no statement but only commands or directions. The problem then becomes what exactly mathematicians are told to do.

It is probable that the answer to this vexed question as to the nature of mathematics will be found to consist of a combination of these varied doctrines. There is no good reason for supposing that mathematics is fundamentally homogeneous, although its possession of a single symbol system makes it appear so. The known readiness with which not only single symbols but whole systems of symbols may acquire supernumerary uses should make us ready to allow this possibility. It is plain that some parts of mathematics are concerned in a special way with the discussion of other parts. "It may be that when logic is wholly emancipated from metaphysics, logicians will devise a grammar of logistic language. Perhaps they will then call it the grammar of logic, and logistic language will be called logic. All that is valuable in the so-called logic will remain as component elements of a grammar—a grammar of the science of reasoning with language."[1]

Returning from this excursus, it is important to remember that a reference, as described above at page 62, is a set of external and psychological contexts linking a mental process to a referent. Thus it is extremely unlikely that any two references will ever be *strictly* similar. In asking, therefore, whether two symbols are used by the same reference—especially when the users thereof are two persons with their different histories—we are raising a question of degree.

[1] J. W. Powell, *Twentieth Annual Report of the Bureau of American Ethnology* (1903), p. clxx.

It is better to ask whether two references have sufficient similarity to allow profitable discussion. When such discussion is possible the references are said to be 'the same.' No means are at present available for directly comparing references. We have to judge by indirect evidence derived mainly from observing the further behaviour of the parties concerned. We notice whether doubt and certainty arise at the same points, whether both admit alternatives at the same points, and so on. But for many important questions in the theory of Grammar, especially when discussing the degree to which the emotive functions of language interfere with the referential, there is urgent need for some more easily applicable test. The only hope is in further analysis of the contexts operative in reference, with a view to selecting from the many contextual factors those which are determinative; and meanwhile a clear realization of the complexities involved may prevent unnecessary dogmatism.

When a symbol seems to stand for two or more referents we must regard it as two or more symbols, which are to be differentiated. This Canon guards against the most obvious kind of ambiguity, that of top (mountain), and top (spinning), for instance. We differentiate these symbols by the aid of a Second Canon which concerns what is usually called Definition, and is also of the utmost importance.

When we encounter a symbol which we do not comprehend we take steps, if interested, to have another symbol, which we can interpret, provided, whose referent is the same. Then we can say "I know what symbol A means; it means the same as symbol B." (When scholars say 'chien' means 'dog,' they *should* say that 'chien' and 'dog' both mean the same.) Similarly if a symbol is long or awkward to use, or likely to be misunderstood, we take a new convenient symbol and use it instead. In both cases the same process, Definition, is occurring. The details of the technique of definition, as required constantly in discussion, call for special study and will be dealt with in Chapter VI. below. A foundation-stone is laid in the Second Canon of Symbolism, the Canon of Definition :—

II.—*Symbols which can be substituted one for another symbolize the same reference.*

By means of this Canon we substitute for the ambiguous symbol 'top' the synonym 'mountain top' or 'spinning top,' and the ambiguity is removed. But this is not the only use which we make of the Canon. Its importance is belied by its modest simplicity. It is the guarantor of mathematics. The systematization of our symbols (for which we may substitute the phrase "the organization of our thought") is achieved by its application. It is plain for instance that the two symbols 'The King of England' and 'the owner of Buckingham Palace' have the same referent. They do not however symbolize the same reference, quite different psychological contexts being involved in the two cases. Accordingly they are not substitutes one for another in the sense required in this Canon. Symbols which are substitutes and so can be used to 'define'[1] one another not only have the same referent but symbolize the same reference. Such symbols are usually said to have the same 'connotation,' a misleading and dangerous term, under cover of which the quite distinct questions of application of reference and correctness of symbolization (*cf.* p. 102 below) are unwittingly confused. Connotation will be further discussed in Chapter IX.

But there are more dangerous booby-traps in language than the plain equivoque, and "certain it is," as Bacon has it, "that words like a Tartar's bow do

[1] As we shall see in the following chapter, this rigorous form of definition is chiefly of service in the construction of deductive symbol systems. The freer forms of definition, in which it is sufficient if the referents alone of the two symbols are identical, are indispensable in general discussion.

shoot back upon the understanding and mightily entangle and pervert the judgment." Those complex symbols, known as propositions, which 'place' referents (cf. Canon VI *infra*) can be either Contracted or Expanded. "Hamlet was mad" is a contracted symbol, needing to be expanded before it can be discussed. "Hamlet was mad on the stage" or "in my interpretation of the play" may be expanded symbols for what is referred to. The question is of the greatest importance because of its bearing on the distinction between true and false. It leads to the Third Canon of Symbolism, the Canon of Expansion:—

III.—*The referent of a contracted symbol is the referent of that symbol expanded.*

The consequences of infringing this Canon are sometimes called Philosophy, as little by little we shall proceed to show.

It is an obvious result of this Canon that the first thing to do when a disputed symbol is encountered is to expand it, if possible, to its full form—to such a form, that is, as will indicate the sign-situations behind the reference it symbolizes. Instances of this expansion occur continually in all scientific discussion. In the last chapter we had occasion to expand 'table' and 'see' and later on we shall endeavour to expand 'meaning' in all possible directions. Unfortunately in the absence of any systematic theory of interpretation, no definite ordering of the levels at which we refer has hitherto been made. The idea even of a level of reference remains vague. Yet when we refer to 'that animal,' and then later, after further study of its footprints perhaps, to 'that lynx,'[1] our reference will be to the same referent but at different levels of interpretation

[1] For certain sciences, zoology, geology, botany, etc., at certain stages, the technique of genus and species arrangement serves this purpose excellently. But this technique is not of great service at earlier or later stages, or outside such sciences.

in a definite sense involving the number of applications of interpretative processes and the complexity of these processes. In such relatively simple cases matters are easy to set straight ; in more complicated cases—if we speak of government, credit, patriotism, faith, beauty, emotion, etc.—it is not so. All our usual discussion of subjects of general interest suffers from the uncertainty, difficult even to state, as to the *level* of interpretation, of reference, at which we are symbolizing. All those engaged in education know what 'levels of reference' stand for. The fuller analysis of the question is of great urgency. Something towards it was attempted in Chapter IV. It is a pity, however, that those very persons who by their analytic ability would be most likely to succeed, should be so reluctant to take up problems until they have been elaborately formulated.

Meanwhile such is the chaos of symbolic apparatus in general that, instead of expansions, mere symbolic overgrowths are most usually what are provided by way of elucidation of doubtful symbols, thus leading to greater confusion than would the contractions which they replace. Instances are given in the following paragraph. Both contractions and pseudo-expansions have the same result—the peopling of the universe with spurious entities, the mistaking of symbolic machinery for referents. The only permanent cure is the discovery of the appropriate expansion by inquiry into the sign-situation leading to the reference which is doubtfully symbolized.[1]

It can in fact be recognized without difficulty that until this is done it is idle to raise such further questions as its truth or its relations to other symbols ; for a contracted symbol does not make plain the 'place' of its referent, and so cannot be investigated. The distinction between true and false symbols is a matter

[1] In simple but loose words, we only know for certain what is said when we know why it is said, though we must not include motives in the 'why.'

which cannot be discussed profitably in general terms, *i.e.*, by means of contractions or linguistic shorthand. It must be left in each case to the specialist, who being familiar with the actual sign-situations involved can decide within his particular field of reference which symbols are true and which not. It is owing to such a discussion in contracted symbols that what is known as the Problem of Truth has arisen. Instead of treating each case of adequacy on its own merits, epistemologists will have it that because they can use one word as a convenient shorthand sign to refer to all true symbols, there must be something for them to investigate apart from true and false propositions. No problem arises over any true proposition when recognized as such, and to raise a bogus problem here is quite as unnecessary as to assume a universal 'redness' because red things are every one of them red. Classes are now recognized as symbolic fictions, and logisticians will only be logical when they admit that universals are an analogous convenience. The World of Pure Being will then be definitively denuded of its quondam denizens, for which the theory of Universals was an attempted explanation. It should be noted that our symbolic machinery (similarity, etc.), becomes both more valuable and more comprehensible when these desiccated archetypes have faded away.

By way of explanation of these symbolic conveniences a few considerations may be added. Modifications of our sense organs, and 'things' as we come to know them through the interpretation of these signs, are always complex or parts of a complex. Even the tiny speck which, in virtue of a certain disturbance in the colour apparatus of an eye, we call a barely visible star is surrounded by a dark field. All that there is in such a sign for us to talk about is this complex, and we can talk about it in various ways. We can say "the speck is in the field" or "surrounded by the field" or "part of the field" or "related to the field by the relation of being enclosed by"; or we can say "this which has the property of being a speck is related to that which has the property of being a field by the relation of inclusion." These are alternative locutions, equally true. 'Speck in field' is a name, and so is 'speck.' On other occasions, however, we wish to symbolize references under circumstances in which the same names are correctly reapplied. We have to economize in our symbolic material; we have to use it over and over again, and in a systematic fashion, under pain of failure to communicate. Now if instead of the name 'this speck' we use the more luxuriant symbolic growth, 'this which has the property of being a speck,' we shall be tempted to suppose that the 'thises' on different occasions stand for different referents but that 'the property of being a speck' stands for one and the same.

In this way universal 'qualities' arise, phantoms due to the refractive power of the linguistic medium; these must not be treated as part of the furniture of the universe, but are useful as symbolic accessories enabling us to economize our speech material. Universal 'relations' arise in a precisely similar fashion, and offer a similar temptation. They may be regarded in the same way as symbolic conveniences. The claims of 'similarity' and 'dissimilarity' which on account of purely symbolic arguments (*cf.* Russell, *Some Problems of Philosophy*, p. 150) are often supposed to be peculiar are in no way different.

In all cases, even in this case of similarity, the invention of non-existent entities in order to account for the systematic use of symbols is an illegitimate procedure. Were there other evidence for them not deriving merely from *symbolic* necessities[1] it would be

[1] Grammatical exigencies. It must be remembered, disconcerting though the fact may be, that so far from a grammar—the structure of a symbol system—being a reflection of the structure of the world, any supposed structure of the world is more probably a reflection of the grammar used. There are many possible grammars and their differences

a different matter. As it is they stand on the same footing as the 'faculty' of knowing in psychology. The occurrence of similars does not compel us to recognize 'similarity,' a universal, any more than the occurrence of knowledge forces us to recognize a faculty of knowing. It merely compels us to recognize that similars do occur. That things are similar is natural knowledge. To make it, by exploiting the economy of symbolisms, into a basis of metaphysical knowledge —into a proof of another world of pure being where entities 'subsist' but do not exist—is unwarrantable. No argument about the world is valid if based merely upon the way a symbol system behaves.[1] Such argu-

are fundamental. Their several developments appear to reflect, if they reflect anything, the features of the early experiences of the races in which they occur, their dominant interests, their effective organizations and perhaps the structure of their central nervous systems. Although it is true that a grammar may mirror the needs and the outlook of a given race, and that owing to the similarity of these needs there may even be a common structure in all primitive and demotic language, it does not follow (though it is, of course, possible) that the finely-meshed language most adequate to serve the needs of science would retain anything of this structure, or would itself directly correspond in structure to the structure of the world. To suppose that this *must* be so is to forget the indirectness, through reference, of the relations of thoughts to things. These questions are further considered in Appendix A, on Grammar.

[1] It is interesting to compare with this argument against 'universals' the view taken by the late Mr. F. P. Ramsey of King's College, Cambridge (*Mind*, October, 1925, pp. 404-5): "In 'Socrates is wise,' Socrates is the subject, wisdom the predicate. But suppose we turn the proposition round and say, 'Wisdom is a characteristic of Socrates,' then wisdom formerly the predicate is now the subject. Now it seems to me as clear as anything can be in philosophy, that the two sentences 'Socrates is wise,' 'Wisdom is a characteristic of Socrates' assert the same fact. . . . They are not, of course, the same sentence, but they have the same meaning, just as two sentences in two different languages can have the same meaning. Which sentence we use is a matter either of literary style or of the point of view from which we approach the fact . . . and has nothing to do with the logical nature of Socrates or wisdom, but is a matter entirely for grammarians."

Mr Ramsey claims that "the above argument throws doubt upon the whole basis of the distinction between particular and universal"; and he proceeds to "argue that nearly all philosophers, including Mr Russell, have been misled by language in a far more far-reaching way" than that of supposing that all propositions must be of the subject-predicate form, and "that the whole theory of particulars is due to mistaking for a fundamental characteristic of reality, what is merely a characteristic of language." Yet some eighteen months previously, as a believer in universals, he wrote in the same Journal (*Mind*, January, 1924, p. 109) of the present work that the authors "fail to see the existence of logical problems, and propose to replace ments can give knowledge only about the symbol system in question. This knowledge is often of great value. All methods of distinguishing symbols proper, *i.e.*, names, from symbolic accessories are important.

We have spoken above of reflection and refraction by the linguistic medium. These metaphors if carefully considered will not mislead. But language, though often spoken of as a medium of communication, is best regarded as an instrument; and all instruments are extensions, or refinements, of our sense-organs. The telescope, the telephone, the microscope, the microphone, and the galvanometer are, like the monocle or the eye itself, capable of distorting, that is, of introducing new relevant members into the contexts of our signs. And as receptive instruments extend our organs, so do manipulative instruments extend the scope of the motor activities. When we cannot actually point to the bears we have dispatched we tell our friends about them or draw them; or if a slightly better instrument than language is at our command we produce a photograph. The same analogy holds for the emotive uses of language: words can be used as bludgeons or bodkins. But in photography it is not uncommon for effects due to the processes of manipulation to be mistaken by amateurs for features of the objects depicted. Some of these effects have been exploited by experts so as greatly to exercise the late Sir Arthur Conan Doyle and his friends.[1] In a similar fashion language is full of elements with no representative or symbolic function, due solely to its manipulation; these are similarly misinterpreted or exploited by metaphysicians and their friends so as greatly to exercise one another—and such of the laity as are prepared to listen to them.

The fictitious entities thus introduced by language

philosophy by 'the science of symbolism' and psychology." The relegation of problems to the grammarian, however, is not the same thing as failure to see their existence.

[1] Cf. *The Case against Spirit Photographs*, by W. Whately Smith and C. V. Patrick, pp. 33-36. Cf., now (1946) *Mind*, July, 1945, p. 225.

form a special variety of what are called fictions. But, as Vaihinger's own use shows, this term is very vague and so-called fictions are often indistinguishable from hypotheses, which are simply unverified references. Certain abstractions, like the 'economic man,' are of this nature, though, being purely methodological, they are not believed in; on the other hand, many idealizations and imaginative creations, such as Don Juan and the Übermensch, may some day find their referents. Hamlet and Goethe's *Urtier* appear not to be hypotheses, since they are dated and placed where history has no room for them; they are fictitious in the sense that Shakespeare or Goethe's thought had no single referent. We, of course, may refer to these thoughts; more usually we attempt only to reproduce them. But all fictions of this kind must be clearly distinguished from those due to manipulations of language itself. Vaihinger has not sufficiently emphasized this distinction; owing perhaps to an incomplete analysis of the relations of language and thought—shown by his use of the terms 'Begriff' and 'begreifen' in the discussion of abstractions and knowledge.[1] Linguistic fictions occur in two ways, either through a misunderstanding of the function of symbolic accessories such as 'liberty' or 'redness,' so that in making a reference to free actions or red things the user supposes himself to be referring to something not in time and space; or through hypostatization of such connective structural machinery as 'or,' 'if,' 'not,' etc., to which only logicians are prone.

The use of the term 'concept' is particularly misleading in linguistic analysis. There is a group of words, such as 'conception,' 'perception,' 'excitation,' which have been a perpetual source of controversy since the distinction between happenings inside and happenings outside the skin was first explicitly recognized. Processes of perceiving caused in an interpreter by the action on him of external objects have been

[1] *Philosophie des Als Ob* (1920), pp. 51, 393.

commonly called 'perceptions,' and so, too, by a very intelligible confusion, discussed in our next chapter as the 'utraquistic fallacy,' have those objects themselves. Other processes, more abstract or less obviously caused references, have similarly been called 'conceptions.' But whereas the double sense of the term 'perception' involves merely a confusion between two possible referents or sets of referents, the one inside the head and the other outside, the term 'concept' when thus duplicated has been a special inducement to the creation of bogus entities. It has often been assumed that the referents of these more abstract processes, since they appeared to be simple, were quite different from those of the mental processes which occurred when the referents were 'given' in perception. A transcendental world of 'concepts' has therefore been envisaged by philosophers; while even psychologists who elected to call themselves 'conceptualists' in recognition of the fact that concepts are mental—as opposed to the transcendental (scholastic 'realist') or the non-psychological (nominalist) account—have frequently been led by their terminology to take an inaccurate view of symbol situations.

In discussions of method or of mental processes, 'concepts' or abstract references may, of course, be themselves talked about; and in this special case words will properly be said to stand for ideas. But it is not true to say that in ordinary communication we are thus referring to our own mental machinery rather than to the referents which we talk 'about' by means of that machinery. Words, as we have seen, always *symbolize* (cf. p. 11) thoughts, and the conceptualist is apt to imply that the very special case of the construct or concept imagined for the purpose of an attempted scientific reference or classification, and then itself examined, can be generalized. He then states that the word is not a mere word as the nominalist holds, but stands for a conceptual symbol. In opposition to the believer in a single discoverable entity for which words symbolizing general references stand, he is right; but by those who do not admit that they are talking 'about' nothing when they appear to have referred to unjustifiable entities, his vocabulary is likely to be misunderstood.[1]

Such linguistic accessories may be used without danger, provided they are recognized for what they are. They are conveniences in description, not necessities in the structure of things. This is shown by the fact that various alternatives are open to us in describing any referent. We can either use a grammar of 'substantives' and 'attributes'[2] (nouns and adjectives), or one of 'Events' and 'Objects,'[3] or of 'Place' and 'Referent,'[4] according as we favour an Aristotelian outlook, or that of Modern Physics, or a pictorial exposition of the views here advocated. To discuss such questions in any other spirit than that in which we decide between the merits of different Weed killers is to waste all our own time and possibly that of other people.

In a similar way, from the question, What is Truth? an apparently insoluble problem has arisen. In Chapter III. however the problem was seen to be soluble as part of the theory of Interpretation. It will

[1] Crookshank, for example, *Influenza* (1922), p. 3, in his statement that Influenza is "a universal and nothing more," has been supposed to be denying the occurrence of illness, though in the sequel he makes the implications of his attack on the medical 'realists' quite plain. Cf. also Supplement II.

Except in combating the very crudest transcendentalism, such a terminology is as injudicious as that which obliges Sapir (*Language*, p. 106; cf. *supra*, Chapter I., p. 7), to speak of Concrete, Derivational, Concrete Relational and True Relational Concepts, when an account in terms of names, linguistic accessories and referents would enable the fundamental distinction between thoughts, words and things to be preserved.

[2] Johnson, *Logic*, Part 1, p. 100.

[3] Whitehead, *The Concept of Nature*, pp. 77, 169.

[4] P. 105, *infra*. It is interesting in this connection to note that Indian schools of philosophy, such as the Vaiçesika, at various periods developed logical machinery as unlike most of these Western grammars as they are unlike one another. Praçastapada, for instance, propounded a theory of particularity as an independent reality residing in eternal substances and distinguishing them from one another. Other divisions hardly reproducible in intelligible terms may readily be found.

be convenient here to define a true Symbol as distinguished from a true Reference. The definition is as follows :—A true symbol = one which correctly records an adequate[1] reference. It is usually a set of words in the form of a proposition or sentence. It correctly records an adequate reference when it will cause a similar reference to occur in a suitable interpreter. It is false when it records an inadequate reference.

It is often of great importance to distinguish between false and incorrect propositions. An incorrect symbol is one which in a given universe of discourse[2] causes in a suitable interpreter a reference different from that symbolized in the speaker. Thus if we say, "Charles I. died in his bed, making witty remarks," our symbol is more likely to be incorrect than our reference false, for it is no rash suggestion that the referent is Charles II.'s death in *his* bed. But in many cases such an audacious exegetic is unwarranted, and it will then be a more difficult matter to decide which is occurring. In the opposite case when, *e.g.*, we say, "The sun is trying to come out," or "The mountain rises," we may clearly be making no different references than if we were to give a scientific description of the situation, but we *may* mean these assertions to be taken 'literally.' By taking an assertion literally is meant interpreting our symbols as primary symbols, *i.e.*, as names used with a reference fixed by a given universe of discourse. When for any reason, such as poverty of language, no symbol is at hand we can choose a symbol whose referent is

[1] It is useful in English to have a term such as 'adequacy' by which to distinguish the sense in which a symbol may be true from that in which a reference is true. In such sentences as "What he said was untrue," the ambiguities are obvious ; we are left uncertain whether his symbol or his reference was false. In more subtle cases, where the word 'proposition' is casually introduced confusions often arise which without this distinction are hard to disentangle. The term 'adequacy' has the advantage of suggesting the difficult question whether and in what sense reference is capable of degree.

[2] A Universe of discourse is a collection of occasions on which we communicate by means of symbols. For different universes of discourse differing degrees of accuracy are sufficient, and (cf. Chapter VI., p. 111) new definitions may be required.

analogous to our referent and transfer this symbol. Then if the speaker fails to see that such symbols are metaphorical or approximative only, *i.e.*, takes them literally, falsity arises, namely the correct symbolization of a false reference by which the interpreter could be misled. If on the other hand the speaker makes a true reference, but uses symbols such that a suitable *interpreter*, rightly interpreting, makes a false reference, then the symbol is incorrect.

Incorrectness may plainly have degrees, for if, when my pipe is out, I say, "My pipe is alight," then this symbol, "My pipe is alight," is sufficiently correct to characterize its referent but not to place it. In other words, it is good enough for the investigator to be able to look for its referent among events, and to exclude it on the ground that the place it claims is filled by the referent of "My pipe is out." It may also be good enough, according to the actual context, for him to go and look for it among other likely orders of referents, gustatory, olfactory and thermal sensations, images and so forth. If he can find it he may be able to expand the incorrect symbol, possibly changing every word in the process. Similarly, once convinced that my pipe is out, I may be able myself to expand my symbol to "My pipe feels as though it were alight."

A group of questions arise out of this instance, which require a Fourth Canon, the Canon of Actuality, to clarify the situation :—

IV.—*A symbol refers to what it is actually used to refer to; not necessarily to what it ought in good usage, or is intended by an interpreter, or is intended by the user to refer to*

The assertion considered above may or may not have referred to a referent like that for which it would be correctly used. I may admit or deny that my referent was some feeling and not burning tobacco. Accordingly, by Canon I., we have here a group of symbols appearing to be one symbol, and we must select that which is actually being used. When we cannot so select, nothing more can be done beyond framing a collection of unambiguous symbols for future use in analogous cases.[1] But suppose that we were led to state, after the manner of formal logicians, that a referent such as 'non-existent combustion of tobacco' is involved, we should appear to be confronted by a problem as to how we can refer to what is not there to be referred to. This problem, which is of no interest in itself, is mentioned here because it is typical of the difficulties which arise through treating an incomplete system of defective symbols as though it were a complete system of perfect symbols. Within a minor system of symbols which has been wrought into a high degree of complexity, such contradictions, if they ensue from a legitimate manipulation of symbols, are a helpful indication of some imperfection still remaining. Mathematics is a case in point. Faced with such a contradiction, the mathematician proceeds to improve his symbolism, and we should follow his example rather than suppose that we have proved some curious eccentricity in the universe.

Two other questions arise which deserve an answer. The first is "How do we know that 'pipe alight now' claims the same place as 'pipe out now,' while 'pipe foul now' does not?" The answer is, in the words of the old tale, "By experience." We possess in familiar fields vast accumulations of such knowledge. We know, for instance, that 'x is green' and 'x is red' and 'x is blue' all claim the same place for their referents; as do 'x is dark' and 'x is light.' We also know that 'x is green' and 'x is dark' and 'x is vivid' do not make conflicting claims. In fields with which we are unfamiliar the main difficulty is pre-

[1] To the technique required for this operation Chapters VI. and VII. are devoted, and in Chapter IX. the methods developed are applied to the arch-ambiguity, Meaning.

cisely in gaining such knowledge. We need this knowledge in order to perfect our symbols, just as we need perfected symbols in order to advance our knowledge.

The other question is, "Why not say that since no referent for 'My pipe is out' was to be found where we were led to look for it, there was no referent?" But there was a reference—though not to the referent suggested at first sight. The problem of finding the actual referent is here, as always, that of tracing out the causal connections or contexts involved, in the manner indicated in Chapter III.

One special difficulty with regard to complex symbols calls for a Canon whose functions may not be evident at first sight, though it is necessary for the avoidance of nonsense in our discourse. It concerns the building up of complex symbols from those which are simple or less complex. It is plain that if we incorporate in one symbol signs which claim the same place, whether *e.g.*, colour (red—yellow) or shape (round—square), our proposed symbol is void. This Fifth Canon is called the Canon of Compatibility :—

V.—*No complex symbol may contain constituent symbols which claim the same 'place.'*

It is therefore important at once to make clear what is done when a symbol 'places' a referent. Since the days of Aristotle, three formulæ, traditionally known as the Laws of Thought, have received much attention, civil and uncivil, from logicians. They have been variously interpreted as laws which the mind obeys but which things need not, as laws which things obey but which the mind need not, as laws which all things (the mind included) obey, or as laws which nothing need obey but which logic finds strangely useful. For Symbolism they become a triad of minor Canons which help to keep the Cathedral of Symbolism in due order. First comes the Law of identity—quaintly formulated as 'A is A'; a symbol is what it is; *i.e.*, *Every symbol has a referent.* The second is the Law of Contradiction—'A is not not-A'; no symbol refers to what it does not refer to; *i.e., No referent has more than one place in the whole order of referents.* The third is the Law of Excluded Middle—'A is either B or not B'; a symbol must have a given referent or some other; *i.e., Every referent has a fixed place in the whole order of referents.* For this triad, by Canon II. we may substitute the following formula, which is then the Sixth Canon of Symbolism: The Canon of Individuality—

VI.—*All possible referents together form an order, such that every referent has one place only in that order.*

One difficulty with regard to 'place' may be usefully commented on. It is rather a symbolic accessory (cf. p. 94 above) than an actual symbol. In any false assertion, we have implied, two things must be clearly distinguished (1) the referent to which we are actually referring (2) an alleged referent to which we believe ourselves to be referring. Only the first of these has a 'place' in the whole order of referents.

We can, using alternative language, say either that in a false assertion we are believing a referent to be in a 'place' in which it is not, or that we are believing ourselves to be referring to a different referent from that to which we are actually referring. We can for instance either say that in two contradictory assertions we are referring to the same referent but assigning to it different 'places,' or we can say that we are referring to two different referents and assigning them to the same 'place.' These alternative locutions involve subtle shifts in the references using both 'referent' and 'place,' and accentuate the important consideration that the distinction between the reference of these terms is merely artificial. There is no difference between a referent and its place. There can be no referent out of a place, and no place lacking a referent. When a referent is known its place also is known, and a place can only be identified by the referent which fills it. 'Place,' that is, is merely a symbol introduced as a convenience for describing those imperfections in reference which constitute falsity.

We have shown that for all references, between the referent and the act there are always intervening sign-situations. In the simplest case, that of the true direct judgment of perception, there may be only one such sign-situation (discussed in Chapter III.). In a false proposition there will be a similar sign chain with the difference that some misinterpretation occurs. It is not however always necessary in order to *translate* a false proposition into a true one to discover where the misinterpretation occurred; a new sign chain abutting on the same referent may be substituted. In *expansion*, however, such discovery is necessary, and the difficulty explains our preference for Translation over Expansion. In education and controversy the discovery of the misinterpretation is usually the more essential step.

In these six Canons, Singularity, Expansion, Definition, Actuality, Compatibility, and Individuality, we have the fundamental axioms, which determine the right use of Words in Reasoning. We have now a compass by the aid of which we may explore new fields with some prospect of avoiding circular motion. We may begin to order the symbolic levels and investigate the process of interpretation, the 'goings-on' in the minds of interpreters. In particular it will be possible now, though not always easy, to show when a symbol is merely an abbreviation; and to specify the various kinds of definition suitable on different occasions. It might not seem unreasonable in the meantime to call a halt in such discussions as would be affected by these discoveries—

> "Seal up the mouth of outrage for a while
> Till we can clear these ambiguities,
> And know their spring, their head, their true descent."

These Canons control the System of Symbols known as Prose. If by themselves they do not prove sufficient to keep our speech from betraying us, any others which may be required will be of the same nature. A set of symbols will only be well organized, or form a good prose style, when it respects these Canons. Only such a set will allow us to perform with safety those transformations and substitutions of symbols by which scientific language endeavours to reflect and record its distinctions and conclusions—those operations which, as we have seen, appeared to primitive man to partake of the nature of magic. Moreover, only such a set will enable the philosopher to discuss more important matters than his own or his colleagues' peculiarities of expression.

CHAPTER VI

THE THEORY OF DEFINITION

The first cause of absurd conclusions I ascribe to the want of method; in that they begin not their ratiocination from definitions.—*Hobbes.*

" Do, as a concession to my poor wits, Lord Darlington, just explain to me what you really mean."—" I think I had better not, Duchess. Nowadays to be intelligible is to be found out."—
Lady Windermere's Fan.

THERE is at present no theory of Definition capable of practical application under normal circumstances. The traditional theory, in so far as it has not been lost in the barren subtleties of Genus and Differentia, and in the confusion due to the term 'Connotation,' has made little progress—chiefly on account of the barbarous superstitions[1] about language which have gathered on

[1] The Magic of Names is often potent where we should least expect it, and the distress of Sachs on the discovery of Uranus, which found expression in his query—" What guarantee have we that the planet regarded by astronomers as Uranus is *really* Uranus ? "—is only one degree more primitive than Herbert Spencer's contention that " By comparing its meanings in different connections, and observing what they have in common, we learn the *essential meaning* of a word . . . let us thus ascertain the meaning of the words ' good,' " etc.

The italics are ours, and no one who does not believe with Nansen's Greenland Eskimos " that there is a spiritual affinity between two people of the same name," can fail to see the futility of such attempts to define by Essence. The doctrine derives from the view already referred to that words are in some way parts of things (a charge which Spencer himself, curiously enough, brings elsewhere against Greek speculation in general). If, as was supposed everything has its proper name, the existence of a name enables us to look with confidence for the thing or ' idea ' to which it belongs, and, in general, things possessing the same name will have something in common which the process of definition must endeavour to find. The search for the quiddity of things, the *hæcceitas*, as Duns Scotus called it, probably has its origin in the same attitude to Words, though it is unfair to attribute to Aristotle the linguistic absurdities of his followers. Some of the most curious implications of these traditions, both in the history of philosophy

the confines of logic from the earliest times. Four difficulties have stood in the way and must first be removed.

Firstly, do we define things or words? To decide this point we have only to notice that if we speak about defining words we refer to something very different from what is referred to, meant, by 'defining things.' When we define *words* we take another set of words which may be used with the same referent as the first, *i.e.*, we substitute a symbol which will be better understood in a given situation. With *things*, on the other hand, no such substitution is involved. A so-called definition of a horse as opposed to the definition of the word 'horse,' is a statement about it enumerating properties by means of which it may be compared with and distinguished from other things. There is thus no rivalry between 'verbal' and 'real' definitions.[1]

The words by means of which these properties are enumerated do, of course, give us a substitute symbol—either a complete analysis, or as abbreviated by classificatory methods (the usual 'genus and differentia' type)—with the same referent (the horses) as the original symbol; but rather by way of corollary than as the main purpose of the analysis. Moreover, this process is only possible with complex objects which have been long studied by some science. With simple objects, or those which for lack of investigation are not known to be analysable, as well as with everything to which classificatory methods have not yet been applied, such a method is clearly not available, and here other symbols must be found as the substitutes which symbol-definition seeks to provide. Such, in outline, is the solution of the long-standing dispute between the advocates of real and symbolic definitions.

and in the most recent developments of logic, are admirably treated by Professor L. Rougier in his *Paralogismes du Rationalisme*, pp. 146 ff., 368 ff., 386 ff.

[1] See Leibnitz, *New Essays concerning Human Understanding*, 1916, pp. 316-7, for an example of the way in which the distinction has been envisaged.

The second difficulty is closely related to the above. Though definition be symbol-substitution, definitions have usually, for grammatical reasons, to be stated in a form which makes them appear to be about things. This is because we are in the habit of abbreviating such symbols as "the word 'fire' refers to the same referent as the words 'what burns'" to "fire is what burns"; and of saying "*Chien* means 'dog,'" when we ought to say "the word *chien* and the word 'dog' both mean the same animal."[1]

Thirdly, all definitions are essentially *ad hoc*. They are relevant to some purpose or situation, and consequently are applicable only over a restricted field or 'universe of discourse.' For some definitions, those of physics, for instance, this universe is very wide. Thus for the physicist 'energy' is a wider term than for the schoolmaster, since the pupil whose report is marked "without energy" is known to the physicist as possessing it in a variety of forms. Whenever a term is thus taken outside the universe of discourse for which it has been defined, it becomes a metaphor, and may be in need of fresh definition. Though there is more in metaphor than this, we have here an essential feature of *symbolic* metaphorical language. The distinction between this and *emotive* metaphorical language is discussed later at pages 239-40.

Fourthly there is the problem of 'intensive' as opposed to 'extensive' definition which comes to a head with the use of the terms 'denote' and 'connote.' In Chapter IX. the artificiality of these distinctions will be urged. Here it is only necessary to point out that two symbols may be said to have the same connotation when

[1] It may be noted that when we say "Fire burns" we appear to be conveying information about fire and not about symbols, whereas with such a combination of synonyms as "*Chien* is 'dog'" we seem unable to advance the knowledge of anyone. This is because in saying "Fire burns," 'fire' and 'burns' are used with differing definitions. If we defined *chien* as "domestic wolf-like animal" and 'dog' as "barking quadruped" we could say "*Chien* is 'dog'" (="Dogs bark"), which would convey information.

they symbolize the same reference. An intensive or connotative definition will be one which involves no change in those characters of a referent in virtue of which it forms a context with its original sign. In an extensive definition there may be such change. In other words when we define intensively we keep to the same sign-situation for definiendum and definiens, when we define extensively this may be changed.

We are now in a position to grapple with the difference between definitions and ordinary assertions. "Gorillas are animals" and "Gorillas are affable" are unlike one another in the respect that the first appears to be certainly true as soon as we understand it, while the second may be doubted. From "This is a gorilla" it follows directly that "This is an animal," but not that it is an affable one. If we look for a distinction in essential connection between animality and gorillarity on the one hand, and gorillarity and affability on the other we shall make but indifferent use of our leisure. But if the difference be sought in its proper place, that is, between or in[1] the references, it will be found that the definition actually used in the first case includes animal, so that in speaking of a gorilla we have spoken of an animal, and are therefore able to refer again without diffidence to what we have already referred to; while affability was not so included. The relevant definition, in fact, is the one actually used.[2]

[1] As a typical bogus question we might ask: Where *does* difference Reside?

[2] This point has its bearing upon the controversy as to whether relations, all or some, are internal or external. An Internal relation would seem to be a defining relation, and any relation used as such to be internal. 'Internal' and 'defining' are thus synonyms, *e.g.*, the relation of whole to part, since a whole is automatically defined as containing its parts, is internal; and similarly if a part be defined as contained in a whole, the relation of part to whole. An External relation is any relation other than a defining relation. If Prof. G. E. Moore's relation 'entails' (*Philosophical Studies*, p. 291) were a relation of substitution, partial or complete, between symbols, based upon identity of reference, then this account of internal relations would not differ greatly from that given by Prof. Moore. It is, however, exceptionally difficult to discover what the several parties to this controversy are asserting; and indeed each is apt to lament his inability to understand the others.

To attempt now a fresh attack upon the essential problem of how we define, or attain the substitute symbols required in any discussion. We know[1] that 'A symbol refers to what it has actually been used to refer to.' We shall cease then to assume that people are referring to what they 'ought' to have referred to, and consider only what they actually do refer to. The point to be met in every discussion is the point actually advanced, which must be first understood. We have, that is, in all cases *to find the referent.* How can this best be done?

The answer is simple and obvious. Find first, it runs, a set of referents which is certainly common to all concerned, about which agreement can be secured, and locate the required referent through its connection with these.

It is fortunate that the types of fundamental connections with which discussions are concerned are few in number, though we are apt to believe, such is the multifarious complexity of our talk, that things are connected in any number of ways. Whether this poverty is due to the trammelling influence of language, a larger number of connections being quite, not merely partially, unmanageable by naïve talkers, whether it is due to the structure of the brain, or whether it is due to an actual simplicity in the universe, need not here be considered. For practical purposes the fundamental connections which can be used in definition are limited to those which the normal mind can think of when directly named. Let us consider, for instance, the growth of the abstraction which we name a spatial relation. In all our references to spatial objects certain common elements or strands are active. Originally to think of space as opposed to spatial objects we had to think in rapid succession of a variety of spatial objects in order that the common elements in the references should stand out. In time we became able to use these

[1] By Canon IV.—Chapter V.

common, *i.e.*, general references independently without requiring them to be built up anew on each occasion. We are now able to use them merely upon the vicarious stimulus of the symbol 'spatial relation.' A normal mind, however, except in the few cases in which such abstractions have universal value, still requires the aid of instances, analogies and metaphors. The fewness of these abstractions saves the linguistic situation. If we employed, say, a hundred radically different types of connections (still a small number) the task of limiting the misunderstandings due to the variety in our references would have proved impossible.

The fundamental connections being thus so few, the task of a theory of definition narrows itself down to the framing of a list. All possible referents are connected in one or other, or several, of these fundamental ways with referents which we can all succeed in identifying. We must not assume in referring to any given fixed point of agreement from which we find we are able to start that we do more than agree in identifying this. We must be careful to introduce our starting-points in such a way that they do not raise fresh problems on their own account. That is to say, we must select them with reference to the particular universe of discourse in which our definienda fall. Thus, if we wish to indicate what we are referring to when we use the word 'Beauty' we should proceed by picking out certain starting-points, such as nature, pleasure, emotion, or truth, and then saying that what we refer to by 'Beauty' is anything lying in a certain relation (*imitating* nature, *causing* pleasure or emotion, *revealing* truth) to these points. How this may be done is shown in detail in the following chapter.

When someone asks where Cambridge Circus is, we say, "You know where the British Museum is, and you know the way down Shaftesbury Avenue. If you go down Shaftesbury Avenue you will come to it." We may note—

(1) The starting-point must be familiar, and this can in practice only be guaranteed when it is either something with which we are directly, not symbolically acquainted (we do not merely know its name), or something with a wide and vague extension involving no ambiguity in the context in which it is used. Thus anyone in Kensington Gardens with a quarter of an hour to spare and a desire to view Cambridge Circus, if told that the said Circus is beyond Leicester Square, will postpone his visit as readily as if he were told (equally vaguely for another purpose) that it is in Soho.

(2) For the stricter purposes we shall almost always require starting-points taken outside the speech situation; things, that is, which we can point to or experience. In this way we can utilize in our symbols the advantages of gesture languages mentioned above. Thus it is easier to point to an Antimacassar, when one of these safeguards is present, than to describe it.

The importance of starting-points having thus been indicated, namely, to act as signs by which the required referents may be reached, we may now enumerate some of the main routes which are useful in finding our way about the field of reference. The sign-situations here involved, we must not forget, arise only through and upon many other simpler interpretations of the kind discussed in the preceding chapters. It is easy symbolically to make the situation which arises when we define appear simple, but if we realize the delicacy of the processes and adaptations required we shall not place overmuch trust in face-value comparisons of symbols (the usual method), but will attempt instead to consider what actually is happening.

When in a discussion we are asked, 'Can you define your terms?' or complain 'I do not understand what you mean by the words you use,' we endeavour to discover some route by which understanding, *i.e.*, identification of referents, may be secured.

A person thoroughly acquainted with his subject

and with the technique of Definition should be able, like the man up aloft in a maze, to direct travellers from all quarters to any desired point; and it may be added that to go up the ladder and overlook the maze is by far the best method of mastering a subject.

Although in no case, as we have already seen, are relations to be regarded as part of the stuff of nature, and although when we appear to speak of them we are merely using them as tools, which does not involve actual referents corresponding to them, yet when they are so used there are various distinctions which it is desirable to make as a matter of convenience. At the beginning of our inquiry we described the relation which could be said to hold between symbol and referent as an imputed relation. To have described it simply as an indirect relation would have omitted the important difference between indirect relations recognized as such, and those wrongly treated as direct. Thus the relation between grandfather and grandson is much more indirect than that between father and son, and can be analysed into two paternal relations—'being the father of the father (or mother) of.' Few people would suppose that a direct relation was here involved, since all family relations are highly indirect. But love, hate, friendship, sympathy, etc., are very commonly spoken of and regarded as direct, though on examination their indirectness is at once discovered. The whole of social psychology is, however, infested with imputed relations of this type, for an explanation of which such hypotheses as that of group-consciousness are often invoked.

The distinction between simple and complex relations on the other hand is somewhat different. Indirectness is only one kind of complexity, and direct relations need not be simple. For instance, the relation of 'being a benevolent uncle to' is complex; it is a blend of the two relations 'well disposed towards' and 'avuncularity.' The similarity between one pea and another is complex, being a blend of similarities in respect of greenness, hardness, edibility, etc. These considerations, elementary though they may appear, are of use whenever we have to treat of relations.

The routes, then, which we seek in our endeavour to reach a desired referent are the obvious relations in which that referent stands to some known referent. The number of possible relations is indefinitely large, but those which are of practical use fortunately fall, as we have already explained, into a small number of groups. So that as a preliminary classification[1] we get such a list as this :—

1. *Symbolization*

This is the simplest, most fundamental way of defining. If we are asked what 'orange' refers to, we may take some object which is orange and say "'Orange' is a symbol which stands for This." Here the relation which we use in defining is the relation discussed in Chapter I. as constituting the base of our triangle. It is, as we mentioned, an imputed relation reducible to a relation between symbol and act of reference and a relation between act of reference and referent. Our starting-point is the word 'orange,' our route of identification is this relation. The required referent is This. What we are doing in fact here is directly *naming*.

But, it will be said, This merely tells us that 'orange' is applicable in *one* case; what we wish to know is how it is applicable in general; we wish to have the definition extended so as to cover all the referents for which 'orange' is a suitable symbol. This generalization may be performed for all types of definitions in the same manner by the use of similarity relations. We may say "'Orange' applies to this and to all things similar in respect of colour to this." In practice the discrimination of one similarity relation from others generally requires the use of

[1] Cf. further *Psyche*, Vol. X, No. 3, January, 1930, pp. 9 and 29.

parallel instances, analogies in fact, of the simplest order.

2. *Similarity*

Thus similarity itself may be used as a defining relation. Our required referent is *like* a chosen referent. If we are asked what the symbol 'orange' refers to, we may define this symbol by taking something which is orange and saying "To anything which is like this thing in respect of colour the symbol 'orange' is applicable." Here we have substituted for 'orange' 'like this in respect of colour,' and the referents of both symbols are the same. Our starting-point is This and the relation is Likeness, and anyone who knows what 'This' stands for (*i.e.*, is not blind) and knows what 'Likeness' stands for will get there.

3. *Spatial Relations*

In, On, Above, Between, Beside, To the right of, Near, Bigger than, Part of, are obvious examples. "'Orange' is a symbol for the colour of the region between red and yellow in a spectrum (and of any colour like this)." It will be noted that the naming relation is involved in this as in every definition, and that the definition is always extendable by a similarity relation. It is curious that some of these symbols for spatial relations are unsymmetrical. Thus we have 'on'='above and in contact with,' but no abbreviation for 'under and in contact with,' except such ambiguous words as 'supporting.' We may further note that most of the common uses of 'on' are so strangely metaphorical that it has even been doubted whether there is not some simple unanalysable relation which has not yet been noticed. The right approach to problems of metaphorical extension will be considered later in this chapter.

4. *Temporal Relations*

'Yesterday' is the day before to-day; 'Sunday'

is the first day of the week; 'The end of the war' is x months after event y; 'Lighting-up time' is x minutes after sunset.

5. *Causation: Physical*

'Thunder' is what is caused (not by two clouds bumping but) by certain electrical disturbances. 'Sawdust' is what is produced, etc.

6. *Causation: Psychological*

'The Unconscious' is what causes dreams, fugues, psychoses, humour and the rest. 'Pleasure' is 'the conscious accompaniment of successful psychic activity.'

7. *Causation: Psycho-physical*

In addition to the examples given in the following chapter in connection with Beauty, we may define 'A perception of orange' as 'the effect in consciousness of certain vibrations falling on the retina.'

Causal relations are probably the routes of identification most commonly employed in general discussion, as well as in science. Thus a view of great historical consequence defines the Deity as the Cause of the Universe, while the importance of Embryology in zoological classification is due to the causal defining relations which are thereby provided.

8. *Being the Object of a Mental State*

The right-hand side of our triangle, Referring, is one of these; so are Desiring, Willing, Feeling, etc. Thus 'Piteous things' may be defined as those towards which we feel pity, and 'Good things' are those which we approve of approving.

9. *Common Complex Relations*

Some definitions are most conveniently formulated in complex form. While capable of being analysed out into sets of simple relations falling under one or other of the above headings, they are more readily applicable as popularly symbolized.

Examples are 'utility' (analysable into Nos. 7 and 8), 'Imitation' (2 and 7), 'Implication' (1 and 8).

10. *Legal Relations*

These are so frequently employed and implied, though often disguised, that it seems worth while to give them a separate heading; moreover, they are subject to an arbitrary test—satisfying the judge.

Examples: 'Belonging to' (when = 'owned by'), 'Subject of,' 'Liable to,' 'Evidence of.' All legal definitions are highly complex, though none the less serviceable.

The above relations are those which considerable experience has shown to be commonly employed in definitions. Any other relations which might be required for special purposes equally deserve to be included in a complete list—Shape, Function, Purpose, or Opposition, for example. It is therefore neither claimed that the first eight groups exhaust the relevant elementary relations, nor that those complex relations which we have cited can be reduced without remainder to relations of these types. The whole classification is on a pragmatic basis, and merely on the level of the most usual universes of discourse.

It has also proved unnecessary to discuss whether and in what sense all relations may be logically reducible to one or more ultimate kinds,[1] for any such reduction would make no difference to the value of the definitions we have been considering in their appropriate field. Even definitions of considerable complexity, involving a variety of theories, can be reduced without difficulty to discussable morsels, and their validity as substitutes the better examined. This further illustrates the fact that definitions often go by stages, as when our inquirer for Cambridge Circus is not

[1] Thus, on Alexander's hypothesis, for instance (*Space, Time and Deity*, I., p. 239), "in the end all relation is reducible to spatio-temporal terms."

familiar with the British Museum and requires first to be directed thither *via* the Tube from the Marble Arch.

The question of multiple relations raises no difficulty in this connection. A multiple relation holds between a number of terms greater than two. Thus, Perceiving, as Dr Whitehead has recently insisted, is a multiple relation holding between a percipient, an object, and the conditions; and Giving is a multiple relation holding between a philanthropist, a donation, and a beneficiary. In defining any of these terms, or in taking any of them as a starting-point for a route of definition, we proceed in exactly the same fashion as with dual relations—except that bearings must be taken from more than one landmark, when the universe of discourse demands special accuracy. Otherwise the Definiendum is not reached. Thus, in defining some object as what so-and-so saw, it may on some occasions be necessary to state the conditions—as in a séance we need to know the strictness of the test; or in identifying a passing train as an Express we have to consider the speed of our own train. But much discussion can be profitably undertaken without such complex situations arising.

The practical aspect of the above list of routes of definition deserves to be insisted upon. The reason for using definitions at all is practical. We use them to make discussion more profitable, to bring different thinkers into open agreement or disagreement with one another. There is, it is true, a more recondite use of definition derived from this simple primitive use. Definitions are of great importance in the construction of deductive, scientific systems, those automatic thinking-machines for which logic and mathematics are, as it were, the rules or instructions. In such a deductive system as mechanics, for example, it is through the definitions employed that the parts of the symbolic system are linked together, so that a given manipulation of the symbolism will yield comparable results even when their precise nature is not foreseen by the manipulator. Thus, for such systems there comes to be something which is regarded as *the* definition of a particular symbol. Given the system, there will be one and only one definition of a symbol which is the right or proper definition, in the sense that the working of the system depends upon the employment of this definition.

Specialists who are much concerned with such systems naturally tend to regard all definitions in the same manner. Yet for many of the most interesting topics of discussion a quite different attitude and habit of mind as regards definitions is not only desirable, but, in fact, necessary, if fruitful discussion is to be possible. In æsthetics, politics, psychology, sociology, and so forth, the stage of systematic symbolization with its fixed and unalterable definitions has not been reached. Such studies as these are not far enough advanced for anyone yet to decide which system is most advantageous and least likely to exclude important aspects. The most highly systematized sciences are those which deal with the simplest aspects of nature. The more difficult and to many people, naturally, the more attractive subjects are still in a stage in which it is an open question which symbolization is most desirable. At this stage what has chiefly to be avoided is the veiled and hidden strife between rival systems in their early forms, which more than anything else prevents mutual understanding even between those who may be in agreement. Many terms used in discussions where 'faith,' 'beautiful,' 'freedom,' 'good,' 'belief,' 'energy,' 'justice,' 'the State' constantly occur are used with no distinct reference, the speaker being guided merely by his linguistic habits and a simple faith in the widespread possession of these habits. Hence the common sight of anger aroused by the hearer's apparent obtuseness and wrong-headedness "where the matter is surely self-evident."

But even in those rarer discussions in which the speakers are capable of greater explicitness, the curious instinctive tendency to believe that a word has its own true or proper use, which we have seen has its roots in magic, too often prevents this ability to produce definitions from taking effect. No doubt other factors are involved. Lack of practice, literary fetishes concerning elegance of diction, reluctance to appear pedantic, defensive mimicry and other protective uses of language all contribute. But far more important than these is the instinctive attitude to words as natural containers of power, which has, as we have shown, from the dawn of language been assumed by mankind, and is still supported and encouraged by all the earlier stages of education.

The correction for this persistent tendency is a greater familiarity with the more common routes of definition, and a lively sense, which might easily be awakened as a part of education, that our use of any given word to stand for our referent on any occasion is not due to any particular fitness of the word for that particular referent, but is determined by all sorts of odd accidents of our own history. We ought to regard communication as a difficult matter, and close correspondence of reference for different thinkers as a comparatively rare event. It is never safe to assume that it has been secured unless both the starting-points and the routes of definition, whereby the referents of at least a majority of the symbols employed have been reached, are known.

In this chapter we are, for the sake of simplicity, confining our attention to reference alone. In actual discussion terms are used at least as much for the sake of their suasory and emotive effects as for their strictly symbolic value. Any substitute for 'beautiful,' for example, inevitably falls so flatly and heavily that many people prefer to use the term with all its dangers rather than the psychological jargon which they may agree is more satisfactory from a scientific as opposed to an emotive point of view.

It is often, indeed, impossible to decide, whether a particular use of symbols is primarily symbolic or emotive. This is especially the case with certain kinds of metaphor. When the Psalmist cries of his enemies, "They have sharpened their tongues like a serpent; adders' poison is under their lips," it is hard to determine whether an elusive similarity between the reptile and the persons he is describing is enabling him metaphorically to state something about them, or whether the sole function of his utterance is not to express his abhorrence of them and to promote similar attitudes towards them in his hearers. Most terms of abuse and endearment raise this problem, which, as a rule, it is, fortunately, not important to settle. The distinction which is important is that between utterances in which the symbolic function is subordinate to the emotive act and those of which the reverse is true. In the first case, however precise and however elaborate the references communicated may be, they can be seen to be present in an essentially instrumental capacity, as means to emotive effects. In the second case, however strong the emotive effects, these can be seen to be by-products not essentially involved in the speech transaction. The peculiarity of scientific statement, that recent new development of linguistic activity, is its restriction to the symbolic function.

If this restriction is to be maintained, and if scientific methods of statement are to be extended to fields such as those traditionally tended by philosophers, certain very subtle dangers must be provided for. Amongst these is the occurrence, in hitherto quite unsuspected numbers, of words which have been erroneously regarded without question as symbolic in function. The word 'good' may be taken as an example. It seems probable that this word is essentially a collection of homonyms, such that the set of things, roughly, those in connection with which we heard it pronounced in early years (a good bed, a good kick, a good baby, a good God) have no common characteristic. But another use of the word is often asserted to occur, of which some at least of those which we have cited are supposed to be degenerations, where 'good' is alleged to stand for a unique, unanalysable concept. This concept, it is said, is the subject-matter of Ethics.[1] This peculiar ethical use of 'good' is, we suggest, a purely emotive use. When so used the word stands for nothing whatever, and has no symbolic function. Thus, when we so use it in the sentence, '*This* is good,' we merely refer to *this*, and the addition of 'is good' makes no difference whatever to our reference. When on the other hand, we say '*This* is red,' the addition of 'is red' to 'this' does symbolize an extension of our reference, namely, to some other red thing. But 'is good' has no comparable *symbolic* function; it serves only as an emotive sign expressing our attitude to *this*, and perhaps evoking similar attitudes in other persons, or inciting them to actions of one kind or another.

The recognition that many of the most popular subjects of discussion are infested with symbolically blank but emotively active words of this kind is a necessary preliminary to the extension of scientific method to these questions. Another is some technique by which to ascertain which words are of this nature and on what occasions. Whether experimental and physiological methods can at present yield any result may be doubted, but the ultimate settlement of the matter can hardly be expected until tests in some

[1] Cf. G. E. Moore, *Principia Ethica*, Chap. I. Of course, if we define 'the good' as 'that of which we approve of approving,' or give any such definition when we say "This is good," we shall be making an assertion. It is only the indefinable 'good' which we suggest to be a purely emotive sign. The 'something more' or 'something else' which, it is alleged, is not covered by any definition of 'good' is the emotional aura of the word.

way independent of the opinion of the speaker are obtained.

In all discussions we shall find that what is said is only in part determined by the things to which the speaker is referring. Often without a clear consciousness of the fact, people have preoccupations which determine their use of words. Unless we are aware of their purposes and interests at the moment, we shall not know what they are talking about and whether their referents are the same as ours or not.

Purpose affects vocabulary in two ways. Sometimes without affecting reference it dictates the choice of symbols specially suited to an occasion. Thus, the language of a teacher in describing his spectroscope to a child may differ from that in which he describes it to his colleague or to his fiancée without there being any difference in his reference. Or an elegant writer will ring the changes on a series of synonyms [1] without changing his reference. On the other hand, a physicist uses different language from that employed by his guide in order to discuss the Spectre of the Brocken ; their different purposes affect their language in this case through altering their references.

It is plain that cases of the first kind are much simpler than those of the second ; only the latter are likely to lead to vain controversies. Thus, if one disputant talks of public opinion he *may* be referring to what others would call the views of certain newspaper owners, in which case an argument as to whether the Press influences public opinion would tend to be inconclusive in the absence of some third party familiar with the technique of definition. Such arguments are of constant occurrence even in the most intelligent circles, although when examined in the clear light of criticism they usually appear too foolish to be possible.

But how should a discussion whose aim is the

[1] Complete synonyms, *i.e.*, words alike in *all* their functions, probably do not occur. But partial synonyms which are used for the same reference are not uncommon.

removal of uncertainty as to whether the parties to it are referring to the same things or not be conducted?

The first necessity is to remember that since the past histories of individuals differ except in certain very simple respects, it is probable that their reactions to and employment of any general word will vary. There will be some to whom a word is merely a stimulus to the utterance of other words without the occurrence of any reference—the psittacists, that is to say, who respond to words, much as they might respond to the first notes of a tune which they proceed almost automatically to complete. At the other extreme there will be some for whom every word used symbolizes a definite and completely articulated reference. With the first we are not here concerned, but as regards the others, unless we have good evidence to the contrary we should assume that, clear though their ideas may be, they will probably not be ideas of the same things. It is plain that we can only identify referents through the references made to them. Different references then, *may* be to the same referent, sufficiently similar ones must be; and it is only by ensuring similarity of reference that we can secure identity in our referents. For this it is desirable to symbolize references by means of the simple routes of definition discussed above. We must choose as starting-points either things to which we can point, or which occur freely in ordinary experience. The routes by which we link these starting-points to our desired referents must be thoroughly familiar, which in practice confines us to four main routes and combinations of these. They are those which we must know and unerringly recognize if we are to survive—Similarity, Causation, Space and Time. In practice, however, it is often sufficient to start from less primitive initial points and follow more complicated and dangerous routes. Thus 'razor' = 'instrument used for shaving' unambiguously, without it being necessary to reduce 'used for' any further by analysis.

At what point our definitions are thorough enough must be left for the occasion to decide. In *viva voce* discussion, unless unduly prolonged and pertinacious, little can be hoped for except stimulus and hints which will be of use in more serious endeavours. But where there is reason to suppose that a slippery term is being employed, it is a wise policy to collect as wide a range of uses as possible *without* at this stage seeking for a common element. A good dictionary attempts this for certain words, but usually from an historical standpoint and on no theoretical principle. The next step is to order these uses with a view to discovering which main routes of identification have been adopted for the referents concerned. It is not necessary that the separate definitions so formulated should be mutually exclusive ; very often they will cover the same referents but with different references. In such cases we may be confronted by the problem of levels of reference above alluded to. 'Animal' in current speech, and 'mammal' in zoology stand for almost the same referents ; but the references differ very greatly in the definiteness and complexity of the sign-chains involved. These differences should, if possible, be indicated in the formulation of the definitions. What is required is that each definition should unmistakably mark out a certain range of referents. If two definitions mark out the same range no harm is done, the essential consideration being that each range should be clearly separated from the others so as to be capable of treatment on its own merits.

The natural tendency of those accustomed to traditional procedure is to expect that since what appears to be one word is being defined, the alternative substitute symbols will stand for referents with some common character of a more or less recondite nature. This may sometimes occur, but the inquiry as to whether there is such a common character should be postponed to a much later stage. The slightest study of the way in which words in ordinary speech gain occasional derivative and supernumerary uses through metaphorical shifts of all degrees of subtlety, and through what can be called linguistic accidents, is enough to show that for a common element of any interest or importance to run through all the respectable uses of a word is most unlikely. Each single metaphorical shift does, of course, depend upon some common element which is shared by the original reference and by the reference which borrows the symbol. Some part of the two contexts of the references must be the same. But the possible overlaps between contexts are innumerable, and there is no reason to expect that any word at all rich in context will always be borrowed on the strength of the same similarity or overlap. Thus, Beautiful^{A} and Beautiful^{B} may symbolize references with something in common ; so may Beautiful^{B} and Beautiful^{C}, but it by no means follows that these common elements will be the same or that the three symbols will stand for referents which share anything whatever of interest. Yet few writers who concern themselves with such wandering words resist the temptation to begin their inquiry with a search for essential or irreducible meanings.

The temptation has been greatly increased by the tendency of dictionaries to isolate an arbitrary nucleus of uses in the interests of conciseness, and to treat as 'dead' or 'accidental' just those senses which are likely to prove most troublesome in discussion. In some cases historical changes as well as phonetic modifications in the symbol itself are readily distinguishable. Thus with *persona—person—parson* the shifts can be seen at a glance in the following scheme :[1]—

1.	A	Mask.
2.	A+B	Character indicated by a mask.
3.	B	Character or rôle in a play.
4.	B+C ..	One who represents a character.
5.	C ..	Representative in general.
6.	C+D	Representative of church in parish.
7	D	Parson.

[1] Greenough and Kittredge, *Words and their Ways in English Speech*, p. 268.

The whole of this development took place in Latin, but when in English the word was borrowed in the form *persoun*, which Chaucer uses, a transference and fading out of the metaphor in B produces B1, the shift to 'personage'; and *parson* is a phonetic spelling of this older form. In this manner about a dozen uses of a word may often be found; and where the historical or phonetic separation is not clearly defined confusion is inevitable unless the objects referred to are so readily distinguishable as to encourage the punster.

If we wish to mediate between rival views it is far better to assume that the disputants are terminologically independent than to assume that they must in all respects use their words alike. With the first procedure, if there actually is a common element involved, we shall be in a good position to discover it. With the second we shall inevitably tend to misrepresent all the views concerned and to overlook most of their really valuable and peculiar features. The synthesis of diverse opinions, if it is attempted at all, should be postponed until each view has been examined as completely as possible in isolation. Premature efforts, to which all our natural attitudes to symbols conspire to tempt us, are an unfailing source of confusion.

For those whose approach to symbols is unreflective it is often difficult to believe that such convenient words as 'beauty,' 'meaning,' or 'truth' are actually not single words at all, but sets of superficially indistinguishable yet utterly discrepant symbols. The reasons why this is so are, however, not hard to point out. Language, which has developed chiefly to satisfy the exigencies of everyday practical intercourse, presents a remarkable unevenness in the density of distribution of its units when we regard it from the standpoint of our theoretical needs. Thus it constantly happens that one word has to serve functions for which a hundred would not be too many. Why language is often so recalcitrant to growth at these points is a puzzling problem. Shortage of terms in the established sciences is met without difficulty by the introduction of new terms. But with sciences in their initial stages, before they have developed into affairs for specialists, and while they are still public concerns, the resistance to new terms is very great. Probably the explanation of this is to be found in the lack of emotive power which is a peculiarity of all technicalities.

The result of this scarcity of terms is that any reference whatever made to these symbolically starved topics is forced to make use of the few words which are available, no matter how distinct its referents may be from those of other references which also use the same words. Thus any reference to human activities which are neither theoretical nor practical tends to be symbolized by the word 'æsthetic'; and derivatively anything which we are not merely concerned either to know or to change tends to be described as beautiful. And this, no matter how many fundamentally different attitudes to things we may come to distinguish. We have here a cause for the extravagant ambiguity of all the more important words used in general discussion; one which supplements and reinforces the processes of metaphorical shift just considered.

At the beginning, then, of any serious examination of these subjects we should provide ourselves with as complete a list as possible of different uses of the principal words. The reason for making this list as complete as possible, subject, of course, to common sense and ordinary discretion, is important. It is extraordinarily difficult in such fields to retain consistently what may be called a 'sense of position.' The process of investigation consists very largely of what, to the investigator, appear to be flashes of insight, sudden glimpses of connections between things and sudden awareness of distinctions and differences. These, in order to be retained, have to be symbolized, if, indeed, they do not, as is most often the case, originally occur in an already symbolized state.

Without such a map of the separable fields covered by the investigation any *constatation géniale* is liable to be confused with another, to their common detriment, or to yield an apparent contradiction of purely verbal origin. If, however, we are able at once to locate the idea in its proper province, the accident that we have to use the same words as totally distinct symbols is deprived of its power to disturb our orientation. The mere *ad hoc* distinction between two or perhaps three senses of a word made in response to particular exigencies of controversy is insufficient. We can never foretell on what part of the total field light will next be vouchsafed, and unless we know in outline what the possibilities are we are likely to remain ignorant of what it is into which we have had insight.

Not all words are worth so much trouble. It might be supposed that it is rather certain subjects which do not merit attention, but closer scrutiny suggests that these subjects, of which Theology appears to be a good example, are themselves merely word systems. But even the most barren fields have their psychological interest, and those who approach a discussion armed with a symbolic technique and able to apply such principles as the Canons dealt with in the last chapter may hope every day and in every way to find themselves better and better.

Something, however, can be achieved even by those who shrink from the severities of the Six Canons. In his *Art of Controversy*, of which he remarked "I am not aware that anything has been done in this direction although I have made inquiries far and wide," Schopenhauer says, "It would be a very good thing if every trick could receive some short and obviously appropriate name, so that when a man used this or that particular trick, he could be at once reproached for it." This suggestion is supported by Professor Dewey's characterization of the verbal sign as a fence; a label; and a vehicle: that is to say it selects and detaches meanings from out of the void, and makes what was dim and vague stand out as a clear-cut entity—secondly, it conserves the meaning thus fixed for future use, and, thirdly, enables it to be applied and transported to a new context and a new situation. Or in less metaphysical language, a symbol assists us in separating one reference from another, in repeating a reference we have already made, and in making partially analogous references in other contexts. In all these ways a notation of the devices of the controversialist would be very desirable.

Three such tricks may thus be readily stigmatized. The first, the Phonetic subterfuge, would be considered too simple to be dangerous if history bore no testimony to its effects. It consists in treating words which sound alike as though their expansions must be analogous. The most famous case is Mill's use of 'desirable' as though it must expand in the same way as 'visible' or 'knowable.' The subterfuge is to be charged against language rather than against Mill, and is plainly verbal. 'Desirable,' in the sense equivalent to 'ought to be desired,' may be reducible to 'can be desired by a mind of a certain organization,'[1] but is not on all fours as a symbol with 'visible' in the sense of 'able to be seen by somebody.'

The second subterfuge, the Hypostatic, is more difficult to discourage because it is a misuse of an indispensable linguistic convenience. We must, if we are ever to finish making any general remark, contract and condense our language, but we need not hypostatize our contractions. The point has been referred to in connection with Universals, but how popular and how influential is this practice may be

[1] This theory of value is developed in *op. cit.*, *Principles of Literary Criticism*, where arguments against it as a 'naturalistic fallacy' are disposed of.

shown by such a list of terms as the following :—Virtue, Liberty, Democracy, Peace, Germany, Religion, Glory. All invaluable words, indispensable even, but able to confuse the clearest issues, unless controlled by Canon III.

The third, the Utraquistic subterfuge, has probably made more bad argument plausible than any other controversial device which can be practised upon trustful humanity. It has long been recognized that the term 'perception' may have either a physical or a mental referent. Does it refer to what is perceived, or to the perceiving of this? Similarly, 'knowledge' may refer to what is known or to the knowing of it. The Utraquistic subterfuge consists in the use of such terms for both at once of the diverse referents in question. We have it typically when the term 'beauty' is employed, reference being made confusedly both to qualities of the beautiful object and to emotional effects of these qualities on the beholder.

Sometimes two or more of these subterfuges may be located in the same word. Thus 'Beauty' on most occasions is a double offender, both hypostatic and utraquistic.

In addition to this labelling of controversial tricks, a further set of Rules of Thumb may be laid down for practical guidance in conformity with the six Canons. In a recent Symposium of the Aristotelian Society on Mental Activity, carried on for the most part in inverted commas, it was not surprising to find Professor Carveth Read remarking once more that "the commonest cause of misunderstanding has long been recognized to lie in the ambiguity of terms, and yet we make very little progress in agreeing upon definitions. Even if we sometimes seem to be agreed upon the use of an important word, presently a new interest awakens or an old interest acquires new life ; and then, if its adherents think it would be strengthened by using that word in another sense they make no scruple about altering it."

Over two years later at the tenth annual meeting of the American Philosophical Association we find Professor Lovejoy breaking in on a similar series of misunderstandings with the remark, "More adherence to definitions is required if we are to come to an understanding. Appoint a committee to define the fundamental terms which are to be used in the discussion."

When we consider the amount of time we spend to-day in such discussion and the number of words we utter in the course of a single day—it is calculated that when vocal we emit between 150 and 250 words per minute—it is of some importance to recognize certain classes of these words which are liable to mislead in controversy.

"In Psychology what seems 'is'" it has been happily said. Is what 'seems' Real? "Everything," replies Bosanquet, "is Real so long as we do not take it for what it is not." "I somewhat uncautiously speak of mind as a Thing," confessed Professor Alexander—and still more regretfully "I have used the unfortunate word Phenomenon. I have made up my mind that I shall never use the word Phenomenon again without carefully defining its meaning. How Mr Stout can say I describe the mind as if it were not a Phenomenon passes my comprehension. I meant by the word Almost Nothing at all." This is reminiscent of Croce's dictum with regard to the Sublime: "the Sublime is everything that is or will be so called by those who have employed or shall employ the name." The chief function of such terms in general discussion is to act as Irritants, evoking emotions irrelevant to the determination of the referent. This is an abuse of the poetical function of language to which we shall return.

There is much scope for what may be called the Eugenics of Language, no less than for the Ethics of Terminology.

Foreshadowing the conscious process of Linguistic

elimination Mr Alfred Sidgwick has drawn attention under the title "Spoilt Words" to terms ambiguous beyond remedy. But having thus stated the problem, he leaves it. Language, as we know, was made before people learned to think: in the phraseology of Mill, by the 'vulgar'; and it is still being so made in the form in which we use it in conversation, however much we may regret the fact. It is very questionable how far we do but add to the existing confusion by endeavouring to restrict the meaning of these Unfortunates. When we remember that it is not round words only that emotional and other associations gather, but that Victor Hugo, for instance (as Ribot has pointed out), saw in each letter, even, a symbolic representation of some essential aspect of human knowledge,[1] it is somewhat optimistic to put trust in the efficacy of restriction of meaning in discussion. "I believe," said Max Müller, "that it would really be of the greatest benefit to mental science if all such terms as impressions, sensations—soul, spirit, and the rest, could, for a time, be banished, and not be readmitted till they had undergone a thorough purification." And in his remarkable analysis of the *Economics of Fatigue and Unrest* (1924) Dr Sargant Florence has successfully employed this method by eliminating altogether the terms 'fatigue' and 'unrest' in the earlier stages (Chapters V.-XI.) of his argument.

"Never change native names, for there are Names in every nation God-given, of unexplained power in the mysteries." So says a Chaldean Oracle with true insight. But in prose discussions which aim at the avoidance of mysteries, both Irritants and Degenerates must be ruthlessly rejected—Irritants because of their power to evoke disturbing emotions, and Degenerates because of the multiplicity of their associated referents.

[1] The importance of calligraphy in Chinese writing is an instance of æsthetic intrusion in a system of prose signs—even where the pictorial appeal of the signs themselves has vanished.

It is not necessary here to compile the Index Expurgatorius from 'Appearance' to 'Reality,' or as near Z as possible.

There is another class of words which may profitably be placed beyond the range of legitimate dispute. Matthew Arnold speaks of "terms thrown out, so to speak, at a not fully grasped object of the speaker's consciousness." So long as the true function of these Mendicants, as they might be designated, is recognized, they will cause little trouble. They must never receive harsh treatment; decasualization is the remedy.

To be distinguished from Mendicants, which may be assumed to possess the homing instinct, are Nomads, whose mode of life was first described by Locke.

> "Men having been accustomed from their cradle to learn words which are easily got and retained, before they knew or had framed the complete ideas which they express, they usually continue to do so all their lives; and without taking the pains necessary to settle in their minds determined ideas, they use their words for such unsteady and confused notions as they have; contenting themselves with the same words as other people use, as if the very sound necessarily carried with it the same meaning. This (although men make a shift with it in ordinary occurrences of life, yet when they come to reason concerning their Tenets) it manifestly fills their discourse with abundance of empty noise and jargon—especially in moral matters where the bare sound of the words are often only thought on, or at least very uncertain and obscure notions annexed to them.
>
> Men take the words they find in use amongst their neighbours, and that they may not seem ignorant what they stand for use them confidently without much troubling their heads about a certain fixed meaning, whereby besides the ease of it they obtain this advantage that as in such discourse they are seldom in the right so they are seldom to be convinced they are in the wrong, it being all one to draw these men out of their mistakes, who have no settled notions, as to dispossess a Vagrant of his habitation, who has no settled abode. This I guess to be so; and every one may observe in himself or others whether it be so or not."

We can still agree to-day that there is little doubt as to whether it be so or not; and if we were able more readily to recognize these Nomads, we should spend less time in the frenzied rifling of Cenotaphs which is at present so much in favour.

When we enter the Enchanted Wood of Words, our Rules of Thumb may enable us to deal not only with such evil genii as the Phonetic, the Hypostatic and the Utraquistic subterfuges, but also with other disturbing apparitions of which Irritants, Mendicants and Nomads are examples; such Rules, however, derive their virtue from the more refined Canons, whose powers we have already indicated.

It may, however, be asked, What is the use of knowing the nature of definition, for does not the difficulty consist in hitting upon the precise definition which would be useful? There are two answers to this. In the first place, the ability to frame definitions comes for most people only with practice, like surgery, diagnosis or cookery, but, as in these arts, a knowledge of principles is of great assistance. Secondly, such a knowledge of general principles renders any skill acquired in the course of special study of one field available at once when we come to deal with other but similar fields. In all the main topics of discussion —Æsthetics, Ethics, Religion, Politics, Economics, Psychology, Sociology, History—the same types of defining relations occur, and thus a theoretical mastery of any one of them gives confidence in the attack upon the others.

CHAPTER VII

THE MEANING OF BEAUTY

This I have here mentioned by the bye to show of what Consequence it is for Men to define their Words when there is Occasion. And it must be a great want of Ingenuity (to say no more of it) to refuse to do it: Since a Definition is the only way, whereby the precise Meaning of moral Words can be known.—*Locke.*

" Disputes are multiplied, as if everything was uncertain, and these disputes are managed with the greatest warmth, as if everything was certain. Amidst all this bustle 'tis not reason which gains the prize, but eloquence; and no man need ever despair of gaining proselytes to the most extravagant hypothesis, who has art enough to represent it in any favourable colours. The victory is not gained by the men at arms, who manage the pike and sword; but by the trumpeters, drummers, and musicians of the army."—*Hume.*

In order to test the value of the account of Definition given in the previous chapter, we may best select a subject which has hitherto proved notoriously refractory to definitive methods. Many intelligent people indeed have given up æsthetic speculation and take no interest in discussions about the nature or object of Art, because they feel that there is little likelihood of arriving at any definite conclusion. Authorities appear to differ so widely in their judgments as to which things are beautiful, and when they do agree there is no means of knowing *what* they are agreeing about.

What in fact do they mean by Beauty? Prof. Bosanquet and Dr Santayana, Signor Croce and Clive Bell, not to mention Ruskin and Tolstoi, each in his own way dogmatic, enthusiastic and voluminous, each leaves his conclusions equally uncorrelated with those of his predecessors. And the judgments of experts on one another are no less at variance. But if there is no reason to suppose that people are talking about the same thing, a lack of correlation in their remarks need not cause surprise. We assume too readily that similar language involves similar thoughts and similar things thought of. Yet why should there be only one subject of investigation which has been called Æsthetics? Why not several fields to be separately investigated, whether they are found to be connected or not? Even a Man of Letters, given time, should see that if we say with the poet:

> "'Beauty is Truth, Truth Beauty'—that is all
> Ye know on earth, and all ye need to know,"

we need not be talking about the same thing as the author who says:

> "The hide of the rhinoceros may be admired for its fitness; but as it scarcely indicates vitality, it is deemed less beautiful than a skin which exhibits mutable effects of muscular elasticity."

What reason is there to suppose that one æsthetic doctrine can be framed to include all the valuable kinds of what is called Literature.

Yet, surprising though it may seem, the only author who appears to have expressly admitted this difficulty and recognized its importance is Rupert Brooke. "One of the perils attending on those who ask 'What is Art?' is," he says, "that they tend, as all men do, to find what they are looking for: a common quality in Art. . . . People who start in this way are apt to be a most intolerable nuisance both to critics and to artists. . . . Of the wrong ways of approaching the subject of 'Art,' or even of any one art, this is the worst because it is the most harmful." He proceeds to point out how "Croce rather naïvely begins by noting that 'æsthetic' has been used both for questions of Art and for perception. So he sets out to discover what meaning it can really have to apply to both. He takes it for the one necessary condition a true answer about 'Æsthetics' must satisfy, that it shall explain how Art and Perception are both included. Having found such an explanation, he is satisfied." The same lively awareness of linguistic pitfalls which enabled Rupert Brooke wisely to neglect Croce also allowed him to detect the chink in Professor G. E. Moore's panoply, and so to resist the inexorable logic of the Cambridge Realists, then at the height of their power. "Psychologically," he says, "they seem to me non-starters. In the first place I do not admit the claims of anyone who says 'There *is* such a thing as Beauty, because when a man says, "This is beautiful," he does not *mean* "This is lovely."' . . . I am not concerned with what men may *mean*. They frequently mean, and have meant, the most astounding things. It is, possibly, true that when men say, 'This is beautiful' they do not mean 'This is lovely.' They may *mean* that the æsthetic emotion exists. My only comments are that it does not follow that the æsthetic emotion does exist; and that, as a matter of fact, they are wrong."[1]

His own sympathies, at least as they appear in the volume from which we quote, were with views of type XI. in the list given below, though he does not seem to have considered the matter very deeply, and had no opportunity of following up the promise of his admirable approach.

Whenever we have any experience which might be called 'æsthetic,' that is whenever we are enjoying, contemplating, admiring or appreciating an object, there are plainly different parts of the situation on which emphasis can be laid. As we select one or other of these so we shall develop one or other of the main æsthetic doctrines. In this choice we shall, in fact, be

[1] *John Webster and the Elizabethan Drama*, pp. 1-7.
Rupert Brooke clearly did not understand that the argument here being refuted professed to supply a proof not of existence but of *subsistence*. Common sense, however, sometimes succeeds where logical acumen overreaches itself.

deciding which of the main Types of Definition we are employing. Thus we may begin with the object itself; or with other things such as Nature, Genius, Perfection, The Ideal, or Truth, to which it is related; or with its effects upon us. We may begin where we please, the important thing being that we should know and make clear which of these approaches it is that we are taking, for the objects with which we come to deal, the referents to which we refer, if we enter one field will not as a rule be the same as those in another. Few persons will be equally interested in all, but some acquaintance with them will at least make the interests of other people more intelligible, and discussion more profitable. Differences of opinion and differences of interest in these matters are closely interconnected, but any attempt at a general synthesis, premature perhaps at present, must begin by disentangling them.

We have then to make plain the method of Definition which we are employing. The range of useful methods is shown in the following table of definitions, most of which represent traditional doctrines, while others, not before emphasized, render the treatment approximately complete. It should be remarked that the uses of 'beautiful' here tabulated are not by any means fully stated. Any definition is sufficiently explicit if it enables an intelligent reader to identify the reference concerned. A full formulation in each of these cases would occupy much space and would show that the field of the beautiful is for some of them more extensive than that of works of art, while certain restrictions, such as those which would exclude the Police from No. VIII., for example, will readily occur to the reader.

A { I *Anything is beautiful—which possesses the simple quality of beauty.*
II *Anything is beautiful—which has a specified Form.*

B

III *Anything is beautiful—which is an imitation of Nature.*

IV *Anything is beautiful—which results from successful exploitation of a Medium.*

V *Anything is beautiful—which is the work of Genius.*

VI *Anything is beautiful—which reveals* (1) *Truth,* (2) *the Spirit of Nature,* (3) *the Ideal,* (4) *the Universal,* (5) *the Typical.*

VII *Anything is beautiful—which produces Illusion.*

VIII *Anything is beautiful—which leads to desirable Social effects.*

IX *Anything is beautiful—which is an Expression.*

C

X *Anything is beautiful—which causes Pleasure.*

XI *Anything is beautiful—which excites Emotions.*

XII *Anything is beautiful—which promotes a Specific emotion.*

XIII *Anything is beautiful—which involves the processes of Empathy.*

XIV *Anything is beautiful—which heightens Vitality.*

XV *Anything is beautiful—which brings us into touch with exceptional Personalities.*

XVI *Anything is beautiful—which induces Synæsthesis.*[1]

It will be noticed that each of these definitions illustrates one or more of the fundamental defining relations discussed in the last chapter. Thus, the definitions in Group C, Definitions X.–XVI., are all in terms of the effects of things upon consciousness and so are cases of type VII. Of the two definitions in Group A, the first is a case of simple naming, type I. We postulate a quality Beauty, name it, and trust the identification of this mythological referent to the magical efficacy of our name. The discussion of the

[1] A detailed discussion of the views defined in these ways is provided in *The Foundations of Æsthetics* by the authors and Mr James Wood (1921, Second Edition, 1926); and a survey of the most recent work in the light of the above classification will be found in the *Encyclopædia Britannica*, Thirteenth Edition, New Volumes (1926), *sub.* "Æsthetics."

Beautiful in terms of an intrinsic quality Beauty is in fact an excellent example of the survival of primitive word-superstitions, and of the risks run by any discussion which is symbolically uncritical. The second Definition (II.), by Form, is either Spatial or Temporal according to the Art to which it is applied. If any others than these relations seem to be involved on any occasion, we shall find on examination that the definition has had its starting-point surreptitiously changed and has become actually psychological, a change which can easily occur in this field, without any immediately apparent change in the symbolism. As a glaring instance the use of the word 'great' in literary and artistic criticism shows this process, the transition, without symbolic indication, from the 'objective' to the 'subjective' as they used to be called.

The Definitions in Group B are all more or less complex.

Both Imitation (III.), and Exploitation (IV.), the definition by reference to the capacities of the medium, are evidently compounded of Causation, Similarity, Cognizing and Willing Relations; Exploitation being in fact as fine an instance as can be found of a complex definition easy to understand in its condensed shorthand form and difficult or impossible to analyse. Few people, however, will suffer any temptation to postulate a special property of being an exploitation, though such devices are the penalty we usually have to pay for convenient short cuts in our symbolization.

The other definitions of Group B offer similar problems in analysis. The degree to which routes of type VIII., mental attitudes of believing (VI. and VII.) or approving (VIII.), appear is an interesting feature, which again helps to account for the tendency of such views to become psychological (Group C). Thus definition XVI. tends to absorb and replace VI.; and XV. in a refined and explicit form often supersedes V. These variations in reference, even for definitions of symbols specially provided to control such inconstancy, serve to remind us of the paramount importance of Canon IV. for all discussion. The use of a symbolic theory of definition lies not in any guarantee which it can offer against ambiguity, but in the insight which it can give as to what, since we are using symbols, will be happening; and in the means provided of detecting and correcting those involuntary wanderings of the reference which are certain in all discourse to occur.

In the case of the above definitions our 'starting-points,' synæsthesis, specific emotion, desirable social effects, etc., are plainly themselves arrived at by intricate processes of definition. For the particular purposes for which definitions of 'beautiful' are likely to be drawn up these starting-points can be assumed to be agreed upon, and the methods by which such agreement can be secured are the same for 'emotion' or 'pleasure,' as for 'beautiful' itself.

Equally we can proceed from these definitions or from any one of them, to terms cognate (Ugliness, Prettiness, Sublimity) or otherwise related (Art, Æsthetic Decoration), and to define these in their turn we may take as starting-points either some one of the now demarcated fields of the beautiful and say:—Æsthetics is the study of the Beautiful, or:—Art is the professed attempt to produce Beauty, or we may return to our starting-point for the definition of Beauty and box the compass about it.

The fields indicated by the above definitions may in some cases be co-extensive, *e.g.*, V. and XV.; or they may partially overlap, *e.g.*, X. and XIII.; or they may be mutually exclusive, a condition not realized here or indeed in any probable discussion. The question whether two such fields do co-extend, do overlap or do exclude, is one to be decided by detailed investigation of the referents included in the fields. The ranges of overlap between fields, in fact, give rise to the special empirical problems of the sciences. Thus, for instance, we find that beautiful things defined as Imitations of Nature (III.) only coincide with beautiful things defined as producers of Illusion (VII.) under certain strict conditions among which is to be found the condition that neither shall be included in the range defined by IV. The investigation of such correlations and the conditions to which they are subject is the business of Æsthetic as a science.

The advantage of a grammatically extensional form for the definitions is that, so put, the symbols we use are least likely to obscure the issues raised, by making questions which are about matters of fact into puzzling conundra concerning the interlinking of locutions.

The fields reached by these various approaches can all be cultivated and most of them are associated with well-known names in the Philosophy of Art.

Let us, then, suppose that we have selected one of these fields and cultivated it to the best of our ability; for what reasons was it selected rather than some other? For if we approach the subject in the spirit of a visitor to the Zoo, who, knowing that all the creatures in a certain enclosure are 'reptiles,' seeks for the common property which distinguishes them as a group from the fish in the Aquarium, mistakes may be made. We enter, for example, Burlington House, and, assuming that all the objects there collected are beautiful, attempt similarly to establish some common property. A little consideration of how they came there might have raised serious doubts; but if, after the manner of many æstheticians, we persist, we may even make our discovery of some relevant common property appear plausible.

We have seen (pp. 124-5) how widely such a respected word as 'good' may wander; and there are good reasons for supposing that 'beauty' will not be more faithful to one particular kernel of reference. In discussion we must in fact always bear in mind that there is an indefinitely large number of ways in which any symbol may acquire derivative uses; any similarity, any analogy may provide a sufficient reason for an extension of 'meaning,' or semantic shift. It no more follows that the two or more symbols which it then becomes (cf. p. 91) will stand for referents with some relevant common property, than it would follow from the common name of a man's step-mother and his daughter-in-law that they share his gout or his passion for the turf.

If, therefore, terms such as Beauty are used in discussion for the sake of their emotive value, as is usually the case, confusion will inevitably result unless it is constantly realized that words so used are indefinable, *i.e.*, admit of no substitution, there being no other equally effective stimulus-word. Such indefinable uses are no doubt what have often led to the assumption of a simple quality of Beauty (Definition I.) to account for verbal difficulties; as was also suggested above in the case of Good (p. 125). If, on the other hand, the term Beauty be retained as a short-hand substitute, for some one among the many definitions which we have elicited, this practice can only be justified as a means of indicating by a Word of Power that the experience selected is regarded as of outstanding importance; or as a useful low-level shorthand.

In addition to providing a test case for any general technique of definition a consideration of the problem of Beauty is perhaps the best introduction to the question of the diverse functions of language. As is well known, those whose concern with the arts is most direct often tend to deprecate a scientific approach as being likely to impair appreciation. This opinion if carefully examined will be found to be a typical symptom of a confusion as to the uses of language so constantly present in all discussions that its general recognition would be one of the most important results which a science of symbolism could yield.

If we compare a body of criticism relating to any

of the arts with an equally accredited body of remarks dealing with, let us say, physics or physiology, we shall be struck by the frequency, even in the best critics, of sentences which it is impossible to understand *in the same way* as we endeavour to understand those of physiologists. "Beautiful words are the very and peculiar light of the mind," said Longinus. According to Coleridge "the artist must imitate that which is within the thing, that which is active through form and figure, and discourses to us by symbols—the *Naturgeist*, or spirit of nature." "Poetry," Dr Bradley writes, "is a spirit. It comes we know not whence. It will not speak at our bidding, nor answer in our language. It is not our servant; it is our master."[1] And Dr Mackail is even more rhapsodic: "Essentially a continuous substance or energy, poetry is historically a connected movement, a series of successive integral manifestations. Each poet, from Homer to our own day, has been to some extent and at some point, the voice of the movement and energy of poetry; in him poetry has for the moment become visible, audible, incarnate, and his extant poems are the record left of that partial and transitory incarnation. . . . The progress of poetry . . . is immortal."[2]

No one who was not resolved to waste his time would for long try to interpret these remarks in the same way as he would, let us say, an account of the circulation of the blood. And yet it would be a mistake to regard them as not worth attention. It is clear that they require a different mode of approach. Whether their authors were aware of the fact or not, the use of words of which these are examples is totally distinct from the scientific use. The point would be made still more plain, if sentences from poetry were used for the experiment. What is certain is that there is a common and important use of words which is different from the

[1] *Oxford Lectures on Poetry*, p. 27.
[2] *Lectures on Poetry*, pp. xi., xiii.

scientific or, as we shall call it, the strict *symbolic* use of words.

In ordinary everyday speech each phrase has not one but a number of functions. We shall in our final chapter classify these under five headings; but here a twofold division is more convenient, the division between the *symbolic* use of words and the *emotive* use. The symbolic use of words is *statement;* the recording, the support, the organization and the communication of references. The emotive use of words is a more simple matter, it is the use of words to express or excite feelings and attitudes. It is probably more primitive. If we say "The height of the Eiffel Tower is 900 feet" we are making a statement, we are using symbols in order to record or communicate a reference, and our symbol is true or false in a strict sense and is theoretically verifiable. But if we say "Hurrah!" or "Poetry is a spirit" or "Man is a worm," we may not be making statements, not even false statements; we are most probably using words merely to evoke certain attitudes.

Each of these contrasted functions has, it will be seen, two sides, that of the speaker and that of the listener. Under the symbolic function are included both the symbolization of reference and its communication to the listener, *i.e.*, the causing in the listener of a similar reference. Under the emotive function are included both the expression of emotions, attitudes, moods, intentions, etc., in the speaker, and their communication, *i.e.*, their evocation in the listener. As there is no convenient verb to cover both expression and evocation, we shall in what follows often use the term 'evoke' to cover both sides of the emotive function, there being no risk of misunderstanding. In many cases, moreover, emotive language is used by the speaker not because he already has an emotion which he desires to express, but solely because he is seeking a word which will evoke an emotion which he desires to have; nor, of course, is it necessary for the speaker himself to experience the emotion which he attempts to evoke.

It is true that some element of reference probably enters, for all civilized adults[1] at least, into almost all use of words, and it is always possible to import a reference, if it be only a reference to things in general. The two functions under consideration usually occur together but none the less they are in principle distinct. So far as words are used emotively no question as to their truth in the strict sense can directly arise. Indirectly, no doubt, truth in this strict sense is often involved. Very much poetry consist of statements, symbolic arrangements capable of truth or falsity, which are used not for the sake of their truth or falsity but for the sake of the attitudes which their acceptance will evoke. For this purpose it fortunately happens, or rather it is part of the poet's business to make it happen, that the truth or falsity matters not at all to the acceptance. Provided that the attitude or feeling is evoked the most important function of such language is fulfilled, and any symbolic function that the words may have is instrumental only and subsidiary to the evocative function.

This subtle interweaving of the two functions is the main reason why recognition of their difference is not universal. The best test of whether our use of words is essentially symbolic or emotive is the question—"Is this true or false in the ordinary strict scientific sense?" If this question is relevant then the use is symbolic, if it is clearly irrelevant then we have an emotive utterance.

But in applying this test we must beware of two

[1] It is desirable to make the reservation, if only for educational purposes, for according to some authorities "ninety-nine per cent. of the words used in talking to a little child have no meaning for him, except that, as the expression of attention to him, they please him." Moreover, before the age of six or seven children "cannot hold a meaning before their minds without experiencing it in perceptual symbols, whether words or otherwise. . . . Hence the natural desire of the child to talk or be talked to, if he is asked even for a few minutes to sit still."—(W. E. Urwick *The Child's Mind*, pp. 95, 102.)

dangers. There is a certain type of mind which although it uses evocative language itself cannot on reflection admit such a thing, and will regard the question as relevant upon all occasions. For a larger body of readers than is generally supposed poetry is unreadable for this reason. The other danger is more important. Corresponding in some degree to the strict sense of true and false for symbolic statements (True^{S}), there are senses which apply to emotive utterances (True^{E}). Critics often use True^{E} of works of art, where alternative symbols would be 'convincing' in some cases, 'sincere' in others, 'beautiful' in others, and so on. And this is commonly done without any awareness that True^{E} and True^{S} are different symbols. Further there is a purely evocative use of True—its use to excite attitudes of acceptance or admiration; and a purely evocative use of False—to excite attitudes of distrust or disapprobation. When so used these words, since they are evocative, cannot, except by accident, be replaced by others; a fact which explains the common reluctance to relinquish their employment even when the inconvenience of having symbols so alike superficially as True^{S} and True^{E} in use together is fully recognized. In general that affection for a word even when it is admitted to be ambiguous, which is such a common feature of discussion, is very often due to its emotive efficiency rather than to any real difficulty in finding alternative symbols which will support the same reference. It is, however, not always the sole reason, as we shall see when we come in our final chapter to consider the condition of word-dependence.

This disparity of function between words as supports or vehicles of reference and words as expressions or stimulants of attitudes has, in recent years, begun to receive some attention, for the most part from a purely grammatical standpoint. That neglect of the effects of our linguistic procedure upon all our other activities which is so characteristic of linguists has, however, deprived such studies as have been made of most of their value. G. von der Gabelentz for instance, though he declares that "Language serves a man not only to express something but also to express himself," seems in no way to have considered what extreme consequence this intermingling of functions has for the theory as well as for the form of language. And to take the most recent work upon the subject, Vendryes, in his chapter upon Affective Language, keeps equally strictly to the grammarian's standpoint. "The logical element and the affective element," he says, "mingle constantly in language. Except for technical languages, notably the scientific languages, which are by definition outside life, the expression of an idea is never exempt from a nuance of sentiment." "These sentiments have no interest for the linguist unless they are expressed by linguistic means. But they generally remain outside language; they are like a light vapour which floats above the expression of the thought without altering its grammatical form," etc. The two chief ways in which the affective side of language concerns the linguist he finds, first in its effect upon the order of words and secondly as determining the vocabulary. Many words are dropped or retained, for affective reasons. "It is by the action of affectivity that the instability of grammars is to a great extent to be explained. The logical ideal for a grammar would be to have an expression for each function and only one function for each expression. This ideal supposes for its realization that the language is fixed like an algebra, where a formula once established remains without change in all the operations in which it is used. But phrases are not algebraic formulæ. Affectivity always envelops and colours the logical expression of the thought. We never repeat the same phrase twice; we never use the same word twice with the same value; there are never two absolutely identical linguistic facts. This is due to the circumstances which ceaselessly modify the conditions of our affectivity."[1]

It is perhaps unfair to ask from grammarians some consideration of the wider aspects of language. They have their own difficult and laborious subject to occupy all their attention. Yet from a book the promise of which was the cause of the abandonment by Couturat of his projected "Manual of the logic of language" a more searching inquiry might be expected. It still remains true that linguists, of whom M. Vendryes is one of the most distinguished, abound, but investigators into the theory of language are curiously lacking.[2]

From the philosophical side also, the speculative approach to this duality of the symbolic and evocative functions has been made recently under various disguises. All such terms as Intuition, Intellect, Emotion, Freedom, Logic, Immediacy, are already famous for their power to confuse and frustrate discussion. In general, any term or phrase, 'élan vital,' 'purely logical analysis' . . . which is capable of being used either as a banner[3] or as a bludgeon, or as both, needs, if it is to be handled without disaster, a constant and conscious understanding of these two functions of language. It is useless to try to sterilize our instruments without studying the habits of the bacteria. Not even mathematics is free as a whole from emotive complications; parts of it seem to be, but the ease with which mathematicians turn into mystics ("Even were there no things at all, there would still be the property of being divisible by 107")

[1] *Le Langage* (1922), pp. 163, 165, 182. E. T., *Language* (1924), Part II., Chapter IV.

[2] An exception might be made of Professor Delacroix, who in his (*op. cit.*) *Le Langage et la Pensée* (1924) devotes considerable space to the subject, but treats the emotive function in a purely academic spirit without more regard for its far-reaching effects upon discussion than the Logical Positivists (cf. Carnap, *The Logical Syntax of Language*, 1937).

[3] Cf. Nietzsche's dictum: "Words relating to values are merely banners planted on those spots where a new blessedness was discovered—a new feeling."

when they consider its foundations, shows what the true situation is.

One of the best known of these disguised discussions of the emotive function of language centres about the teaching of Bergson on the nature of knowledge. To quote from a recent exposition: "The business of philosophy, according to Bergson, is not to explain reality, but to know it. For this a different kind of mental effort is required. Analysis and classification, instead of increasing our direct knowledge, tend rather to diminish it."[1] As Bergson himself says: "From the infinitely vast field of our virtual knowledge we have selected, to turn into actual knowledge, whatever concerns our action upon things; the rest we have neglected."[2] And as his expositor continues: "The attitude of mind required for explaining the facts conflicts with that which is required for knowing them. From the point of view simply of knowing, the facts are all equally important and we cannot afford to discriminate, but for explanation some facts are very much more important than others. When we want to explain, therefore, rather than simply to know, we tend to concentrate our attention upon these practically important facts and pass over the rest."[3]

The processes of explanation as described by Bergson bear a close resemblance to what we have called reference when this is supported by symbolism. Owing to his peculiar view of memory, however, he is unable to make the use of mnemic phenomena which, as we have seen, is essential if mysticism, even as regards this kind of 'knowledge' is to be avoided.

The other kind of knowledge, 'virtual knowledge,' the knowledge which is 'creative duration,' the only kind of knowledge of 'really real reality' Bergsonians will allow, is, as he presents it, unavoidably mystical.

[1] K. Stephen, *The Misuse of Mind*, p. 19.
[2] Bergson, *La Perception du Changement*, p. 12.
[3] K. Stephen, *op. cit.*, p. 22.

Not only because any description of it must involve the expositor in self-contradiction—as we have seen any repudiation of orthodox symbolic machinery has this consequence[1]—but also because it requires an initial act of faith in the existence of a vast world of 'virtual knowledge' which is actually unknown. None the less, those who have no such faith, and merely follow the advice of Bergsonians to neglect the actual terms in the descriptions given and to perform instead an 'act of synthesis,' can easily become persuaded that they understand what 'virtual knowledge' is, and even that they can possess it.

We have above (p. 81) insisted that knowledge in the sense of reference is a highly indirect affair, and hinted that though we often *feel* an objection to admitting that our mental contact with the world is neither close nor full, but on the contrary distant and schematic, our reluctance might be diminished by a consideration of our non-cognitive contacts. These, too, are for the most part indirect, but they are capable of much greater fullness. The more clear and discriminating reference becomes, the slighter, relatively to similar but cruder reference, is our link with what we are referring to—the more specialized and exquisite the context involved. With all that Bergson has to say about the tendency for precise, discriminating, analytic attention to whittle down our connection with what we are attending to, we can agree. Bergson, moreover, has well emphasized the part played by language in reinforcing and exaggerating this tendency. Thinking casually of conies, the context involved may be of immense complexity, since a large part of our past experience with these animals is operative. Thinking discriminatingly of the same objects as 'small deer,' our context becomes specialized, and only those features of conies need be involved which they share with their co-members of the

[1] Mrs Stephen writes with great lucidity upon this question. Cf. especially pp. 57-61.

class in question. The others *need* not be lost, but we can agree that there is a strong tendency for them to disappear, and in any really difficult feats of discrimination they will certainly be best omitted.

At the extreme of consciousness most removed from analytic and abstract attention we have not one but a variety of possible states, according to the kind and extent of the contexts, to which the experience in question belongs. The state may be comparatively simple, as when we are engaged in some ordinary *perceptual* activity, such as throwing dice; or it may be predominantly emotional; or leaping for our lives from the onrush of motor cyclists we may again experience simple throbs of pure unsophisticated experience. But certain of these concrete, immediate, unintellectualized phases of life have in their own right a complexity and richness which no intellectual activities can equal. Amongst these æsthetic experiences figure prominently. Many to whom Bergson's recommendation of immediacy, and his insistence upon the treasures awaiting those who regain it, make their appeal will admit that this is because he seems to them to be describing what happens when they are most successful in artistic contemplation. We cannot enter here into the details of what, from the standpoint of more or less conventional psychology, may be supposed to happen in these states of synæsthesis.[1] What, however, from this standpoint is indisputable is that the more important of them derive their value from the peculiar fashion in which impulses formed by and representing the past experience of the contemplator are set working.

Thus in a quite precise sense, though one which can only be somewhat elaborately formulated, the states of æsthetic contemplation owe their fullness and richness to the action of memory; not memory narrowed

[1] Those who desire to pursue the matter may be referred to *The Foundations of Æsthetics*, cited above.

down and specialized as is required in reference, but memory operating in a freer fashion to widen and amplify sensitiveness. In such conditions we are open to a more diffused and more heterogeneous stimulation, because the inhibitions which normally canalize our responses are removed.

Partly because of certain of the felt characters of the states we have been describing, a sense of repose and satisfaction not unlike the repose which follows a successful intellectual effort, though due to quite different causes—partly for other reasons, it is not surprising that these states should have been often described as states of knowledge. The temptation to a philosopher when concerned with a subject in which he feels a passionate interest, to use all the words which are most likely to attract attention and excite belief in the importance of the subject is almost irresistible. Thus, any state of mind in which anyone takes a great interest is very likely to be called 'knowledge,' because no other word in psychology has such evocative virtue. If this state of mind is very unlike those usually so called, the new "knowledge" will be set in opposition to the old and praised as of a superior, more real, and more essential nature. These periodic raids upon æsthetics have been common in the history of philosophy. The crowning instance of Kant, and the attempted annexation of æsthetics by Idealism are recent examples.

The suggestion is reasonable, therefore, that when the pseudo-problems due to cross vocabularies are removed and the illusory promise of a new heaven and a new earth, which Bergsonians somewhat weakly hold out, has been dismissed, the point at issue in the intuitionist-intellectualist controversy will be found to be removable by an understanding of the dual function, symbolic as well as emotive, of the word 'knowledge.' To deny that 'virtual knowledge' is in the symbolic sense knowledge is in no way derogatory to the state (according to the view here maintained, a state, or set of states, of specially free response to stimulation) called by that name. It is merely to apply a rule which all those who are aware of the functions of language will support, namely, that in discussion, where symbolic considerations are supposed to be prior to all others, the evocative advantages of terms are only to be exploited when it is certain that symbolically no disadvantage can result.

But a more general consciousness of the nature of the two functions is necessary if they are to be kept from interfering with one another; and especially all the verbal disguises, by which each at times endeavours to pass itself off as the other, need to be exposed. It ought to be impossible to pretend that any scientific statement can give a more inspiring or a more profound 'vision of reality' than another. It can be more general or more useful, and that is all. On the other hand it ought to be impossible to talk about poetry or religion as though they were capable of giving 'knowledge,' especially since 'knowledge' as a term has been so overworked from both sides that it is no longer of much service. A poem—or a religion, though religions have so definitely exploited the confusion of function which we are now considering, and are so dependent upon it, as to be unmistakably pathological growths—has no concern with limited and directed reference. It tells us, or should tell us, nothing. It has a different, though an equally important and a far more vital function—to use an evocative term in connection with an evocative matter. What it does, or should do, is to induce a fitting[1] attitude to experi-

[1] Instead of 'fitting' we might have said 'valuable.' But since the value of an attitude depends in part upon the other attitudes which are possible and in part upon the degree to which it leaves open the possibility of other attitudes for other circumstances, we use the term 'fitting'; not, however, to imply any narrow code of the proper attitudes to be adopted upon all occasions. The term 'attitude' should throughout this discussion be understood in a wide sense, as covering all the ways in which impulses may be set ready for action; including those peculiar settings from which no overt action results, often spoken of as the 'æsthetic moods' or 'æsthetic emotions.'

ence. But such words as 'fitting,' 'suitable' or 'appropriate' are chilly, having little or no evocative power. Therefore those who care most for poetry and who best understand its central and crucial value, tend to resent such language as unworthy of its subject. From the evocative standpoint they are justified. But once the proper separation of these functions is made it will be plain that the purpose for which such terms are used, namely to give a strictly symbolic description of the function of poetry, for many reasons[1] the supreme form of emotive language, cannot conflict with the poetic or evocative appraisal of poetry, with which poets as poets are concerned.

Further, the exercise of one function need not, *if the functions are not confused*, in any way interfere with the exercise of the other. The sight of persons irritated with science because they care for poetry ("Whatever the sun may be, it is certainly not a ball of flaming gas," cries D. H. Lawrence), or of scientists totally immune from the influences of civilization, becomes still more regrettable when we realize how unnecessary it is. As science frees itself from the emotional outlook, and modern physics is becoming something in connection with which attitudes seem rather *de trop*, so poetry seems about to return to the conditions of its greatness, by abandoning the obsession of knowledge and symbolic truth. It is not necessary to know what things are in order to take up fitting attitudes towards them, and the peculiarity of the greatest attitudes which art can evoke is their extraordinary width. The description and ordering of such attitudes is the business of æsthetics. The evaluation of them, needless to say, must rest ultimately upon the opinions of those best qualified to be judges by the range and delicacy of their experience and their freedom from irrelevant preoccupations.

[1] Cf. Chapter X., pp. 239-240 *infra*; also *Principles of Literary Criticism*, Chapters XXIII.-XXXV.

CHAPTER VIII

THE MEANING OF PHILOSOPHERS

What do you read, my lord ?—*Polonius.*
Words, words, words.—*Hamlet.*

"O wondrous power of words, by simple faith
Licensed to take the MEANING that we love."

Thus the poet ; and observation does not invalidate the perspicacious remark. It might, however, have been supposed that logicians and psychologists would have devoted special attention to meaning, since it is so vital for all the issues with which they are concerned. But that this is not the case will be evident[1] to anyone who studies the Symposium in *Mind* (October 1920 and following numbers) on "The Meaning of 'Meaning.'"

It is perhaps unnecessary to point out that such brief extracts from lengthy philosophical disquisitions as the limits of this chapter allow, cannot fairly represent any given author's views upon that, whatever it may be, if anything, for which he uses the word 'meaning.' Some quotations, however, do tell their own tale ; but even where no actual absurdity transpires, the resort

[1] The following passage in *Nuces Philosophicæ*, by one Edward Johnson, published in 1842, is worth recalling :

"A. I confess I am surprised that all this time you have never yet once asked me what I *mean* by the word *meaning*.
"B. What then do you mean by the word meaning ?
"C. Be patient. You can only learn the meaning of the word *meaning* from the consideration of the *nature of ideas*, and their connection with things."

Half a century later, Lady Welby quoted from this author in *Mind* (1896), and complained that "Sense *in the meaning sense* has never yet been taken as a centre to work out from : attention, perception, memory, judgment, etc., have never been cross-examined from the direction of their common relation to a 'meaning.'" And after the lapse of a further twenty-five years we find Mr Russell admitting ("On Propositions : What they are and how they mean." *Proc. Arist. Soc.* 1919) with the approval of Dr Schiller in the symposium "that logicians have done very little towards explaining the relation called 'meaning.'"

to such a term in serious argument, as though it had some accepted use, or as though the author's use were at once obvious, is a practice to be discredited.

Dr Schiller began by announcing that the Greek language is "so defective that it can hardly be said to have a vocabulary for the notion" of meaning at all; and in proceeding to state his own view that "MEANING is essentially personal . . . . what anything MEANS depends on *who* MEANS it," he found it necessary to traverse Mr Russell's dictum that "the problem of the MEANING of words is reduced to the problem of the MEANING of images." Mr Russell replied by endeavouring "to give more precision to the definition of MEANING by introducing the notion of 'mnemic causation'" and succeeded thereby in evolving an instructive description of metaphysics. "A word," he explained, "which aims at complete generality, such as 'entity,' for example, will have to be devoid of mnemic effects, and therefore of MEANING. In practice, this is not the case: such words have *verbal* associations, the learning of which constitutes the study of metaphysics." Mr Joachim, who elected to stand aside from the discussion, professed to find Mr Russell "asserting that nobody can possibly *think*," and confined himself to an analysis of the function of images, drawing attention in a foot-note to the fact that for Mr Russell meaning appeared (amongst other things) as 'a relation,' that "a relation 'constitutes' meaning, and that a word not only 'has' meaning, but is related 'to its meaning.'"

This whole episode was characterized by Dr Schiller six months later (April, 1921, p. 185) as presenting "the usual features of a philosophic discussion. That is to say, it reads like a triangular duel, in which each participant aims at something different, and according to the other misses it, and hits a phantom." In dealing with details he quotes Mr Russell's remark that "all the *words* in which Dr Schiller endeavours to describe his unobservable entities *imply* that after all he can observe them," as a typical case of "the overriding of actual MEANING by verbal, which could hardly be surpassed from the writings of Mr Bradley."

In July Mr Alfred Sidgwick explained (p. 285) that "MEANING depends on consequences, and truth depends on MEANING;" and Professor Strong intervened (p. 313) as a 'critical realist' to meet Dr Schiller's objections to Mr Russell and to render the latter's theory intelligible to Mr Joachim. He illustrated his rendering by imagining an explosion. When we hear what we call an explosion, "the sound has not so much acquired, as become converted into a MEANING. . . . What is non-concrete and non-sensuous is always a MEANING, a sense of that unfathomed beyond which we cannot contemplate but only intend. . . . To MEAN something is to conceive or rather treat it as not wholly revealed to the mind at the moment."

To this Dr Schiller rejoins that Dr Strong always confines his attention to the case "in which an 'object' is said to 'MEAN so-and-so.'" This, he thinks, "imposes on him the duties of deriving the personal MEANING, and of explaining the relativity of 'the' MEANING of an object to various cognitive purposes and personal MEANINGS" (p. 445). He concludes (p. 447) that "the existence of personal MEANING remains a pitfall in the path of all intellectualism." The controversy is presumably still in progress.

Contemporaneously with the Symposium on Meaning which appeared in *Mind*, an inquiry into the nature of Aphasia was appearing in *Brain*[1] and during the discussion of Dr Head's views the question of meaning came to the front. A special memorandum suggested by the treatment of 'semantic aphasia,' was handed in by Dr J. Herbert Parsons,[2] and it throws interesting

[1] 1920. Vol. XLIII., Parts II. and IV.

[2] "The Psychology of 'Meaning' in its Relation to Aphasia." *Ibid.*, p. 441.

light on the degree of assistance which neurologists can be expected to derive from the work of philosophers in this field. According to Dr Parsons, at the lowest biological level "it would be unwise to deny the presence of a plus or minus affective tone—and this is the primitive germ of 'MEANING.'" At the perceptual level, however, "the relatively undifferentiated psychoplasm is differentiated into specialized affective and cognitive elements, which are reintegrated, thus undergoing a synthesis which is the 'MEANING' of the given experience. Perceptual 'MEANING' suffused with affective tone, issues in instinctive conative activity." Thus at the end of the completed reaction "the 'MEANING' has become enriched and complicated. . . . This altered 'MEANING' is stored up, and, though depressed below the threshold of consciousness, is capable of being revived. . . . The integration and synthesis of the already more plastic psychoplasm results in a higher, more complex type of 'MEANING.'" Later the influence of social environment makes itself felt, and in the complicated process of social intercourse "the ultimate results are equivalent to an interaction of old and new 'MEANINGS,' resulting in an infinity of still newer, richer and more refined 'MEANINGS.'" At this stage "the creative activities assume a synergy at a higher level," and "show a projicience hitherto absent." The child's "gestures are no longer merely passive signs of his mind's activities, but active indications of his feelings and desires. This is the dawn of language."

A detailed analysis of the *Mind* Symposium might have been instructive as a preliminary to the framing of a set of definitions, but its technique was unusually disappointing,[1] and since in any case the metaphysical arena of the Old World inevitably suggests to many an atmosphere of barren logomachy, we may more

[1] Owing largely to the temperamental incompatibility of the symposiasts. Mr Russell, moreover, has now superseded his contribution by the relevant chapters of his *Analysis of Mind*, to which reference has already been made (p. 54).

profitably deal with the confusions which arise as occasion allows and cite here the procedure of the latest co-operative product of the New. The *Essays in Critical Realism*, which made their appearance in 1920, are the work of seven American Professors who have revised and redrafted their language until it met the approval of all the other essayists. They are the fruits of a decade of controversy in a limited controversial field, where "our familiarity with one another's MEANING has enabled us to understand methods of expression from which at first we were inclined to dissent." The main issues of the controversy had already been elaborated, as the result of conferences begun in 1908-9, in a similar co-operative volume by six Neo-realists. The final outcome may be regarded as the clarification of the life's work of a dozen specialists, all of whom have been continuously improving their mutual terminology in the full view of the public for over a decade.

With the earlier volume we need not here concern ourselves except to note that in the Introduction, where a scrupulous use of words and the importance of clear definitions are insisted on, there occur the following remarks :—

> "In exact discourse the MEANING of every term must be reviewed."
>
> "If we cannot express our MEANING in exact terms, let us at least cultivate literature."
>
> "Idealism has MEANT nothing to the actual psychologist."

—while in the final essay we find Professor Pitkin objecting at a crucial point that Alexander and Nunn "treat only the *stuff* of hallucinatory objects as real, leaving the erroneous MEANINGS more or less products of a construing mind."

Since that date, 1912, the word 'meaning' has not ceased to play a decisive part in every dispute, and as the Critical Realists have had such ample opportunity of avoiding any ambiguities into which the Neo-

Realists may have fallen, we may, as far as Realism is concerned, confine ourselves to their efforts.

First comes Professor Drake, of Vassar:—

"The very MEANING of 'existence' involves a definite locus" (p. 16).

"The *very MEANING of the term* 'relation' includes reference to something related" (p. 19).

These two statements are used to lead up to the view that perceptual data "cannot be the same existents as their causes," and that we "get back somewhere to qualities."

It would be a large undertaking, continues Professor Lovejoy, to "analyse the MEANINGS" of the formulations of Pragmatism, which "began as a theory concerning the conditions under which concepts and propositions may be said to possess MEANING, and concerning the nature of that in which all MEANINGS must consist." The pragmatist, he holds, ignores the patent fact that "many of our MEANINGS are retrospective. . . . No logical *hocus-pocus* can transubstantiate the MEANING 'yesterday' into the MEANING 'to-morrow' . . . . It is, in very truth, a MEANING intrinsically incapable of directly-experienced fulfilment. . . . Without ever actually experiencing the fulfilment of these MEANINGS, we nevertheless have an irresistible propensity to believe that some of them are in fact valid MEANINGS. . . . A judgment is its own master in deciding what it MEANS, though not in deciding as to the fulfilment of its MEANINGS."

According to Professor Pratt, the Neo-Realists "performed a most fruitful piece of analysis in insisting that the data presented to our thought consist of MEANINGS or natures," but they did not distinguish "between these MEANINGS and the sensational part of our mental states on the one hand and the existential physical objects to which the MEANINGS are attributed on the other." A number of people might describe their conception of anything differently though all

"MEANT, or thought of, the same thing." He proceeds to distinguish (p. 90) between the MEANING which one entertains in conception "and images which are the 'vehicle' of our MEANING. This MEANING is that which we find directly given to our thought," and he holds "this MEANING or datum is often capable of exact definition, *i.e.*, it has, or rather *is*, a definable nature." Perception, equally with conception, "contains not merely sensuous and revived images but a large element of MEANING as well." Usually, "*All* the *sensed* qualities are included within those *MEANT*." As regards outer reference (p. 92) "this may be regarded as part of the datum or MEANING of perception, but it is an easily distinguishable part." Thanks to past reactions, the quality-group "of which one is aware, directly *MEANS* more than it is. As a result of all one's past experience it has come to *stand for* an active entity." This quality-group "*MEANS*, or *immediately implies* to the individual the presence and, to a considerable extent, the nature of some active entity of which it is well for him to be aware. It is in short *the means of his perceiving the object*." In conclusion he maintains that though Critical Realists "do not pretend to an exhaustive knowledge of the inner nature of physical entities, we have defined them sufficiently to know what we *MEAN* by them, and to make that MEANING perfectly plain to every one but the perversely blind."

Professor Rogers of Yale, who deals with Error, complains that Bosanquet failed to understand the question of "degrees of truth" because of his "annoying refusal to keep sharply separate the varying MEANINGS of terms. It is not a question whether the same form of words MEANS the same thing to different people. It is a question whether any given MEANING singly, *whatever* it may be, is successful in corresponding to the fact" (p. 123). Of Mr Joachim's account of things in terms of systems, he remarks that "If we insist on defining the MEANING of a fact in terms of its place in a system, naturally it will cease to have that MEANING outside the system" (p. 125).

As regards identity "we naturally make a clear distinction between the characters of things as embodied in MEANINGS which we attribute to them, and the real existence of these characters in the things themselves. . . . The 'identity of indiscernibles' applies to abstract logical MEANINGS, not to existents. MEANINGS we may call the same—provided we can detect no difference in them—just because their 'character' is all there is to them; but things are not necessarily the same when they are alike" (p. 131). Professor Holt's analysis is, he thinks, an "approximately correct account of what the critical realist intends to refer to under the head of essences, or human MEANINGS. But for him the problem of knowledge consists, not merely in the presence of these MEANINGS or data, but in their reference to the actual object" (p. 133). Professor Perry's difficulties as regards error vanish if we grant the distinction "between the something as an existent *about* which I have a belief, and the something (as an intellectual content or MEANING or essence) *which* I believe about it." When in error, we have a "MEANING before the mind," and wrongly suppose that it characterizes a real object.

Dr Santayana urges that though without our animal bodies "appearance would lose its seat and its focus, and without an external object would lose its significance," we can yet take appearance absolutely and "inhibit all reaction and understanding"; but since even the passive and immediate data of appearance, "its bare signals and language when stupidly gazed at" have æsthetic reality, "the special and insidious kind of reality opposed to appearance must MEAN an underlying reality, a *substance:* and it had better be called by that name." And he introduces to us Essences = Universals = Intuited æsthetic data—"symbols of sense or thought" (p. 165), which may be identical with the essences embodied in the substance though "the intention and the embodiment remain different in existence, origin, date, place, substance, function and duration."

That the individual's field of experience "has a certain structure, and is shot through with MEANINGS and affirmations," seems to Professor Sellars of Michigan "a matter of undeniable fact." The chief error of much contemporary thought is the refusal to recognize "that thinghood and perception go together"; in other words, in the percipient, "we have the content of perception, and over against it in a qualifying way, the motor complex of adjustment combined with the realistic MEANINGS and expectations which are characteristic of perception." What is needed is, he holds, "a patient and persistent analysis which is able to go forward step by step while doing justice to the structure and MEANINGS of the individual's experience" (p. 197). And as regards knowledge of the past, "we can MEAN a reality which no longer exists equally with a reality which exists at the time of the intention" (p. 215).

Professor Sellars makes the following distinction:

> "Knowledge of other concurrences is different from knowledge of the physical world. It is a knowledge through asserted identity of content, whereas knowledge of the physical world is information about data. Thus when I interpret an expression on the face of my friend as MEANING amusement I use the expression as a symbol of an experience which I regard as in its essentials the same for him as for me" (p. 217).

Finally Professor Strong who examines the nature of the 'datum,' which he replaces by Santayana's 'essence' (which, as we have seen, is regarded by Critical Realism as also equivalent to 'meaning'), concludes that data are in their nature "not existences but universals, the bare natures of the objects, in such wise that the essence embodied and the essence given may be the same."

"What is given to us in sense-perception," we learn (p. 235), "is the sensation as a MEANING, or to speak more correctly what is given is the MEANING and not the sensation . . . . That this significance, or MEANING, or essence is not an existence and not in time and space, but, like the MEANING when we think of a universal, a purely logical entity, is quite credible"; moreover, the datum "is not properly a sensible fact. We cannot actually find it as a feeling, we can only tend towards it or MEAN it. . . . A MEANING here is not to be understood as a peculiar kind of feeling, but as a *function* which the feeling discharges" (p. 237).

We need not here attempt to correlate these different uses of the term in what claims to be the last achievement of co-ordinated symbolization. As might have been expected this statement with its challenge to Neo-Realists, Pragmatists, and Idealists aroused abundant controversy, but the one inevitable source of misunderstanding and disagreement, the omnipresence of the term Meaning, was allowed to pass unchallenged. It seems to have been accepted without question into the vocabulary of American philosophy, for use on all occasions of uncertainty,[1] though to the English reader it still happily sounds strange in most of its typical contexts.

But lest the uninitiated should suppose that Metaphysicians and Critical Realists are peculiar in their method, we may turn to the use made of the word by a psychologist. For over twenty years the writings of Professor Hugo Münsterberg exercised a powerful influence on thought in England and in Germany, no less than in America. His *Eternal Values* (1909) appeared first in German and then in an improved and revised form in English. It claims to be carefully and system-

[1] The treatment of the term 'meaning' by Professor Sellars in his independent volumes, *Critical Realism* (1916) and *Evolutionary Naturalism* (1921), is exemplified by the following dictum in the former (p. 282): "As a MEANING, knowledge precedes truth, which is a reflective deepening of the sense of knowledge in the light of an awakened doubt."

atically written, a protest against the impressionistic American style of philosophizing, much of which "has become antagonistic to the real character of philosophy." Already in his Preface he assures us that sincere conviction gave the real aim and MEANING to his work. On his first page his way of admitting that tastes may differ is to say that "the beauties of one school may MEAN ugliness to another"; on his second the words "To profess idealism never MEANS to prove it right" indicate that asseveration and proof are not the same; on his third he informs us that "the world longs for a new expression of the MEANING of life and reality." On page 4 we read that for the sciences to urge criticism of their foundations "MEANS that they ask about the real value of truth"; that in practical affairs "the MEANING of life is in danger"; that we need "a new philosophy which may give MEANING to life and reality." Page 5—

> "The MEANING of what is valuable must decide our view of the world."
>
> "Philosophy needs to understand what the fundamental MEANING of any valuation is."
>
> "The philosopher keeps for his own inquiry what the real MEANING of special facts may be, and what it MEANS to have knowledge of the world at all."

Part I is entitled 'The Meaning of Values' and on the six pages 74-79 which reveal "the deciding fact" the term 'meaning' appears no less than sixteen times. The deciding fact is that we demand that things recur. "We demand that there be a world; that MEANS that our experience be more than just passing experience. Here is the original deed which gives eternal MEANING to our reality" (p. 75). The world becomes a world by its identical recurrence, and this identity MEANS fulfilment, MEANS satisfaction, MEANS value" (p. 79).

In passing it may be noted that identity does not exclude change, for it is postulated that whatever changes "must still present an identity in its changes by showing that the change belongs to its own

MEANING." Indeed "our question as to the validity of pure values can have no other MEANING except in reference to this true world," the world "of our experiences in so far as they assert themselves;" and "it would be MEANINGLESS to deny the question.

To complete the argument with this accommodating linguistic material, it would seem that since its identical recurrence presumably *is* the 'meaning' of anything, and since the 'meaning' of anything is presumably its value, the statement above that "identical recurrence means value" might equally well have appeared in the form MEANING MEANS MEANING.

So stated it may lose in force what it gains in clarity, but so stated it suggests that we may pass rapidly to the final chapter in which the celebrated psychologist sums up his ultimate theory of value, merely noting from the intervening pages such dicta as the following :—

"The will of Napoleon, if we want to understand it in its historical MEANING, does not come to us as an object. The act is completely grasped when it is understood in the MEANING of its attitude. If Napoleon's will is completely understood in its MEANING, there remains nothing to be understood by other inquiries" (p. 144),

which explains the meaning of History.

"The world in its over-personal MEANING is absolutely valuable by the fact that the glow of happiness illuminates human souls" (p. 202),

which explains the meaning of Happiness.

"The real has its MEANING in the expectation which it awakens,"

which explains the meaning of Reality.

"The inner agreement of our desires finally gives to our life its perfect MEANING. . . . The tones to which our life gives MEANING express a will which asserts itself" (p. 253),

which explains the MEANING both of Life and Music.

Finally then we proceed to the message of the final chapter which deals with the values of Absoluteness. In this chapter, covering forty-six pages, the word 'meaning' occurs no less than fifty-eight times. As the climax approaches ("We now stand before a new ultimate value, the absolute of philosophy, the fundamentally absolute which bears all reality in itself," p. 39), the key-word stands out in almost every sentence. At page 400 "we can already take a wide outlook." If our will towards identification is satisfied "it cannot have any possible MEANING to ask further as to the value of the world."

"Our whole experience now gains its unity, its rest, its final MEANING. . . . The MEANING of the value enters into connection with the over-experience of the over-self. . . . Here for the last time we might separate outer-world, fellow-world, and inner-world, and examine for each realm how it enlarges its MEANING in the relation to the over-reality. . . . An inquiry into the 'stuff' of the world can have a MEANING only when there are sufficient stuffs which can be discriminated. When everything is equally will it cannot have any MEANING to find out what this will really is. . . . To reach a goal MEANS that the will maintains its object in a new form. . . . The MEANING of the world is an aiming towards a greater abundance of aiming which yet remains identical with itself. . . . In the deed itself the not-yet and the no-longer are one. Their temporal, mutual relation gives unity and MEANING to the deed."

Ten pages later (p. 416) it is still going on :—

"Only when we view mankind in this metaphysical connection do we recognize the ultimate MEANING of its inexhaustible activity. . . . When the MEANING of the social work towards values becomes metaphysically deepened, at the same time the counter-will which foolishly destroys values must be sharpened in its contrast. The world-will which gives MEANING to reality is a principle annulled by the conscious denial of values; suddenly everything has become MEANINGLESS. . . . Each of us is a member of mankind, and the MEANING of our single self then lies in the part which we take in the upbuilding of the values. . . . We will indicate once more the purest MEANING of our view of the world. We have come to understand how the world and mankind and the self are embedded in the deed of the over-self for eternity. For eternity! We have reached the highest point from which the MEANING of eternity unveils itself. . . . In the deed therefore past and future are one and that alone is the MEANING of eternity. . . . Every new stage realizes the ultimate MEANING of the preceding stages. But just that MEANT to us progress. . . . Deed

MEANS fulfilment and completion. . . . From here we understand the task and the MEANING of our individual selfhood. . . . Our life has MEANING and purpose. Banished is the anxiety that the over-reality may be MEANINGLESS. . . . It would be MEANINGLESS to hope for more from life than such a fulfilment of the over-will. . . . The mere desire for pleasure cannot possibly be the goal of our life if it is to maintain MEANING and value at all. . . . A mere skipping and a mere sudden transition from one state to another would never have MEANING. . . . To unfold his own will MEANS for every one to help the up-building of the same common world."

And so, on the next page (430), the last of the book, we conclude with the assurance that "To progress in the sense of the self-assertion of the will in will-enhancement remains for mankind, too, the ultimate MEANING of duty."

A study of these extracts in the German version of Münsterberg's work is an interesting exercise in comparative linguistic, and the contribution of the term 'meaning' to the cogency of the argument is considerable. There may be those who find it hard to believe that any writer responsible for such a verbal exploit could also enjoy a reputation as a thinker of the first rank. There is, however, another ambitious modern attempt by an American theorist to deal specifically with the fundamentals of psychology; and in the preface to this work[1] we find a reference to Münsterberg's "illuminating work on the great problems of philosophy and of natural and mental science. . . . It may be truthfully said that in his death America has lost its one great theoretical psychologist." Professor Moore has no occasion to quote largely from the particular work selected above, but his extracts (pp. 107-110) from Münsterberg's *Psychology General and Applied*, and *Psychotherapy* are equally bespattered with the term. And as might be expected Professor Moore's own treatment is also vitiated at its most crucial points by his too hospitable attitude to this plausible nomad.

[1] *The Foundations of Psychology*, by Jared Sparks Moore, 1921.

To understand the nature of psychology as a science we must, he holds, carefully distinguish Science from Metaphysics, and "the key-word of the problem of metaphysics is *Interpretation*. To interpret anything is to determine its MEANING. If the fundamental presupposition of all science is that every fact has a cause; the fundamental presupposition of metaphysics is that every fact has a MEANING" (p. 97). In other words, in philosophy as opposed to science, "each fact is treated not as the effect of some antecedent cause, but as the expression of a Meaning." Science must precede metaphysics—"We cannot know what facts MEAN until we know what the facts are, we cannot interpret the facts until we have described them."

But, objects the critic (p. 100), "is it not true that the very essence of a mental process is its MEANING?" No. Titchener has given six good reasons why mental processes are "not intrinsically MEANINGFUL" (p. 101). But, the critic insists (p. 102), Do not all our experiences "in their inmost nature MEAN something. Do we ever experience a 'MEANINGLESS' sensation?" We have no reason, the reply runs, to believe that the mind "began with MEANINGLESS sensations, and progressed to MEANINGFUL perceptions. On the contrary we must suppose that the mind was MEANINGFUL from the very outset."

And here we pause at the very pertinent question: "What then from the psychological point of view *is* this MEANING?" The answer is given without hesitation and in italics—"From the psychological point of view, MEANING *is context*." To explain: In every perception, or group of sensations and images, "the associated images form as it were a context or 'fringe' which binds together the whole and gives it a definite MEANING," and it is this "fringe of MEANING that makes the sensations not 'mere' sensations but symbols of a physical object." So when we see an orange it is the contextual images of smell and taste "which enable us to 'recognize' the object—*i.e.*, give a MEANING to the sensations" of colour and brightness. Similarly (p. 103) "every *idea* has a core or nucleus of images, and a fringe of associated images . . . which give MEANING to the nuclear images."

To sum up:

"In all these cases, the MEANING of the perception or idea is 'carried' by the contextual images or sensations, and it is context which gives MEANING to every experience, and yet it would be inaccurate to say that the MEANING of a sensation or symbolic image is through and through nothing but its associated images or sensations, for this would be a violation of the principle that psychology is not concerned with MEANINGS. All that is implied is that the MEANINGS of our experiences are represented in the realm of mental processes by 'the fringe of related processes that gathers about the central group of sensations or images.' Psychologically MEANING is context, but logically and metaphysically MEANING is much more than psychological context; or, to put it the other way round, whatever MEANING may be, psychology is concerned with it only so far as it can be represented in terms of contextual imagery" (p. 103).

It is a curious approach to the problems of sign-interpretation, this account of Meaning which (psychologically) *is* context, which is *carried by* context, which is *much more than context*, which is *expressed by facts*, with which *psychology is not concerned*—and yet *is concerned*, so far as it can be represented by contextual imagery.[1]

[1] In a letter printed by *Mind* (April 1924), but unfortunately marred by four *lapsus calami* (' nuclear image ' for *nuclear images*, ' 102 ' for 103, ' 193 ' for 293, and ' 541 ' for 544) Professor Moore, after drawing attention to three typist's errors in the above (now corrected) complains that this paragraph " makes chaos of my whole position by ridiculing my account " of Meaning. Says he : " My whole point is that Meaning is ' much more than context ' though ' carried ' or ' represented ' in the mind by context ; and that *for this reason*, ' psychology is not concerned with Meaning, but only with its representatives in the mind.' " He adds : " I nowhere say that Meaning ' *is* context,' or that psychology

But there are stranger things to follow, for here True Meaning makes its appearance—in connection with a bell. "The true MEANING of the percept of the bell is its reference to the real objective bell," and this reference is represented in the mind by contextual images which "constitute its MEANING 'translated into the language of' psychology. So the true MEANING of an idea lies in its logical reference to an objective system of ideas" (p. 104); and a little later (p. 111) we find that "all experiences are expressions of the inner MEANINGS of the self."

It is hard to believe that Professor Moore would have been satisfied with such a vocabulary had he attempted to investigate the psychology of signs and symbols; and this investigation could not but have shown him how much of his present work had its origin in an unfortunate choice of, and attitude towards, symbols. As it is, the constant appeal to an esoteric Doctrine of Meaning is reminiscent of the dialectical devices of mediæval theologians, and we may conclude by noting that the Doctrine is specifically invoked in relation to Religion.

> "Psychology may discuss as freely the mental processes involved in religious experience as it does those concerned in our experience of physical things; but in neither case can its decisions affect the question of the MEANING . . . of those experiences. The question of the nature of the processes undergone by the human mind in any spheres of activity is a question of *fact*, calling for analytical description and explanation in causal terms: the problem of the validity or truth-value of these processes is a question of MEANING, calling for interpretation" (p. 122).

For those who regard interpretation as a purely causal process, and consider that when the meaning of anything is interpreted it is but explained in causal terms (while at the same time recognizing a totally

'is concerned' with Meaning itself." *Our* whole point is that Professor Moore constantly shifts his uses of meaning without elucidating any of them. We were not concerned to discuss his view but to exhibit his linguistic technique, and we are glad to notice that the sentences quoted from his letter supplement the exhibit.

distinct sense of meaning in which the 'meaning' of a poem or a religion would be the emotion or attitude evoked through it), the extent to which this symbol can change places with its other selves should provide material for reflection.

Our object here, however, is rather to provide instances of its use in current constructive and controversial literature, and it remains only to group together a few further typical examples.

"Strictly," says Professor Broad, "a thing has MEANING when acquaintance with or knowledge about it either enables one to infer or causes one by association to think of something else."[1] But so 'strict' an account has not always found favour with philosophical writers. "We may, for convenience sake," explains Professor Nettleship,[2] "mentally hold apart a certain fraction of the fact, for instance, the minimum of MEANING which justifies us in using the word triangularity"—while Lord Haldane[3] can write, "The percipient is an object in his universe, but it is still the universe including himself that there is for him, and for its MEANING it implies the presence of mind." And here are some of the propositions advanced by so influential a thinker as Professor Royce:[4]—

"The melody sung, the artist's idea, the thought of your absent friends: all these not merely have their obvious internal MEANING as meeting a conscious purpose by their very presence, but also they at least appear to have that other sort of MEANING,

[1] *Perception, Physics and Reality*, 1914, p. 97. In reviewing J. Ellis McTaggart's "The Nature of Existence" in *The Hibbert Journal* (1921, p. 173) Dr Broad notes that "McTaggart seems to have taken over without question from Russell's *Principles of Mathematics*, the doctrine that an infinite regress is vicious when, and only when, it concerns the 'MEANING' of some concept." According to Russell (*Mind*, 1920, p. 401), "MEANING is an observable property of observable entities." Professor John Laird goes further than this, and in his opinion "MEANING is directly perceptible just like sound and colour. . . . Continuants are conveyed to us through the intrinsic MEANING of what we perceive intermittently. . . . The MEANING directly perceived in the filling of space and time has the seeds of causality in it." (*A Study of Realism*, pp. 27, 29, 98.)

[2] R. L. Nettleship, *Philosophical Remains*, I., p. 220.

[3] *The Reign of Relativity*, 1921, p. 181.

[4] *The World and the Individual*, pp. 36, 176.

that reference beyond themselves to objects. . . . This external MEANING, I say, appears to be very different from the internal MEANING, and wholly to transcend the latter.

"Just what the internal MEANING of an idea already imperfectly but consciously is, namely, purpose relatively fulfilled, just that and nothing else the apparently external MEANING when truly comprehended also proves to be, namely, the entire expression of the very Will that is fragmentarily embodied in the life of the flying conscious idea. . . . To be MEANS simply to express to embody the complete internal MEANING of a certain absolute system of ideas, a system, moreover, which is genuinely implied in the true internal MEANING of every finite idea, however fragmentary.

"The mystic knows only Internal MEANINGS, precisely as the realist considers only External MEANINGS."

"We have direct acquaintance with the ideas or MEANINGS about which we have thoughts and which we may be said to *understand*," declared the late Lord Keynes; and again, "We are able to pass from direct acquaintance with things to a knowledge of propositions about the things of which we have sensations or understand the MEANING."[1] So helpful a term is equally in demand as a carminative in ecclesiastical controversy,[2] as a *vade mecum* in musical criticism,[3] as an indication of the precise point where doctors differ,[4] and as a lubricant for the spinning-wheel of the absolute relativist.[5] "If education cannot be

[1] J. M. Keynes, *A Treatise on Probability*, Part I., Fundamental Ideas, pp. 12, 13.

[2] "This House recognizes the gain which arises from inquiry into the MEANING and expression of the Faith."—The Upper House of Convocation, May 2nd, 1922.

[3] "Miss A's programme last night became stimulating in virtue of the abounding health and freshness of her outlook, conveyed through an admirable technique. Probably Beethoven's Sonata in A, Op. 101, will reveal a deeper MEANING to her in full maturity, but her present reading was eloquently truthful."—*The Morning Post*, June 24th, 1922.

[4] "The importance of symptoms is so imperfectly realized that a description of the MEANING, mechanism and significance of symptoms is nowhere to be found, and this constitutes a great defect in medical knowledge."—Sir James Mackenzie, *op. cit.*, p. 2.

[5] "The concrete universal MEANS that reality in the full MEANING of the word is of the nature of the concept. . . . Universality MEANS that the whole is present in every part. . . . If there be nothing absolute in our objective universe, it follows that the absolute is within us. It is not within, however, in any abstract MEANING, any MEANING which would isolate the subject of experience from its object. . . . Also

identified with mere instruction, what is it? What does the term MEAN?" asks the educationist. "I answer, it must MEAN a gradual adjustment to the spiritual possession of the race."[1] Meaning is therefore just the sort of word with which we may attempt to probe the obscure depths of the souls of fishes. "Let us fix attention on the state of the mind of the goldfish. . . . Suddenly comes a new element into consciousness—the conscious counterpart of the stimuli of the eye caused by the bread falling into the water. . . . The food is an object in space and time for the fish and has its MEANING, but when the food is eaten both percept and MEANING disappear. . . . This is an instance of percept and MEANING tied."[2]

Turning now to official Psychology, we have six current Professorial utterances which invite comparison :—

"The Object of simple apprehension is whatever the mind MEANS or intends to refer to.

"The sight of the word sugar MEANS its sweetness.

"The only general word which is at all appropriate for expressing this kind of consciousness is the word MEANING."[3]

"All that is intended is never given in the mental state. The mental content merely MEANS what we are thinking about; it does not reproduce it or constitute it."[4]

"Perceptions have MEANING. No sensation MEANS, a sensation simply goes on in various attributive ways: intensely, clearly, spatially, and so forth. All perceptions MEAN: they go on, also, in various attributive ways; but they go on MEANINGLY." "An idea MEANS another idea, is psychologically the MEANING of that other idea, if it is that idea's context."[5]

"The affective-volitional MEANING, or worth, of an object becomes explicit only on the cognitive level. It is the actualization of the dispositional tendency, either in feeling or desire,

there is pre-established harmony of the monads, if we impart to this new term the old MEANING."—H. Wildon Carr, *A Theory of Monads* (1922), pp. 299-300, 318.

[1] Nicholas Murray Butler, *What is Education*? (1906), p. 17.

[2] W. E. Urwick, *The Child's Mind* (1907), p. 68.

[3] Stout, *Manual of Psychology*, pp. 104, 180, 183.

[4] Pillsbury, *Fundamentals of Psychology*, p. 269.

[5] Titchener, *A Text-book of Psychology*, p. 367; and *Experimental Psychology of the Thought-Processes*, p. 175.

through these cognitive acts, which gives to the feeling or desire that MEANING described as worth. . . . What are the possible MEANINGS of reality as employed in reflective valuation, or what is the common logical cue of all these MEANINGS."[1]

"MEANING may be something MEANT, or it may be—well, just MEANING. . . . If, then, MEANING, in my interpretation, is just part of a process itself, why does it so persistently elude our most patient search for it among the juxtaposed or compounded products of mental process?"[2]

"MEANING is the essential part of a thought or a consciousness of an object . . . MEANING has no immediate physiological correlate in the brain that could serve as its substitute and discharge its functions."[3]

As a specimen of the language of Psycho-analysts, on the other hand, the following by the late Professor J. J. Putnam[4] of Harvard may be considered:—

"It seems, and is, a small matter to walk in the country without one's coat, but a similar insufficiency of costume, if occurring in a dream, may be a circumstance of far wider MEANING. . . . It will be obvious from the foregoing that the term 'sexual' as defined in the psycho-analytic vocabulary, is of far wider MEANING than is ordinarily conceived. . . . The next point has reference to 'sublimation.' This outcome of individual evolution, as defined by Freud, has a strictly social MEANING. . . .

The logical end of a psycho-analytic treatment is the recovery of a full sense of the bearings and MEANINGS of one's life.

A man's sense of pride of his family may be a symptom of narcistic self-adulation; but like all other signs and symbols, this is a case where two opposing MEANINGS meet. . . ."

The Pragmatists made a bold attempt to simplify the issue. "That which is suggested is MEANING," wrote Professor Miller,[5] and Professor Bawden[6] is equally simple—"Feeling is the vague appreciation of the value of a situation, while cognition is a clear and distinct perception of its MEANING." The trouble begins, however, with the first attempts at elaboration.

[1] Urban, *Valuation*, pp. 95, 387.
[2] Lloyd Morgan, *Instinct and Experience*, pp. 277, 278.
[3] W. McDougall, *Body and Mind*, pp. 304, 311.
[4] *Addresses on Psycho-analysis*, 1921, pp. 146, 151, 306.
[5] I. Miller, *The Psychology of Thinking*, 1909, p. 154.
[6] H. Heath Bawden, *The Principles of Pragmatism*, p. 151.

"An experience is *cognitional*," says Professor Dewey[1] "which is contemporaneously aware of MEANING something beyond itself. Both the MEANING and the thing MEANT are elements in the same situation. . . . One is present as not-present-in-the-same-way-in-which-the-other-is. . . . We may say that the smell of a rose, when involving conscious MEANING or intention, is mental."

Historians, of philosophy[2] and childhood,[3] Reformers, social[4] and grammatical,[5]—all have their own uses of the word, obvious yet undefined. Even the clearest thinkers refrain from further analysis. Throughout Professor G. E. Moore's writings 'meaning' plays a conspicuous part, and in *Principia Ethica* we may read:—

"Our question 'What is good?' may have still another MEANING. We may, in the third place, MEAN to ask not what thing or things are good, but how 'good' is to be defined. . . . That which is MEANT by 'good' is, in fact, except its converse

[1] J. Dewey, *The Influence of Darwin upon Philosophy*, 1910, pp. 88, 104.

[2] "Ideas, we may say generally, are symbols, as serving to express some actual moment or phase of experience and guiding towards fuller actualization of what is, or seems to be, involved in its existence or MEANING. . . . That no idea is ever wholly adequate MEANS that the suggestiveness of experience is inexhaustible." Forsyth, *English Philosophy*, 1910, pp. 180, 183.

[3] "Babies learn to speak words partly by adopting sounds of their own and giving them a MEANING, partly by pure imitation. . . . Whether the baby invents both sounds and MEANING seems doubtful. . . . Certainly they change the MEANING of words." E. L. Cabot, *Seven Ages of Childhood*, 1921, pp. 22, 23, 24.

[4] "The MEANING of Marriage! How really simple it is for you and me to ascertain its precise MEANING, and yet what desperate and disappointing efforts have been made to discover it. . . . If our children knew all about them they would yet have missed the essential MEANING of human marriage. A knowledge of life outside humanity would not enlighten us as to what marriage MEANT for men and women. . . . Manifestly, if we desire to know the MEANING of marriage, we ought to search out homes where the conditions are favourable. . . . We may ungrudgingly pay a well-deserved tribute to the mother cat. Motherhood MEANS already much in the animal world!" G. Spiller, *The Meaning of Marriage*, 1914, pp. 1-3.

[5] Strictly speaking, the image is often both a part of the MEANING and a symbol of the rest of it. As part it gives one of the MEANING'S details. Part of the MEANING of an idea is its fixed reference to some objective identity. . . . MEANING alone passes between mind and mind. A. D. Sheffield, *Grammar and Thinking*, pp. 3-4.

'bad,' the *only* simple object of thought which is peculiar to Ethics.

It would be absolutely MEANINGLESS to say that oranges were yellow, unless yellow did in the end MEAN just 'yellow' . . . We should not get very far with our science if we were bound to hold that everything which was yellow MEANT exactly the same thing as yellow.

In general, however, ethical philosophers have attempted to define good without recognizing what such an attempt must MEAN."[1]

Nor is it only in Ethics that important philosophical positions are based on this arbitrary foundation. "Things, as we know, are largely constructions," says one modern metaphysician[2]—"a synthesis of sense elements and MEANINGS. . . . The concept is no mere word, because it has MEANING. . . . A universal, as the object of a MEANING, is not a mental act." It is impossible, urges another,[3] who also speaks of "analysing the MEANING of a process of change from a conceptual point of view," to imagine "that we ourselves can be analysed into sense-data, for sense-data are 'given' or 'presented' by the very MEANING of the term." And again, "It is doubtless true that 'body' and 'mind' are used with more than one MEANING to which a reasonable significance may be attached."[4] Meanings to which significance is attached have also the authority of Lotze,[5] who held that "historical persons and events, in spite of all the significance attached to their MEANING, are often very insignificant

[1] Pp. 5, 14, 15.

We may compare Professor Perry's method of approach:

"What can the realization of goodness MEAN if not that what is natural and necessary, actual and real shall also be good?

"If it be essential to the MEANING of Philosophy that it should issue from life, it is equally essential that it should return to life. But this connection of philosophy with life does not MEAN its reduction to the terms of life as conceived in the market-place.

"The present age is made insensible to the MEANING of life through preoccupation with its very achievements." R. B. Perry, *The Approach to Philosophy*, pp. 422, 426, 427.

[2] D. H. Parker, *The Self and Nature*, 1917, pp. 158, 190.

[3] C. A. Richardson, *Spiritual Pluralism*, 1920, pp. 10, 40.

[4] *Ibid.*, p. 184.

[5] *Outlines of Æsthetics*, in the English translation by Professor G. T. Ladd of Yale, p. 86.

in the external form of their appearance," and who also informs us that in Moorish architecture "the soaring pointed bow of horse-shoe shape has no properly *constructive* MEANING, but rather recalls the mighty opening of a cleft" (p. 66), while a landscape in pictorial composition "has a MEANING only as a part of the actual world" (p. 82).

Æsthetics, however, has always flourished on loose usage, and non-philosophic writers have here been more than usually persistent in their invocation of the word at all critical points. "Colour as colour," writes Van Gogh, "MEANS something; this should not be ignored, but rather turned to account."[1] The poet, too, we read, "said what he MEANT, but his MEANING seems to beckon away beyond itself, or rather to expand into something boundless which is only focussed in it."[2]

And so on in a crescendo of reiteration as the emotions of the cosmologist soar through the Empyrean:—

"Thought transformed the whole status of life and gave a new MEANING to reality. . . . Our age is great in opportunity to those who would wrest from life a MEANING and a value."[3]

"All reasoning as to the MEANING of life leads us back to the instincts. . . . As soon as we deny sensation any other significance beyond that which belongs to it as a regulator of activity, the various values of life that have been promulgated since the dawn of civilization become quite MEANINGLESS."[4]

"Just as the artist finds his own MEANING in the successful struggle to express it, so, from our point of view, God realizes His own intention in the process of effecting it. . . . In the world, novelty is part of its MEANING, and this is particularly true of an experience such as we found the Divine experience must be, where the Future is the dominant element of Time."[5]

"God is both fact and ideal; not merely in the common way of a value attaching to a fact or truth, as utility attaches to my inkstand, but in the peculiar way in which a MEANING attaches

[1] *Letters of a Post-Impressionist*, p. 29.
[2] A. C. Bradley, *Oxford Lectures on Poetry*, 1901, p. 26.
[3] R. Eucken, *The Meaning and Value of Life*, 1909, pp. 38, 147.
[4] I. Harris, *The Significance of Existence*, 1911, p. 319.
[5] W. Temple, *The Nature of Personality*, 1911, p. 107.

to that which symbolizes it. . . . The objective symbol or emblem is attributed or assigned to this MEANING, to represent it vicariously. . . .

"Reality in the last analysis is what we MEAN by reality. Reality apart from all MEANING for experience is an absurdity or a mere word."[1]

"The *actual* side of every moment of consciousness only possesses value or MEANING as a token of the vast potentiality beyond itself. . . .

"Cosmological theories of world-process often halt and become MEANINGLESS through a refusal to introduce the notion of infinity."[2]

"In order to have a clearer view of these consequences, we should consider the scope of these MEANINGS more clearly; examine whether they can, like the MEANINGS of words, be taken away . . . As by the MEANING of a word I know, or as it were see, into another man's thought, so by the MEANING of my spirit I see into that Being which I call God. . . . By God is MEANT an *Eternal* or Infinite *Spirit*."[3]

[1] J. M. Baldwin, *Genetic Theory of Reality*, 1915, pp. 108, 227.
[2] E. Belfort Bax, *The Real, the Rational, and the Alogical*, 1920, pp. 233, 243.
[3] Professor K. J. Spalding, *Desire and Reason*, 1922, p. 8.

CHAPTER IX

THE MEANING OF MEANING

Father! these are terrible words, but I have no time now but for Meanings.—*Melmoth the Wanderer.*

A STUDY of the utterances of Philosophers suggests that they are not to be trusted in their dealings with Meaning. With the material which they have provided before us, let us see whether more creditable results can be achieved by the technique which we have already elaborated.

To begin with it is not difficult to frame two definitions corresponding to those of Group A in the case of Beautiful. In two ways it has been easy and natural for philosophers to hypostatize their definiendum; either by inventing a peculiar stuff, an intrinsic property, and then saying let everything which possesses this be said to possess meaning, or by inventing a special unanalysable relation, and saying let everything related by this relation to something else be said to have a meaning.

With the second of these two definitions a grammatical alternative is opened up which reappears in all the other suggested definitions and tends very greatly to confuse the discussion. We may either take Meaning as standing for the relation between A and B, when A means B, or as standing for B. In the first case the meaning of A will be its relation to B, in the second it will be B. This ambiguity once it is understood gives rise to little difficulty, but the avoidance of it by the symbols 'reference' and 'referent' is one of the distinct advantages of that vocabulary.

The other definitions show again a similarity with those of Beautiful in that they are preponderantly psychological definitions. It should not however, be concluded from these two examples that all definition problems develop into psychology. If we were attempting to define 'bathing' or 'absorption,' let us say, we should find the emphasis upon quite different defining routes. 'Meaning' evidently is a symbol some of whose elucidations must rest upon psychology, and the example of Beauty was chosen because that symbol, too, lies though less deeply in the same predicament.

The following is a representative list of the main definitions which reputable students of Meaning have favoured. Meaning is—

A
- I An Intrinsic property.
- II A unique unanalysable Relation to other things.

B
- III The other words annexed to a word in the Dictionary.
- IV The Connotation of a word.
- V An Essence.
- VI An activity Projected into an object.
- VII (a) An event Intended.
  - (b) A Volition.
- VIII The Place of anything in a system.
- IX The Practical Consequences of a thing in our future experience.
- X The Theoretical consequences involved in or implied by a statement.
- XI Emotion aroused by anything.

C
- XII That which is Actually related to a sign by a chosen relation.
- XIII (a) The Mnemic effects of a stimulus. Associations acquired.
  - (b) Some other occurrence to which the mnemic effects of any occurrence are Appropriate.

(c) That which a sign is Interpreted as being of.

(d) What anything Suggests.

In the case of Symbols.

That to which the User of a Symbol actually refers.

C

XIV That to which the user of a symbol Ought to be referring.

XV That to which the user of a symbol Believes himself to be referring.

XVI That to which the Interpreter of a symbol

(a) Refers.

(b) Believes himself to be referring.

(c) Believes the User to be referring.

With Group A we need be no further concerned. Let us consider Group B. The first (III) Dictionary meaning, or the philologist's signification, is, in spite of its comical appearance as formulated above, very widely used; and in the domain of philology it has undoubted value, as will be shown when we come to discuss, in the light of definition XIV, the kindred questions of Good Use and Communication.

Connotation (IV) the 'meaning' of traditional logic, and Essence (V) the 'meaning' of the Critical Realists who follow Dr Santayana as quoted above, may be considered together, for 'Essences' by those who do not let their realism overpower their criticism may best be regarded as Connotation hypostatized.

The term Connotation has been adopted by those logicians who follow Mill in the practice of discussing as though they were primary and paramount two senses in which a *symbol* may be said to mean: (1) It means the set of things to which it can be correctly applied; and the members of this set are said to be denoted or indicated by the word, or to be its denotation. (2) It means the properties used in determining the application of a symbol, the properties in virtue of which anything is a member of the set which is the denotation ; these properties are said to be the connotation of a symbol, or sometimes simply its meaning. The relation of denotation to connotation has been conveniently summed up as follows : The connotation of a word determines its denotation which in turn determines its comprehension, *i.e.*, the properties common to the things to which it can be applied. The term connotation is, however, often used with the same sense as comprehension.

It will be plain to all who consider how words are used that this account is highly artificial. Neither denoting nor connoting can be used as if it were either a simple or a fundamental relation. To take denotation first, no word has any denotation apart from some reference which it symbolizes. The relations between a word and the things for which it stands are indirect (cf. diagram, Chapter I., p. 11), and, we have urged, causal. When we add the further complications introduced by correct usage, we get a result so artificial that the attempt to use 'denoting' as the name of a simple logical relation becomes ludicrous. The case is still worse with 'connoting.' The connotation is a selection of properties or adjectives ; but properties are not to be found by themselves anywhere; they are fictitious or nominal entities which we are led to feign through the influence of the bad analogy by which we treat certain parts of our symbols as though they were self-complete symbols. We have no justification, beyond this bad analogy, for treating adjectives as though they were nouns. The sole entities in the real world are propertied things which are only symbolically distinguishable into properties and things. This does not, of course, make symbolization, which proceeds as though properties and things were separable, any less desirable upon occasion. No convenient symbolic device is objectionable so long as we know that it is a device and do not suppose it to be an addition to our knowledge. To let a convenience turn into an argument, and decide for us as to the nature of the universe in the fashion of Dr Santayana's 'Essences' is a gratuitous tactic. On the other hand as linguistic machinery there is no harm and much service in universals. For instance, in expounding the causal or contextual theory of reference we made free use of the terms 'character' and 'relation' as though these might stand for independent and respectable elements in the real world. There is a *linguistic* necessity for such procedure but to exalt this into a logical necessity for the 'subsistence' of such elements is to forget what the world is like.

Thus, to begin with, the connotation of a word is a set of nominal entities, but we have still to decide which these shall be. One method would be by linguistic usage; "a knowledge of the usage of language alone is sufficient to know what a phrase means," says Mr Johnson (*Logic*, p. 92). According to this method, if strictly followed, the connotation of a word would become indistinguishable from its meaning in the sense of "the other words annexed to a word in the dictionary" (III). But another method is possible, the consideration of which will show more plainly still the artificiality of connotation and the little reliance which can be placed in it for logical purposes; for instance, in definition. We can in part translate the convenient formula given above as follows: The reference employing (or symbolized by) a word determines its referents (*i.e.*, denotation) which in turn determine what different references may be made to them. Two symbols would then have the same connotation when they symbolize similar references. But in our account of reference anything becomes a referent for a given process or act of referring only in virtue of certain characters through which it becomes a completing member of the context including the sign for the process. Thus the connotation of a reference (and derivatively of the words symbolizing it) would be those characters of its referent in virtue of which this is what is referred to. Bearing in mind that these characters are but nominal entities we can now see how easy it has been for logicians through the formidable shorthand of 'denotation' and 'connotation' as applied to words to overlook the causal nature of the relations they were unwittingly discussing. It is not surprising that the attempt to explain the relation of meaning to denotation for phrases like 'The King of France' by such shorthand methods should have been found difficult.[1]

One further point amusingly shows the artificiality of the traditional account, namely, the impossibility of applying it to *names*, which without undue rashness may be regarded as the simplest symbols out of which all our other symbolic machinery has developed. Mill concluded that proper names are non-connotative. Mr Johnson in agreeing with him (and "all the best logicians") makes a reservation:[2]—

"This does not amount to saying that the proper name is non-significant or has no meaning; rather we find, negatively, that the proper name does not mean the same as anything that could be meant by a descriptive or connotative phrase; and positively, that it does precisely mean what could be indicated by some appropriate descriptive phrase." Further shifts[3] are

[1] As for instance by Russell "On Denoting," *Mind*, 1905. "Thus it would seem that 'C' and C are different entities such that 'C' denotes C; but this cannot be an explanation, because the relation of 'C' to C remains wholly mysterious; and where are we to find the denoting complex 'C' which is to denote C? Moreover, when C occurs in a proposition, it is not only the denotation that occurs; yet on the view in question C is only the denotation, the meaning being wholly relegated to 'C.' This is an inextricable tangle, and seems to prove that the whole distinction of meaning and denotation has been wrongly conceived." The fresh conceptions, however, designed to save the situation have only led to further intricacies which logicians are once more endeavouring to unravel.

[2] *Logic*, Vol. I., 1921, p. 96.

[3] "The word 'courage' or the phrase 'not shrinking from danger' is of such a nature that there is no distinction between what it means and what it indicates or denotes. It is only phrases prefixed by an article or similar term for which the distinction between meaning and indication arises."—*Ibid.*, p. 92.

then necessary, but serve only to destroy 'meaning' as a useful symbol.

VI, though it appeals to Empathists, Croceans and Solipsists, is most charitably regarded as a metaphor, in which case it is a strange and striking way of phrasing views closely similar to XIII. Dr Schiller's way of putting it, "Meaning is an activity taken up towards objects and energetically projected into them like an *α* particle," obscures his actual agreement with the mnemic causation which he is combating; since when he speaks of "a demand we make upon our experience" as "selecting the objects of attention," he appears to be describing in activist language the very processes (cf. XIII (a) *infra*) which he is so unwilling to admit. The dispute between 'act' and 'process' as fundamental psychological terms is obviously subsequent to a full discussion of the problem of Meaning. As is also indicated by Professor Strong's contribution[1] we presumably have here an instance of a common controversial predicament, the use for the same referents of symbols taken out of different, but to a large extent translatable, symbol systems.

We pass to VII, which arises from the study of such remarks as

They *meant* no harm.
He *means* well.
I *meant* to go.
What I *meant* was what I said.
A mechanistic universe is without *meaning*.

If, as is usually the case when these phrases are used, we can substitute the word 'intend' for 'mean' it will be clear that we have a quite different kind of 'meaning' from any involved when 'intention' cannot

[1] "The enlargement of the sensationalist-behaviourist theory which appears necessary is, then, to recognize that the sound as a meaning is distinct from the sound as a sensuous state, and that distinct from both is the thing meant, without the existence of which this meaning would have no meaning."—*Mind*, July, 1921.

be so substituted.[1] My 'meaning' or 'intention,' as that which I endeavour to promote, is something wished, as distinguished from something known or referred to ('intended,' or 'tended towards,' in the terminology of certain American writers). Thus between this sense and that with which we have to deal in such sentences as "'Chien' and 'Dog,' both mean the same thing," there is no contradiction. There is, however, a pun, and thanks to the practice of disputants who compound the sense of reference with the sense of intention in the phrase "What I *meant* was" (="What I intended to refer to was" or "what I intended you to refer to was") —we have a dangerous source of confusion. The difficulty of making a close examination of the matter under discussion is greatly increased, for what I intended to refer to may be quite other than what I did refer to, a fact which it is important to remember if it is hoped to reach mutual comprehension, and eventually agreement or disagreement.

The intention of the speaker may very naturally be used in conjunction with reference in order to provide complex definitions of meaning for special purposes. To quote from a recent article: "Is the meaning of a sentence that which is in the mind of the speaker at the moment of utterance or that which is in the mind of the listener at the moment of audition? Neither, I think.

[1] Logicians are sometimes led by philological accident to dispute this. Thus Joseph, *Introduction to Logic*, p. 131, says: "'Intension' naturally suggests what we intend or mean by a term."

Lady Welby, who for twenty years eloquently exhorted philosophers and others to concentrate attention on the meaning of meaning, particularly in her articles on "Sense, Meaning and Interpretation," to which reference was made above (*Mind*, 1896, p. 187, etc.), may have failed to carry conviction by contenting herself with a vague insistence on Meaning as human intention. The distinctions necessary in this field are not always such as could be arrived at merely by a refined Linguistic sense, and neither in her book, *What is Meaning?* nor in the later *Significs and Language* (1911), where the following occurs (p. 9):

> "The one crucial question in all Expression is its special property, first of Sense, that in which it is used, then of Meaning as the intention of the user, and, most far-reaching and momentous of all, of implication, of ultimate Significance,"

is the necessary analysis undertaken; while the issue is further confused by echoes of the phraseology of an earlier religious phase.

Certainly not that which is in the mind of the listener, for he may utterly misconstrue the speaker's purpose. But also not that which is in the mind of the speaker, for he may intentionally veil in his utterance the thoughts which are in his brain, and this, of course, he could not do if the meaning of the utterance were precisely that which he held in his brain. I think the following formulation will meet the case: *The meaning of any sentence is what the speaker intends to be understood from it by the listener.*"[1]

'To be understood' is here a contraction. It stands for: (*a*) to be referred to + (*b*) to be responded with + (*c*) to be felt towards referent + (*d*) to be felt towards speaker + (*e*) to be supposed that the speaker is referring to + (*f*) that the speaker is desiring, etc., etc.

These complexities are mentioned here to show how vague are most of the terms which are commonly thought satisfactory in this topic. Such a word as 'understand' is, unless specially treated, far too vague to serve except provisionally or at levels of discourse where a real understanding of the matter (in the reference sense) is not possible. The multiple functions of speech will be classified and discussed in the following chapter. There it will be seen that the expression of the speaker's intention is one of the five regular language functions. It should not be stressed unduly, and it should be remembered that as with the other functions its importance varies immensely from person to person and from occasion to occasion.

The realization of the multiplicity of the normal language function is vital to a serious approach to the problem of meaning. Here it is only desirable to point out that 'meaning,' in the sense of 'that which the speaker intends the listener to refer to,' and 'meaning,' in the sense of 'that which the speaker intends the listener to feel and to do,' etc., are clearly distinguishable.

[1] A. Gardiner, *Brit. Jour. of Psych.*, Vol. XII., Part iv., 1922, p. 361.

In many of the more subtle speech situations these distinctions must be recognized and used.

The first of these is particularly concerned in those cases of misdirection which we saw in our first chapter to be so universal. In the case of a successful lie the person deceived makes the reference which the deceiver intends he shall, and if we define 'meaning' as 'that which the speaker intends the listener to refer to,' the victim will have interpreted the speaker aright. He will have grasped his meaning. But let us consider a more astute interpreter, who, by applying a further interpretative process (based, say, upon his knowledge of business methods) arrives either at a mere rejection of the intended reference or at another reference quite different from that intended. In the latter case, if he has hit upon the reference from which the suggested false reference was designed to divert him, he would often be said to have understood the speaker, or to have divined his 'true meaning.' This last meaning, it should be observed, is non-symbolic. The sagacious listener merely takes the speaker's behaviour, including the words he utters, as a set of signs whence to interpret to an intention and a reference in the speaker which no words passing on the occasion symbolize. The batsman who correctly plays a 'googly' is making exactly the same kind of interpretation. He guesses the 'meaning' of the bowler's action by discounting certain of the signs exhibited.

All cases of 'duplicity,' whether deliberate (intentional) or not, may be analysed in the same manner;[1] the special instance of self-deception as it concerns introspective judgments, which are discussed below, being of most importance for the general theory. Here great care is required in avoiding any confusion between the speaker's intended or professed references and his actual references.

[1] On this point Martinak's treatment (*Psychologische Untersuchungen zur Bedeutungslehre*, p. 82) of the art of the orator, the diplomat, the trickster and the liar is instructive.

This particular ambiguity is indeed one of the most undesirable of those with which we have to deal. Unless the referential and the affective-volitional aspects of mental process are clearly distinguished, no discussion of their relation is possible; and the confusion of reference, with one very special form of the latter aspect, namely 'intending,' is disastrous. To bring the point out by a play of words, we very often mean what we do not mean; *i.e.*, we refer to what we do not intend, and we are constantly thinking of things which we do not want to think of. 'Mean' as shorthand for 'intend to refer to,' is, in fact, one of the unluckiest symbolic devices possible.

The distinction between the two aspects of mental process from the standpoint of the context theory may be briefly and therefore vaguely indicated as follows: Given the psychological context to which a sign belongs, then the reference made by the interpretation of the sign is fixed also. But it is possible for the same sign (or for signs with very similar characters) to belong to different psychological contexts. Certain geometrical figures, that may be seen, more or less 'at will,' either as receding or as extruding from the plane upon which they are drawn offer well-known and convenient examples. If now we raise the question, How does the sign come to belong to the context to which it does belong, or how does it pass from one context to another? we are raising questions as to the affective-volitional aspect. The facts, concerning habit-formation, desire, affective tone, upon the basis of which these questions must be answered, are to some extent ascertained; but pending the discovery of further facts and an hypothesis by which they can be interpreted and arranged, it remains possible to speculate upon the matter either in activist or in automatist language. Which kind of language gives scientifically the most adequate symbolism, or whether a neutral symbolism is not possible, are matters as to which it is premature to decide. Meanwhile there is no excuse for making a confused statement of an unsolved and difficult problem into a chief instrument of all our inquiries, which is what we should be doing if we admitted 'meaning' in the sense here discussed as a fundamental conception.

As regards VII (b) those who are not clear as to the scope of the equation, "His meaning is certain," = "He has definite wishes," often find themselves led to the conclusion that 'meaning' = 'wishes' = 'volition' (a mental event), *i.e.*, is entirely psychological, or as they are often pleased to say, purely personal.[1] The same linguistic ambiguity often arises again when the Universe is regarded as showing evidence of a will or design, and if 'meaning' is substituted for the 'intention' or 'purpose' of such a will, then the meaning of anything will be its purpose—as conceived by the speaker *qua* interpreter of the divine plan; or, for biological teleologists with a partiality for the *élan vital*—its function. Such a phrase as the Meaning of Life (cf., for example, Professor Münsterberg's treatment above) usually implies such a view, but there is sometimes another possible interpretation when Meaning is equated with 'Significance' (VIII). Here the notion of purpose is not always implied, and the meaning of anything is said to have been grasped when it has been understood as related to other things or as having its place in some system as a whole.

Good examples of both these uses are provided by Mr Russell, and it is hardly necessary to add that, as here used by him, both are innocuous and convenient locutions. At the close of the immortal account by Mephistopheles of the history of our cosmos, we read: "Such, in outline, but even more purposeless, more void of meaning, is the world which Science presents

[1] Another mode of introducing the personal touch is to equate 'my meaning' with 'my ideas,' whether of, or not of, anything; as when a disputant declares that she has expressed her meaning imperfectly, but claims that ideas are so personal and intangible that they can never be adequately 'expressed.'

for our belief." And again, in relation to the haphazard treatment of mathematics in text-books: "The love of system can find free play in mathematics as nowhere else. The learner who feels this impulse must not be repelled by an array of meaningless examples or distracted by amusing oddities."[1]

The kind of system within which the thing, said in this sense to have 'meaning,' is taken as fitting is not important. Designs or intentions, human or other, form one sub-class of such systems, but there are many others. For example, some people were said to be slow in grasping the 'meaning' of the declaration of war; in other words, they did not easily think of the consequences of all kinds which were causally linked with that event. Similarly we may ask what is the 'meaning' of unemployment.

The theologian will elucidate the 'meaning' of sin by explaining the circumstances of Adam's fall and the history and destiny of the soul. Similarly the 'meaning' of top hats may flash across the mind of a sociologist when he recognizes them as part of the phenomena of conspicuous ostentation.

"I doubt," says Mr Stanley Leathes, "if numerical dates have any meaning to the majority of children. I once asked a Sunday school boy: How long ago Our Lord had lived? He replied: 'Forty days.'"[2] The complaint is not that the dates do not 'suggest' anything, but presumably that their 'significance' in the general measurement of time has not been grasped by the puerile mind. The figures for the distances of remote stars are similarly said to be without 'meaning' for us all.

But 'meaning' in this sense is too vague to be of much service even to orators. Is the meaning of unemployment its causes or its effects, its effects taken sociologically, or as the unemployed individual suffers

[1] *Op. cit., Mysticism and Logic*, pp. 47 and 66.
[2] *What is Education ?*, p. 178.

them? Accordingly various restrictions are commonly introduced by aid of which more specific senses of 'meaning,' as place within some system, are obtained. Two of them are sufficiently important to rank as independent definitions of meaning, since each has been made the keystone of a metaphysical edifice, namely 'meaning' as the *practical* and as the *theoretical* consequences. In both cases the 'meaning' is the rest of the system within which whatever has the 'meaning' is taken. We shall find another narrower and a more scientific variety of this 'meaning' in use when we come to consider natural signs.

The account of meaning in terms of Practical Consequences (IX) is chiefly associated with the pragmatists. William James himself considers that "the meaning of any proposition can always be brought down to some particular consequence in our future practical experience, whether passive or active,"[1] or as he puts it in *Pragmatism* (p. 201): "True ideas are those that we can assimilate, validate, corroborate, verify. False ideas are those that we can not. That is the practical difference it makes to us to have true ideas; that, therefore, is the meaning of truth, for it is all that truth is known as."

Correspondingly there are those who introduce the word 'means' into their prose as a synonym for 'involves' or 'logically implies' (X). All or any of the theoretical consequences of a view or statement are thus included in common philosophic parlance in its 'meaning,' as when we are told (*Mind*, 1908, p. 491) that " while to Spinoza insistence on ends alone means ignorance of causes, to Prof. Laurie insistence on causes alone means ignorance of ends."

XI (Emotion) requires little comment. It is a definite sense of meaning which except amongst men of letters is not likely to be brought in to confuse other issues. A separate treatment of the emotional use of

[1] W. James, *The Meaning of Truth*, p. 210.

language will be found in the following chapter, where what has already been said on this subject receives application. Some typical instances of the emotional use of meaning were provided in the preceding chapter. The word is often purely emotive (cf. 'Good' p. 125), and on these occasions, if the writer is what is known as a stylist, will have no substitute nor will a sensible reader attempt a symbolic definition.

The detailed examination of this sense of meaning is almost equivalent to an investigation of Values, such as has been attempted by Professor W. M. Urban in his formidable treatise on the subject, where 'worth-predicates' appear as 'funded affective-volitional meanings.' "The words 'God,' 'love,' 'liberty,' have a real emotional connotation, leave a trail of affective meaning. . . . We may quite properly speak of the emotional connotation of such words as the funded meaning of previous emotional reactions and the affective abstracts which constitute the psychical correlates of this meaning as the survivals of former judgment-feelings."[1] It is regrettable that Urban's taste for the collocation of forbidding technicalities should have prevented a more general acquaintance with views for the most part so sound and so carefully expounded.

Proceeding then to the third group we have first (XII) the definition which embodies the doctrine of natural signs. Any one event will, it is generally assumed, be connected with other events in a variety of ways. Any one event will be actually related causally or temporally or in some other way to other events so that, taking this event as a sign in respect of some one such relation, there will be another event which is its meaning, *i.e.*, the relatum so related. Thus the effect of the striking of a match is either a flame, or smoke, or the head falling off, or merely a scraping noise or an exclamation. In this case the

[1] *Valuation*, p. 133.

actual effect is the meaning of the scrape, if treated as a sign in this respect, and *vice versa*.

It is in this sense that the Psycho-analyst often speaks of the meaning of dreams. When he discovers the 'meaning' of some mental phenomenon, what he has found is usually a conspicuous part of the cause, and he rarely makes any other actual use of the word. But by introducing theories of unconscious wishes, 'meaning' in the sense of something unconsciously intended, and by introducing 'universal symbols,' kings, queens, etc., 'meaning' in the sense of some intrinsic property of the symbol, may easily come to be what he believes himself to be discussing. In other words, for him as for all natural scientists the causal sign-relations are those which have the greatest interest.

In passing from this sense of 'meaning' to XIII, which must be carefully distinguished, we have to recall the account of interpretation given above. All thinking, all reference, it was maintained, is adaptation due to psychological contexts which link together elements in external contexts. However 'universal' or however 'abstract' our adaptation, the general account of what is happening is the same. In this fashion we arrive at a clear and definite sense of 'meaning.' According to this the meaning of A is that to which the mental process interpreting A is adapted.[1] This is the most important sense in which words have meaning.

In the case of simple interpretations, such as the recognition of a sound, this adaptation is not difficult to explain. In more complex interpretations such as the reader is attempting to carry out at this moment, a detailed account is more difficult, partly because such interpretations go by stages, partly because few important psychological laws have as yet been ascertained and these but vaguely. To take an analogous case, before Newton's time scientists were in much doubt

[1] Cf. Chapter III., *supra*, pp. 53, 75.

as to the 'meaning' of tidal phenomena, and peculiar 'sympathy' and 'affinity' relations used to be postulated in order to connect them with the phases of the moon 'the ruler of the waters.' Further knowledge of more general uniformities made it possible to dispense with such phantom relations. Similarly more accurate knowledge of psychological laws will enable relations such as 'meaning,' 'knowing,' 'being the object of,' 'awareness' and 'cognition' to be treated as linguistic phantoms also, their place being taken by observable correlations.

The most usual objections to such a view as this derive from undue reliance upon introspection. Introspective judgments like other judgments are interpretations. Whether we judge 'I am thinking of rain,' or, after looking at the barometer, judge 'It is going to rain'; we are equally engaged in a sign situation. In both cases we are making a secondary adaptation to a previous adaptation as sign, or more usually to some part or concomitant of the adaptation; such as, for instance, the words symbolizing the reference about which we are attempting to judge in introspection, or, failing words, some non-verbal symbol, or, failing even that, the obscure feelings accompanying the reference. It is possible of course to respond directly to our own responses. We do this constantly in long trains of habitual and perceptual actions; but such responses being themselves non-conscious, *i.e.*, conscious of nothing, do not lead to introspection judgments of the kind which provide evidence for or against any view as to the nature of thinking. Such judgments, since they must appear to rest upon the reflective scrutiny of consciousness itself, are interpretations whose signs are taken from whatever conscious elements accompany the references they are about. It is certain that these signs are unreliable and difficult to interpret; often they are no more than dim, vague feelings. We therefore tend to introduce symbolization, hoping so to gain additional and clearer signs. When, for instance, we attempt what is called the analysis of a judgment by direct introspection our procedure leads as a rule to the provision of alternative symbols which we endeavour to convince ourselves symbolize the same reference. We then say that one symbol is what we mean by the other. In most modern arguments concerning fundamentals some positive or negative assertion of this form can be found as an essential step. It is thus very important to consider what kind of evidence is available for such assertions.

The usual answer would be that it is a matter not of evidence but of immediate conviction. But these direct certainties notoriously vary from hour to hour and are different in different persons. They are in fact feelings, and as such their causes, if they can be investigated, will be found not irrelevant to the question of their validity. Now the main cause of any conviction as to one symbol being the correct analysis of another, *i.e.*, as to the identity of the references symbolized by both, is to be found in the similarity of any other signs of the references in question which may be obtainable. These, since imagery is admittedly often irrelevant, will be feelings again :—feelings accompanying the references, feelings of fitness or unfitness, due to the causal connections of symbols to references, and feelings due to the mere superficial similarities and dissimilarities of the symbols. Thus it is this tangled and obscure network of feelings which is the ground of our introspective certainties. It is not surprising that the task of clarifying our opinions by the method of direct inspection and analysis should be found difficult, or that the results obtained should give rise to controversy.

Those who have attempted to decide what precisely they are judging when they make the commonest judgments, such as 'I am thinking,' 'That is a chair,' 'This is good' will not be in haste to dispute this.

It is indeed very likely that we more often make mistakes in these secondary judgments than in most others, for the obvious reason that verification is so difficult. Nobody's certainty as to his reference, his 'meaning,' is of any value in the absence of corroborative[1] evidence, though this kind of self-confidence dies hard.

It is because the non-verbal sensations and images which accompany references are such unreliable signs that symbols are so important. We usually take our symbolization as our guide to our meaning, and the accompanying sign feelings become indistinguishably merged in the feelings of our symbols. The fact, however, that on some occasions all the available symbols can be felt to be inappropriate to the reference which they are required to symbolize, shows that other feeling-signs are attainable. We are thus not *completely* at the mercy of our symbols.

None the less, there are obvious reasons for that prodigious trustfulness in symbols as indications of what we are meaning which is characteristic of mathematical and other abstract thinkers. Symbols properly used are for such subjects indispensable substitutes for feeling accompaniments not so easily distinguished. The feeling accompanying, for instance, a reference to 102 apples is not easily distinguishable from that accompanying a reference to 103, and without the symbols we should be unable to make either reference as distinct from the other. In abstract thought as a rule and for most thinkers, instead of our references determining our symbols, the linkage and interconnection of the symbols determines our reference.

[1] The precise kinds of this corroborative evidence and their value, *i.e.*, the allied signs or the relevant behaviour, are matters for investigation. Most word-association experiments, for instance, are conducted on dubious assumptions. The problem of the relation of non-verbal signs and verbal signs (*i.e.*, symbols) to the judgment processes of which they are signs, has therefore not often been raised. Since so much experimental psychology must stand or fall with the quite uncritical assumptions as to the value of symbolization as evidence of reference upon which such experiments are conducted, this problem would seem to be worthy of attention.

We merely watch that no violation of certain rules of procedure is brought about. Some of these rules are of no great importance, those recorded in the parts of grammar which deal with literary usage and the conventions of sentence formation. Others however are of quite a different standing and are due to nothing less than the nature of things in general. In other words these rules are logical laws in the sense that any symbol system which does not obey them must break down as a means of recording references, no matter to what the references be made. These fundamental necessities of a symbol system and the mere rules of polite speech above mentioned have historically been subjected to some confusion. We had occasion to discuss some of the former in Chapter V.; some of the latter will receive mention and comment when we come to deal with Symbol Situations in our final chapter.

Subject to these logical requirements we are able, largely by means of symbols defined in terms of one another, to compound references, or, in other words, to abstract common parts of different references—to distinguish, to compare and to connect references in, to, and at, various levels of generality. The compounding of these diverse modes of adaptation into a specific judgment is the process generally alluded to as Thinking, this activity being commonly maintained through any long train by the use of symbols. These, as substitutes for stimuli not available at any given instant, as retaining the product of elaborate concatenations of adjustments, and as affording means for the rearrangement of these adjustments, have become so powerful, so mechanical and so intricately interconnected as to conceal from us almost entirely what is taking place. We come to regard ourselves as related to a variety of entities, properties, propositions, numbers, functions, universals and so forth—by the unique relation of knowledge. Recognized for what they are, *i.e.*, symbolic devices, these entities may be of great use. The attempt to investigate them as referents leads, as we have seen, to Philosophy, and constitutes the unchallenged domain of philosophers.

It will be noticed that definitions (XII) and (XIIIb) for the case of true interpretations have the same effect. The meaning (XIIIb) of a sign adequately interpreted will be that to which it is actually related by the sign relation. But for the case of false interpretations the two 'meanings' will be different. Another point of interest is that this account removes the necessity for any 'Correspondence Theory of Truth' since an adequate reference has as its referent not something which *corresponds* to the fact or event which is the meaning of a sign by definition (XII) but something which is identical with it. We may if we please say that a reference corresponds with its referent, but this would be merely shorthand for the fuller account of reference which we have given.

With these considerations before us we can now understand the peculiarities of Symbols with their twofold 'meaning' for speaker and hearer. A symbol as we have defined it (cf. pp. 11, 12 *supra*) symbolizes an act of reference; that is to say, among its causes in the speaker, together no doubt with desires to record and to communicate, and with attitudes assumed towards hearers, are acts of referring. Thus a symbol becomes when uttered, in virtue of being so caused, a sign to a hearer of an act of reference. But this act, except where difficulty in understanding occurs, is of little interest in itself, and the symbol is usually taken as a sign of what it stands for, namely that to which the reference which it symbolizes refers. When this interpretation is successful it follows that the hearer makes a reference similar in all relevant respects to that made by the speaker. It is this which gives symbols their peculiarity as signs. Thus a language transaction or a communication may be defined as a use of symbols in such a way that acts of reference occur in a hearer which are similar in all relevant respects to those which are symbolized by them in the speaker.

From this point of view it is evident that the problem for the theory of communication is the delimitation and analysis of psychological contexts, an inductive problem exactly the same in form as the problems of the other sciences. Owing, however, to the difficulty of observing psychological events and the superficial nature of the uniformities hitherto observed, the methods employed in testing whether communication has or has not taken place are indirect. Since we are unable to observe references directly we have to study them through signs, either through accompanying feelings or through symbols. Feelings are plainly insufficient and symbols afford a far more sensitive indication.[1] But symbols also mislead and some method of control has to be devised ; hence the importance of definition. Where there is reason to rely upon the indicative power of symbols, no doubt a language purged of all alternative locutions is scientifically desirable. But in most matters the possible treachery of words can only be controlled through definitions, and the greater the number of such alternative locutions available the less is the risk of discrepancy, provided that we do not suppose symbols to have 'meaning' on their own account, and so people the world with fictitious entities.

The question of synonyms leads us naturally to the consideration of (XIV) Good Use. We have already seen what correctness of symbolization involves. A symbol is correet when it causes a reference similar to that which it symbolizes in any suitable interpreter. Thus for any given group of symbol users there will arise a certain fixity of something which will be called

[1] The extent to which we rely upon symbols to show us what we are doing, is illustrated by the recently reported case of the Bishop who mislaid his railway ticket.

"It's quite all right, my lord!" said the Inspector, who was also a Churchwarden.

"No, it isn't," replied the Bishop. "How can I know where I am going to without it?"

proper meaning or Good Use. This something tends to be spoken of as *the* meaning of the words in question. What is fixed is the reference which any member of this group will make in interpreting a symbol on any occasion within the relevant universe of discourse. It is no doubt very important that these meanings should not vary beyond narrow limits. But we may be legitimately anxious to maintain uniform standards of comparison without finding it necessary to suppose them supernaturally established or in their own nature immutable. The belief which is so common that words necessarily mean what they do derives from the ambiguity of the term 'necessary,' which may stand either for the fact that this is a requisite of communication or for the supposed possession by words of intrinsic 'meanings.' Thus it has been argued that such a word as Good has no synonym and is irreplaceable, so that persons making good use of this word will have an idea which they cannot otherwise symbolize—from which it is held to follow that, since the word is certainly used, there must be a unique and simple ethical idea, or, as is sometimes said, a unique property or predicate, whether possessed by anything or not. In a precisely similar fashion mathematicians are apt to aver that if nothing whatever existed, there would yet be the property of 'being 107 in number.'

These fixities in references are for the most part supported and maintained by the use of Dictionaries, and for many purposes 'dictionary-meaning' and 'good use' would be equivalents. But a more refined sense of dictionary-meaning may be indicated. The dictionary is a list of substitute symbols. It says in effect: "This can be substituted for that in such and such circumstances." It can do this because in these circumstances and for suitable interpreters the references caused by the two symbols will be sufficiently alike. The Dictionary thus serves to mark the overlaps between the references of symbols rather than to define their fields.

The two remaining definitions of our list (XV., XVI.) arise through this difficulty in the control of symbols as indications of reference. As we have seen, the reference which the user of a symbol believes himself, thanks to his trust in the symbol, to be making may be quite different from that which he is actually making; a fact which careful comparison of locutions often reveals. Similarly the reference made by a hearer will often be quite unlike that made by the speaker. The final case, in which the meaning of a symbol is what the hearer believes the speaker to be referring to, is perhaps the richest of all in opportunities of misunderstanding.

CHAPTER X

SYMBOL SITUATIONS

For one word a man is often deemed to be wise and for one word he is often deemed to be foolish. We ought to be careful indeed what we say.—*Confucius.*

Abba Ammon asked Abba Sisoes, saying, " When I read in the Book my mind wisheth to arrange the words so that there may be an answer to any question." The old man said unto him, " This is unnecessary, for only purity of heart is required. From this it ariseth that a man should speak without overmuch care."—*Palladius,* " *The Book of Paradise.*"

THE context theory of interpretation as applied to the use of words may now be sketched in outline. Let us consider first the hearer's side of the matter, returning later to the more difficult case of the speaker. As a preliminary to any understanding of words, we necessarily have a very simple kind of interpretation which may be called sensory discrimination, or sensory recognition. At this level[1] we can be said to be discriminating between sounds as sounds (the case where what is discriminated is a movement of the organs of articulation, or an image of this or of a sound, is quite parallel); and thus we are here interpreting an initial sign. Clearly unless one sound or image be distinguished, consciously or unconsciously, from another no use of words is possible. Usually the discrimination

[1] One interpretative process is said to be on a higher level than another when its occurrence requires the preceding occurrence of that other (cf. Chapter V., *apud* Canon III.). Whether the level is said to be higher or lower is immaterial. Here it will be said to be higher.

is unconscious, our use of words being habitual; it can, however, become conscious, as in learning a foreign tongue. One of the chief distinctions also between poetry and strict scientific prose is that in poetry we must consciously attend to the sensory characters of the words, whereas in prose we need not do so. This conscious attention to words as sounds does, however, tend to impede our further interpretations.

The next stage of interpretation takes us from the mere recognition of the initial sign as sound of a certain kind to the recognition of it as a word. The change is due to a change in the psychological context of the sign. To recognize it as a sound with a distinctive character we require a context consisting of the sign and of other past sound sensations more *and* less similar. To recognize it as a word requires that it form a context with further experiences[1] other than sounds. In what precise fashion we first come to know that there are words, or to take some sounds as words but not others, is still to be experimentally investigated, but as infants we do not make this step by guessing straight off that people are talking to us. Long before this surmise could become possible we have developed an extensive private language through the fact that certain sounds have come into contexts with certain other experiences in such a way that the occurrence of the sound is a sign interpreted by a response similar to that aroused by the other associated experience. This interpretation also may be conscious or unconscious. Normally it is unconscious, but again if difficulty arises it tends to become conscious. When we understand with ease we are as a rule less aware of the words used than when, through unfamiliarity of diction or the strangeness of the referent, we are checked in our interpretation.

These considerations are of importance in education.

[1] A general term here used to cover sensations, images, feelings, etc., and perhaps unconscious modifications of our mental state.

Many children appear more stupid than they are, not through misinterpreting words but through failure to recognize them first as sounds ; and adults also differ greatly in their ability to distinguish vocal sounds when spoken rapidly or with an 'accent.' This ability greatly affects the ease with which languages are acquired.

With the recognition of the sound as a word the importance of the prior recognition of the sound appears to be decreased. This cannot actually be the case. It is true that we can recognize a word whether it be pronounced high or low, quickly or slowly, with a rising intonation or a falling and so on. But however different two utterances of one word may be as sounds, they must yet have a common character ;[1] otherwise they could not be recognized as the same word. It is only in virtue of this character that the two sounds are in similar psychological contexts and so interpreted alike. We may be unable consciously to detect this common character, but this need not surprise us. In general it seems plausible to assume that simpler stages of interpretation tend to lapse out of consciousness as more elaborate developments grow out of them, provided that they are successfully and easily carried out. Difficulty or failure at any level of interpretation leads in most cases to the re-emergence of the lower levels into consciousness and to a kind of preoccupation with them which is often an adverse condition for the higher interpretations whose instability has led to their emergence.

So far we have reached the level of the understanding of simple names and statements, and a considerable range of reference can be recorded and communicated by this means alone. A symbol system of this simple type is adequate for simple referents or aggregates of simple referents, but it fails at once for complex

[1] It should be remembered that such constitutive characters of contexts may be of the form ' being either A or B or C, etc.'

referents, or groups of referents which have a structure more intricate than mere togetherness. To symbolize references to such complex referents complex symbols with specialized structures are required; although it does not appear to be necessary that the symbol should in any very close way reflect or correspond to the complexity of the referent. Possibly in primitive languages this correspondence is closer. In highly developed languages the means by which complex symbols are formed, by which they receive their structure as symbols, are very many and various. Complex symbols with the same referent may be given alternative forms even when the simple symbols, the names, contained remain unaltered. The study of these forms is a part of grammar, but a more genuine interest in, and awareness of, psychological problems than it is usual for grammarians to possess is required if they are to be fruitfully discussed.

We may now consider a few of the easier cases of these complex symbols. Let us begin with the contrast between proper names and descriptive phrases. We saw above that particular references require contexts of a much simpler form than general references, and any descriptive phrase involves for its understanding a context of the more complicated form. To use such a symbol as the name of an individual—let us call him *Thomas*—we need merely that the name shall be in a context with Thomas-experiences. A few such experiences are usually sufficient to establish this conjunction; for every such experience, since we rarely encounter an acquaintance without realizing that he has a name and what that name is, will help to form the context. Contrast with this the understanding of such a descriptive name as 'my relatives.' Here the experiences required will not be in all cases the same. At one time a grandfather, at another a niece will present themselves; but not upon all occasions will their relationship to us be in any degree a dominant feature, nor is the relationship which they agree in bearing to their grandson and uncle respectively an obvious one. Thus a range of experiences differing very widely one from another is necessary if the required context is to be built up.

'Relatives' is in fact an abstraction, in the sense that the reference which it symbolizes cannot be formed simply and directly by one grouping of experience, but is the result of varied groupings of experiences whose very difference enables their common elements to survive in isolation. This process of selection and elimination is always at work in the acquisition of a vocabulary and the development of thought. It is rare for words to be formed into contexts with non-symbolic experience directly, for as a rule they are learnt only through other words. We early begin to use language in order to learn language, but since it is no mere matter of the acquisition of synonyms or alternative locutions, the same stressing of similarities between references and elimination of their differences through conflict is required. By these means we develop references of greater and greater abstractness, and metaphor, the primitive symbolization of abstraction, becomes possible Metaphor, in the most general sense, is the use of one reference to a group of things between which a given relation holds, for the purpose of facilitating the discrimination of an analogous relation in another group.[1] In the understanding of metaphorical language one reference borrows part of the context of another in an abstract form.

There are two ways in which one reference may appropriate part of the context of another. Thus a reference to man may be joined with a reference to sea, the result being a reference to seamen. No metaphor is involved in this. When, on the other hand, we take arms against a sea of troubles, that part of the context

[1] For other forms of Metaphor, see *Principles of Literary Criticism*, Chapter XXXII.

of the reference to sea which is combined with the other references appears in an abstract form, *i.e.*, the relevant characters of the sea will not include attraction by the moon or being the resort of fishes. The poetic value of the metaphor depends in this case chiefly on the way in which the ceaseless recurrence of the waves accentuates the sense of hopelessness already present—as the Cuchulain legend well shows.

In fact the use of metaphor involves the same kind of contexts as abstract thought, the important point being that the members shall only possess the relevant feature in common, and that irrelevant or accidental features shall cancel one another. All use of adjectives, prepositions, verbs, etc., depends on this principle. The prepositions are particularly interesting, the kinds of contexts upon which they depend being plainly different in extent and diversity of members. 'Inside' and 'outside,' it would appear, are the least complicated in context, and consequently, as might be expected, are easily retained in cases of disturbance of the speech functions. The metaphorical aspects of the greater part of language, and the ease with which any word may be used metaphorically, further indicate the degree to which, especially for educated persons, words have gained contexts through other words. Very simple folk with small and concrete vocabularies do on the other hand in some degree approximate to the account given above (p. 211), since the majority of their words have naturally been acquired in direct connection with experience. Their language has throughout many of the characteristics of proper names. Hence in part their comparative freedom from confusions, but hence also the naïve or magical attitude to words. Such linguists may perhaps be said to be beneath the level at which confusion, the penalty we pay for our power of abstraction, becomes possible.

In what has been said hitherto we have dealt chiefly

with the listener, who interprets symbols as they are given to him. We have yet to examine the processes by which references, as they proceed in a speaker, are symbolized. This in some respects is the reverse of the preceding case, but in others what happens is entirely different. For the listener the word is the sign, and without it the required reference does not occur. Possibly for some mental types an exactly similar process occurs in the speaker, with the sole difference that the words are not given from without, but arise through some sort of internal causation. Here there are not two distinct processes, reference and symbolization, but only one—reference through symbols; the situation being such that the reference is governed by the symbol.

With most thinkers, however, the symbol seems to be less essential. It can be dispensed with, altered within limits and is subordinate to the reference for which it is a symbol. For such people, for the normal case that is to say, the symbol is only occasionally part of the psychological context required for the reference. No doubt for us all there are references which we can only make by the aid of words, *i.e.*, by contexts of which words are members, but these are not necessarily the same for people of different mental types and levels; and further, even for one individual a reference which may be able to dispense with a word on one occasion may require it, in the sense of being impossible without it, on another. On different occasions quite different contexts may be determinative in respect of similar references. It will be remembered that two references, which are sufficiently similar in essentials to be regarded as the same for practical purposes, may yet differ very widely in their minor features. The contexts operative may include additional supernumerary members. But any one of these minor features may, through a change in the wider contexts upon which these narrower contexts depend, become an essential element instead of a mere accompaniment. This appears to happen in the change from word-freedom, when the word is not an essential member of the context of the reference, to word-dependence, when it is.

The practical consequences of these differences between individuals, and between occasions for the same individual, are important. In discussion we have constantly to distinguish between those who are unable to modify their vocabularies without extensive disorganization of their references, and those who are free to vary their symbolism to suit the occasion. At all levels of intellectual performance there are persons to be found to whom any suggestion that they should change their symbols comes, and must come, as a suggestion that they should recant their beliefs. For such people to talk differently is to think differently, because their words are essential members of the contexts of their references. To those who are not so tied by their symbolism this inability to renounce for the moment favourite modes of expression usually appears as a peculiar localized stupidity.[1] But it need not necessarily betoken a crude and superstitious view of the relations of words to things, for we should be ready to recognize that such adherence to special words as though they had sovereign and talismanic virtue, may be a symptom that for the speaker the word is a necessary part of the reference context: either because it was so when the reference was first made, or because non-verbal signs alone would be insufficient to avoid confusion. On the other hand, too great a readiness to use any and every suggested symbol

[1] Not to be confused with the obstinacy of official persons and others which is often displayed in verbal intransigence: as in the darky anecdote which C. S. Peirce was wont to relate.—" You know, Massa, that General Washington and General Jackson was great friends, dey was. Well, one day General Washington he said to General Jackson, 'General, how tall should you think this horse of mine was?' 'I don't know, General,' says General Jackson. 'How tall is he, General Washington?' 'Why,' says General Washington, 'he is sixteen feet high.' 'Feet, General Washington?' says General Jackson, 'feet, General Washington? You mean hands, General.' 'Did I say feet, General Jackson?' said General Washington. 'Do you mean to say that I said that my horse was sixteen feet high? Very well, then, Gen'ral Jackson, if I *said* feet, *if* I said feet, then I sticks to it.' "

may also be a symptom of a low power of discrimination between references; suggesting to the observer that the speaker is making no fixed reference whatever.

But the symptomatology of language behaviour is an intricate matter and little trust can be put in observations which are not able to be checked by a wide knowledge of the general behaviour of the subject. These instances are here outlined merely to indicate the kind of work which is still necessary. It is the sort of work at which many people are by nature very successful; they can often readily decide merely from the way in which words proceed out of the mouth of a speaker, and quite apart from the particular words, whether he is worth listening to. A study of the mannerisms of politicians and preachers is, however, useful as a check upon too hasty conclusions. In general, the distinction between those for whom reference governs symbol and those for whom symbol governs reference, is constantly required, although as we have already pointed out the two conditions, word-independence and word-dependence as they may be called, can rarely be found in isolation, and most speakers alternate from one condition to the other. In spite of this practical difficulty the distinction between word-dependence and freedom is one of the starting-points for linguistic investigation, because the symptoms of nonsense-speech, verbiage, psittacism or whatever we may elect to call the devastating disease from which so much of the communicative activity of man suffers, are quite different for the two conditions, and, indeed, without the distinction, are conflicting and ambiguous. Most writers or speakers will agree from their own experience that on some occasions their speech proceeds slowly, heavily and importantly, because, while they are word-dependents, the necessary words without which nothing whatever would happen occur slowly and have to be waited for, whereas on other occasions the words are emitted in the same fashion because, being word-free for the moment, they are choosing the symbolism most suited to the reference and to the occasion, with a view to some finality of statement.

Neither of these speech processes can be dogmatically established as the only right or proper process. Word-dependence, for instance, must on no account be identified with psittacism, or be regarded as necessarily tending thereto. Psittacism is the use of words without reference; and the fact that a word is necessary to a reference is, as will easily be seen, in no way an indication of an absence of reference. None the less if we consider those other activities, such as eating or bicycling, which are similar to speech in that they are subject to a variable degree of control, there is reason perhaps to decide in favour of a speech procedure which should be a mingling of the two extremes of word-dependence and word-freedom. At certain points in serious utterances, the degree of deliberate control should be at its maximum, *i.e.*, the psychological context into which the word fits and to which the reference is due should contain as many varied members as possible. The rest of the symbolization should be left to the guidance of those systems of narrow contexts which are called verbal habits, speech-mechanisms, or the linguistic senses.

Considerable light upon the use of symbols is thrown, as is always the case in psychological investigation, by pathology. Much may be expected from the work now in progress on aphasia.[1] Meanwhile it

[1] See in particular Henri Piéron, *Thought and the Brain* (*Int. Lib. Psych.*, 1926), Part III., pp. 149-227, and Kinnier Wilson, *Aphasia* (*Psyche Miniatures*, 1926), where both the emotive and the symbolic aspects are dealt with.

Dr Henry Head distinguished four varieties of speech disorders, named from " the most salient defect in the use of words," as follows:

(1) *Verbal Aphasia.* " Essentially a disturbance of word-formation. . . . As speech returns, commands given in spoken or written words can be executed, but orders which necessitate the evocation of some word or phrase may be carried out badly."

(2) *Syntactical Aphasia.* The patient " tends to talk jargon; not only is the articulation of the word ill-balanced, but the rhythm of the phrase is defective, and there is want of grammatical coherence.

is interesting to consider some of the difficulties which occur in the normal use of language. Corresponding to the hierarchies of interpretations described above we have as many levels of possible failure. We may fail to recognize a word *qua* sound, both when the word is spoken to us and when we are about to utter it ourselves. Secondly, although we are successful in this, the context required for the understanding of a word may lapse. This disturbance may be due either to physiological, or, as the psycho-analysts have shown, to emotional, interference. The failure may occur over a name, and in such cases there is reason to suspect emotional influence; or it may occur over a descriptive phrase, or indeed any abstract symbol, in which case, since many delicate adaptations to widely differing experiences having only a slender common part are involved, failure to discriminate this part is likely to be accompanied by failure over the general abstract field.[1]

. . . Single words can be written correctly but any attempt to convey a formulated statement is liable to end in confusion."

(3) *Nominal Aphasia.* "Essentially a defective use of names and want of comprehension of the nominal meaning of words or other symbols." In this connection Dr Head remarks that "the separation of word-formation from naming and its allied functions is an entirely new feature in the classification of the aphasias." This seems extraordinary.

(4) *Semantic Aphasia.* "The affection comprises want of recognition of the full significance or intention of words and phrases." The patient "has lost the power of appreciating the ultimate or non-verbal meaning of words and phrases, and fails to recognize the intention or goal of actions imposed upon him."

Whatever the clinical value of the above classification, it is by no means satisfying theoretically, and Dr. Head's uses of the word 'meaning' involve the dangers and obscurities inseparable from such a terminology. As Kinnier Wilson remarks (*op. cit.*, p. 78): "Until further advance is made a psychological arrangement has the serious disadvantage of losing touch with cerebral function, and this is not compensated for by the greater scientific legitimacy which is claimed for it."

[1] Which kinds of words vanish first has long been a disputed point. Thus Ribot, in his classic treatment of Memory (*Les Maladies de la Mémoire*, Chapter III.), cites a number of authorities to the effect that "amnesia progresses from the particular to the general. It first affects proper names" . . . etc. But the degree of abstractness of a word is certainly not less important in this connection than its generality; nor must it be forgotten that there may be a diversity of functional disturbances which are indifferently described as 'amnesia' and 'aphasia.' As Ribot well says, "the psychologist is helpless until anatomy and physiology have made further progress." It is, however,

Those periodical moments of stupidity to which we are all prone, in which all abstract remarks appear pedantic and incomprehensible, seem very often to be physiologically determined.

Passing again to a higher level, there may be no inability to understand those symbols which are components of a complex symbol, and yet we may fail to interpret the whole sentence. In this case we should be said not to appreciate the logical form of the symbol. Logical form might here be defined as what is common to such complex symbols as "Crusoe landed from the wreck," and "Quixote fell off Rosinante," where the components[1] may be subjected to a one for one substitution. We have suggested above that the problem of logical form requires further attention which it is not likely to receive on current logical assumptions. It is fatal to regard it as an ultimate notion, for what is involved in interpreting a complex symbol is that the contexts of the component symbols should, together with the whole symbol, form a context of higher type. All discursive symbolization involves this weaving together of contexts into higher contexts, and interpretation of such complex symbols is of the same nature as that of simple symbols, with the difference only that the members of these higher contexts are themselves contexts. The same mechanisms of abstraction, metaphor, etc., occur, and the same levels at which failure is possible repeat themselves. Thus many people are able to understand such a symbol as "The fire is hot," though baffled by predicative facts or if called upon to consider relational attributes.

The study of the form or structure of complex refer-

also clear that any given word may be at different levels of abstractness and generality in different speakers. It may be true in general that "the new is more vulnerable than the old and the complex than the simple" (cf. Piéron, *op. cit.*, *Thought and the Brain*, p. 165), but which of these is which can only be decided on any particular occasion by the aid of some such context theory as that outlined in Chapter III. above.

[1] To what degree these particular symbols are of the same logical form might give rise to subtle discussion.

ences together with the form or structure of their symbols is fundamental both for Logic and for what is usually called grammar, which may be regarded as the Natural History of symbol systems. This science has, for obvious reasons, occupied the attention of educationists and students of language, to the detriment of more far-reaching inquiries. As normative, grammar tends to confine itself to a verbal analysis of How the King Talks, and, though sometimes suggestive, applies no real critical apparatus. In particular it is not realized that a Usage is only Good for a given universe of discourse, and the ordering of these different classes of occasions on which words may be used has never been seriously approached.

A science which can justify itself as a discipline imparting insight into the nature of the language medium has at present no such status either with instructors or instructed. The appointment, fashionable in philological circles, of Standing Joint Committees, to deal with the preliminaries of the science, is an indication that it is still in the state which led Smart to exclaim in 1831, "God help the poor children who are set to learn the definitions in elementary grammar." But indeed the traditional problems of grammar, the establishment of usage, the analysis of sentences, the classification of the parts of speech, are secondary problems of minor importance. They are not open to investigation until the primary problem of the nature of the language medium to which Symbolism addresses itself has been explored. If this fundamental investigation can be carried a very little further it is probable that these later problems upon which grammarians have lavished the treasures of human industry and acumen, will be seen in some cases to be purely artificial, in others to be concerned with points of detail.[1]

The wider educational problems which concern the

[1] See Appendix A.

acquisition of language in infancy have frequently received attention, and much useful material has been amassed by Sully, Meumann, O'Shea, and Piaget; but psychologists still make assumptions which prevent any advantage accruing from the investigation. "The Infant begins by imitating spoken words without understanding them and then understands them," says Münsterberg. Fortunate infant to reach the second stage! But unluckily the ingenuous little one does nothing of the kind. Far more accurate is Rousseau's view in his *Thoughts on Education*—"Inattention on our part to the real way in which words are understood by children appears to me the cause of their first errors; and these, even when removed, have a great influence on their turn of mind the remainder of their lives." The whole question of the acquisition and use of language requires a fresh foundation, and must be treated concretely with a view to the free development of the interpretative faculties.

As an example of the kind of procedure which is desirable, we may instance the ordering of the levels at which, as we saw in Chapter IV. (p. 86), 'chair,' 'wood,' 'fibres,' and so forth become correct symbols for what we are perched upon. It was there pointed out in what way the set of confusions known as metaphysics has arisen through lack of this true grammatical approach, *the critical scrutiny of symbolic procedure.* In the same manner our analyses of Beauty and Meaning are typical instances of what grammar might long ago have achieved had grammarians only possessed a better insight into the necessities of intelligent intercourse, and a livelier sense of the practical importance of their science. Preoccupied as is natural by the intricate details of a vast subject-matter, and master of an imposing technique and an elaborate semi-philosophic nomenclature, the grammarian has unwittingly come to stand somewhat fixedly in the way of those who wish to approach the questions—How are words used?

and, How should they be used? The grammarian also is studying questions somewhat similar at first sight, namely—Which words are used when? and, Which should be used when? He resents the suggestion that his work may be of small importance through his having mistaken his question. In short, a normative examination of words cannot be begun without a normative examination of thinking, and no important question of verbal usage can be considered without raising questions as to the rank or level and the truth or falsity of the actual references which may employ it. Symbols cannot be studied apart from the references which they symbolize and, this being admitted, there is no point at which our examination of these references may stop with safety, short of the fullest possible investigation.

Returning now to complexities in references and in their symbols, the attempt to trace correspondence leads to the adoption of two distinct sets of considerations as guiding principles. With one of these, with the study of reference, we have here been throughout concerned. Symbolic form varies with variation of reference. But there are other causes for its variation upon which we have said something above (pp. 148-9). Besides symbolizing a reference, our words also are signs of emotions, attitudes, moods, the temper, interest or set of the mind in which the references occur. They are signs in this fashion because they are grouped with these attitudes and interests in certain looser and tighter contexts. Thus, in speaking a sentence we are giving rise to, as in hearing it we are confronted by, at least two sign-situations. One is interpreted from symbols to reference and so to referent; the other is interpreted from verbal signs to the attitude, mood, interest, purpose, desire, and so forth of the speaker, and thence to the situation, circumstances and conditions in which the utterance is made.

The first of these is a symbol situation as this has been described above, the second is merely a verbal sign-situation like the sign-situations involved in all ordinary perception, weather prediction, etc. Confusion between the two must be avoided, though they are often hard to distinguish. Thus we may interpret from a symbol to a reference and then take this reference as a sign of an attitude in the speaker, either the same or not the same as that to which we should interpret directly from his utterance as a verbal sign.

The ordering of verbal sign-situations is a large subject in which various branches may be distinguished. The following seem, together with strict symbolization, which it will be convenient to number as (i), to cover the main functions of language as a means of communication.

(ii) There are the situations which derive from attitudes, such as amity or hostility, of the speaker to his audience. In written language many of the most obvious signs for these attitudes[1] are necessarily lost. Manner and tone of voice have to be replaced by the various devices, conventional formulæ, exaggerations, under-statements, figures of speech, underlining, and the rest familiar in the technique of letter-writing. Word order is plainly of especial importance in this connection, but, as we shall see, no general literary device can be appropriated to any one of the functions of speech, it is sure to be borrowed on occasion by the others. Thus for this function almost any symbolic

[1] Not only attitudes but symbolic and syntactic elements have vocal tones as signs. Accents in Hebrew are a good example of the way in which a written language may attempt to preserve the distinctions which in speech are given by pause and intonation. Of the Distinctive accents there are four main classes corresponding roughly with English stops. In addition there are eleven Conjunctive accents, showing that the word to which they are attached is closely connected in sense with that which follows. Their neglect has been responsible for a number of mistranslations which have, nevertheless, become classic. Thus Isaiah xl. 3: "The voice of him that crieth in the wilderness, Prepare ye the way of the Lord." The voice, as the R.V. notes, is not in the wilderness, but cries, "Prepare ye in the wilderness the way of the Lord." And again Gen. iii. 22: "The Lord God said, Behold the man is become as one of us to know good and evil," where a proper accentuation gives, "Behold the man who hath been like one of us, is come to know good through evil." (Cf. Saulez, *The Romance of the Hebrew Language*, p. 99.)

transformations can be brought in. For instance telescoped or highly summarized phraseology is often used, even where on referential grounds it is unsuitable, as a mark of courtesy or respect to the hearer, or to avoid the appearance of pedantry or condescension which an expanded statement might produce. A speaker will naturally address a large audience in terms different from those which he employs in familiar conversation; his attitude has changed.

(iii) In a similar fashion our attitude to our referent in part determines the symbols we use. Here again complicated cases occur in which it may be uncertain whether our attitude is itself stated, or merely indicated through verbal signs. Æsthetic judgments in particular present this difficulty, and often the speaker himself would be unable to decide which was taking place. Emphasis, redundance, and all forms of reinforcement can be, and are commonly, used for these reasons, though equally they are used for the sake of their effects upon hearers (iv); or as rallying-points, rests or supports in case of difficulty of reference (v).

(iv) The structure of our symbols is often determined by our *Intention*, the effects which we endeavour to promote by our utterance. If we desire a hearer to commit suicide we may, on occasion, make the same remarks to him whether our reason for desiring such action is benevolent interest in his career or a dislike of his personal characteristics. Thus the symbol modification due to the effect intended must not be confused with that due to the attitude assumed towards an interlocutor, although often, of course, they will coincide.

(v) Besides their truth, or falsity, references have a character which may be called, from the accompanying feelings, Ease or Difficulty. Two references to the same referent may be true but differ widely in this ease, a fact which may be reflected in their symbols. The two symbols, "I seem to remember ascending Mount Everest," and "I went up Everest," *may*, on occasion, *stand for* no difference in reference and thus owe their dissimilarity solely to degrees of difficulty in recalling this uncommon experience. On the other hand this may, of course, be a real symbolic difference which does not merely *indicate* difference of difficulty but *states* it. This ease or difficulty should not be confused with certainty or doubt, or degree of belief or disbelief, which come most naturally under the heading (iii) of attitude to the referent. Each of these non-symbolic functions may employ words either in a symbolic capacity, to attain the required end through the references produced in the listener, or in a non-symbolic capacity when the end is gained through the direct effects of the words.

If the reader will experiment with almost any sentence he will find that the divergence which it shows from a purely symbolic notation governed solely by the nature of the reference which it symbolizes, will be due to disturbing factors from one or more of the above four groups. Further, what appears to be the same difference will sometimes be due to one factor, at other times to another. In other words, the plasticity of speech material under symbolic conditions is less than the plasticity of human attitudes, ends and endeavours, *i.e.*, of the affective-volitional system; and therefore the same modifications in language are required for quite different reasons and may be due to quite different causes. Hence the importance of considering the sentence in the paragraph, the paragraph in the chapter, and the chapter in the volume, if our interpretations are not to be misleading, and our analysis arbitrary.

It is somewhat surprising that grammarians should have paid so little attention to the plurality of functions which language has to perform. We have discussed above (p. 152) the half-hearted fashion in which from time to time they have admitted an affective side to their problems. But even this recognition is rarely made prominent. The five functions here enumerated—

(i) Symbolization of reference ;

(ii) The expression of attitude to listener;
(iii) The expression of attitude to referent;
(iv) The promotion of effects intended;
(v) Support of reference;
appear to be exhaustive.

It is, of course, not difficult to mention other factors which modify the form or structure of symbols. A hiccup, for instance, may do this, or laryngitis or brachydactyly; so will the distance of the audience, and more seriously the character of the occasion; or if the speaker is excited or irritated for some extraneous reason, his diction may show traces of this affect. The whole past linguistic history both of the individual and of the race to which he belongs obviously exercise enormous influence; the Scot does not naturally talk Yiddish. But all these influences upon linguistic form, though the last is of paramount importance to the comparative linguist, are not language functions in the sense here considered.[1] The state of the diaphragm, of the throat, or of the fingers, the acoustics of a church or a parade ground are no concern of the Theory of language; and although Comparative Philology has often been regarded as in itself comprising the whole field of the science, it is clear that this study belongs essentially to history. In saying this we do not minimize the interest and importance of the data which

[1] The means by which writers can attain their ends must not be confused with the ends themselves. "Surplusage! The true artist will dread that," says Walter Pater, "as the runner on his muscles. For in truth all art does but consist in the removal of surplusage, from the last finish of the gem-engraver blowing away the last particle of invisible dust, back to the earliest divination of the finished work to be, lying somewhere, according to Michelangelo's fancy in the rough-hewn block of stone." Or as Sydney Smith remarked with great acumen, a prose style may often be improved by striking out every other word from each sentence when written. Professor Conington, however (*Miscellaneous Writings*, Vol. I., p. 197. Edited by J. A. Symonds, 1872), points out that "there are occasions when a certain amount of surplusage may sometimes be admitted into harmonious prose for no better reason than to sustain the balance of clause against clause, and to bring out the general rhythmical effect"—the question being clearly one of purpose. In any case, style, balance, rhythm, etc., are not ends in themselves, but may be employed in connection with any of the functions.

it provides. The functions we are examining are those necessarily operative in all communication, the ways in which the work of speech is performed, the essential uses which speech serves.

Whether our list is exhaustive or not, it is at any rate certain these functions cannot be reduced in number without great loss of clarity and the omission of considerations in many cases vital to the understanding of the detail of language behaviour.

In translation, for example, the lack of such an analysis of the ways in which words are used has led to much confusion. Faced by the unaccountable failure of apparently accurate renderings, linguists have been too ready to accept the dicta of philosophers on this point, as well as their vague vocabulary. Thus, according to Sapir, "all the effects of the literary artist have been calculated, or intuitively felt, with reference to the formal 'genius' of his own language; they cannot be carried over without loss or modification. Croce is therefore perfectly right in saying that a work of literary art can never be translated. Nevertheless, literature does get itself translated, sometimes with astonishing adequacy."[1] So a problem appears to arise, and as a solution it is suggested that "in literature there are intertwined two distinct kinds or levels of art—a generalized, non-linguistic art, which can be transferred without loss into an alien linguistic medium, and a specifically linguistic art that is not transferable. I believe the distinction is entirely valid, though we never get the two levels pure in practice. Literature moves in language as a medium, but that medium comprises two layers, the latent content of language—our intuitive record of experience—and the particular conformation of a given language—the specific how of our record of experience. Literature that draws its sustenance mainly—never entirely—from the lower level, say a play of Shakespeare's, is translatable

[1] *Op. cit.*, *Language*, pp. 237-239.

without too great a loss of character. If it moves in the upper rather than in the lower level—a fair example is a lyric of Swinburne's—it is as good as untranslatable." And to illustrate this distinction, literature is compared with science; a scientific truth is said to be impersonal, "in its essence untinctured by the linguistic medium in which it finds expression. . . . Nevertheless it must have some expression, and that expression must needs be a linguistic one. Indeed, the apprehension of the scientific truth is itself a linguistic process, for thought is nothing but language denuded of its outward garb." Literature, on the other hand, is "personal and concrete. . . . The artist's intuition, to use Croce's term, is immediately fashioned out of a generalized human experience. . . . Certain artists whose spirit moves largely in the non-linguistic (better, in the generalized linguistic layer), even find a certain difficulty in getting themselves expressed." Whitman and others are supposed to be, as it were, "striving for a generalized art language, a literary algebra. . . . Their art expression is frequently strained, it sounds at times like a translation from an unknown original—which indeed is precisely what it is."

If we attempt to deal with the difficulties of translation in terms of the 'formal genius' and 'latent content' of the linguistic medium, and of the 'non-linguistic layer' in which 'intuition' moves, mysteries are inevitable. But a recognition of the richness of the means at the disposal of poetry, with which we shall shortly be concerned, allows us to dispense with the doubtful assistance of the Neapolitan dialectic. Translation, in fact, may succeed or fail for several quite intelligible reasons. Any purely symbolic use of words can be reproduced if in the two vocabularies similar symbolic distinctions have been developed. Otherwise periphrases or new symbols will be required, and the degree of possible correspondence is a matter which can be simply investigated. On the other hand, the more the emotive functions are involved the less easy will be the task of blending several of these in two vocabularies. And further, the greater the use made in the original of the direct effects of words through rhythm, vowel-quality, etc., the more difficult will it be to secure similar effects in the same way in a different sound-medium. Thus some equivalent method has to be introduced, and this tends to disturb the other functions so that what is called the 'success' of a translation is often due chiefly to its own intrinsic merits. With an understanding both of the functions of language and of its technical resources the criticism of translations provides a particularly fascinating and instructive method of language study.

The view that speech on almost all occasions presents a multiple, not a single, sign-situation throws a fresh light upon many problems of traditional grammar. In particular the treatment of sentence formation and syntax will have to be undertaken afresh. From this point of view we may note as typical a philologist[1] content with merely a dual language function in his definitions of the word and the sentence.

A word is an articulate sound symbol in its aspect of denoting something which is spoken about.

A sentence is an articulate sound symbol in its aspect of embodying some volitional attitude of the speaker to the listener.

Dr Gardiner's 'volitional attitude' would appear to be included in No. IV of our list of functions. It will be generally agreed that no use of speech can be admitted to be an attempt at *communication* unless this function is concerned.

The utility to grammarians of the terms so defined is not obvious. What is of importance is the heterogeneity which the author rightly insists upon between the two functions of speech mentioned. The other

[1] Dr A. Gardiner in *art. cit.*, *The British Journal of Psychology* (General Section), Vol. XII, Part iv., April, 1922. See, however, his *The Theory of Speech and Language*, 1932, p. 98.

functions which need to be considered in any comprehensive analysis of Language are not less heterogeneous.

The charge is sometimes brought against writers on psychology that they have neglected the side of the listener. It is certainly true that preoccupation with 'expression' as the chief function of language[1] has been disastrous. But this is not so much because of the neglect of the listener thereby induced as because of the curiously narcotic effect of the word 'expression' itself. There are certain terms in scientific discussion which seem to make any advance impossible. They stupefy and bewilder, yet in a way satisfy, the inquiring mind, and though the despair of those who like to know what they have said, are the delight of all whose main concern with words is the avoidance of trouble. 'Expression' is such an one, 'embody' is another, and we have just been concerned with 'meaning' in detail. What is wanted is a searching inquiry into the processes concealed by such terms, and as our analysis shows the introduction of the listener does little to throw light upon the matter. Moreover, psychologists and others, when they have been concerned with the fact that Speech does imply a listener, have not failed to insist upon the point. Thus Dittrich, the holder of one of the few recognized Chairs of the subject, wrote in 1900: "For linguistic science it is fundamental that language is an affair not merely of *expression* but also of *impression*, that communication is of its essence, and that in its definition this must not be overlooked." He accordingly includes in his own definition the words, 'in so far as understanding could be attempted by at least *one* other individual."[2] What such additional words contribute to a science may be doubted; but it is certain that von Humboldt went too far in this direction when he said:[3] "Man only understands himself when he has experimentally tested the intelligibility of his words on others."

[1] As, for example, Wundt, *Völkerpsychologie*, 3rd ed., I., p. 43.

[2] O. Dittrich, *Die Probleme der Sprachpsychologie*, pp. 11-12.

[3] *Sprachphilosophische Werke*, edited by Steinthal (1884), p. 281.

Steinthal's insistence on the part played by the listener in the origin and development of language is also well known;[1] and de Saussure in his standard treatment of speech functions which, as we saw in our first chapter, was otherwise unsatisfactory, goes so far as to draw pictures of the listener attending to the speaker and so completing the 'language circuit.'[2] A similar circuit for volitional signs is diagrammatically completed by Martinak through the fulfilment of the wish by the listener;[3] while Baldwin devotes over seventy pages of the second volume of his *Thought and Things* to language as affected by its functions in intercourse, and the relations of speaker and listener in what he calls "predication as elucidation" and "predication as proposal."[4]

But the most important practical recognition of the fact that language has many functions is to be found in Brunot's massive onslaught on current grammatical procedure.[5] Already, in 1903, the *doyen* of French scholarship had convinced himself of the necessity of abandoning the so-called 'parts of speech,' either as a method of approach or in actual teaching; and in 1908, as Professor at the Sorbonne, he recorded this conviction with clarity and vigour. For fifteen years, in ten revisions, he worked over the debated ground: "After each revision I returned to the same conclusion—that no tinkering with the old scheme, no re-grouping of the facts of language would be satisfactory so long as the classification by parts of speech was retained. We must make up our minds to devise methods of language-study no longer drawn up on the basis of signs but on the basis of ideas." Unlike the majority of linguists, Professor Brunot is fully aware that a purely psychological analysis of the speech situation lies behind this

[1] *Abriss der Sprachwissenschaft*, Vol. I., 2nd ed. (1881), p. 374.
[2] *Op. cit.*, *Cours de Linguistique Générale* (1916), p. 28.
[3] *Op. cit.*, *Psychologische Untersuchungen zur Bedeutungslehre* (1901), p. 65.
[4] Vol. II., p. 152.
[5] *La Pensée et la langue* (1922).

functional approach to language, and it is interesting to find that his exhaustive account of French idiom is in accordance with the fivefold division proposed above.

We may now state the connection of reference to symbol, subject to these disturbing factors, more accurately. The reference of a symbol we see now, is only one of a number of terms which are relevant to the form of a symbol. It is not even the dominant factor in most cases, and the more primitive the speech which we investigate, the less important does it appear to be. None the less, since, for all our finer dealings with things not immediately present—*i.e.*, not in very close and simple contexts with our present experience—since for all our more complicated or refined reference we need supports and distinguishing marks, this strictly symbolic function of words easily becomes more important than any other. It is thus natural in an account of the functions of words in ordinary usage to begin with strict symbolization.

In the normal case not one, but a variety of symbol forms is possible so far as the reference which they have to accompany is concerned. The reference could be accompanied let us say by A, or by B, or by C, or by D; these being symbols of different forms or structure. Any one of these is a possible member of the context upon which the reference depends, in the sense that its inclusion would not alter the reference. It is this range of possible forms which enables the symbol to perform so many different services, to be a sign in so many distinct though contemporary situations.

Suppose now the speaker, in addition to referring, assumes some attitude towards his audience, let us say amity. Then among these symbolic forms A, B, C, D, there may be one, say D, which is more suitable to the special shade of this attitude than the others, in the sense that it is a possible member of the context of the attitude, one of that group of symbols whose utterance would not alter the attitude. If this were all that were involved D would be uttered, since any other suitable remark would presumably involve some change in the reference.

Suppose further that the speaker feels, let us say, disgust, towards his referent. This will lead in similar fashion to further modification of the symbol. So again will the speaker's hopes, desires and intentions with regard to the effects of his remarks. Often the same modifications will satisfy both these conditions, but sometimes, when for instance the speaker's own attitude and that which he wishes to promote are for any reason discrepant, the natural word-attitude contexts must lapse, and judicious symbolization becomes for some people more difficult. In a similar fashion the speaker's own clearness or vagueness in reference has often to be disguised or to submit to compromise. His certainty or uncertainty, his doubt or degree of belief may as we have above remarked, be best ranked with general attitudes to referents.

Most writing or speech then which is of the mixed or rhetorical kind as opposed to the pure, or scientific, or strictly symbolic, use of words, will take its form as the result of compromise. Only occasionally will a symbolization be available which, without loss of its symbolic *accuracy*, is also *suitable* (to the author's attitude to his public), *appropriate* (to his referent), *judicious* (likely to produce the desired effects) and *personal* (indicative of the stability or instability of his references). The odds are very strongly against there being many symbols able to do so much. As a consequence in most speech some of these functions are sacrificed. In 'good morning' and 'good-bye' the referential function lapses, *i.e.*, these verbal signs are not symbols, it is enough if they are suitable. Exclamations and oaths similarly are not symbols; they have only to satisfy the condition of appropriateness, one of the easiest of conditions at the low-level of subtlety to which these emotional signs are developed. The only contexts required here would seem to be of the simplest order possible in psychology, as simple as the toothache-groan context. Orders or commands must satisfy reference and purpose conditions, but may, indeed often must, avoid both suitability and appropriateness in the senses used above, as for instance in many military orders. Threats on the other hand can easily dispense with reference, *i.e.*, be meaningless, and may be governed only by the purpose intended. Questions and requests are similar to commands in the respects above mentioned and differ from them merely in the means through which the effects desired are sought.

These instances of the dropping of one or more of the language functions lead us naturally to the most remarkable and most discussed case of such variation, the distinction, namely, between the prose and the poetic uses of language. In these terms the distinction is not happily symbolized, poetry being best defined for the most general and most important purposes by relation to the state or states of mind produced by the 'poem' in suitable readers and without any relation to the precise verbal means. Instead therefore of an antithesis of prose and poetry we may substitute that of symbolic and emotive uses of language. In strict symbolic language the emotional effects of the words whether direct or indirect are irrelevant to their employment. In evocative language on the other hand all the means by which attitudes, moods, desires, feelings, emotions can be verbally incited in an audience are concerned. We have already discussed at some length (p. 159) the importance of distinguishing between these two uses of language, and we may here add a few further considerations dealing with the means by which evocative languages secure their effects.

These accessory effects of words have often been described by men of letters, without much having been done towards their detailed study. Lafcadio Hearn, for instance, writes that for him "words have colour, form character. They have faces, ports, manners, gesticulations: they have moods, humours, eccentricities: they have tints, tones, personalities. I write for beloved friends who can see colour in words, can smell the perfume of syllables in blossom, can be shocked with the fine elfish eccentricity of words. And in the eternal order of things, words will eventually have their rights recognized by the people."

Words or arrangements of words evoke attitudes both directly as sounds, and less directly in several different ways through what are called loosely 'associations.' The effects of the words due directly (*i.e.*, physiologically) to their sound qualities are probably slight and only become important through such cumulative and hypnotic effects as are produced through rhythm and rhyme. More important are the immediate emotional accompaniments due to past experience of them in their typical connections. To get these, there is no need for the connections themselves to be recalled. Thirdly there are the effects ordinarily alluded to as the emotions due to associations, which arise through the recall of whole situations. So far we have confined our attention to verbal languages, but the same distinction and the same diversity of function arise with non-verbal languages. When we look at a picture, as when we read a poem, we can take up one or both of two attitudes. We can submit to it as a stimulus, letting its colour-qualities and form-qualities work upon us emotionally. Or with a different attitude we can interpret its forms and colours (its words). The first of these attitudes is not an indispensable preliminary to the second. To suppose so would be to mistake the distinction. Mr Clive Bell has performed a useful service in pointing out that many people are accustomed to pass, in the case of pictures, to the second of these attitudes, omitting the first entirely. Such omission, of course, deprives the picture of its chief part. Professor Saintsbury has performed a similar service for hasty readers.

But although the first of these attitudes, submission to the work of art as a stimulus, is in need of encouragement, the second attitude, that of interpretation, is equally necessary. At this point both critics become over zealous for an aspect of the truth. After allowing pure forms to affect us, we must, in most cases, go on to interpret if we are to allow the picture or poem to produce its full result. In so doing, there are two dangers which good sense will avoid. One is the danger of personal associations, concerning which nothing need be said. The other is the danger of confusing the evocation of an attitude towards a situation with the scientific description of it. The difference between these very different uses of language is most clearly apparent in the case of words. But all that we have said will apply equally to the contrast between art and photography. It is the difference between the presentation of an object which makes use of the direct emotional disturbances produced by certain arrangements, to reinstate the whole situation of seeing, or hearing, the object, together with the emotions felt towards it, and on the other hand, a presentation which is purely scientific, *i.e.*, symbolic. The attitude evoked need not necessarily be directed towards the objects stated as means of evoking it, but is often a more general adjustment. It will make these distinctions more plain if we consider them in the closely analogous field of painting, where emotions do not enter in different ways but only with an increased difference and distinction between them in accordance with the ways by which they enter. Exactly as we may distinguish the direct emotional effects of sound qualities and stresses, so we can distinguish the similar direct effects of colour and form. Just as, for instance, vowel and consonantal quality may conflict with rhythm, so colour may conflict with form: that is, they may evoke incongruous emotions. Similarly, it is admitted that colours acquire emotional effects through experience, emotional effects which are not the emotional effects of their associations. An Eskimo and a Moor, for instance, are differently affected by English colouring, because different selections of it are familiar, quite apart from association.

Emotional effects are naturally disregarded in the scientific use of language; it is evident that by including them language may be made to serve a double function. If we wish, for instance, to describe how, when we are impatient, a clock seems to go slowly, we may either describe psychologically the peculiarities in the expansion of our sense of duration, using symbols for the elements of the situation, and disregarding the emotional evocations of these symbols, or we may use symbols for a selection of these elements only, and so dispose them that they reinstate in the listener the appropriate emotions. We find in practice that these two methods of using language conflict in most cases, though not in all; Professor Mackenzie has urged that when Shelley wrote

> "Hail to thee blithe spirit,
> Bird thou never wert,"

he "did not really mean to deny that the lark belongs to the class Aves"; and conversely a statement adequate symbolically may have little emotional effect. Exceptions occur, but this conflict is so general that the usual antithesis between analysis and intuition, between science and art, between prose and poetry, are justified. They are due simply to the fact that an arrangement of symbols which will reinstate a situation by evoking emotions similar to those originally involved will, as things happen, very rarely be an adequate symbol for it. M. Bergson and the analysts are therefore both in the right, each maintaining the importance of one of the two functions of language. They are in the wrong only in not seeing clearly that language must have these two functions. It is as though a dispute arose whether the mouth should be for speaking or for eating.

The complexities and ambiguities in the use of

language for purposes of evocation are admittedly not less than those from which scientific language suffers. But when two people differ in what they are in ordinary usage perfectly correct in calling "their interpretations" of a poem or a picture, the procedure to be adopted is quite other than that advisable should they differ in their interpretations of a physicist's remarks. None the less, there is, in the two cases, an underlying similarity due to the fact that both are sign-situations though only the second is symbolic in the strict sense of the term.

The difference between the two uses may be more exactly characterized as follows: In symbolic speech the essential considerations are the correctness of the symbolization and the truth of the references. In evocative speech the essential consideration is the character of the attitude aroused. Symbolic statements may indeed be used as a means of evoking attitudes, but when this use is occurring it will be noticed that the truth or falsity of the statements is of no consequence provided that they are accepted by the hearer.

The means by which words may evoke feelings and attitudes are many and offer an alluring field of study to the literary psychologist. As sounds, and again as movements of articulation, and also through many subtle networks of association, the contexts of their occurrences in the past, they can play very directly upon the organized impulses of the affective-volitional systems. But above all these in importance, heightening and controlling and uniting these subordinate influences, are the rhythmic and metrical effects of word arrangements. If, as may reasonably be supposed, rhythms and especially metres have to a small degree an hypnotic effect, the very marked difference in evocative power between words so arranged and words without recurrent system is readily accounted for. Some degree of hyperæsthesia would be a convenient assumption to explain further the greater sensitiveness to vowel and consonantal characters which accompanies metrical reading, and the flat or tinny effect of the same syllables occurring in *vers libres*. Emotionality, exaggeration of belief-feelings, the occulting of the critical faculties, the suppression of the questioning—'Is this so as a matter of fact?'—attitude, all these are characteristics of metrical experiences and fit in well with a hypnosis assumption. When we add to these effects of metre, its powers of indirect representation (as the words 'swinging', 'rolling', 'heavy', 'rushing', 'broken', applied to rhythms indicate) its powers of directly controlling emotions (as the words 'lulling', 'stirring', 'solemn', 'gay' indicate) and its powers of unification (as at a low level its use as a mere mnemonic shows), we shall not be surprised to find it so extensively present in the evocative use of speech.

The indirect means of arousal which are possible through words need not be dwelt upon here at length. Through statement; through the excitement of imagery (often effected at low levels of refinement by the use of metaphor); through metaphor itself—used not, as in strict symbolizing, to bring out or stress a structural feature in a reference, but rather to provide, often under cover of a pretence of this elucidation, new sudden and striking collocations of references for the sake of the compound effects of contrast, conflict, harmony, interinanimation and equilibrium which may be so attained, or used more simply to modify and adjust emotional tone; through association; through revival; and through many subtle linkings of mnemic situations, words are capable of exerting profound influence quite apart from any assistance from the particular passions, needs, desires or circumstances of the hearer. With the further aid of these there is, as has often been illustrated in history, no limit to their evocative range.

The characteristic feature of these forms of evocation which occur in the arts, where severance from such personal particular circumstances is necessary for the sake of universality, is the constant mingling of direct and indirect means. The neglect or underestimation of the direct means available in poetry is, however, common in those who do not use the medium, and has often led to attempts to exclude poetry from the arts on the ground that its appeal is indirect only, through ideas, and not sensory in character. This contention is due merely to ignorance.

It is unfortunately very necessary to insist upon the importance of the distinction between these two functions of speech. Confusion between them leads to wrangles in which Intellect and Emotion, Reason and Feeling, Logic and Intuition, are set in artificial opposition to one another: though as is easily perceived, these two functions need not in any way trespass upon one another's provinces.[1] None the less, analogous sets of recording symbols have developed for each use—a Truth, Reality and Universality for symbolic speech and a Truth, Reality and Universality for evocative speech. This formal parallelism is very misleading, since the words Truth^{S} and Truth^{E} are totally distinct as symbols, the first being defined in terms of reference, while the second is equivalent to appropriate and genuine, and does not involve reference. It is unfortunate that devotees of literature should so often pass their whole active mental existence under the impression that through their antitheses of Intuition and Logic in this field they are contemplating a fundamental issue.

The chaos to which uncritical reliance upon speech has reduced this topic, together with so many others which rightly arouse intense interest, is by itself a powerful argument for the prosecution of the inquiry into Symbolism. When we remember the fruitless questionings and bewilderment caused by the irrelevancies and the intrinsic peculiarities of words, not only to children but to all who endeavour to pass beyond the mere exchange of accepted and familiar references, we

[1] For a fruitful application of the distinction in the treatment of disorders of speech, see Kinnier Wilson, *op. cit.*, *Aphasia* (1926), pp. 53-62.

shall not be tempted to think that the proposal seriously to investigate language must be either a joke or a form of pedantry—as those do who, having never been troubled by thought, have never found any difficulty in expressing it. The view that language gives rise to no such difficulties can be dispelled for all intelligent people either by observation or by personal experience. The opposite view that the difficulties are too formidable to be overcome, though more worthy of the human mind, must be rejected for similar reasons. What language already does, is the ground for hope that it may in time be made fully to perform its functions. To this end the Theory of Signs and Education must co-operate. No formal apparatus of Canons and Rules, no demands that abuses of language shall be reformed, will take effect, unless the habits which will enable language to be freely used are developed. What is required is not only strictness of definition and rigidity of expression, but also plasticity, ease and freedom in rapid expansion when expansion is needed. These abilities can only be developed through the training which at present is devoted to matters for whose understanding an adequate language is a prerequisite.

A new Science, the Science of Symbolism, is now ready to emerge, and with it will come a new educational technique. Language is the most important instrument we possess. At present we attempt to acquire and to impart a knowledge of its use by mimicry, by intuition, or by rule of thumb, in contented ignorance of its nature. It is not by his own efforts that the modern child is in so many ways better equipped than Aristotle; for such improvement must be the result of co-operative endeavour. Those who are not satisfied by the solutions of linguistic problems offered in these pages will, it is to be hoped, discover better. If, however, our claim to have provided a new orientation is a just one, the far-reaching practical results which we have discussed are already capable of attainment.

SUMMARY

At the close of a long discussion involving the detailed examination of many separate problems, elaborate examples of the application of method, historical illustrations and special criticisms of vicious tendencies, a brief outline of the main topics dealt with is desirable in order to give a general impression of the scope and task of the Science of Symbolism. Only by excluding all allusion to many subjects not less important than those here mentioned, can we avoid the loss of perspective inevitably entailed by the list of Contents to which the reader is referred.

1.—*Thoughts, Words and Things.*

The influence of language upon Thought is of the utmost importance. Symbolism is the study of this influence, which is as powerful in connection with everyday life as in the most abstruse speculation.

There are three factors involved when any statement is made, or interpreted.

1. Mental processes.
2. The symbol.
3. A referent—something which is thought 'of.'

The *theoretical* problem of Symbolism is—

How are these three Related?

The *practical* problem, since we must use words in discussion and argument, is—

> *How far is our discussion itself distorted by habitual attitudes towards words, and lingering assumptions due to theories no longer openly held but still allowed to guide our practice?*

The chief of these assumptions derives from the magical theory of the name as part of the thing, the theory of an inherent connection between symbols and referents. This legacy leads in practice to the search for *the* meaning of words. The eradication of this habit can only be achieved by a study of Signs in general, leading up to a referential theory of Definition by which the phantom problems resulting from such superstitions may be avoided. When these have been disposed of, all subjects become more accessible and more interesting.

2.—*The Power of Words.*

The magic of words has a special place in general magic. Unless we realize what have been the natural attitudes towards words until recent years we shall fail to understand much in the behaviour of logicians and others among modern mystics, for these same attitudes still persist in underground and unavowed fashion. At the same time the theory of signs can throw light upon the origins of these magical beliefs and their persistence.

3.—*Sign-situations.*

In all thinking we are interpreting signs.

In obvious cases this is readily admitted. In the more complex cases of mathematics and grammar more complicated forms of the same activity only are involved.

This is hidden from us by an uncritical use of symbols, favouring analyses of 'meaning' and 'thinking' which are mainly occupied with mirages due to 'linguistic refraction.'

We must begin therefore with Interpretation.

> Our Interpretation of any sign is our psychological reaction to it, as determined by our past experience in similar situations, and by our present experience.

If this is stated with due care in terms of causal contexts or correlated groups we get an account of judgment, belief and interpretation which places the psychology of thinking on the same level as the other inductive sciences, and incidentally disposes of the 'Problem of Truth.'

A theory of thinking which discards mystical relations between the knower and the known and treats knowledge as a causal affair open to ordinary scientific investigation, is one which will appeal to commonsense inquirers.

Sign-situations are always linked in chains and the simplest case of such a sign-chain is best studied in Perception.

4.—*Signs in Perception.*

The certainty of our knowledge of the external world has suffered much at the hands of philosophers through the lack of a theory of signs, and through conundrums made possible by our habit of naming things in haste without providing methods of identification.

The paradoxes of really round pennies which appear elliptical, and so forth, are due to misuses of symbols; principally of the symbol 'datum.'

What we 'see' when we look at a table is first, modifications of our retinæ. These are our initial signs. We interpret them and arrive at fields of vision, bounded by surfaces of tables and the like. By taking beliefs in these as second order signs and so on, we can proceed with our interpretation, reaching as results tables, wood, fibres, cells, molecules, atoms, electrons, etc. The later stages of this interpretative effort are physics. Thus there is no study called 'philosophy' which can add to or correct physics, though symbolism may contribute to a systematization of the levels of discourse at which 'table' and 'system of molecules' are the appropriate symbols.

The method by which confusions are to be extirpated in this field is required wherever philosophy has been applied. It rests partly upon the theory of signs, partly upon the Rules of Symbolization discussed in the next chapter.

5.—*The Canons of Symbolism.*

Underlying all communication, and equally fundamental for any account of scientific method, are the rules or conventions of symbolism.

Some of these are obvious enough when stated, but, perhaps for this reason, have been generally neglected. Others have been cursorily stated by logicians, concerned hitherto with a narrow range of traditional problems. When, however, all are fully set forth in the forms implied by systematic discourse, the solutions of many long-standing problems are found to be *de facto* provided.

Examples of such problems are those of Truth, Reality, Universals, Abstractions, Negative Facts, Virtuous Triangles, Round-squares and so forth.

The rules or postulates in question which most need formulation are Six in number, and appear as the *Canons of Symbolism.* They derive from the nature of mental processes, but, being required for the control of symbolization, are stated in terms of symbols and referents.

The observance of these Canons ensures a clear prose style, though not necessarily one intelligible to men of letters.

6.—*Definition.*

In any discussion or interpretation of symbols we need a means of identifying referents. The reply to the question what any word or symbol refers to consists in the substitution of a symbol or symbols which can be better understood.

Such substitution is Definition. It involves the selection of known referents as starting-points, and the identification of the definiendum by its connection with these.

The defining routes, the relations most commonly used for this purpose, are few in number, though specialists in abstract thought can employ others. In fact they may be pragmatically generalized under eight headings. Familiarity with these defining routes not only conduces to ease of deportment in reasoning and argument, but offers a means of escape from the maze of verbal cross-classifications which the great variety of possible view-points has produced.

7.—*The Meaning of Beauty.*

The application of this procedure in practice may be demonstrated by taking one of the most bewildering subjects of discussion, namely Æsthetics.

Beauty has been very often and very differently defined—and as often declared to be indefinable. If, however, we look for the characteristic defining relations, we find that the definitions hitherto suggested reduce conveniently to sixteen.

Each of these then provides a distinct range of referents, and any such range may be studied by those whom it attracts. If in spite of the disconcerting ambiguity thus revealed (and all freely-used terms are liable to similar ambiguity) we elect to continue to employ the term Beauty as a shorthand substitute for the definition we favour, we shall do so only on grounds of ethics and expediency and at the risk of all the confusions to which such behaviour must give rise.

In addition to its symbolic uses 'Beauty' has also its emotive uses. These have often been responsible for the view that Beauty is indefinable, since as an emotive term it allows of no satisfactory verbal substitute. Failure to distinguish between the symbolic and emotive uses is the source of much confusion in discussion and research.

8.—*The Meaning of Philosophers.*

Proceeding on the same principles to 'Meaning' itself, we find a widely divergent set of opinions in the writings of the best philosophers. The recent discussions in *Mind* and in *Brain* show the helplessness of expert disputants in dealing with the resultant ambiguities of the term. The procedure of the ables and most practical group of American thinkers, the Critical Realists of 1921, reveals the same incompetence, while the use made of the word by so influential an authority as Professor Münsterberg is equally open to objection. In fact, a careful study of the practice of prominent writers of all schools leads to the conclusion that in spite of a tacit assumption that the term is sufficiently understood, no principle governs its usage, nor does any technique exist whereby confusion may be avoided.

9.—*The Meaning of Meaning.*

When, however, the problem is scientifically approached, we find that no less than sixteen groups o definitions may be profitably distinguished in a field where the most rigid accuracy is desirable.

In other cases ambiguity may be fatal to the particular topic in which it occurs, but here such ambiguity even renders it doubtful what discussion itself is. For some view of 'meaning' is presupposed by every opinion upon anything, and an actual change of view on this point will for a consistent thinker involve change in all his views.

The definitions of Meaning may be dealt with under three headings. The first comprises Phantoms linguistically generated; the second groups and distinguishes Occasional and erratic usages; the third covers Sign and Symbol situations generally.

One interesting effect of such an exposition is that

it forces us for the time being to abandon the term 'meaning' itself, and to substitute either other terms, such as 'intention,' 'value,' 'referent,' 'emotion' for which it is being used as a synonym, or the expanded symbol which, contrary to expectation, emerges after a little trouble.

A careful study of these expansions leaves little room for doubt that what philosophers and metaphysicians have long regarded as an abstruse and ultimate notion, falling entirely within their peculiar domain and that of such descriptive psychologists as had agreed to adopt a similar terminology, has been the subject of detailed study and analysis by various special sciences for over half a century. During the last few years advances of biology, and the physiological investigation of memory and heredity have placed the 'meaning' of signs in general beyond doubt, and it is here shown that thought and language are to be treated in the same manner.

10.—*Symbol Situations.*

The first stage of the Development of Symbolism as a Science is thus complete, and it is seen to be the essential preliminary to all other sciences. Together with such portions of grammar and logic as it does not render superfluous it must provide both what has been covered by the title Philosophy of Mathematics, and what has hitherto been regarded as *Meta*-physics—supplementing the work of the scientist at either end of his inquiry.

All critical interpretation of Symbols requires an understanding of the Symbol situation, and here the main distinction is that between the condition in which reference is made possible only by symbols (Word-dependence) and that for which a free choice of symbols can be made (Word-freedom). The examination of language processes in their perfection or in their degeneration must also start from this distinction. It is further important to notice that words have further functions in addition to that of strict symbolization. The study of these evocative aspects leads naturally to an account of the resources of poetical language and of the means by which it may be distinguished, from symbolic or scientific statement. Thus the technique of Symbolism is one of the essential instruments of the æsthetics of literature.

Its practical importance will be found in its application to Education and to Discussion in general; for when the Influence of Language upon Thought is understood, and the Phantoms due to linguistic misconception have been removed, the way is open to more fruitful methods of Interpretation and to an Art of Conversation by which the communicants can enjoy something more than the customary stones and scorpions.

APPENDIX A

ON GRAMMAR

" Incomprehensible abstractions, pretentious yet for the most part empty definitions, false rules, indigestible lists of forms, one has only to turn over a few pages of any text book to find variegated specimens of these sins against reason, truth and education." These are strong words in which to condemn the bulk of modern grammatical teaching, but, as we have seen above in Chapter X. (p. 232), Professor Brunot, after fifteen years of further work on linguistic analysis since their publication,[1] found no reason to modify them. Considering the medley of verbal superstition, obsolete philosophy, and ill-comprehended logic, which we have found in the course of these pages doing duty for a theory of verbal function, it is not surprising that the best-informed philologists should feel that no words can be too strong for the grammatical fare on which the twentieth-century child is still nourished.

After giving examples of current grammatical classification, on which he remarks : " Oh ! ces classifications grammaticales ! Quels modèles pour les autres sciences ! " Brunot continues—

" Le même verbiage se remarquera dans l'analyse dite 'grammaticale.' Voici un modèle : *Ils enlevèrent tout ce qui s'y trouvait.*

Tout, adjectif indéfini, masculin singulier, détermine *ce* (!!) ;
ce, pronom démonstratif, mis pour : *le matériel* (!) complément direct de *enlevèrent ;*
qui, pronom relatif, ayant pour antécédent *ce*, 3me personne du singulier, sujet de *se trouvait ;*
s', mis pour *se*, pronom personnel (?!), 3me personne du singulier, *complément direct* (?!) de *trouvait.*

(*Courrier des examens* de 1908, p. 302).

" Que de beautés ! Un mot *indéfini*, qui cependant *détermine !*

[1] *L'Enseignement de la Langue Française*, p. 3.

un pronom *ce*, qui, nécessairement, remplace un nom sous-entendu! et le pronom de '*se trouvait,*' devenu *personnel*, et *complément direct!* Ce *matériel*, qu'on a imaginé, et qui finit par se trouver lui-même!!"

His final comment is: "A profound pity overcomes one in thinking of the hundreds of thousands of children compelled to undergo an education composed of such aberrations."[1]

It is with a view to the elimination of the most patent of these absurdities that the various Committees on Grammatical Terminology have been labouring in various countries since the 1906 conferences at the Musée pédagogique in Paris. The Recommendations of the English Committee were issued in 1911, and efforts are now being made by the various Language Associations to have them applied. In such an application, however, two distinct problems are involved. One is the elimination of outstanding absurdities in a grammatical terminology for any one language; and as to the desirability of a reformed terminology and the value of the work of the Committee in this respect, as far as it goes, there is little room for controversy. The other concerns "the importance of adopting from the first, in all grammar teaching, a terminology which should be capable of being employed, with the minimum of variation, for the purposes of any other language that is subsequently learnt."[2] It is true that "a uniform terminology brings into relief the principles of structure common to all allied languages; needless variation of terms conceals the substantial unity,"[3] but it must be remembered that insistence on supposed similarities of structure by Indo-European grammarians has been a chief hindrance to ethnologists in their study of primitive speech, that most vitally important branch of their subject. Within such a group of languages as that to which English belongs it is useful to have a system to mark similarities,[4] but there is always the risk that the uniformity

[1] *Ibid.*, p. 12.

[2] *Report of Government Committee on Classics*, p. 163.

[3] *Report of Government Committee on Modern Languages*, p. 55.

[4] Even here the danger of an historical approach is considerable. "I do not say one word against a uniform terminology," writes Professor Jespersen in the controversy to which reference is made at the end of this Appendix, "but I am strongly against that falsification of the facts of English grammar which is too often the consequence of the preoccupation with Latin grammar. . . . The Committee on Grammatical Terminology makes the five languages treated appear more similar than they are in reality. They speak of five cases in English, though the absurdity of this was seen clearly by Madvig as early as 1841. If it was the object of the Committee, as Professor Sonnenschein says, to simplify grammar, not to make it more complicated, they have here accomplished the very opposite of what they

thus stressed may come to be regarded as a necessity of all language, and indeed, of thought itself. It is then natural for these alleged necessities of expression to appear as reflections of the actual nature of the things spoken about themselves.

It is doubtful how far grammarians have explicitly considered the problem of the correspondence of word-symbols with things, as raised by Mr Bertrand Russell in his Introduction to Wittgenstein's *Tractatus Logico-Philosophicus*. Four problems as regards language are there enumreated :

"First, there is the problem what actually occurs in our minds when we use language with the intention of meaning something by it ; this problem belongs to psychology. Secondly, there is the problem as to what is the relation subsisting between thoughts, words, or sentences, and that which they refer to or mean ; this problem belongs to epistemology. Thirdly, there is the problem of using sentences so as to convey truth rather than falsehood ; this belongs to the special sciences dealing with the subject-matter of the sentences in question. Fourthly, there is the question : what relation must one fact (such as a sentence) have to another in order to be *capable* of being a symbol for that other ? This last is a logical question, and is the one with which Mr Wittgenstein is concerned. He is concerned with the conditions for *accurate* Symbolism, *i.e.*, for Symbolism in which a sentence 'means' something quite definite."

It is with the last of these four questions that we are here concerned and, whether with a full sense of its implications or not, the procedure of grammarians—in their treatment of subject and predicate, for instance—has often seemed tacitly to assume Wittgenstein's answer : "To the configuration of the simple signs in the propositional sign corresponds the configuration of the objects in the state of affairs."[1] This unplausible conclusion rests on the arbitrary identification of the indirect relation 'standing for,' discussed in our first chapter, with representation. "In order to be a picture a fact must have something in common with what it pictures" runs Prop. 2.16, and further 2.171, "The picture can represent every reality whose form it has . . . 2.182, Every picture is also a logical picture . . . 3, The logical picture of the facts is the thought . . . 3.1, In the proposition the thought is expressed perceptibly through the senses . . . 3.12, The sign through which we express the thought I call the

aimed at." It is unnecessary to take sides as to the classificatory or pedagogical merits of 'cases' in order to agree that philological discussion of the principle of uniformity has not been very profound.

[1] *Tractatus*, Prop. 3.21.

propositional sign. 3.2, In propositions thoughts can be so expressed that to the objects of the thoughts correspond the elements of the propositional sign." If every word must here be understood in a special sense, such an account of a symbol situation resembles the pronouncements of the Pre-Socratic aphorists ; yet to call it a ' logical ' and not a psychological account is, on the whole, an unconvincing apologetic.

Two steps are made in this argument. The first purports to secure a common structure in thoughts and things in order to explain how a thought can be ' of ' a thing. But on a causal theory this assumption of correspondence in structure is unnecessary and highly improbable.[1] The second step, the assertion of correspondence between the structure of the propositional sign and the structure of the facts is even more bold and baseless. In a simple case, as when we make diagrams and in such notations as those of chemistry and music, we can no doubt secure some degree of correspondence, because, as was pointed out in the chapter cited, the elements of such mimetic language approximate to simple signs. In the case of notations, it has been the deliberate effort of generations of scientists to force their symbols into simple correspondence with the things for which they are to stand. Again, in any primitive tongue there may come a time when, through the simplicity of the distinctions made by the race amongst the things surrounding them, their language will show an analogous set of distinctions. Here, however, the correspondence is through the correspondence of references to things and of kinds of words to kinds of references. But it is plain that such a language cannot keep pace with the additional distinctions in their thought and with its growing complexity. New kinds of words and new verbal structures would be desirable for new aspects and structures which they wish to distinguish. The old machinery, therefore, has to be strained and recourse is

[1] It is hardly less unplausible than the similar belief in a strict correspondence between words and thoughts, which appears frequently in the writings of the nineteenth-century philologists, and was, perhaps, stated most emphatically by Donaldson (*The New Cratylus*, p. 69) : " We find in the internal mechanism of language the exact counterpart of the mental phenomena which writers on psychology have so carefully collected and classified. We find that the structure of human speech is the perfect reflex or image of what we know of the organization of the mind : the same description, the same arrangement of particulars, the same nomenclature would apply to both, and we might turn a treatise on the philosophy of mind into one on the philosophy of language, by merely supposing that everything said in the former of the thoughts as subjective is said again in the latter of the words as objective."

had to fictitious entities, due to linguistic elements and structures no longer fulfilling their proper function but inadequately serving purposes for which they were not originally developed. Thus ' Energy ' in modern physics seems to be the wrong kind of word for the referents concerned, and no other word belonging to any of the recognized grammatical categories is likely to be better fitted. Hence some difficulties of the Quantum theory.

The attempt to generalize from the exceptional cases in which symbols and referents partially correspond, to a necessity for such correspondence in all communication is invalid. The extent of the correspondence in any given case can only be settled by an empirical inquiry ; but the result of such an inquiry is not doubtful. Such a correspondence may give to scientific symbol systems vastly increased scope and accuracy, and render them amenable to deductive processes ; but it can only be imposed when limited to the simplest and most schematic features, such as number or spatial relations. Ordinary language, as a rule, dispenses with it, losing in accuracy but gaining in plasticity, facility, and convenience. Nor is the loss so great as is sometimes supposed, for by straining language we are able to make and communicate references successfully, in spite of the misleading character of our symbols if taken literally.[1] For some, such as Wittgenstein himself, the possibility of this correspondence and the impossibility of doing more leads to a dissatisfaction with language ; and to an anti-metaphysical mysticism. For others, such as Bergson,[2] the alleged impossibility of this correspondence

[1] To take a metaphor or hypostatization 'literally' is to overlook the fact that a symbol or symbolic accessory is not occurring in its original use. Cf. Chapter V., *apud* Canon III.

[2] *Introduction to Metaphysic*, pp. 40-41. " Analysis operates always on the immobile, whilst intuition places itself in mobility, or, what comes to the same thing, in duration. There lies the very distinct line of demarcation between intuition and analysis. The real, the experienced and the concrete are recognized by the fact that they are variability itself, the element by the fact that it is invariable. And the element is invariable by definition, being a diagram, a simplified reconstruction, often a mere symbol, in any case a motionless view of the moving reality. . . . The error consists in believing that we can reconstruct the real with these diagrams."

In connection with these mystical doctrines and their linguistic justification, it is interesting to recall the scholastic problem : *an Deus nominabilis sit.* S. Bonaventura, not content with the dogma of the Fathers that the Deity could not be ' named,' advanced three reasons from the nature of language itself for the negative conclusion : (i) Nomen proportionem et similitudinem aliquam habet ad nominatum (but God is infinite and language finite) ; (ii) Omne nomen imponitur a forma aliqua (but God is without form) ; (iii) Omne nomen significat substantiam cum qualitate (but in God there is mere substance without quality).

based upon the assumed nature of reality, leads to a different kind of dissatisfaction ; and to a mystical metaphysics.

For the grammarian these ultimate issues may appear to be remote, but none the less he cannot have a view upon the relations of language with fact, or a basis for the discussion of true linguistic function in the sense defined in Chapter X. (which is, of course, different from the functions of words in sentence formation) without raising these issues.

We may consider, as a typical instance of a language function which has been supposed to be derived from a fundamental feature of reality, and to be capable of direct treatment by common sense without resort to a theory of reference, the problem of the proposition and the subject-predicate relation. Since all traditional views on this matter derive from Aristotle it is worth while to recall the way in which it was first approached. What is signified for Aristotle by words (whether single or in combination), says his clearest modern exponent, is some variety of mental affections[1] " or of the facts which they represent. But the signification of a term is distinguished in an important point from the signification of that conjunction of terms which we call a Proposition. A noun, or a verb, belonging to the aggregate called a language, is associated with one and the same phantasm or notion, without any conscious act of conjunction or disjunction, in the minds of speakers and hearers : when pronounced, it arrests for a certain time the flow of associated ideas, and determines the mind to dwell upon that particular group which is called its meaning. But neither the noun nor the verb, singly taken, does more than this ; neither one of them affirms, or denies, or communicates any information true or false. For this last purpose, we must conjoin the two together in a certain way, and make a Proposition. The signification of the Proposition is thus specifically distinct from that of either of its two component elements. It communicates what purports to be matter of fact, which may be either true or false ; in other words, it implies in the speaker, and raises in the hearer, the state of belief or disbelief, which does not attach either to the noun or to the verb separately. Herein the Proposition is discriminated from other significant arrangements of words (precative, interrogative, which convey no truth or falsehood), as well as from its own com-

[1] The scholastics in commenting on the *De Interpretatione,* where this reference to *passiones animæ* occurs, characteristically substituted *conceptiones intellectus* in the spirit of the Nominalist-Realist controversy (cf. Duns Scotus *D.I.*, III., § 3).

ponent parts. Each of these parts, noun and verb, has a significance of its own; but these are the ultimate elements of speech, for the parts of the noun or of the verb have no significance at all."[1]

In this statement may be found all the uncertainty and hesitation which since Aristotle's time have beset both grammarians and logicians. Notably the doubt whether words signify 'mental affections' or the facts which these 'represent,' and the confusion between the assertive character of the proposition (which is here used as equivalent to sentence) and the states of belief and disbelief which may occur in connection with it.

With the first source of confusion we have dealt at length, but the second demands further attention if it is to be avoided. Recent psychological research, especially into the nature of suggestion and into the effects of drugs upon the feelings, has done nothing to invalidate William James' view as to the relation of belief to reference. "In its inner nature, belief, or the sense of reality, is a sort of feeling more allied to the emotions than to anything else." Belief and disbelief as opposed to doubt are "characterized by repose on the purely intellectual side," and "intimately connected with subsequent practical activity."[2] Belief and disbelief, doubt and questioning, seem to be what nowadays would be called affective-volitional characteristics of mental states, and thus theoretically separable from the states to which they attach. The same reference, that is to say, may at one time be accompanied by belief and at another by disbelief or doubt. For this reason, so far as language is modified by the nature of the belief-feelings present, these modifications come under the heading of expression of attitude to referent, the third of the language functions distinguished in Chapter X.

This separation greatly assists a clear analysis of the most important character of the proposition, namely, the way in which it seems to symbolize assertion, to stand for a complete object of thought, a character lacking to the parts of a simple sentence. A noun by itself or a verb by itself somehow differs from the whole which is made up when they are suitably juxtaposed, and this difference has been the pivotal point upon which not merely grammatical analysis, but logic and philosophy have also turned ever since Aristotle s time.

The confusion has been further aggravated by the introduction of the problem of truth in an unsolved condition. Propositions have been almost universally regarded as the only objects to

[1] Grote, *Aristotle*, Vol. I., p. 157.
[2] *Principles of Psychology*, Vol. II., p. 284.

which the words 'true' and 'false' are properly applied; though this unanimity has been somewhat disguised by differences of view as to whether true propositions are those which express true beliefs or whether true beliefs are those whose objects are true propositions. In these controversies the various shifts of the symbol 'proposition', standing, as it does, at one time for a sentence, at another for a referent, and yet another for a relational character of a mental act or process, provide a fascinating field for the Science of Symbolism to explore. But in view of what has been said above in Chapter III. on the analysis of the differences which distinguish a complex symbol such as 'Snow chills' from the single symbols such as 'snow' and 'chills' which compose it, the apparent complications due to the introduction of truth raise no difficulty. They are merely a bewildering, because imperfectly parallel, re-naming of the problem.

According to the theory of signs all references, no matter how simple they may be, are either true or false, and no difference in this respect is to be found between the reference symbolized by 'snow' and that symbolized by 'snow chills.' This statement requires to be guarded from over-hasty interpretation. It is easy to use single words in such a way that they are not symbols, and so do not stand for anything. When this is done no doubt some stray images and other mental goings-on may be aroused, and if we are not careful in our use of 'meaning' we may then suppose that non-symbolic words so considered have meaning just as much and in the same sense as they do when present symbolically in a proposition. The single word, whether noun or verb, only has meaning in the sense here required, when taken in such a way that it enters a reference contest of the normal kind; and only so taken is it a symbolic (as distinguished from an emotive) component of a proposition. Any word so considered comes to be, *qua* symbol of a reference to some state of affairs, capable of truth and falsehood; and in this respect it differs in no way from a sentence used symbolically for purposes of statement.

We have yet to see, therefore, in what the marked difference between single words and sentences consists; and, as we should expect from the nature of the symbol situation, we find the difference to be not one but several, none of which is always or necessarily present although some may be said to be normally involved.[1] In the first place the references of the symbols will

[1] This multiple function of the noun-verb combination is recognized as an important feature for analysis by Sheffield (*Grammar and Thinking*,

often differ structurally. Thus the reference of ' larks sing,' since it has two components, will differ from that of ' larks ' just as do ' soaring larks ' or ' lark pie,' being also dual references. This difference is therefore unessential, though most complex references do in fact use the propositional form. One reason for the use of this form is because it is the normal means by which the togetherness of the component references is symbolized in cases where ambiguity is possible. Thus the sentence is the chief, but not the only symbolic device by which the togetherness of references is made plain. It is this which is usually described as the ' synthetic ' function of the proposition,[1] an unsatisfactory term, since verbal arrangements which are not of the propositional form, such as ' lark pie ', or ' this lark pie ' [2]—are equally synthetic. In logic the translation of all propositions into the subject-copula-predicate form has been a convention to avoid ambiguity, though modern logicians have found that more elaborate conventions are desirable for relational propositions.

But the sentence also serves emotively in various ways.[3] It is the conventional mode of *Address*, since listeners expect some special signal that a reference is occurring before they incline their ears cognitively. Further, it is the conventional verbal sign of the presence of *Belief*, of feelings of acceptance, rejection or doubt, in the speaker ; and a stimulus to similar feelings in the

p. 34), though his use of the word ' meaning ' may have obscured the value of his distinctions for the grammarians whom he criticizes.

[1] Cf. *e.g.*, Baldwin's treatment in *Thought and Things*, Vol. II., Experimental Logic, p. 262.

[2] Cf. C. Dickens, *Works*, Autograph Edition, 1903, Vol. I., p. 16.

[3] Subject and Predicate reappear at this point in the writings of the modern Leipzig glotto-psychologists, Professor Dittrich and his followers. For them the *Generalsubjekt* or *Protosubjekt* seems to correspond in great part with the Referent in our terminology, while the *Generalprädikat* or *Protoprädikat* is the attitude (assent, doubt, desire, or any other emotion) adopted towards this state of affairs. The *protosubjekt* is a constant (Dittrich, in his *Probleme*, p. 61), the *protoprädikat* a variant. In comparison with these two components, ' subject ' and ' predicate ' are regarded as secondary in character, ' noun ' and ' verb ' as tertiary. " Fall in Home Rails " is on this view a sentence, its *protosubjekt* is ' fall in Home Rails,' its *protoprädikat* a feeling of assent. The sentence would thus contain no expressed subject ; ' fall ' being regarded as an unindexing impersonal *prädikativum*. The reason why the subject of ' fall ' is not expressed is said to be because it is not of interest here ; and it must on this view be sought in all that is capable of falling, in the *Aussagegrundlage*. With these elaborations we are not here concerned, and the reader is referred to Appendix D and the work of Dittrich for the terminology of Gomperz, on which this system is based. It is sufficient to remark that this use of the traditional terms ' subject ' and ' predicate ' is likely to confuse those not well acquainted with the writings of this school. The new use has little in common with that already familiar.

hearer. It may, of course, also express intentions, desires, and so forth, on the part of the speaker that these attitudes shall be adopted by the hearer.

With this account of the sentence before us we may consider the traditional view both as to the distinction between noun and verb and as to the necessity of combining them in all assertion. There is some reason to suppose that in primitive languages the separation of verbs and nouns reflected the distinction between the actions of the speaker and the objects which surrounded him. At a later stage, by a natural formal analogy, this division in linguistic material was extensively used to mark the distinction between things or particulars and the states, qualities, and changes which 'belong' or 'happen' to these particulars. As has been argued, these supposed entities are in all cases of linguistic *provenance*, but this did not prevent the antithesis between particular and universal, thing and property, subject and predicate, substantive and adjective, noun and verb, confusedly named in all these forms, from appearing as the most fundamental with which thought could be concerned.[1] For Aristotle neither particular nor universal was separately conceivable, and it is not too much to see in his doctrine of the proposition an application of this metaphysic. On his assumption that words 'correspond' to reality, neither the noun alone, standing for a particular, nor the verb alone, standing for a universal could in itself have a complete 'meaning.' There could be no better instance of the influence both of the belief that different words and word-arrangements must stand for different kinds of referents, and of the belief that different kinds of referents require different kinds of words. Both these assumptions we have seen to be unfounded.

But even should the truth of the above contentions be granted, the moral, it may be said, is surely that grammarians should avoid all commerce with fundamentals and confine themselves to so-called 'common sense' classifications. It must, however, be remembered that 'common sense' in matters of linguistic is itself only an elaborate and confused theory, some of whose tenets figure in our second chapter. Moreover, the current distinctions as well as the terminology which the grammarian proposes to employ are the legacy not only of Aristotelian dogma,

[1] Thus Sapir is voicing a view very prevalent amongst philologists, when he writes, as though dealing with some ultimate characteristic of the universe, "There must be something to talk about and something must be said about this subject of discourse once it is selected. . . . The subject of discourse is a noun. . . . No language wholly fails to distinguish noun and verb" (*op. cit.*, p. 126).

but of that "Century of metaphysical syntax," which, as Professor Hale has pointed out,[1] followed on the application of the Kantian theory of Categories to Grammar by Hermann in 1801. Since, therefore, a searching inquiry into the psychology of language cannot in any case be avoided, if more is to result from an ancient and honoured science than the mere standardization of a score or so of convenient names for groups of words, it is important that the issue should be squarely faced. We would by no means belittle the serious endeavour of grammarians to produce a certain order out of the present chaos, or underestimate the time and energy which go to achieve this end. The division of opinion between two of the first authorities in Europe manifested recently[2] as to the legitimacy of the terms 'subjunctive-equivalent' and 'future in the past' (recommended in the *Report of the Committee on Grammatical Terminology*, pp. 35-6) in elucidation of the sentence 'I should write to him if I knew his address', is, however, a good instance of the kind of nomenclature which is being evolved. But granted that a respectable nomenclature can be extracted from the litter of scholastic vocables now in use, what would have been achieved? We should not have done more than *name* the principal forms of speech, and this clearly would not justify the present restriction of Grammar to the learning of these names and to the acquisition of respect for the standard usage of the locutions named. What is wrong with Grammar is not its defective terminology but the lack of interest displayed by Grammarians in the less arid and familiar portions of the field which it professes to cover. It is for this reason that dissatisfaction with Grammar is so prevalent, and if as a 'subject' it is not to disappear from the curriculum, and with it all theoretical study of language as an instrument of communication, its reform must not be delayed too long.[3]

The understanding of the functions of language, of the many

[1] St Louis Congress (1904) *Proceedings*. Cf. the same author's "The Heritage of Unreason in Syntactical Method" in the Classical Association's *Proceedings*, 1907.

[2] See Professor Jespersen's letter in controversy with Professor Sonnenschein (*Times Literary Supplement*, June 29, 1922, p. 428). This writer's *Philosophy of Grammar* (1925) unfortunately fails to discuss any of the more fundamental problems raised by a psychological approach to language, and especially the critical aspects of language reform.

[3] A suggestive attempt to avoid the whole apparatus of grammatical terminology in teaching by the use of diagrams has been made by Miss Isabel Fry, in *A Key to Language* (1925). The method might profitably be extended to the more difficult problems of language analysis here discussed.

ways in which words serve us and mislead us, must be an essential aim of all true education. Through language all our intellectual and much of our social heritage comes to us. Our whole outlook on life, our behaviour, our character, are profoundly influenced by the use we are able to make of this, our chief means of contact with reality. A loose and insincere use of language leads not only to intellectual confusion but to the shirking of vital issues or the acceptance of spurious formulæ. Words were never a more common means than they are to-day of concealing ignorance and persuading even ourselves that we possess opinions when we are merely vibrating with verbal reverberations.

How many grammarians still regard their science as holding the keys of knowledge ? It has become for them too often merely a technical exercise of strictly limited scope, instead of the inspiring study of the means by which truth is acquired and preserved. No doubt the founders of the science sufficiently misconceived the actual powers of language, but they realized its importance. We have examined in the course of our study the means by which we may be put on our guard against the pitfalls and illusions due to words. It should be the task of Grammar to prepare every user of symbols for the detection of these. Training in translation (p. 107), and above all in expansion (p. 93) ; in the technique of substitution (p. 113), and the methods of preventing and removing misunderstanding at different levels (p. 222) ; in the discrimination of symbolic from emotive words and locutions (p. 149) ; and in the recognition of the five main functions of language (p. 224)—all are amongst the indispensable preliminaries for the right use of language as a means of communication, and consequently the business of Grammar.

APPENDIX B

ON CONTEXTS

For a simple case of expectation, when both sign and referent are sensations, the causal theory of reference outlined in Chapter III., pp. 54 ff.—see especially pp. 56 and 62—may be stated as follows :—

Let *i* be a mental process or occurrence.

If, now, there preceded *i* a sensation *s* (*e.g.*, a sound), such that :—

> *s* has some character *S* (*e.g.*, being a harsh sound) which is a constitutive character of 'Proximity' contexts (dual in this case) determinative in respect of their other constitutive character *F* (being a flaring sensation) and (denoting members of such contexts by s_1, f_1, s_2, f_2 . . .)
> s_1, f_1, s_2, f_2 . . . *s*, *i*,
> form in virtue of characters *S*, *F*, *S*, *F*. . . . *S*, *I* a context determinative in respect of *I*,

then *i* is said to be an ***interpretation*** of *s* in respect of *S*, and *I* is said to be its character relevant to *s*, and *s* is said to be a *Sign*. In this case *i* is a belief that something will happen which is a flaring sensation and in proximity with *s*.

Now if there be anything (say *f*) which forms with *s* in virtue of *SF* a Proximity context determinative in respect of *s*, then *f* is said to be the *Referent* of *i qua* interpretation of *s* in this respect. It will be noticed that *f* has by definition the character *F* and is in proximity with *s*.

If there be something having these properties, then *i* is said to be a *true* interpretation of *s* in respect of *S* ; but if there be nothing with the required properties, then *i* is said to be a *false* interpretation in the same respect.

In more informal language, when, as a result of hearing a match scrape, we expect a flame sensation, our belief is a process which is a member of a psychological context united by a multiple mnemic relation, among whose other members are past sensations of scrapes and flames, themselves united in dual contexts by the relation of proximity. If now the scrape is related by this relation to a flame, our belief is true ; this sensation is the referent of our belief. If there is no flame to which the scrape is so related our belief is false. We have discussed (p. 71) what, if anything, may be said to be the referent in this case.

For those who find diagrams of service in considering complicated matters, the following depiction of the above account is not misleading and throws some light upon additional complexities not there included. The central dotted line separates psychological from external contexts ; brackets and continuous lines indicate contexts ; s, f, etc., stand for stimuli. *s*, *f*, etc., for corresponding sensations :—

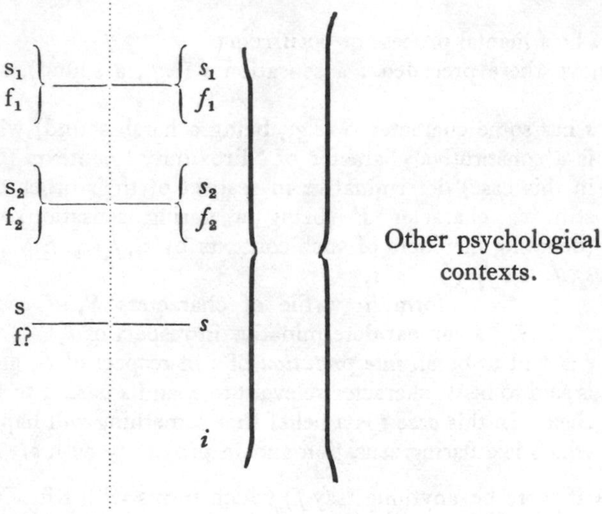

It will be noticed that the above account deals merely with contexts whose members are sensations. In the diagram 'stimulus-sensation' contexts are also included. Any actual instances of interpretation will naturally be far more complicated than any account or diagram which can be put on paper. The bracket including other psychological contexts indicates one reason for this. There must be some sense in which one context can be said to be dependent upon others. To take a concrete instance, the action of a penny-in-the-slot machine may be treated as a simple dual context (insertion of penny—appearance of chocolate) provided that certain vast multiple contexts involving the growth of the cocoa-tree, the specific gravity of copper, and the regular inspection of the contrivance recur uniformly. Psychology is throughout concerned with similar situations, but it is less easy to analyse the contexts involved in this fashion. It is peculiarly difficult, indeed, in Psychology to discover contexts whose members are few in number. Even a stimulus-sensation context, in order to be determinative in respect of the character of the sensation, must ordinarily include other psychological members, amongst which will be other sensations and the conditions to which we allude when we use the word 'attention.'

APPENDIX C

AENESIDEMUS' THEORY OF SIGNS

WHAT we know of the views of Aenesidemus is derived chiefly from brief references in the writings of Sextus Empiricus; but the fourth book of his lost work Πυῤῥωνίων λόγοι was devoted to the Theory of Signs. The main arguments are summarized by Sextus in §§ 97-134 of his Hypotheses, though it is not always clear how much has been added by Sextus himself.

According to Photius,[1] Aenesidemus held that invisible things cannot be revealed by visible signs, and a belief in such signs is an illusion. This is confirmed by a passage in Sextus,[2] which shows that the views of the Epicureans are here being attacked. The argument is thus expounded:—

"If phenomena appear in the same way to all observers who are similarly constituted, and if, further, signs are phenomena, then the signs must appear in the same way to all observers similarly constituted. This hypothetical proposition is self-evident; if the antecedent be granted the consequent follows. Now, continues Sextus, (1) phenomena do appear in the same way to all observers similarly constituted. But (2) signs do not appear in the same way to all observers similarly constituted. The truth of proposition (1) rests upon observation, for though, to the jaundiced or bloodshot eye, white objects do not appear white, yet to the normal eye, *i.e.*, to all observers similarly constituted, white objects invariably do appear white. For the truth of proposition (2) the art of medicine furnishes decisive instances. The symptoms of fever, the flush, the moisture of the skin, the high temperature, the rapid pulse, when observed by doctors of the like mental constitution, are not interpreted by them in the same way. Here Sextus cites some of the conflicting theories maintained by the authorities of his age. In these symptoms Herophilus

[1] *Biblioth.*, 170, p. 12.
[2] *Adv. Math.*, VIII., 215 sqq.

sees a mark of the good quality of the blood; for Erasistratus they are a sign of the passage of the blood from the veins to the arteries; for Asclepiades they prove too great tension of corpuscles in interspaces, although both corpuscles and interspaces, being infinitesimally small, cannot be perceived by sense but only apprehended by the intellect. Sextus, having borrowed this argument from Aenesidemus, has developed it in his own fashion, and is probably himself responsible for the medical instances which he has selected."[1]

Sextus, however, is not content with disproving the Epicurean account of signs as sensible objects. He goes on to attack the view of the Stoics, and to show that they cannot be apprehended by reason or intellect. Aenesidemus himself may not have gone beyond the demonstration that (in the words of Photius) "there are no signs, manifest and obvious, of what is obscure and latent," and there are those who think it probable that Sextus himself was chiefly responsible for the distinction familiar to the later Sceptics between two classes of signs—signs 'commemorative' and signs 'demonstrative.'[2] According to this distinction "there are signs which act, as we should say, by the law of association, reminding us that in past experience two phenomena were conjoined, as smoke with fire, a scar with a wound, a stab to the heart with subsequent death. If afterward one of the two phenomena is temporarily obscured and passes out of immediate consciousness, the other, if present, may serve to recall it; we are justified in calling the one which is present a sign, and the other, which is temporarily absent, the thing signified. With the term 'sign,' as thus understood, the sign commemorative or reminiscent, Sextus has no quarrel. By its aid prediction is justified; we can infer fire from smoke, the wound from the scar, approaching death from the fatal stab, for in all these cases we proceed upon past experience. Sextus reserves his hostility for another class of signs which we may call the sign demonstrative. When one of two phenomena assumed to be the thing signified never has occurred in actual experience but belongs wholly, by its own nature, to the region of the unknown, the dogmatists nevertheless maintained that, if certain conditions were fulfilled, its existence was indicated and demonstrated by the other phenomenon, which they called the sign. For instance, according to the dogmatists, the movements of the body indicate and demon-

[1] R. D. Hicks, *Stoic and Epicurean*, p. 390.

[2] *Ibid.*, p. 391: the source being *Pyrrh. Hyp.*, II., 100; cf. the context, 99-102; *Adv. Math.*, VIII., 148-158.

strate the existence of the soul ; they are its sign. It is ' sign ' then, in this latter sense, the indicative or demonstrative sign, whose existence Sextus disputes and undertakes to refute."

If such an interpretation of their views is correct it is clear that with their account of reminiscent signs the Sceptics came very near to formulating a modern theory of scientific induction, while their scepticism about demonstrative signs amounts to a denial of the possibility of inferring to the transcendental. Given a fact, or as the Stoics called it, a ' sign,' we cannot determine *a priori* the nature of the thing signified. That the main terms in which the discussion was conducted suffered from confusions which still haunt their modern equivalents, is not surprising ; there can be no signs of things to which we cannot refer, but things can be referred to which are not experienced.

When the excavation of Herculaneum is accomplished, the lost treatise of Philodemus on the Epicurean theory of signs and inference which is likely to become available, together with other similar documents relative to this remarkable controversy, may throw more light on the progress which had been made in these early times towards a rational account of the universe ; and so enable us to realize something of what a healthy scepticism might have achieved had theological interests not so completely dominated the next fifteen hundred years.

APPENDIX D

SOME MODERNS

THOSE unfamiliar with the literature of Meaning will find it difficult to realize how strange and conflicting are the languages which the most distinguished thinkers have thought fit to adopt in their attempts to deal with Signs, Symbols, Thoughts and Things. In our eighth chapter sundry examples were given with a brevity which, though necessary, may have inclined the fair-minded to question whether there has not been an occasional injustice. We therefore append more lengthy examples, which can be judged on their merits, from the pens of the most eminent specialists who have dealt with the question in recent years. It is hoped by this means to justify the assertion made at the outset that a fresh approach was necessary.

§1. *Husserl*

We may begin with what is perhaps the best known modern attempt to deal comprehensively with the problem of Signs and Meaning, that of Professor Edmund Husserl. And it is important for the understanding of Husserl's terminology to realize that everything he writes is developed out of the " Phenomenological Method and Phenomenological Philosophy " which he has been elaborating since 1910, as Professor of Philosophy, first at Göttingen and later at Freiburg. In June, 1922, in a course of lectures at London University, he gave an exposition of his system to a large English audience, and the following sentences are taken from the explanatory *Syllabus* in which he, or his official translator, endeavoured to indicate both his method and his vocabulary.

> " There has been made possible and is now on foot, a new *a priori* science extracted purely from concrete phenomenological intuition (*Anschauung*), the science, namely, of transcendental phenomenology, which inquires into the totality of ideal possibilities that fall within the framework

> of phenomenological subjectivity, according to their typical forms and laws of being.
>
> In the proper line of its explication lies the development of the originally ' egological ' (referred to the ego of the philosophizing subject for the time being) phenomenology into a transcendental sociological phenomenology having reference to a manifest multiplicity of conscious subjects communicating with one another. A systematically consistent development of phenomenology leads necessarily to an all-comprehensive logic concerned with the correlates ; knowing-act, knowledge-significance, knowledge-objectivity."

And as one of his conclusions Husserl explains that " the transcendental monadism, which necessarily results from the retrospective reference to absolute subjectivity, carries with it a peculiar *a priori* character over against the constituted objectivities, that of the essence-requirements of the individual monads and of the conditions of possibility for a universe of ' compossible ' monads. To this ' metaphysical ' inquiry there thus belongs the essence-necessity of the ' harmonious accord ' of the monads through their relation to an objective world mutually constituted in them, the problems of teleology, of the meaning of the world and of the world's history, the problem of God."

Such are the formulæ through which Husserl desired his system to be approached, and in the narrower field of Meaning the selection of essentials has similarly been undertaken by his disciple, Professor J. Geyser, of the University of Münster, in his *Neue und alte Wege der Philosophie*, which is devoted to a summary of Husserl's main contributions to the theory of knowledge in the *Logische Untersuchungen*, and *Ideen zu einer reinen Phenomenologie*.

According to Husserl, the function of expression is only directly and immediately adapted to what is usually described as the *meaning* (Bedeutung) or the *sense* (Sinn) of the speech or parts of speech. Only because the meaning associated with a word-sound expresses something, is that word-sound called ' expression ' (*Ideen*, p. 256 f). " Between the *meaning* and the *what is meant*, or what it expresses, there exists an *essential relation*, because the *meaning* is the expression of the *meant* through its own content (Gehalt). What is meant (dieses Bedeutete) lies in the ' object ' of the thought or speech. We must therefore distinguish these three—Word, Meaning, Object." [1]

[1] Geyser, *op. cit.*, p. 28.

The *object* is that about which the expression says something, the *meaning* is what it says about it. The statement is therefore related to the object by means of its meaning. But Husserl maintains explicitly: " The object never coincides (*zusammenfällt*) with the meaning " (*L.U.*, II., i., p. 46). He bases this assertion on the fact " that several expressions can have the same meaning, but different objects, and again, different meanings, but the same object " (*Ibid.*, p. 47). " The two expressions ' equiangular and equilateral triangle ' have for example a different *meaning*, but name the same object. Conversely a different object but the same meaning is signified when Bucephalus and a cart-horse are described as ' horse.' The meaning of an expression becomes an object only when an act of thought turns towards it reflectively."[1]

The sense of the expression ' meaning ' which, according to Geyser (p. 33) is as a rule synonymous with ' concept ' (was meist als Begriff bezeichnet wird), Husserl illustrates by the comparison of two cases. In the perception of a white object, we can be satisfied by perceiving it and eventually distinguishing something or other in it. For this function, expression and meaning are not necessary. But we can also pass on to the thought: " This is white." The perceiver has now added to the perceiving a mental act, which *expresses*, *means* the thing perceived and the thing distinguished in what is perceived, that is to say, the objective. The expression is therefore, to state the matter generally, a form which raises the sense " into the kingdom of the ' Logos ' of the *conceptual* and thereby the ' general ' " (*Ideen*, p. 257). The function of the expression, of this peculiar intention, " *exhausts itself in expressing*, and that with this newly entering *form of the conceptual* " (*Ibid.*, p. 258). Further, ' expressing ' is an imitative, and not a productive function.

By the words ' expression ' and ' meaning,' Husserl describes in the first place concepts, but also judgments and conclusions: " Pure logic, wherever it deals with concepts, judgments, conclusions, has in fact to do exclusively with these *ideal* unities, which we here call *meanings* " (*L.U.*, II., i., p. 916). In general, it is " evident that logic must be knowledge of meanings as such, of their essential kinds and differences, as well as of the laws purely grounded in them (that is to say *ideal*). For to these essential distinctions belong also those between meanings, with and without objects, true and false. . . . " (*Ibid.*, p. 92). All thought has a certain appropriate range of acts of expressing or meaning, which are neither identical with the sensory word nor

[1] Geyser, *op. cit.*, p. 29.

with the objects of cognition. " It is not easy to realize clearly that actually after abstraction of the sensory word-sound stratum, a stratification is found of the kind that we suppose here ; that is to say in every case—even in that of unclear, empty, and merely verbal thought—a stratum of expressing meaning and a sub-stratum of expressed. Still less easy is the understanding of the essential connections of these strata " (*Ideen*, p. 259).

Husserl proceeds to distinguish between what he calls ' meaning-intentions ' (Bedeutungsintentionen) and ' realized meanings ' (erfüllte Bedeutungen) ; between ' meaning-conferring ' and ' meaning-realizing ' acts (*L.U.*, i., p. 38) ; and between the psychological and objective-phenomenological treatment of meaning.[1] Phenomenologically, when we ask the meaning of the expression ' prime-number ' we refer to (meinen) this expression in itself and as such, not in its particularity (Besonderheit), as it is spoken by a given individual in a lecture, or as it is found in such and such a book written in such and such a way. Rather we simply ask : What does *the* expression ' Prime-number ' mean ? Similarly we do not ask what at this or that moment was the meaning of the expression thought and experienced by such and such a man ; we ask in general about its meaning as such and in itself. Husserl expresses this state of affairs by saying that in such questions it is a matter of the expression and the meaning ' in specie,' ' as species,' ' as idea,' ' as ideal unity ' ; for what is referred to is *one and the same meaning*, and one and the same expression, however these may be thought or spoken (*L.U.*, II., i., p. 42 f). Hence : Meanings, ideal objects, must have being, since we predicate truly of them—as when we say that four is an even number (*Ibid.*, p. 125) ; but their existence does not depend on their being thought. They have eternal, ideal, existence.[2] " What Meaning is can be given to us as immediately as colour and tone. It cannot be further defined ; it is a descriptive ultimate. Whenever we complete or understand an expression, it means something to us and we are actually conscious of its sense." Distinctions between meanings are also directly given, and we can classify these in the Phenomenology of meaning, as ' symbolic-empty ' ' intuitively realized,' etc. ; such operations as identification and distinction, relating, and generalizing abstraction, give us " the fundamental logical concepts, which are nothing but ideal conceptions of the primitive distinctions of meaning " (*Ibid.*, p. 183).

[1] Geyser, p. 22.
[2] *Ibid.*, p. 36.

§2. *Bertrand Russell*

Mr Russell's best known view (which must now, however, be read in connection with his more acceptable psychological account discussed in our third chapter, and with his *Monist* articles 1918-1919) is to be found at page 47 of his *Principles of Mathematics*. He is there concerned with the connection of his doctrine of adjectives with certain traditional views on the nature of propositions, and with the theory of Bradley [1] " that all words stand for ideas having what he calls *meaning*, and that in every judgment there is a something, the true subject of the judgment," which is not an idea and does not have *meaning*. " To have meaning," says Mr Russell, " is a notion confusedly compounded of logical and psychological elements. *Words* all have meaning, in the simple sense that they are symbols which stand for something other than themselves. But a proposition, unless it happens to be linguistic, does not itself contain words : it contains the entities indicated by words. Thus meaning, in the sense in which words have meaning, is irrelevant to logic. But such concepts as *a man* have meaning in another sense : they are, so to speak, symbolic in their own logical nature, because they have the property which I call *denoting*. That is to say, when *a man* occurs in a proposition (*e.g.*, ' I met a man in the street '), the proposition is not about the concept *a man*, but about something quite different, some actual biped denoted by the concept. Thus concepts of this kind have meaning in a non-psychological sense. And in this sense, when we say ' this is a man ', we are making a proposition in which a concept is in some sense attached to what is not a concept. But when meaning is thus understood, the entity indicated by *John* does not have meaning, as Mr Bradley contends ; and even among concepts, it is only those that denote that have meaning. The confusion is largely due, I believe, to the notion that *words* occur in propositions, which in turn is due to the notion that propositions are essentially mental and are to be identified with cognitions."

§3. *Frege*

Frege's theory of Meaning is given in his *Begriffsschrift*, *Grundlagen der Arithmetik* and his articles on " Begriff und Gegenstand," and " Sinn und Bedeutung." A convenient summary, which we here follow, is given at p. 502 of his *Principles* by Mr Russell, who holds that Frege's work " abounds in subtle

[1] *Logic*, Book I., Chapter I., §§ 17, 18 (pp. 58-60).

distinctions, and avoids all the usual fallacies which beset writers on Logic." The distinction which Frege makes between meaning (*Sinn*) and indication (Bedeutung) is roughly, though not exactly, equivalent to Mr Russell's distinction between a concept as such and what the concept denotes (*Principles*, §96). Frege did not possess this distinction in the first two of the works under consideration ; but it makes its appearance in *B.u.G.*, and is specially dealt with in *S.u.B.* Before making the distinction, he thought that identity had to do with the names of objects (*Bs.*, p. 13): " A is identical with B " means, he says, that the sign A and the sign B have the same signification (*Bs.*, p. 15)—a definition which, in Mr Russell's view, " verbally at least, suffers from circularity." But later he explains identity in much the same way as Mr Russell did in the *Principles*, §64. " Identity," he says, " calls for reflection owing to questions which attach to it and are not quite easy to answer. Is it a relation ? A relation between Gegenstände or between names or signs of Gegenstände ? " (*S.u.B.*, p. 25). We must distinguish, he adds, the meaning, in which is contained the way of being given, from what is indicated (from the *Bedeutung*). Thus ' the evening star ' and ' the morning star ' have the same indication, but not the same meaning. A word ordinarily stands for its indication ; if we wish to speak of its meaning, we must use inverted commas or some such device. The indication of a proper name is the object which it indicates ; the presentation which goes with it is quite subjective; between the two lies the meaning, which is not subjective and yet is not the object. A proper name *expresses* its meaning, and *indicates* its indication.

" This theory of indication," adds Mr Russell, " is more sweeping and general than mine, as appears from the fact that *every* proper name is supposed to have the two sides. It seems to me that only such proper names as are derived from concepts by means of *the* can be said to have meaning, and that such words as *John* merely indicate without meaning. If one allows, as I do, that concepts can be objects and have proper names, it seems fairly evident that their proper names, as a rule, will indicate them without having any distinct meaning ; but the opposite view, though it leads to an endless regress, does not appear to be logically impossible."

§4. *Gomperz*

The view of H. Gomperz is developed in Vol. II. of his

Weltanschauungslehre (1908), Part I. of which is devoted to Semasiology. It is adopted by Professor Dittrich in his *Probleme der Sprach-psychologie* (1913), on whose exposition the following summary is based :—

In every complete statement (Aussage) we can distinguish: A. The *sounds* (Aussage-laute), *i.e.*, the verbal form of the statement, or better the *phonesis* (Lautung); B. The *import* (Aussage-inhalt), *i.e.*, the *sense* (Sinn) of the statement; C. The foundation (Aussagegrundlage), *i.e.*, the *actual fact* (Tatsache) to which the statement is related. The relations between these three elements can be thus characterized : the sounds (phonesis) are the *expression* (Ausdruck) of the import, and the designation (Bezeichnung) of the foundation, while the import is the *interpretation* (Auffassung) of the foundation. In so far as the sounds are treated as the expressions of the import they are grouped with the statement (Aussage). In so far as the foundation is treated as the fact comprehended by the import, it can be called the *stated fact* (ausgesagte Sachverhalt); or simply, the fact. The relation subsisting between the statement and the fact expressed is called *Meaning* (Bedeutung).[1]

According to Gomperz the sounds which correspond to a full statement, such as " This bird is flying," have a fivefold representative function. The statement, as sound, can thus be considered under five headings :—

1. It represents itself, *qua* mere noise, as perceived by anyone unacquainted with the language.

2. It represents the state of affairs (Tatbestand), ' This bird is flying,' the sense for whose expression it is normally used, the import of the thought which is thought by everyone who enunciates it or hears it.

3. It further represents the fact, ' This bird is flying,' *i.e.*, every bit of reality which can be comprehended by the thought ' This bird is flying ' and denoted by that sound. (This may be very various—a starling, or an eagle, or merely ' Something is moving ').

4. It represents the proposition, ' This bird is flying ' as a significant utterance, wherein the sound, which thus becomes a linguistic sound, expresses the sense or state of affairs ' This bird is flying,' and together with that sense forms the statement.

5. It represents the fact (Sachverhalt) stated in the proposition, which is characteristically distinguished both from the foundation and from the import. " The proposition does not merely state

[1] Gomperz, *loc. cit.*, p. 61.

that a bit of physical reality is present which can be thought of as the possessing of a property or as a process, as active or passive, etc. But it states that a physical process is taking place in which an active object, viz., a bird, an activity (flying), and an immediate presence of that object denoted by 'this,' are to be distinguished. In other words, what the proposition states is 'the flying of this bird.' This is equally a bit of physical reality, but one of univocal articulation. It is not only in general a bit of physical reality, but more precisely a physical process, and quite specifically a physical activity: but these are mere predicates which could not have been stated of the sounds as such. . . . In other words, the foundation can be the same for the three propositions. 'This bird is flying,' 'This is a bird,' and 'I see a living creature,' whereas the fact expressed by these three propositions is different on each occasion. For in the first what it states is the 'flying of *this* bird,' in the second the 'being-a-bird of *this*,' and in the third 'the seeing of a living creature by *me*.' If, then, the foundation of these propositions can be one and the same, while the fact stated is not one and the same, the fact cannot possibly coalesce with the foundation." Nor must the fact be identified with the import or sense (Inhalt oder Sinn), "which is not something physical, but a group of logical determinations (Bestimmungen)."

From all this, says Dittrich, the peculiarly relational character of that element of the statement named *meaning* results. Meaning cannot be identified with mere designation (Bezeichnung). One and the same sound, *e.g.*, 'top' can, he urges, designate very different foundations; and if, with Martinak, we confine meaning to the relation between the sign and what is designated, we cannot reach a satisfactory definition. Interpretation (Auffassung) may similarly be a many-one relation; moreover to use the term meaning for that relation would omit the linguistic element. Nor can meaning be identified with the relation of expression (Ausdruck). Finally, Meaning appears as a definite but complex relation, based on the theory of 'total-impressions' (Totalimpression) and common emotional experiences which distinguishes the pathempiricists.[1] "Any sound whatever can

[1] As regards this view, Dr E. H. F. Beck, whose treatise on *Die Impersonalien* (1922) is an application of the Gomperz-Dittrich analysis and to whom we are indebted for certain of the English equivalents given above, writes to us as follows: "The accent falls on the Gesamteindrucksgefühl. Speaker and hearer have in common certain emotional experiences which have a common object and common reflexes. In every effective communication the reflex—whether

designate any foundation ; but it can only *mean* when it becomes a *statement* through the constitution of a general-typical import, and that becomes the foundation (Grundlage) for a fact (Sachverhalt)." [1]

§5. *Baldwin*

Professor Baldwin's mode of treating the problem of Meaning is best studied in his *Thought and Things*. Vol. II. of this work deals with what he calls 'Experimental Logic,' and Chapter VII. is devoted to the Development of Logical Meaning. "Our most promising method of procedure would seem to be to take the various modes or stages in the development of predication, and to ask of each in turn as to its structural or recognitive meaning, its 'what'— that is, *what it now means*, as an item of contextuated and socially available information. The 'what' is the subject-matter of judgment. Having determined this, we may then inquire into the instrumental use of such a meaning: the 'proposal' that the meaning when considered instrumentally suggests or intends. This latter we may call the question of the 'why' of a meaning: the for-what-purpose or end, personal or social, the meaning is available for experimental treatment. If we use the phrase 'selective thinking,' as we have above, for the entire process whereby meanings grow in the logical mode—the process of 'systematic determination' sketched in the preceding chapter —then we may say that every given meaning is both predication *as* elucidation *of* a proposal, and predication *as* a proposal *for* elucidation. It is as his elucidation that the believer proposes it to another; it is as proposal that the questioner brings it to the hearer for his elucidation. We may then go forward by this method. . . ."

In §10, forty pages later, we "gather up certain conclusions already reached in statements which take us back to our fundamental distinction between Implication and Postulation," as follows :—

> "Implication was defined as meaning so far fixed and reduced by processes of judgment that no hypothetical or problematic intent was left in it. Implication, in other

phonesis, gesture, or written symbol—re-instates the common (typical-general) emotional experience which is referred back to its foundation. The sign—which term, on account of its wider range, might replace phonesis—is therefore the causa cognoscendi proximately of a certain emotional state and ultimately its foundation."

[1] Dittrich, *op. cit.*, p. 52.

> words, is simply meaning by which belief, the attitude of acknowledgment in judgment is rendered. Under this heading, we find two sorts of meaning: first, that which is subject-matter of predication, the content of thought; and second, that which is presupposition of judgment, the control sphere in which the predication holds or is valid. . . ."

Later (p. 299) the question arises: "In what sense can a meaning that is universal as respects community still be singular?" And the answer is as follows: "That it does banish singular meaning from the logical, if by the singular we mean a type of meaning that lacks community. For when a meaning of singularity is rendered in a judgment then precisely the marks that served to make it singular are generalized in one of the modes of community—as recurring in different experiences either for the same or for different persons. The intent of singularity which admits of no generalization has then retreated into the domain of direct appreciation or immediate experience." This, he says, may be illustrated without difficulty. "Suppose I submit the statement 'this is the only orange of this colour.' By so doing I give the orange a meaning in community in two ways. I mean that you can find it the only one with me, or that I myself can find it the same one by repeating my experience of it."

Finally (p. 423), in replying to Professor A. W. Moore's difficulties as regards his terminology, Baldwin explains himself thus:—"Our relativisms are contrast-meanings, dualisms, instrumentalities one to another, and the mediation and abolishing of these contrasts, dualisms, means to ends, removes the relativities and gives the only tenable 'absolute.' This is the 'absolute' that experience is competent to reach. If you ask why this does not develop again into new relativities, I answer, *in fact* it does; but *in meaning* it does not. For the meaning is the universal of all such cases of mediation. If the mediation effected in the æsthetic is one of *typical meaning everywhere in the progression of mental 'dynamic,'* then it is just its value that it discounts in advance any new demands for mediation which new dualisms may make. The æsthetic is absolute then in the only sense that the term can mean anything: it is *universal progression-wise, as well as content or relation-wise*. It mediates the *genetic dynamogenies as well as the static dualisms*." And then he turns to MEANING.

> "As to 'meaning,' I hold that after meaning arises as over against mere present content, then the content of neces-

sity and by contrast also becomes meaning; since consciousness may then intend or mean both, either, or the difference between the two. As I put it in Vol. I., with the rise of meaning there arise *meanings* (in the plural). To hold a content to just its bare presence is to make it a meaning—after consciousness is once able to *mean* '*that only and not anything else.*' Consequently the use of 'meaning' for what is had in mind (as in the phrase 'I *mean* so and so') supersedes the use of it for that merely which is attached to a content (as in 'it means much'). When I say (in the former sense) 'I mean chickens,' I do not intend to restrict 'meaning' to what the chicken suggests beyond the bare image. On the contrary, I intend the *whole bird.*"

It should be added that C. S. Peirce, to whom we now turn, wrote very highly of Professor Baldwin's terminology.

§6. *C. S. Peirce*

By far the most elaborate and determined attempt to give an account of signs and their meaning is that of the American logician C. S. Peirce, from whom William James took the idea and the term Pragmatism, and whose Algebra of Dyadic Relations was developed by Schroeder. Unfortunately his terminology was so formidable that few have been willing to devote time to its mastery, and the work was never completed. "I am now working desperately to get written before I die a book on Logic that shall attract some minds through whom I may do some real good," he wrote to Lady Welby in December, 1908, and by the kindness of Sir Charles Welby such portions of the correspondence as serve to throw light on his published articles on Signs are here reproduced.

In a paper dated 1867, May 14th (*Proc. Am. Acad. Arts and Sci.* (Boston), VII (1868), 295), Peirce defined logic as the doctrine of the formal conditions of the truth of symbols; *i.e.*, of the reference of symbols to their objects. Later, when he "recognized that science consists in inquiry not in 'doctrine'—the history of words, not their etymology, being the key to their meanings, especially with a word so saturated with the idea of progress as science," he came to realize, as he wrote in 1908, that for a long time those who devoted themselves to discussing "the general reference of symbols to their objects would be obliged to make researches into the references to their interpretants, too, as well as into other characters of symbols, and not of symbols alone but of all sorts of signs. So that for the present, the man who makes researches into the reference of symbols to their objects will be forced to make original studies into all branches of the general theory of signs." This theory he called Semeiotic, and its essentials are developed in an article in the *Monist*, 1906, under the title, "Prolegomena to an Apology for Pragmaticism." A sign, it is there stated, "has an *Object* and an *Interpretant*, the latter being that which the Sign produces in the Quasi-mind that is the Interpreter by determining the latter to a feeling, to an exertion, or to a Sign, which determination is the Interpretant. But it remains to point out that there are usually two Objects, and more than two Interpretants. Namely, we have to distinguish the *Immediate Object*, which is the object as the Sign itself represents it, and whose Being is thus dependent upon the Representation of it in the sign, from the *Dynamical Object*, which is the Reality which by some means contrives to determine the Sign to its Representation. In regard to the Interpretant we have equally to distinguish in the first place, the *Immediate Interpretant*, which is the interpretant as it is revealed in the right understanding of the Sign itself, and is ordinarily called the 'meaning' of the sign; while, in the second place, we have to take note of the *Dynamical Interpretant*, which is the actual effect which the Sign, as a Sign, really determines. Finally, there is what I provisionally term the *Final Interpretant*, which refers to the manner in which the Sign tends to represent itself to be related to its Object. I confess that my own conception of this third interpretant is not yet quite free from mist."

Reference is then made to the "ten divisions of signs which have seemed to me to call for my special study. Six turn on the characters of the Interpretant and three on the characters of the Object. Thus the division into Icons, Indices, and Symbols depends upon the different possible relations of a Sign to its Dynamical Object." Only one division is concerned with the nature of the Sign itself, and to this he proceeds as follows:—

"A common mode of estimating the amount of matter in a MS. or printed book is to count the number of words. There will ordinarily be about twenty 'thes' on a page, and, of course, they count as twenty words. In another sense of the word 'word,' however, there is but one word 'the' in the English language; and it is impossible that this word should lie visibly on a page, or be heard in any voice, for the reason that it is not a Single thing or Single event. It does not exist; it only determines things that do exist. Such a definitely significant Form, I propose to term a *Type*. A Single event which happens once and whose identity is limited to that one happening, or a Single Object of a thing which is in some single place at any one instant of time, such an event being significant only as occurring when and where it does, such as this or that word on a single line of a single page of a single copy of a book, I will venture to call a *Token*. An indefinite significant character such as the tone of voice, can neither be called a Type nor a Token. I propose to call a Sign a *Tone*. In order that a Type may be used, it has to be embodied in a Token which shall be a sign of the Type, and thereby of the object the Type signifies. I propose to call such a Token of a Type an Instance of the Type. Thus there may be twenty Instances of the Type ' the ' on a page."

The special interest to Peirce of the distinctions thus christened was their application in explaining and developing a system of ' Existential Graphs,' whereby diagrams are furnished " upon which to experiment, in the solution of the most difficult problems of logic." A diagram, he notes, " though it will ordinarily have Symbolide features, is in the main an Icon of the forms of relations in the constitution of its Object." And in the same terminology it could be said that the footprint which Crusoe found in the sand " was an Index to him of some creature, while as a Symbol it called up the idea of a man." In the material here reproduced we are not concerned with the special applications which its author made of his theory, but in view of his constant insistence on the *logical* nature of his inquiry and his desire to avoid psychology, a further trichotomy [1] of general interest may here be mentioned. *Logic* he defined in an article in the *Monist* (Vol. VII., 1896-7, p. 25) as dealing with the problem, " to what conditions an assertion must conform in order that it may correspond to the ' reality ' " ; *Speculative Grammar* was the name given also by Duns Scotus to " the study of properties of beliefs which belong to them as beliefs " ; and thirdly, " the study of those general conditions under which a problem presents itself for solution, and then under which one question leads on to another," appears as *Universal Rhetoric*. In writing to Lady Welby, he remarks that ' Significs,' the term which she used for the study of Meaning, " would appear from its name to be that part of Semeiotic which inquires into the relation of Signs to the Interpretants (for which,

1 " They seem all to be trichotomies which form an attribute to the essentially triadic nature of the sign."

as limited to Symbols, I proposed in 1867 the name Universal Rhetoric)." He strongly urges her to make a scientific study of Semeiotic, as well as of his Graphs (" I wish you would study my Existential Graphs ; for in my opinion it quite wonderfully opens up the true nature and method of logical analysis—that is to say, of definition ; though how it does so is not easy to make out, until I shall have written my exposition of that art ") ; and in a letter written in 1904, shortly before the publication of his chief *Monist* article, he deals with the classification of Signs at some length.

He prefaces his remarks by insisting that " a sign has *two Objects*, its object as it is represented and its object in itself. It has also *three Interpretants*, its interpretant as represented or meant to be understood, its interpretant as it is produced, and its interpretant in itself." Signs may be divided as to their own material nature, as to their relations to their objects, and as to their relations to their interpretants.

> " As it is in itself a sign is either of the nature of an appearance, when I call it a *qualisign ;* or secondly, it is an individual object or event, when I may call it a *sinsign* (the syllable sin being the first syllable of Semel, simul, singular, etc.) ; or thirdly, it is of the nature of a general type, which I call a *legisign*. As we use the term ' word ' in most cases, saying that ' the ' is one ' word ' and ' an ' is a second ' word,' ' word ' is a legisign. But when we say of a page in a book that it has 250 ' words ' upon it, of which twenty are ' the s,' the ' word ' is a sinsign. A sinsign so embodying a legisign, I term a *replica* of the legisign. The difference between a legisign and a qualisign, neither of which is an individual thing, is that a legisign has a definite identity, though usually admitting a great variety of appearances. Thus &, *and*, and the sound are all one word. The qualisign, on the other hand, has no identity. It is the mere quality of an appearance, and is not exactly the same throughout a second. Instead of identity it has great similarity, and cannot differ much without being called quite a different qualisign."

With regard to the other main divisions of signs he explains that " in respect to their relations to their dynamic objects, I divide signs into *Icons*, *Indices* and *Symbols* (a division I gave in 1867). I define an *Icon* as a sign which is determined by its dynamic object by virtue of its own internal nature. Such is any qualisign like a vision, or the sentiment excited by a piece of music considered as representing what the composer intended. Such may be a sinsign like an individual diagram ; say a curve of the distribution of errors. I define an *Index* as a sign determined by its dynamic object by virtue of being in a real relation to it. Such is a Proper Name (a legisign), such is the occurrence of a symptom of a disease (the symptom itself is a legisign, a general type of a different character. The occurrence in a particular case is a sinsign). I define a *Symbol* as a sign which is determined by its dynamic object only in the sense that it will be so interpreted. It thus depends either upon a convention, a habit[1] or a natural disposition of its interpretant or of the field of its interpretant (that of which the interpretant is a determination). Every symbol is necessarily a legisign ; for it is inaccurate to call a replica of a legisign a symbol."

In respect of its immediate object a sign may either be a sign of quality, of an existent or of a law ; while in regard to its relation to its signified interpretant, it is said to be either a *Rheme*, a *Dicent*, or an *Argument*. " This corresponds to the old division Term, Proposition, and Argument, modified so as to be applicable to signs generally. A Term is simply a class-name or Proper-name. I do not regard the common noun as an essentially necessary part of speech. Indeed, it is only fully developed as a separate part of speech in the Aryan languages and the Basque—possibly in some other out of the way tongues. In the Semitic languages it is generally in form a verbal affair, and usually is so in substance too. As well as I can make out, such it is in most languages. In my universal algebra of logic there is no common noun."

A Rheme is defined as " a sign which is represented in its signified interpretant as if it were a character or mark (or as being so)." It is any sign that is neither true nor false, like most single words except ' yes ' and ' no,' which are almost peculiar to modern languages.

A Dicent is defined as " a sign represented in its signified interpretant as if it were in a real relation to its object (or as being so if it is asserted)." A proposition, he was careful to point out in the *Monist* (1905, p. 172), is for him not the German *Satz*, but " that which is related to any assertion, whether mental and self-addressed or outwardly expressed, just as any possibility is related to its actualization." It is here defined as a dicent symbol.

[1] In the (1906) *Monist* article we read : " A symbol incorporates a habit, and is indispensable to the application of any intellectual habit at least " (p. 495). And again : " Strictly pure symbols can signify only things familiar, and these only in so far as they are familiar."

" A dicent is not an assertion, but a sign capable of being asserted. But an assertion is a dicent. According to my present view (I may see more light in future) the act of assertion is not a pure act of signification. It is an exhibition of the fact that one subjects oneself to the penalties visited on a liar if the proposition asserted is not true. An act of judgment is the self-recognition of a belief; and a belief consists in the deliberate acceptance of a proposition as a basis of conduct. But I think this position is open to doubt. It is simply a question of which view gives the simplest view of the nature of the proposition. Holding then that a Dicent does not assert, I naturally hold that the Argument need not be actually submitted or urged. I therefore define an *Argument* as a sign which is represented in its signified interpretant not as a Sign of that interpretant, the conclusion, but as if it were a Sign of the Interpretant, or perhaps as if it were a Sign of the state of the Universe to which it refers in which the premises are taken for granted."

A sign may appeal to its dynamic interpretant in three ways:—

1. An argument only may be submitted to its interpretant, as something the reasonableness of which will be acknowledged.
2. An argument or dicent may be urged upon the interpretant by an act of insistence.
3. Argument or dicent may be, and a rheme can only be, presented to the interpretant for contemplation.

" Finally, in its relations to its immediate interpretant, I would divide signs into three classes, as follows :—

1. Those which are interpretable in thoughts or other signs of the same kind in infinite series.
2. Those which are interpretable in actual experiences.
3. Those which are interpretable in qualities of feelings or appearances.

The conclusion is that there are ten principal classes of signs :— 1, Qualisigns ; 2, Iconic Sinsigns ; 3, Iconic Legisigns ; 4, Vestiges or Rhematic Indexical Sinsigns ; 5, Proper Names, or Rhematic Indexical Legisigns ; 6, Rhematic Symbols ; 7, Dicent sinsigns (as a portrait with a legend) ; 8, Dicent Indexical Legisigns ; 9, Propositions, or Dicent Symbols ; 10, Arguments."

This treatment of the familiar logical distinction between Term, Proposition, and Argument is somewhat different from the account given in the *Monist* (1906) article, where it is explained that " the first two members have to be much widened," and where we are introduced to Semes, Phemes, and Delomes.

" By a *Seme* I should mean anything which serves for any purpose as a substitute for an object of which it is, in some sense, a representative or Sign. The logical Term, which is a class-name is a Seme. Thus the term ' The Mortality of man ' is a Seme. By a *Pheme* I mean a sign which is equivalent to a grammatical sentence, whether it be Interrogative, Imperative or Assertory. In any case, such a Sign is intended to have some sort of compulsive effect on the Interpreter of it. As the third member of the triplet, I sometimes use the word *Delome* (pronounced deeloam, from δήλωμα), though *Argument* would answer well enough. It is a sign which has the Form of tending to act upon the Interpreter through his own self-control, representing a process of change in thoughts or signs, as if to induce this change in the Interpreter."

A Graph, he says, is a Pheme, " and in my use hitherto, at least, a Proposition. An Argument is represented by a series of Graphs."

There follows a discussion of " the Percept, in the last analysis the immediate object of all knowledge and all thought."

"This doctrine in nowise conflicts with Pragmaticism, which holds that the Immediate Interpretant of all thought proper is Conduct. Nothing is more indispensable to a sound epistemology than a crystal-clear discrimination between the object and the Interpretant of knowledge; very much as nothing is more indispensable to sound notions of geography than a crystal-clear discrimination between north latitude and south latitude; and the one discrimination is not more rudimentary than the other. That we are conscious of our Precepts is a theory which seems to me to be beyond dispute; but it is not a fact of Immediate Perception. A fact of Immediate Perception is not a Percept, nor any part of a Percept; a Percept is a Seme, while a fact of Immediate Perception or rather the Perceptual Judgment of which such fact is the immediate Interpretant is a Pheme that is the direct Dynamical Interpretant of the Percept, and of which the Percept is the Dynamical Object, and is with some considerable difficulty (as the history of psychology shows) distinguished from the Immediate Object, though the distinction is highly significant. But not to interrupt our train of thought, let us go on to note that while the Immediate Object of a Percept is excessively vague, yet natural thought makes up for that lack (as it almost amounts to) as follows:—A late Dynamical Interpretant of the whole complex of Percepts is the Seme of a Perpetual Universe that is represented in instinctive thought as determining the original Immediate Object of every Percept. Of course, I must be understood as talking not psychology, but the logic of mental operations. Subsequent Interpretants furnish new Semes of Universes resulting from various adjunctions to the Perceptual Universe. They are, however, all of them, Interpretants of Percepts.

Finally, and in particular, we get a Seme of that highest of all Universes which is regarded as the Object of every true Proposition, and which, if we name it all, we call by the somewhat misleading title of 'The Truth.'

That said, let us go back and ask this question: How is it that the Percept, which is a Seme, has for its direct dynamical Interpretant the Perceptual Judgment, which is a Pheme? For that is not the usual way with Semes, certainly. All the examples that happen to occur to me at this moment of such action of Semes are instances of Percepts, though doubtless there are others. Since not all Percepts act with equal energy in this way, the instances may be none the less instructive for being Percepts. However, Reader, I beg you will think this matter out for yourself, and then you can see—I wish I could—whether your independently formed opinion does not fall with mine. My opinion is that a pure Perceptual Icon—and many really *great* psychologists have evidently thought that Perception is a passing of images before the mind's eye, much as if one were walking through a picture gallery,—could not have a Pheme for its direct Dynamical Interpretant. I desire, for more than one reason, to tell you why I think so, although that you should to-day appreciate my reasons seems to be out of the question. Still I wish you to understand me so far as to know that, mistaken though I be, I am not so sunk in intellectual night as to be dealing lightly with philosophic Truth when I aver that weighty reasons have moved me to the adoption of my opinion; and I am also anxious that it should be understood that those reasons have not been psychological at all, but purely logical. My reason, then, briefly stated and abridged, is that it would be *illogical* for a pure Icon to have a Pheme for its Interpretant, and I hold it to be impossible for thought not subject to self-control, as a Perceptual Judgment manifestly is not, to be illogical. I dare say this reason may excite your derision or disgust, or both ; and if it does I think none the worse of your intelligence."

There is an interesting letter dated March 14, 1909, in which Lady Welby's own Triad of Interpretation is discussed. "I confess," he writes, "I had not realized before reading your *Encyclopædia Britannica* article, how fundamental your trichotomy of Sense, Meaning and Significance really is. It is not to be expected that concepts of such importance should get perfectly defined for a long time. . . . I now find that my division (of the three kinds of Interpretant) nearly coincides with yours, as it ought to do exactly, if both are correct. I am not in the least conscious of having been influenced by your book in setting my trichotomy." He does not believe that there was even an unconscious reminiscence, and consequently feels "some exultation in finding that my thought and yours nearly agree."

He proceeds to inquire how far there is agreement. "The greatest discrepancy appears to lie in my *Dynamical Interpretant* as compared with your 'Meaning.' If I understand the latter, it consists in the effect on the mind of the Interpreter that the utterer (whether vocally or by writing) of the sign intends to produce. My Dynamical Interpreter consists in direct effect actually produced by a Sign upon an Interpreter of it. They agree in being effects of the Sign upon an individual mind, I think, or upon a number of actual individual minds by independent action upon each. My *Final Interpretant* is, I believe, exactly the same as your Significance ; namely, the effect the Sign *would* produce upon any mind upon which circumstances should permit it to work out its full effect. My *Immediate Interpretant* is, I think, very nearly, if not quite, the same as your 'Sense' ; for I understand the former to be the total unanalysed effect that the Sign is calculated to produce ; and I have been accustomed to identify this with the effect the sign first produces or may produce upon a mind, without any reflection upon it. I am not aware that you have ever attempted to define your term 'Sense,' but I gather from reading over what you say that it is the first effect that a sign would have upon a mind well qualified to comprehend it. Since you say it is Sensal and has no Volitional element, I suppose it is of the nature of an 'impression.' It is thus, as far as I can see, exactly my Immediate Interpretant. You have selected words from vernacular speech to express your varieties, while I have avoided these and have manufactured terms suitable, as I think, to serve the uses of Science. I might describe my Immediate Interpretation as so much of the effect of a Sign as would enable a person to say whether or not the Sign was applicable to anything concerning which that person had sufficient acquaintance."

As regards Meaning and Intention, he continues: "My Interpretant with its three kinds is supposed by me to be something essentially adding to anything that acts as a Sign. Now natural Signs and symptoms have no utterer; and consequently have no Meaning, if Meaning be defined as the intention of the utterer. I do not allow myself to speak of the 'purposes of the Almighty,' since whatever He might desire is done. Intention seems to me, though I may be mistaken, an interval of time between the desire and the laying of the train by which the desire is to be brought about. But it seems to me that desire can only belong to a finite creature." And he sums up as follows :—

> "Your ideas of *Sense*, *Meaning* and *Signification* seem to me to have been obtained through a prodigious sensitiveness of Perception that I cannot rival; while my three grades of Interpretant were worked out by reasoning from the definition of a Sign what sort of thing *ought* to be noticeable and *then* searching for its appearance. My *Immediate Interpretant* is implied in the fact that each Sign must have its own peculiar Interpretability before it gets any interpreter. My *Dynamical Interpretant* is that which is experienced in each act of Interpretation and is different from that of any other; and the *Final Interpretant* is the one Interpretative result to which every Interpreter is destined to come, if the Sign is sufficiently considered. The Immediate Interpretant is an abstraction, consisting in a possibility; the Dynamical Interpretant is a single actual event; the Final Interpretant is that toward which the actual tends."

Peirce's conception of an 'Interpretant' receives further elucidation in a letter written at the end of 1908, from which we have already quoted. He there emphasizes that in all questions of interpretation it is indispensable to start with an accurate and broad analysis of the nature of a sign. "I define a Sign as anything which is so determined by something else, called its Object, and so determines an effect upon a person, which effect I call its Interpretant, that the latter is thereby mediately determined by the former. My insertion of 'upon a person' is a sop to Cerberus, because I despair of making my own broader conception understood. I recognize three Universes which are distinguished by three Modalities of being. One of these Universes embraces whatever has its Being in itself alone, except that whatever is in this Universe must be present to one consciousness, or be capable of being so present to its entire Being." The objects of this Universe he called Ideas or Possibles, the objects of the second or actual Universe being Facts, and of the third Necessitants.

The Mode of Being of signs can be ' possible ' (*e.g.*, a hexagon circumscribed in or about a conic) ; or ' actual ' (as with a barometer) ; or ' necessitant ' (as the word ' the,' or any other in the dictionary). A ' possible ' sign he calls, as in the *Monist* article, a *Tone* ("though I am considering replacing this by ' Mark ' ") ; an ' actual ' sign, a *Token ;* a ' necessitant ' sign a *Type.*

> " It is usual and proper to distinguish two Objects of a Sign, the Mediate without, and the Immediate within the Sign. Its Interpretant is all that the sign conveys ; acquaintance with its Object must be gained by collateral experience. The Mediate Object is the Object outside the Sign ; I call it the *Dynamoid* Object. The Sign must indicate it by a hint ; and this hint, or its substance, is the *Immediate Object*."

When the Dynamoid object is ' possible,' the sign will be *Abstractive* (as the word Beauty), when it is actual the sign will be *Concretive* (any one barometer or a written narrative of any series of events) ; and thirdly, " for a sign whose Dynamoid Object is a Necessitant, I have at present no better designation than a ' *Collective*,' which is not quite so bad a name as it sounds to be until one studies the matter ; but for a person like me, who thinks in quite a different system of symbols to words, it is awkward and often puzzling to translate one's thought into words ! If the Immediate Object is a ' Possible ' (that is, if the Dynamoid Object is indicated, always more or less vaguely, by means of its Qualities, etc.) I call the Sign a *Descriptive ;* if the Immediate is an Occurrence, I call the Sign a *Designative ;* and if the Immediate Object is a Necessitant, I call the Sign a *Copulant ;* for in that case the Object has to be so identified by the Interpreter that the Sign may represent a necessitation."

A Possible can determine nothing but a Possible, and a Necessitant can be determined by nothing but a Necessitant. " Hence," he continues, " it follows from the definition of a Sign that since the Dynamoid Object determines the Immediate object,
which determines the Sign itself,
which determines the Destinate Interpretant,

which determines the Effective Interpretant,
which determines the Explicit Interpretant,
the six trichotomies, instead of determining 729 classes of signs, as they would if they were independent, only yield 28 classes; as I strongly opine (not to say almost approve) there are four other trichotomies of signs of the same order of importance, instead of making 59,049 classes, these will only come to 66. The additional 4 trichotomies are undoubtedly first *Icons* (or Simulacra), *Indices*, *Symbols*, and then three referring to the Interpretants. One of these I am pretty confident is: *Suggestives*, *Imperatives*, *Indicatives*, where the Imperatives include Interrogatives. Of the other two I think that one must be into Signs assuring their Interpretants by *Instinct*, *Experience*, and *Form*. The other I suppose to be what (in the *Monist* (1906) article) I called *Semes*, *Phemes*, and *Delomes*."

[1] The edition of Peirce's *Collected Works*, now in course of publication by the Harvard University Press, has so far brought to light nothing which necessitates a modification or expansion of the above analysis. *Cf.* J. Buchler, *Charles Peirce's Empiricism*, 1939, pp. 4-8, 155-6, and 180-5; also *Psyche*, 1935, pp. 5-7, and Vol. XVIII, 1943, *art. cit.*, "Word Magic."

APPENDIX E

ON NEGATIVE FACTS

We may approach the discussion of Facts from many angles, but perhaps it is best to begin by considering the controversy about Negative Facts in which the issues come clearly to a head. In 1917 Mr Raphael Demos published in *Mind* the results of an interrogatory to which he had subjected his more intelligent non-philosophical acquaintances—as to whether they had ever personally encountered a negative fact. All concurred in the opinion that " every case of knowledge expressed through a negative proposition was in reality of a positive nature, in a fashion which they were unable to comprehend."

In his desire not to oppose this verdict of experience without good reason, the writer ventured to question the orthodox conclusion that negative facts are an essential constituent of the universe, and substituted a theory of contrariety between propositions whereby " John is not in England " is to be construed as a description of some positive proposition (" John is in Paris ") *incompatible* with the positive proposition originally denied (" John is in England "). So intrigued was the author of *Principia Mathematica* by this logical escapade that, in spite of the almost unquenchable desire to escape the admission of negative facts which he had noted as implanted in every human breast, he was constrained to examine the argument minutely and to traverse it by pointing out that, ' incompatible ' being identical with ' not compatible,' a negative fact had been illicitly admitted by the interpretation itself. Should the interpretation be re-applied to eject this, this application again admits an intruder and so on.

It is to be noted, however. that in point of time Mr W. E. Johnson intervened in the pages of *Mind* with the following dictum : " We can only say that ' incompatible ' means ' incompatible with compatible '—or to put it otherwise incompatible is just as ultimate a positive relation as compatible." Further moves in the game were to be expected; some of them, indeed, are to be found in Professor Eaton's *Symbolism and Truth* (1925).

The Doctrine of Symbolism allows us, however, quietly to settle the dispute by turning the attention to what it is about. We can then apply the Theory of Signs upon which the Doctrine depends and point out to what the dispute has been due.

It is about the referents of certain complex symbols; those containing the term 'not' or an equivalent. It is about whether the symbol for one of these is 'negative fact' or 'not a fact,' and about the supposed consequences of this momentous decision. We may best explain by returning at this point to the term Fact, disregarding for the moment the problem of the negative.

The proposition, or complex symbol, "Charles I. died on the scaffold," is used to refer to a certain complex referent. Whenever a form of words has no referent it fails to be a symbol and is nonsense. In this case the referent is admitted by historians to belong to the order of referents which they call 'historical events.'

Similarly, the complex sign, "Alexander VI. became a rat-catcher," has a referent which historians exclude from the historical order. They will do this on the ground that all the places into which this referent might fit are filled by other referents. They say then (if symbolists) that this referent belongs to some other order;[1] either the order of Rabelais' infernal events, or some other order of imaginary events, or events of some imagination—all 'historical' in the wider sense of events which have happened.

When the referent of a given symbol belongs to the order within which we are looking for it, we commonly say "the symbol ('Charles I. died on the scaffold') expresses a fact," or "It is a fact that (the symbol)": more often we say "(The symbol —viz., Charles I., etc.) is true." These locutions have the same referent, the referent more adequately referred to by the complex symbol:—"*The referent belongs to the order to which it is allocated (by context or openly) by a reference.*"

[1] With regard to the symbols 'place' and 'referent' as used here. see Chapter V., p. 106. When we say that a referent is allocated to an 'order,' its 'order' is shorthand for those parts of the reference by the aid of which we attempt verification. Orders most commonly used are 'historical,' 'actual,' 'physical,' 'psychological,' 'imaginary,' 'dream.' Some orders raise special little problems, such as the 'dramatic order.'

When on the other hand the referent belongs to some other order than that within which we are led to seek it, we are apt to say, if our knowledge of this order is sufficient :—

(1) That Charles I. died in his bed is contrary to the fact.
(2) (The symbol, viz., 'Charles I., etc.,') does not express a fact.
(3) (The symbol) expresses what is not a fact.
(4) It is not a fact that (the symbol).
(5) It is a fact that (the symbol, with a ' not ' suitably introduced.)

These locutions can be seen to have the same referent. They illustrate the mutations which signs undergo to serve linguistic convenience and to torture logicians. No. (1) is the most curious. It is a telescoped form of an expansion; and expansion on the way to Mr Demos' theory, as No. (5) is a transformation in his opponent's favour. Instead of " is a fact " we may substitute " is true " or " is a truth," and instead of " is not a fact " we may substitute " is false " or " is not true." How many alternative locutions are then at our disposal with which to avoid monotony in our prose, may be computed by philologists with a statistical penchant. A more adequate complex sign with the referent to which all these refer is the following :—

The referent of (the symbol) belongs to another order of referents than that to which it is allocated (contextually or openly).

More correctly, discarding the symbolic accessories ' referent ' or ' order ' :—*The reference using (the symbol) has as parts references which do not together make up a reference to any event.*

A Fact, therefore, is a referent which belongs to the order to which it is allocated. This definition of ' a fact ' solves the ' problem of negative facts ' with which we began. No other will solve it. The referent in part of the complex symbol (1) " Charles I. did not die on the scaffold " is also the referent in part of the complex symbol (2) " Charles I. died on the scaffold," but with a different allocation. More clearly stated the expanded form of (1) is " *The referent of the symbol ' Charles I. died on the scaffold ' belongs to another order than that of historical events.*" The expanded form of (2) is " *The referent of the symbol ' Charles died on the scaffold ' belongs to the historical order.*" Since historians find the referent of " Charles I. died on the scaffold " in the historical order we can say that (1) is false and (2) is true; but in so doing we are merely using alternative locutions.

The converse case of the symbols (1) " Charles I. did not die in his bed " and (2) " Charles I. died in his bed " is treated in the same fashion. (1) expands to " *The referent of ' Charles I. died in his bed ' belongs to another order than that of historical events*." (2) expands to "*The referent of 'Charles I. died in his bed' belongs to the historical order*." Historians find the ' place ' in the historical order which would be filled by this referent filled by some other referent. We may therefore say that (1) is true and (2) is false, or that (1) refers to a fact and (2) does not so refer, or refers to what is not a fact or to a negative fact ; but in so saying we shall merely be using rival shorthands, developed for the sake of linguistic convenience.

A piece of string will tie up the same parcel whether it has a knot in it or not. There is no further peculiarity about those parcels which happen to be tied by string containing knots. They are neither ' parcels containing knots ' nor ' knotty parcels,' but just honest parcels. Similarly it should now be obvious that though propositions containing negative elements differ, *qua* propositions, from those devoid of nots, the distinction does not imply parallel differences in the objects referred to, or a special class of negative objects. And this is of course equally true when a negative element is used merely as an indication of a relation between *Symbols*, as in Peano's Fourth Postulate " 0 is not the successor of any number," and in the case of objects to which we happen not to be able to refer by other linguistic means. When we dispute as to whether a fact is positive or negative, or whether there *are* ' negative facts,' we are engaged merely in the criticism of rival prose styles.

The moral of neglecting such considerations is perhaps best pointed by a little fable concerning Amœba—

"Realize thyself, Amœba dear," said Will : and Amœba realized herself, and there was no Small Change but many Checks on the Bank wherein the wild Time grew and grew and grew. And in the latter days Homo appeared. How, he knew not ; and Homo called the change Progress, and the How he called God. . . . for speech was ever a Comforter. And when Homo came to study the parts of speech, he wove himself a noose of Words. And he hearkened to himself, and bowed his head and made abstractions, hypostatizing and glorifying. Thus arose Church and State and Strife upon the Earth ; for oftentimes Homo caused Hominem to die for Abstractions hypostatized and glorified : and the children did after the manner of their fathers for so had they been taught. And last of all Homo began also to eat his words.

Now, after much time, there appeared Reason, which said, " Wherefore hast thou done this thing ? "

And Homo said " Speech bewrayèd me."

To whom Reason " Go to now and seek the Doctrine of Symbolism which showeth that the bee buzzeth not in the Head but in the Bonnet."

But Homo hearkened not, and his sin was the greater in that he was proud and obstinate withal. For as Philosopher and Economist he said—" We will tend to give the matter our careful consideration." And as Returning Warrior, he asked : " What, grannie, didst thou say in the Great Wars ? " And as Plain Man he continued to splash solemnly about in the Vocabulary of Ambiguity— and all the while the Noose was tightening and Homo began to grow inarticulate.

Then had Reason compassion on him, and gave him the Linguistic Conscience, and spake again softly : " Go to now, be a Man, Homo ! Cast away the Noose of Words which thou hast woven, that it strangle thee not. Behold ! the Doctrine of Symbolism, which illumineth all things. What are the Laws of Science ? Are they not thine own Conceptual Shorthand ? "

And Man blushed.

And Reason asked again, " What is Number ? Is it not a class of classes : and are not classes themselves thine own convenient Fictions ? Consider the Mountain Top—it Hums not neither does it Spin. Cease then to listen for the noise of the humming. Weary not thyself in unravelling the web that hath never been spun."

And Man replied " Quite."

Then sang Reason and Man the Hymn 1923, " Glory to Man in the Highest for Man is the Master of Words "—nineteen hundred and twenty-three.

And the sound of the Hymn ringeth yet in our ear.

Thus the Realization of Amœba ended in the Realization of an Error.

" God laughed when he made the Sahara," says an old African proverb—but Man may yet discover the uses of Dust.

SUPPLEMENT I

THE PROBLEM OF MEANING IN PRIMITIVE LANGUAGES

By BRONISLAW MALINOWSKI, Ph.D., D.Sc.

Late Professor of Anthropology, University of London.

I. The need of a Science of Symbolism and Meaning, such as is presented in this volume by Ogden and Richards. This need exemplified by the Ethnographer's difficulties in dealing with primitive languages.

II. Analysis of a savage utterance, showing the complex problems of Meaning which lead from mere linguistics into the study of culture and social psychology. Such a combined linguistic and ethnological study needs guidance from a theory of symbols developed on the lines of the present work.

III. The conception of 'Context of Situation.' Difference in the linguistic perspectives which open up before the Philologist who studies dead, inscribed languages, and before the Ethnographer who has to deal with a primitive living tongue, existing only in actual utterance. The study of an object alive more enlightening than that of its dead remains. The 'Sign-situation' of the Authors corresponds to the 'Context of Situation' here introduced.

IV. Language, in its primitive function, to be regarded as a *mode of action*, rather than as a *countersign of thought*. Analysis of a complex speech-situation among savages. The essential primitive uses of speech: speech-in-action, ritual handling of words, the narrative, 'phatic communion' (speech in social intercourse).

V. The problem of Meaning in primitive languages. Intellectual formation of Meaning by apperception not primitive. Biological view of meaning in early non-articulate sound-reactions, which are expressive, significant and correlated to situation. Meaning in early phases of articulate speech. Meaning of words rooted in their pragmatic efficiency. The origins of the magical attitude towards words. Ethnographic and genetic substantiation of Ogden's and Richards' views of Meaning and Definition.

VI. The problem of grammatical structure. Where to look for the prototype of grammatical categories. " Logical ' and ' purely grammatical ' explanations rejected. Existence of Real Categories in the primitive man's pragmatic outlook, which correspond to the structural categories of language. Exemplified on the nature of the noun and of other Parts of Speech.

I

Language, in its developed literary and scientific functions, is an instrument of thought and of the communication of thought. The art of properly using this instrument is the most obvious aim of the study of language. Rhetoric, Grammar and Logic have been in the past and still are taught under the name of Arts and studied predominantly from the practical normative point of view. The laying down of rules, the testing of their validity, and the attainment of perfection in style are undoubtedly important and comprehensive objects of study, especially as Language grows and develops with the advancement of thought and culture, and in a certain sense even leads this advancement.

All Art, however, which lives by knowledge and not by inspiration, must finally resolve itself into scientific study, and there is no doubt that from all points of approach we are driven towards a scientific theory of language. Indeed, for some time already, we have had, side by side with the Arts of Language, attempts at posing and solving various purely theoretical problems of linguistic form and meaning, approached mainly from the psychological point of view. It is enough to mention the names of W. von Humboldt, Lazarus and Steinthal, Whitney, Max Müller, Misteli, Sweet, Wundt, Paul, Finck, Rozwadowski, Wegener, Oertel, Marty, Jespersen and others, to show that the Science of Language is neither new nor unimportant. In all their works, besides problems of formal grammar, we find attempts at an analysis of the mental processes which are concerned in Meaning. But our knowledge of Psychology and of psychological methods advances, and within the last years has made very rapid progress indeed. The other modern Humanistic Sciences, in the first place Sociology and Anthropology, by giving us a deeper understanding of human nature and culture, bring their share to the common problem. For the questions of language are indeed the most important and central subject of all humanistic studies. Thus, the Science of Language constantly receives contributions of new material and stimulation from new methods. A most important impetus which it has thus lately received has come from the philosophical study of symbols and mathematical data, so brilliantly carried on in Cambridge by Mr Bertrand Russell and Dr Whitehead.

In the present book Mr Ogden and Mr Richards carry over the study of signs into the field of linguistics, where it assumes a fundamental importance. Indeed, they work out a new Science of Symbolism which is sure to yield most valuable criteria for the criticism of certain errors of Metaphysics and of purely Formal Logic (cf. Chaps. II, VII, VIII and IX). On the other hand, the theory has not merely a philosophical bearing, but possesses practical importance in dealing with the special, purely scientific problems of Meaning, Grammar, Psychology and Pathology of Speech. More especially, important researches on Aphasia by Dr Henry Head, which promise to throw entirely new light on our conceptions of Meaning, seem to work towards the same Semantic theories as those contained in the present book.[1] Dr A. H. Gardiner, one of the greatest experts in hieroglyphic script and Egyptian grammar—of which he is preparing a new analysis—has published some remarkable articles on Meaning, where he approaches the same problems as those discussed by Mr Ogden and Mr Richards, and solved by them in such an interesting manner, and their respective results do not seem to me to be incompatible.[2] Finally, I myself, at grips with the problem of primitive languages from Papuo-Melanesia, had been driven into the field of general Semantics.[3] When, however, I had the privilege of looking through the proofs of the present book, I was astonished to find how exceedingly well the theories there presented answered all my problems and solved my difficulties; and I was gratified to find that the position to which I

[1] See the preliminary articles in *Brain*, to which the Authors also refer in Chapter X.

[2] See Dr Gardiner's articles in *Man*, January 1919, and in *The British Journal of Psychology*, April 1922.

[3] Cf. my article on "Classificatory Particles in the Language of Kiriwina," *Bulletin of School of Oriental Studies*, Vol. II., and *Argonauts of the Western Pacific*, chapter on "Words in Magic — Some Linguistic Data."

had been led by the study of primitive languages, was not essentially a different one. I was therefore extremely glad when the Authors offered me an opportunity to state my problems, and to outline my tentative solutions, side by side with their remarkable theories. I accepted it the more gladly because I hope to show how important a light the theories of this book throw on the problems of primitive languages.

It is remarkable that a number of independent inquirers, Messrs Ogden and Richards, Dr Head, Dr Gardiner and myself, starting from definite and concrete, yet quite different problems, should arrive, if not exactly at the same results stated in the same terminology, at least at the construction of similar Semantic theories based on psychological considerations.

I have therefore to show how, in my own case, that of an Ethnographer studying primitive mentality, culture, and language, I was driven into a linguistic theory very much on lines parallel to those of the present work. In the course of my Ethnographic researches among some Melanesian tribes of Eastern New Guinea, which I conducted exclusively by means of the local language, I collected a considerable number of texts: magical formulæ, items of folk-lore, narratives, fragments of conversation, and statements of my informants. When, in working out this linguistic material, I tried to translate my texts into English, and incidentally to write out the vocabulary and grammar of the language, I was faced by fundamental difficulties. These difficulties were not removed, but rather increased, when I consulted the extant grammars and vocabularies of Oceanic languages. The authors of these, mainly missionaries who wrote for the practical purpose of facilitating the task of their successors, proceeded by rule of thumb. For instance, in writing a vocabulary they would give the next best approximation in English to a native word.

But the object of a scientific translation of a word is not to give its rough equivalent, sufficient for practical purposes, but to state exactly whether a native word corresponds to an idea at least partially existing for English speakers, or whether it covers an entirely foreign conception. That such foreign conceptions do exist for native languages and in great number, is clear. All words which describe the native social order, all expressions referring to native beliefs, to specific customs, ceremonies, magical rites—all such words are obviously absent from English as from any European language. Such words can only be translated into English, not by giving their imaginary equivalent—a real one obviously cannot be found—but by explaining the meaning of each of them through an exact Ethnographic account of the sociology, culture and tradition of that native community.

But there is an even more deeply reaching though subtler difficulty: the whole manner in which a native language is used is different from our own. In a primitive tongue, the whole grammatical structure lacks the precision and definiteness of our own, though it is extremely telling in certain specific ways. Again some particles, quite untranslatable into English, give a special flavour to native phraseology. In the structure of sentences, an extreme simplicity hides a good deal of expressiveness, often achieved by means of position and context. Returning to the meaning of isolated words, the use of metaphor, the beginnings of abstraction, of generalization and a vagueness associated with extreme concreteness of expression—all these features baffle any attempt at a simple and direct translation. The ethnographer has to convey this deep yet subtle difference of language and of the mental attitude which lies behind it, and is expressed through it. But this leads more and more into the general psychological problem of Meaning.

II

This general statement of the linguistic difficulties which beset an Ethnographer in his field-work, must be illustrated by a concrete example. Imagine yourself suddenly transported on to a coral atoll in the Pacific, sitting in a circle of natives and listening to their conversation. Let us assume further that there is an ideal interpreter at hand, who, as far as possible, can convey the meaning of each utterance, word for word, so that the listener is in possession of all the linguistic data available. Would that make you understand the conversation or even a single utterance? Certainly not.

Let us have a look at such a text, an actual utterance taken down from a conversation of natives in the Trobriand Islands, N.E. New Guinea. In analysing it, we shall see quite plainly how helpless one is in attempting to open up the meaning of a statement by mere linguistic means; and we shall also be able to realize what sort of additional knowledge, besides verbal equivalence, is necessary in order to make the utterance significant.

I adduce a statement in native, giving under each word its nearest English equivalent:

Tasakaulo	*kaymatana*	*yakida*;
We run	front-wood	ourselves;

tawoulo	*ovanu ;*	*tasivila*	*tagine*
we paddle	in place ;	we turn	we see
soda ;	*isakaulo*	*ka'u'uya*	
companion ours ;	he runs	rear-wood	
oluvieki	*similaveta*	*Pilolu*	
behind	their sea-arm	Pilolu	

The verbatim English translation of this utterance sounds at first like a riddle or a meaningless jumble of words ; certainly not like a significant, unambiguous statement. Now if the listener, whom we suppose acquainted with the language, but unacquainted with the culture of the natives, were to understand even the general trend of this statement, he would have first to be informed about the situation in which these words were spoken. He would need to have them placed in their proper setting of native culture. In this case, the utterance refers to an episode in an overseas trading expedition of these natives, in which several canoes take part in a competitive spirit. This last-mentioned feature explains also the emotional nature of the utterance : it is not a mere statement of fact, but a boast, a piece of self-glorification, extremely characteristic of the Trobrianders' culture in general and of their ceremonial barter in particular.

Only after a preliminary instruction is it possible to gain some idea of such *technical terms of boasting and emulation* as *kaymatana* (front-wood) and *ka'u'uya* (rear-wood). The metaphorical use of *wood* for *canoe* would lead us into another field of language psychology, but for the present it is enough to emphasize that 'front' or 'leading canoe' and 'rear canoe' are important terms for a people whose attention is so highly occupied with competitive activities for their own sake. To the meaning of such words is added a specific emotional tinge, comprehensible only against the background of their tribal psychology in ceremonial life, commerce and enterprise.

Again, the sentence where the leading sailors are described as looking back and perceiving their companions lagging behind on the sea-arm of Pilolu, would require a special discussion of the geographical feeling of the natives, of their use of imagery as a linguistic instrument and of a special use of the possessive pronoun (*their* sea-arm Pilolu).

All this shows the wide and complex considerations into which we are led by an attempt to give an adequate analysis of meaning. Instead of translating, of inserting simply an English word for a native one, we are faced by a long and not altogether simple process of describing wide fields of custom, of social psychology and of tribal organization which correspond to one term or another. We see that linguistic analysis inevitably leads us into the study of all the subjects covered by Ethnographic field-work.

Of course the above given comments on the specific terms (front-wood, rear-wood, their sea-arm Pilolu) are necessarily short and sketchy. But I have on purpose chosen an utterance which corresponds to a set of customs, already described quite fully.[1] The reader of that description will be able to understand thoroughly the adduced text, as well as appreciate the present argument.

Besides the difficulties encountered in the translation of single words, difficulties which lead directly into descriptive Ethnography, there are others, associated with more exclusively linguistic problems, which however can be solved only on the basis of psychological analysis. Thus it has been suggested that the characteristically Oceanic distinction of inclusive and exclusive pronouns requires a deeper explanation than any which would confine itself to merely grammatical relations.[2] Again, the puzz ling manner in which some of the obviously correlated sentences are joined in our text by mere juxtaposition would require much more than a simple reference, if all its importance and significance had to be brought out. Those two features are well known and have been often discussed, though according to my ideas not quite exhaustively.

There are, however, certain peculiarities of primitive languages, almost entirely neglected by grammarians, yet opening up very interesting questions of savage psychology. I shall illustrate this by a point, lying on the borderland between grammar and lexicography and well exemplified in the utterance quoted.

In the highly developed Indo-European languages, a sharp distinction can be drawn between the grammatical and lexical function of words. The meaning of a root of a word can be isolated from the modification of meaning due to accidence or some other grammatical means of determination. Thus in the word ***run*** we distinguish between the meaning of the root—rapid

[1] See *op. cit.*, *Argonauts of the Western Pacific*—An account of Native Enterprise and Adventure in the Archipelagoes of Melanesian New Guinea, 1922.

[2] See the important Presidential Address by the late Dr W. H. R. Rivers in the *Journal of the Royal Anthropological Institute*, Vol. LII., January-June, 1922, p. 21, and his *History of Melanesian Society*, Vol. II., p. 486.

personal displacement—and the modification as to time, tense, definiteness, etc., expressed by the grammatical form, in which the word is found in the given context. But in native languages the distinction is by no means so clear and the functions of grammar and radical meaning respectively are often confused in a remarkable manner.

In the Melanesian languages there exist certain grammatical instruments, used in the flection of verbs, which express somewhat vaguely relations of time, definiteness and sequence. The most obvious and easy thing to do for a European who wishes to use roughly such a language for practical purposes, is to find out what is the nearest approach to those Melanesian forms in our languages and then to use the savage form in the European manner. In the Trobriand language, for instance, from which we have taken our above example, there is an adverbial particle *boge*, which, put before a modified verb, gives it, in a somewhat vague manner, the meaning either of a past or of a definite happening. The verb is moreover modified by a change in the prefixed personal pronoun. Thus the root *ma* (come, move hither) if used with the prefixed pronoun of the third singular *i*—has the form *ima* and means (roughly), *he comes*. With the modified pronoun *ay* —or, more emphatical, *lay*—it means (roughly) *he came* or *he has come*. The expression *boge ayna* or *boge layma* can be approximately translated by *he has already come*, the participle *boge* making it more definite.

But this equivalence is only approximate, suitable for some practical purposes, such as trading with the natives, missionary preaching and translation of Christian literature into native languages. This last cannot, in my opinion, be carried out with any degree of accuracy. In the grammars and interpretations of Melanesian languages, almost all of which have been written by missionaries for practical purposes, the grammatical modifications of verbs have been simply set down as equivalent to Indo-European tenses. When I first began to use the Trobriand language in my field-work, I was quite unaware that there might be some snares in taking savage grammar at its face value and followed the missionary way of using native inflection.

I had soon to learn, however, that this was not correct and I learnt it by means of a practical mistake, which interfered slightly with my field-work and forced me to grasp native flection at the cost of my personal comfort. At one time I was engaged in making observations on a very interesting transaction which took place in a lagoon village of the Trobriands between the coastal fishermen and the inland gardeners.[1] I had to follow some important preparations in the village and yet I did not want to miss the arrival of the canoes on the beach. I was busy registering and photographing the proceedings among the huts, when word went round, 'they have come already'—*boge laymayse*. I left my work in the village unfinished to rush some quarter of a mile to the shore, in order to find, to my disappointment and mortification, the canoes far away, punting slowly along towards the beach! Thus I came some ten minutes too soon, just enough to make me lose my opportunites in the village!

It required some time and a much better general grasp of the language before I came to understand the nature of my mistake and the proper use of words and forms to express the subtleties of temporal sequence. Thus the root *ma* which means *come*, *move hither*, does not contain the meaning, covered by our word *arrive*. Nor does any grammatical determination give it the special and temporal definition, which we express by, 'they have come, they have arrived.' The form *boge laymayse*, which I heard on that memorable morning in the lagoon village, means to a native 'they have already been moving hither' and not 'they have already come here.'

In order to achieve the spatial and temporal definition which we obtain by using the past definite tense, the natives have recourse to certain concrete and specific expressions. Thus in the case quoted, the villagers, in order to convey the fact that the canoes had arrived, would have used the word *to anchor*, *to moor*. 'They have already moored their canoes,' *boge aykotasi*, would have meant, what I assumed they had expressed by *boge laymayse*. That is, in this case the natives use a different root instead of a mere grammatical modification.

Returning to our text, we have another telling example of the characteristic under discussion. The quaint expression 'we paddle in place' can only be properly understood by realizing that the word *paddle* has here the function, not of describing what the crew are doing, but of indicating their immediate proximity to the village of their destination. Exactly as in the previous example the past tense of the word to come ('they have come') which we would have used in our language to convey the fact of arrival, has another meaning in native and has to be replaced by another root which expresses the idea; so here the native root *wa*, *to move thither*, could not have been used in

[1] It was a ceremony of the *Wasi*, a form of exchange of vegetable food for fish. See *op. cit.*, *Argonauts of the Western Pacific*, pp. 187-189 and plate xxxvi.

(approximately) past definite tense to convey the meaning of 'arrive there,' but a special root expressing the concrete act of paddling is used to mark the spatial and temporal relations of the leading canoe to the others. The origin of this imagery is obvious. Whenever the natives arrive near the shore of one of the overseas villages, they have to fold the sail and to use the paddles, since there the water is deep, even quite close to the shore, and punting impossible. So 'to paddle' means 'to arrive at the overseas village.' It may be added that in this expression 'we paddle in place,' the two remaining words *in* and *place* would have to be retranslated in a free English interpretation by *near the village*.

With the help of such an analysis as the one just given, this or any other savage utterance can be made comprehensible. In this case we may sum up our results and embody them in a free commentary or paraphrase of the statement:

A number of natives sit together. One of them, who has just come back from an overseas expedition, gives an account of the sailing and boasts about the superiority of his canoe. He tells his audience how, in crossing the sea-arm of Pilolu (between the Trobriands and the Amphletts), his canoe sailed ahead of all others. When nearing their destination, the leading sailors looked back and saw their comrades far behind, still on the sea-arm of Pilolu.

Put in these terms, the utterance can at least be understood broadly, though for an exact appreciation of the shades and details of meaning a full knowledge of the native customs and psychology, as well as of the general structure of their language, is indispensable.

It is hardly necessary perhaps to point out that all I have said in this section is only an illustration on a concrete example of the general principles so brilliantly set forth by Ogden and Richards in Chapters I, III and IV of their work. What I have tried to make clear by analysis of a primitive linguistic text is that language is essentially rooted in the reality of the culture, the tribal life and customs of a people, and that it cannot be explained without constant reference to these broader contexts of verbal utterance. The theories embodied in Ogden's and Richards' diagram of Chapter I, in their treatment of the 'sign-situation' (Chapter III) and in their analysis of perception (Chapter IV) cover and generalize all the details of my example.

III

Returning once more to our native utterance, it needs no special stressing that in a primitive language the meaning of any single word is to a very high degree dependent on its context. The words ' wood ', ' paddle ', ' place ' had to be retranslated in the free interpretation in order to show what is their real meaning, conveyed to a native by the context in which they appear. Again, it is equally clear that the meaning of the expression ' we arrive near the village (of our destination) ' literally : ' we paddle in place ', is determined only by taking it in the context of the whole utterance. This latter again, becomes only intelligible when it is placed within its *context of situation*, if I may be allowed to coin an expression which indicates on the one hand that the conception of *context* has to be broadened and on the other that the *situation* in which words are uttered can never be passed over as irrelevant to the linguistic expression. We see how the conception of context must be substantially widened, if it is to furnish us with its full utility. In fact it must burst the bonds of mere linguistics and be carried over into the analysis of the general conditions under which a language is spoken. Thus, starting from the wider idea of context, we arrive once more at the results of the foregoing section, namely that the study of any language, spoken by a people who live under conditions different from our own and possess a different culture, must be carried out in conjunction with the study of their culture and of their environment.

But the widened conception of *context of situation* yields more than that. It makes clear the difference in scope and method between the linguistics of dead and of living languages. The material on which almost all our linguistic study has been done so far belongs to dead languages. It is present in the form of written documents, naturally isolated, torn out of any *context of situation*. In fact, written statements are set down with the purpose of being self-contained and self-explanatory. A mortuary inscription, a fragment of primeval laws or precepts, a chapter or statement in a sacred book, or to take a more modern example, a passage from a Greek or Latin philosopher, historian or poet—one and all of these were composed with the purpose of bringing their message to posterity unaided, and they had to contain this message within their own bounds.

To take the clearest case, that of a modern scientific book, the writer of it sets out to address every individual reader who will peruse the book and has the necessary scientific training. He tries to influence his reader's mind in certain directions. With the printed text of the book before him, the reader, at the writer's bidding, undergoes a series of processes—he reasons, reflects, remembers, imagines. The book by itself is sufficient to direct the reader's mind to its meaning; and we might be tempted to say metaphorically that the meaning is wholly contained in or carried by the book.

But when we pass from a modern civilized language, of which we think mostly in terms of written records, or from a dead one which survives only in inscription, to a primitive tongue, never used in writing, where all the material lives only in winged words, passing from man to man—there it should be clear at once that the conception of meaning as *contained* in an utterance is false and futile. A statement, spoken in real life, is never detached from the situation in which it has been uttered. For each verbal statement by a human being has the aim and function of expressing some thought or feeling actual at that moment and in that situation, and necessary for some reason or other to be made known to another person or persons—in order either to serve purposes of common action, or to establish ties of purely social communion, or else to deliver the speaker of violent feelings or passions. Without some imperative stimulus of the moment, there can be no spoken statement. In each case, therefore, utterance and situation are bound up inextricably with each other and the context of situation is indispensable for the understanding of the words. Exactly as in the reality of spoken or written languages, a word without *linguistic context* is a mere figment and stands for nothing by itself, so in the reality of a spoken living tongue, the utterance has no meaning except in the *context of situation*.

It will be quite clear now that the point of view of the Philologist, who deals only with remnants of dead languages, must differ from that of the Ethnographer, who, deprived of the ossified, fixed data of inscriptions, has to rely on the living reality of spoken language *in fluxu*. The former has to reconstruct the general situation—*i.e.*, the culture of a past people—from the extant statements, the latter can study directly the conditions and situations characteristic of a culture and interpret the statements through them. Now I claim that the Ethnographer's perspective is the one relevant and real for the formation of fundamental linguistic conceptions and for the study of the life of languages, whereas the Philologist's point of view is fictitious and irrelevant. For language in its origins has been merely the free, spoken *sum total* of utterances such as we find now in a savage tongue. All the foundations and fundamental characteristics of human speech have received their shape and character in the stage of development proper to Ethnographic study and not in the Philologist's domain. To define Meaning, to explain the essential grammatical and lexical characters of language on the material furnished by the study of dead languages, is nothing short of preposterous in the light of our argument. Yet it would be hardly an exaggeration to say that 99 per cent. of all linguistic work has been inspired by the study of dead languages or at best of written records torn completely out of any context of situation. That the Ethnographer's perspective can yield not only generalities but positive, concrete conclusions I shall indicate at least in the following sections.

Here I wish again to compare the standpoint just reached with the results of Messrs Ogden and Richards. I have written the above in my own terminology, in order to retrace the steps of my argument, such as it was before I became acquainted with the present book. But it is obvious that the *context of situation*, on which such a stress is laid here, is nothing else but the *sign-situation* of the Authors. Their contention, which is fundamental to all the arguments of their book, that no theory of meaning can be given without the study of the mechanism of reference, is also the main gist of my reasoning in the foregoing paragraphs. The opening chapters of their work show how erroneous it is to consider Meaning as a real entity, contained in a word or utterance. The ethnographically and historically interesting data and comments of Chapter II show up the manifold illusions and errors due to a false attitude towards words. This attitude in which the word is regarded as a real entity, containing its meaning as a Soul-box contains the spiritual part of a person or thing, is shown to be derived from the primitive, magical uses of language and to reach right into the most important and influential systems of metaphysics. Meaning, the real ' essence ' of a word, achieves thus Real Existence in Plato's realm of Ideas ; and it becomes the Universal, actually existing, of mediæval Realists. The misuse of words, based always on a false analysis of their Semantic function, leads to all the ontological morass in philosophy, where truth is found by spinning out meaning from the word, its assumed receptacle.

The analysis of meaning in primitive languages affords a striking confirmation of Messrs Ogden and Richards' theories. For the clear realization of the intimate connection between linguistic interpretation and the analysis of the culture to which the language belongs, shows convincingly that neither a Word nor its Meaning has an independent and self-sufficient existence. The Ethnographic view of language proves the principle of Symbolic Relativity as it might be called, that is that words must be treated only as symbols and that a psychology of symbolic reference must serve as the basis for all science of language. Since the whole world of 'things-to-be-expressed' changes with the level of culture, with geographical, social and economic conditions, the consequence is that the meaning of a word must be always gathered, not from a passive contemplation of this word, but from an analysis of its functions, with reference to the given culture. Each primitive or barbarous tribe, as well as each type of civilization, has its world of meanings and the whole linguistic apparatus of this people—their store of words and their type of grammar—can only be explained in connection with their mental requirements.

In Chapter III of this book the Authors give an analysis of the psychology of symbolic reference, which together with the material collected in Chapter II is the most satisfactory treatment of the subject which I have ever seen. I wish to remark that the use of the word 'context' by the Authors is compatible, but not identical, with my use of this word in the expression 'context of situation.' I cannot enter here into an attempt to bring our respective nomenclature into line and must allow the reader to test the Relativity of Symbolism on this little example.

IV

So far, I have dealt mainly with the simplest problems of meaning, those associated with the definition of single words and with the lexicographical task of bringing home to a European reader the vocabulary of a strange tongue. And the main result of our analysis was that it is impossible to translate words of a primitive language or of one widely different from our own, without giving a detailed account of the culture of its users and thus providing the common measure necessary for a translation. But though an Ethnographic background is indispensable for a scientific treatment of a language, it is by no means sufficient, and the problem of Meaning needs a special theory of its own. I shall try to show that, looking at language from the Ethnographic perspective and using our conception of *context of situation*, we shall be able to give an outline of a Semantic theory, useful in the work on Primitive Linguistics, and throwing some light on human language in general.

First of all, let us try, from our standpoint, to form a view of the Nature of language. The lack of a clear and precise view of Linguistic function and of the nature of Meaning, has been, I believe, the cause of the relative sterility of much otherwise excellent linguistic theorizing. The direct manner in which the Authors face this fundamental problem and the excellent argument by which they solve it, constitute the permanent value of their work.

The study of the above-quoted native text has demonstrated that an utterance becomes comprehensive only when we interpret it by its context of situation. The analysis of this context should give us a glimpse of a group of savages bound by reciprocal ties of interests and ambitions, of emotional appeal and response. There was boastful reference to competitive trading activities, to ceremonial overseas expeditions, to a complex of sentiments, ambitions and ideas known to the group of speakers and hearers through their being steeped in tribal tradition and having been themselves actors in such events as those described in the narrative. Instead of giving a narrative I could have adduced linguistic samples still more deeply and directly embedded in the context of situation.

Take for instance language spoken by a group of natives engaged in one of their fundamental pursuits in search of subsistence—hunting, fishing, tilling the soil ; or else in one of those activities, in which a savage tribe express some essentially human forms of energy—war, play or sport, ceremonial performance or artistic display such as dancing or singing. The actors in any such scene are all following a purposeful activity, are all set on a definite aim ; they all have to act in a concerted manner according to certain rules established by custom and tradition. In this, Speech is the necessary means of communion ; it is the one indispensable instrument for creating the ties of the moment without which unified social action is impossible.

Let us now consider what would be the type of talk passing between people thus acting, what would be the manner of its use. To make it quite concrete at first, let us follow up a party of fishermen on a coral lagoon, spying for a shoal of fish, trying to imprison them in an enclosure of large nets, and to drive them into small net-bags—an example which I am choosing also because of my personal familiarity with the procedure.[1]

[1] Cf. the writer's article on " Fishing and Fishing Magic in the Trobriand Islands," *Man*, 1918.

The canoes glide slowly and noiselessly, punted by men especially good at this task and always used for it. Other experts who know the bottom of the lagoon, with its plant and animal life, are on the look-out for fish. One of them sights the quarry. Customary signs, or sounds or words are uttered. Sometimes a sentence full of technical references to the channels or patches on the lagoon has to be spoken ; sometimes when the shoal is near and the task of trapping is simple, a conventional cry is uttered not too loudly. Then, the whole fleet stops and ranges itself—every canoe and every man in it performing his appointed task—according to a customary routine. But, of course, the men, as they act, utter now and then a sound expressing keenness in the pursuit or impatience at some technical difficulty, joy of achievement or disappointment at failure. Again, a word of command is passed here and there, a technical expression or explanation which serves to harmonise their behaviour towards other men. The whole group act in a concerted manner, determined by old tribal tradition and perfectly familiar to the actors through life-long experience. Some men in the canoes cast the wide encircling nets into the water, others plunge, and wading through the shallow lagoon, drive the fish into the nets. Others again stand by with the small nets, ready to catch the fish. An animated scene, full of movement follows, and now that the fish are in their power the fishermen speak loudly, and give vent to their feelings. Short, telling exclamations fly about, which might be rendered by such words as: 'Pull in,' 'Let go,' 'Shift further,' 'Lift the net'; or again technical expressions completely untranslatable except by minute description of the instruments used, and of the mode of action.

All the language used during such a pursuit is full of technical terms, short references to surroundings, rapid indications of change—all based on customary types of behaviour, well-known to the participants from personal experience. Each utterance is essentially bound up with the context of situation and with the aim of the pursuit, whether it be the short indications about the movements of the quarry, or references to statements about the surroundings, or the expression of feeling and passion inexorably bound up with behaviour, or words of command, or correlation of action. The structure of all this linguistic material is inextricably mixed up with, and dependent upon, the course of the activity in which the utterances are embedded. The vocabulary, the meaning of the particular words used in their characteristic technicality is not less subordinate to action. For technical language, in matters of practical pursuit, acquires its meaning only through personal participation in this type of pursuit. It has to be learned, not through reflection but through action.

Had we taken any other example than fishing, we would have reached similar results. The study of any form of speech used in connection with vital work would reveal the same grammatical and lexical peculiarities : the dependence of the meaning of each word upon practical experience, and of the structure of each utterance upon the momentary situation in which it is spoken. Thus the consideration of linguistic uses associated with any practical pursuit, leads us to the conclusion that language in its primitive forms ought to be regarded and studied against the background of human activities and as a mode of human behaviour in practical matters. We have to realize that language originally, among primitive, non-civilized peoples was never used as a mere mirror of reflected thought. The manner in which I am using it now, in writing these words, the manner in which the author of a book, or a papyrus or a hewn inscription has to use it, is a very far-fetched and derivative function of language. In this, language becomes a condensed piece of reflection, a record of fact or thought. In its primitive uses, language functions as a link in concerted human activity, as a piece of human behaviour. It is a mode of action and not an instrument of reflection.

These conclusions have been reached on an example in which language is used by people engaged in practical work, in which utterances are embedded in action. This conclusion might be questioned by an objection that there are also other linguistic uses even among primitive peoples who are debarred from writing or any means of external fixation of linguistic texts. Yet even they, it might be urged, have fixed texts in their songs, sayings, myths and legends, and most important, in their ritual and magical formulæ. Are our conclusions about the nature of language correct, when faced with this use of speech ; can our views remain unaltered when, from speech in action, we turn our attention to free narrative or to the use of language in pure social intercourse ; when the object of talk is not to achieve some aim but the exchange of words almost as an end in itself ?

Anyone who has followed our analysis of speech in action and compares it with the discussion of the narrative texts in Section II, will be convinced that the present conclusions apply to narrative speech as well. When incidents are told or discussed among a group of listeners, there is, first, the situation of that moment made up of the respective social, intellectual and emotional attitudes of those present. Within this situation, the narrative creates new bonds and sentiments by the emotional appeal of the words. In the narrative quoted, the boasting of a man to a mixed audience of several visitors and strangers produces feelings of pride or mortification, of triumph or envy. In every case, narrative speech as found in primitive communities is primarily a mode of social action rather than a mere reflection of thought.

A narrative is associated also indirectly with one situation to which it refers—in our text with a performance of competitive sailing. In this relation, the words of a tale are significant because of previous experiences of the listeners; and their meaning depends on the context of the situation referred to, not to the same degree but in the same manner as in the speech of action. The difference in degree is important; narrative speech is derived in its function, and it refers to action only indirectly, but the way in which it acquires its meaning can only be understood from the direct function of speech in action. To use the terminology of this work: the referential function of a narrative is subordinate to its social and emotive function, as classified by the Authors in Chapter X.

The case of language used in free, aimless, social intercourse requires special consideration. When a number of people sit together at a village fire, after all the daily tasks are over, or when they chat, resting from work, or when they accompany some mere manual work by gossip quite unconnected with what they are doing—it is clear that here we have to do with another mode of using language, with another type of speech function. Language here is not dependent upon what happens at that moment, it seems to be even deprived of any context of situation. The meaning of any utterance cannot be connected with the speaker's or hearer's behaviour, with the purpose of what they are doing.

A mere phrase of politeness, in use as much among savage tribes as in a European drawing-room, fulfils a function to which the meaning of its words is almost completely irrelevant. Inquiries about health, comments on weather, affirmations of some supremely obvious state of things—all such are exchanged, not in order to inform, not in this case to connect people in action, certainly not in order to express any thought. It would be even incorrect, I think, to say that such words serve the purpose of establishing a common sentiment, for this is usually absent from such current phrases of intercourse; and where it purports to exist, as in expressions of sympathy, it is avowedly spurious on one side. What is the *raison d'être*, therefore, of such phrases as 'How do you do?' 'Ah, here you are,' 'Where do you come from ? ' ' Nice day to-day '—all of which serve in one society or another as formulæ of greeting or approach ?

I think that, in discussing the function of Speech in mere sociabilities, we come to one of the bedrock aspects of man's nature in society. There is in all human beings the well-known tendency to congregate, to be together, to enjoy each other's company. Many instincts and innate trends, such as fear or pugnacity, all the types of social sentiments such as ambition, vanity, passion for power and wealth, are dependent upon and associated with the fundamental tendency which makes the mere presence of others a necessity for man.[1]

Now speech is the intimate correlate of this tendency, for, to a natural man, another man's silence is not a reassuring factor, but, on the contrary, something alarming and dangerous. The stranger who cannot speak the language is to all savage tribesmen a natural enemy. To the primitive mind, whether among savages or our own uneducated classes, taciturnity means not only unfriendliness but directly a bad character. This no doubt varies greatly with the national character but remains true as a general rule. The breaking of silence, the communion of words is the first act to establish links of fellowship, which is consummated only by the breaking of bread and the communion of food. The modern English expression, ' Nice day to-day ' or the Melanesian phrase, ' Whence comest thou ? ' are needed to get over the strange and unpleasant tension which men feel when facing each other in silence.

After the first formula, there comes a flow of language, purposeless expressions of preference or aversion, accounts of irrelevant happenings, comments on what is perfectly obvious. Such gossip, as found in Primitive Societies, differs only a little from our own. Always the same emphasis of affirmation and consent, mixed perhaps with an incidental disagreement which creates the bonds of antipathy. Or personal accounts of the speaker's views and life history, to which the hearer listens under some restraint and with slightly veiled impatience, waiting till his own turn arrives to speak. For in this use of speech the bonds created between hearer and speaker are not quite symmetrical, the man linguistically active receiving the greater share of social pleasure and self-enhancement. But though the hearing given to such

[1] I avoid on purpose the use of the expression Herd-instinct, for I believe that the tendency in question cannot strictly be called an instinct. Moreover the term Herd-instinct has been misused in a recent sociological work which has, however, become sufficiently popular to establish its views on this subject with the general reader.

utterances is as a rule not as intense as the speaker's own share, it is quite essential for his pleasure, and the reciprocity is established by the change of rôles.

There can be no doubt that we have here a new type of linguistic use—*phatic communion* I am tempted to call it, actuated by the demon of terminological invention—a type of speech in which ties of union are created by a mere exchange of words. Let us look at it from the special point of view with which we are here concerned; let us ask what light it throws on the function or nature of language. Are words in Phatic Communion used primarily to convey meaning, the meaning which is symbolically theirs? Certainly not! They fulfil a social function and that is their principal aim, but they are neither the result of intellectual reflection, nor do they necessarily arouse reflection in the listener. Once again we may say that language does not function here as a means of transmission of thought.

But can we regard it as a mode of action? And in what relation does it stand to our crucial conception of context of situation? It is obvious that the outer situation does not enter directly into the technique of speaking. But what can be considered as *situation* when a number of people aimlessly gossip together? It consists in just this atmosphere of sociability and in the fact of the personal communion of these people. But this is in fact achieved by speech, and the situation in all such cases is created by the exchange of words, by the specific feelings which form convivial gregariousness, by the give and take of utterances which make up ordinary gossip. The whole situation consists in what happens linguistically. Each utterance is an act serving the direct aim of binding hearer to speaker by a tie of some social sentiment or other. Once more language appears to us in this function not as an instrument of reflection but as a mode of action.

I should like to add at once that though the examples discussed were taken from savage life, we could find among ourselves exact parallels to every type of linguistic use so far discussed. The binding tissue of words which unites the crew of a ship in bad weather, the verbal concomitants of a company of soldiers in action, the technical language running parallel to some practical work or sporting pursuit—all these resemble essentially the primitive uses of speech by man in action and our discussion could have been equally well conducted on a modern example. I have chosen the above from a Savage Community, because I wanted to emphasize that such and no other is the nature of *primitive* speech.

Again in pure sociabilities and gossip we use language exactly as savages do and our talk becomes the 'phatic communion' analysed above, which serves to establish bonds of personal union between people brought together by the mere need of companionship and does not serve any purpose of communicating ideas. "Throughout the Western world it is agreed that people must meet frequently, and that it is not only agreeable to talk, but that it is a matter of common courtesy to say something even when there is hardly anything to say "[1]—as the Authors remark. Indeed there need not or perhaps even there must not be anything to communicate. As long as there are words to exchange, phatic communion brings savage and civilized alike into the pleasant atmosphere of polite, social intercourse.

It is only in certain very special uses among a civilized community and only in its highest uses that language is employed to frame and express thoughts. In poetic and literary production, language is made to embody human feelings and passions, to render in a subtle and convincing manner certain inner states and processes of mind. In works of science and philosophy, highly developed types of speech are used to control ideas and to make them common property of civilized mankind.

Even in this function, however, it is not correct to regard language as a mere residuum of reflective thought. And the conception of speech as serving to translate the inner processes of the speaker to the hearer is one-sided and gives us, even with regard to the most highly developed and specialized uses of speech, only a partial and certainly not the most relevant view.

To restate the main position arrived at in this section we can say that language in its primitive function and original form has an essentially pragmatic character; that it is a mode of behaviour, an indispensable element of concerted human action. And negatively: that to regard it as a means for the embodiment or expression of thought is to take a one-sided view of one of its most derivate and specialized functions.

V

This view of the nature of language I have tried to establish by a detailed analysis of examples, by reference to concrete and actual facts. I trust therefore that the distinction which I have explained, between 'mode of action' and 'means of thinking,' will not remain an empty phrase, but that it has received its content from the adduced facts. Nothing, however, establishes the

[1] Cited from Chapter I of the present work.

positive value and empirical nature of a general principle so completely as when it is shown to work in the solution of definite problems of a somewhat difficult and puzzling description.

In linguistics we have an intractable subject of this kind in the Problem of Meaning. It would perhaps be presumptuous for me to tackle this subject in an abstract and general manner and with any philosophical ambition, after it has been shown by Ogden and Richards (Chapters VIII and IX) to be of so highly dangerous a nature. But I simply want to approach it through the narrow avenue of Ethnographic empiricism and show how it looks viewed from the perspective of the pragmatic uses of primitive speech.

This perspective has allowed us to class human speech with the active modes of human behaviour, rather than with the reflective and cognitive ones. But this outside view and wholesale conception must be still supplemented by some more detailed, analytic considerations, if we want to arrive at a clearer idea of Meaning.

In Chapter III of the present work the Authors discuss the psychology of Sign-situations and the acquisition of significance by symbols. I need not repeat or summarize their penetrating analysis, which to me is extremely convincing and satisfactory and forms the corner-stone of their linguistic theory. I wish however to follow up one point in their argument, a point closely related to our pragmatic conception of language.

The Authors reject, and rightly so, the explanations of meaning by suggestion, association or apperception, urging that such explanations are not sufficiently dynamic. Of course new ideas are formed by apperception and since a new idea constitutes a new meaning and receives in due course a new name, apperception is a process by which significance is created. But that happens only in the most highly developed and refined uses of language for scientific purposes. From our previous discussion it should be well established that such a type of formulation of meaning is highly derivative and cannot be taken as the pattern on which to study and explain significance. And this not only with reference to savages, but also in our own linguistic life. For a man who uses his language scientifically has his attitude towards language already developed by and rooted in the more elementary forms of word-function. Before he has ever begun to acquire his scientific vocabulary in a highly artificial manner by apperception—which, moreover, takes place only to a very limited degree—he has learnt to use, used and grown up using words and constructions, the meaning of which has been formed in his mind in quite a different manner. And this manner is primary as regards time, for it is derived from earlier uses ; it is more general, because the vast majority of words thus receive their meaning ; and it is more fundamental, since it refers to the most important and prevalent uses of speech—those which we have indicated above as common to primitive and civilized humanity.

This manner of formation of meaning we must now proceed to analyse more in detail, with reference to our pragmatic view of language. And it will be best done by genetic considerations, by an analysis of infantile uses of words, of primitive forms, of significance and of pre-scientific language among ourselves. Some glimpses of formation of meaning in infancy and childhood will appear the more important, as modern psychology seems to be more and more inclined to assign a permanent influence to early mental habits in the outlook of the adult.

The emission of inarticulate emotional sound and of articulate speech is a biological arrangement of enormous importance to the young and adult of the human species, and is rooted deeply in the instinctive and physiological arrangement of the human organism. Children, savages and civilized adults alike react with vocal expression to certain situations—whether these arouse bodily pain or mental anguish, fear or passion, intense curiosity or powerful joy. These sound reactions are part of the human expression of emotions and as such possess, as has been established by Darwin and others, a survival value or are at least themselves relics of such values. Anyone in contact with infants and small children knows that they express without the slightest ambiguity their mood, their emotion, their need and desire. Concentrating our attention for the moment on infantile utterances of this type, it can be said that each sound is the expression of some emotional state ; that for surrounding people it has a certain significance ; and that it is correlated with the outer situation surrounding and comprising the child's organism—a situation which makes the child hungry or afraid or pleased or interested.

All this is true of the non-articulate sounds emitted by an infant, such as gurgling, wailing, squealing, crowing and weeping. Later on, certain slightly articulated utterances follow, first syllables—*gu*, *ma*, *ba*, etc.—repeated indefinitely, mixed up and blurred by other sounds. These sounds serve in a parallel manner to express certain psycho-physiological states and to expend some of the child's energy. They are a sign of health and they are a form of indispensable exercise. Emission of sounds is at the earliest and at the later stage of verbal development, one of the child's main activities, persistent and passionate, as every parent knows from pleasant and unpleasant experiences alike!

How shall we conceive the formation of meaning at these earliest stages? Here, in this somewhat different approach, the pragmatic view of language obtrudes itself again. The child *acts* by sound at this stage, and acts in a manner which is both adapted to the outer situation, to the child's mental state and which is also intelligible to the surrounding adults. Thus the significance of sound, the meaning of an utterance is here identical with the active response to surroundings and with the natural expression of emotions. The meaning of such a sound is derived from one of the earliest and most important forms of human activity.

When sound begins to articulate, the child's mind develops in a parallel manner and becomes interested in isolating objects from its surroundings, though the most relevant elements, associated with the food and comfort of the infant, have been already singled out previously. At the same time, the child becomes aware of the sounds produced by the adults and the other children of its surroundings, and it develops a tendency to imitate them. The existence of a social milieu surrounding the child is a factor of fundamental biological importance in the upbringing of the human young and it is also an indispensable element in speech formation. Thus the child who begins to articulate certain syllables soon finds these syllables repeated by the adults and this paves the way to a clearer, more articulate enunciation.

It would be extremely interesting to find out, whether and how far some of the earliest articulated sounds have a 'natural' meaning, that is a meaning based on some natural connection between sound and object. The only fact here relevant I can quote from personal observation. I have noticed in two children that at the stage where distinct syllables begin to be formed the repeated sound, *ma*, *ma*, *ma* . . . appears when the child is dissatisfied generally, when some essential want is not fulfilled or some general discomfort is oppressing it. The sound attracts the most important object in its surroundings, the mother, and with her appearance the painful state of mind is remedied. Can it be that the entry of the sound *mama* . . . just at the stage when articulate speech begins—with its emotional significance and its power of bringing the mother to the rescue—has produced in a great number of human languages the root *ma* for *mother?*[1]

However this might be, and whether the child acquires some of its early vocabulary by a spontaneous process or whether all its words come to it from the outside, the manner in which the first items of articulate speech are used is the point which is really interesting and relevant for us in this connection.

The earliest words—*mama*, *dada*, or *papa*, expressions for food, water, certain toys or animals—are not simply imitated and used to describe, name, or identify. Like the previous non-articulate expressions of emotion, these early words also come to be used under the stress of painful situations or strong emotions, when the child cries for its parent or rejoices in her sight, when it clamours for food or repeats with pleasure or excitement the name of some favourite plaything of its surroundings. Here the word becomes the significant reaction, adjusted to situation, expressive of inner state and intelligible to the human milieu.

This latter fact has another very important set of consequences. The human infant, helpless in itself and unable to cope with the difficulties and dangers of its early life, is endowed with very complete arrangements for care and assistance, resulting from the instinctive attachment of the mother and, to a smaller extent, of the father. The child's action on the surrounding world is done through the parents, on whom the child acts again by its appeal, mainly its verbal appeal. When the child clamours for a person, it calls and he appears before it. When it wants food or an object or when it wishes some uncomfortable thing or arrangement to be removed, its only means of action is to clamour, and a very efficient means of action this proves to the child.

To the child, words are therefore not only means of expression but efficient modes of action. The name of a person uttered aloud in a piteous voice possesses the power of materializing this person. Food has to be called for and it appears—in the majority of cases. Thus infantile experience must leave on the child's mind the deep impression that a name has the power over the person or thing which it signifies.

[1] The correspondence between early natural sounds and the nearest kinship terms is well known (cf. Westermarck, *History of Human Marriage*, Vol. I., pp. 242-245). Here I suggest something more: namely that the natural emotional tone of one of these sounds, *ma*, and its significance for the mother, cause her appearance and thus by a natural process form the meaning of the *mama* type of words. The usual opinion is that meaning is given to them, artificially, by adults. "The terms which have been derived from the babble of infants have, of course, been selected, and the use of them has been fixed, by grown-up persons." (Westermarck, *loc. cit.*, p. 245.)

We find thus that an arrangement biologically essential to the human race makes the early articulated words sent forth by children produce the very effect which these words *mean*. Words are to a child active forces, they give him an essential hold on reality, they provide him with the only effective means of moving, attracting and repulsing outer things and of producing changes in all that is relevant. This of course is not the statement of a child's conscious views about language, but it is the attitude implied in the child's behaviour.

Following the manner in which speech is used into the later stage of childhood, we find again that everything reinforces this pragmatic relation to meaning. In all the child's experience, words *mean*, in so far as they act and not in so far as they make the child understand or apperceive. His joy in using words and in expressing itself in frequent repetition, or in playing about with a word, is relevant in so far as it reveals the active nature of early linguistic use. And it would be incorrect to say that such a playful use of words is 'meaningless.' It is certainly deprived of any intellectual purpose, but possesses always an emotional value, and it is one of the child's favourite actions, in which he approaches this or that person or object of his surroundings. When a child greets the approaching person or animal, item of food or toy, with a volley of the repeated name, he establishes a link of liking or disliking between himself and that object. And all the time, up to a fairly advanced age, the name of an object is the first means recurred to, in order to attract, to materialize this thing.

If we transfer now this analysis to conditions of primitive mankind, it will be better not to indulge in essentially imaginary and therefore futile speculations about the beginnings of speech, but simply to cast a glance at the normal uses of language as we see them in empirical observations of savages. Returning to the above examples of a group of natives engaged in a practical pursuit, we see them using technical words, names of implements, specific activities. A word, signifying an important utensil, is used in action, not to comment on its nature or reflect on its properties, but to make it appear, be handed over to the speaker, or to direct another man to its proper use. The meaning of the thing is made up of experiences of its active uses and not of intellectual contemplation. Thus, when a savage learns to understand the meaning of a word, this process is not accomplished by explanations, by a series of acts of apperception, but by learning to handle it. A word *means* to a native the proper use of the thing for which it stands, exactly as an implement *means* something when it can be handled and means nothing when no active experience of it is at hand. Similarly a verb, a word for an action, receives its meaning through an active participation in this action. A word is used when it can produce an action and not to describe one, still less to translate thoughts. The word therefore has a power of its own, it is a means of bringing things about, it is a handle to acts and objects and not a definition of them.

Again, the same view of meaning results from the active uses of speech among ourselves, even among those of us, who, on comparatively rare occasions, can use language in a scientific or literary manner. The innumerable superstitions—the agnostic's fear of blasphemy or at least reluctance to use it, the active dislike of obscene language, the power of swearing—all this shows that in the normal use of words the bond between symbol and referent is more than a mere convention.

The illiterate members of civilized communities treat and regard words very much as savages do, that is as being strongly bound up with the reality of action. And the way in which they value verbal knowledge—proverbs, sayings, and, nowadays, news—as the only form of wisdom, gives a definite character to this implied attitude. But here I encroach on a field amply illustrated and analysed in this book.

Indeed, on anyone who has read the brilliant chapters of Ogden and Richards and grasped the main trend of their argument, it will have dawned before now that all the argument of this Section is a sort of foot-note to their fundamental contention that the primitive, magical attitude towards words is responsible for a good deal in the general use and abuse of language, more especially in philosophical speculation. By the rich material cited in Chapter II, and in *Word Magic*, by the examples of Chapters VII, VIII, and IX, and by much of what is incidentally said, we are made to realize how deeply rooted is the belief that a word has some power over a thing, that it participates of the nature of the thing, that it is akin or even identical in its contained ' meaning ' with the thing or with its prototype.

But whence is this magical attitude derived ? Here the study of the early stages of speech steps in helpfully and the Ethnographer can make himself useful to the Philosopher of Language. In studying the infantile formation of meaning and the savage or illiterate meaning, we found this very magical attitude towards words. The word gives power, allows one to exercise an influence over an object or an action. The meaning of a word arises out of familiarity, out of ability to use, out of the faculty of direct clamouring as with the infant, or practically directing as with primitive man. A word is used always in direct active conjunction with the reality it means. The word acts on the thing and the thing releases the word in the human mind. This indeed is nothing more or less than the essence of the theory which underlies the use of verbal magic. And this theory we find based on real psychological experiences in primitive forms of speech.

Before the earliest philosophical speculation sets in, there emerges the practice and theory of magic, and in this, man's natural attitude towards words becomes fixed and formulated by a special lore and tradition. It is through the study of actual spells and verbal magic as well as by the analysis of savage ideas on magic that we can best understand this developed traditional view of the secret power of appropriate words on certain things. Briefly it may be said that such study simply confirms our theoretical analysis of this section. In magical formulæ we find a preponderance of words with high emotional tension, of technical terms, of strong imperatives, of verbs expressing hope, success, achievement. So much must suffice here and the reader is referred for more data to Chapter II of this book, and to the chapters on 'Magic' and 'The Power of Words in Magic' in the above quoted work of mine.[1]

It may be of interest to interpret the results of our analysis of the earliest stages of meaning on the diagram in which the relations between Symbol, Act of Thought, and Referent are represented by a triangle at the beginning of Chapter I of this book. This diagram represents very adequately the said relations in the developed uses of speech. It is characteristic in this triangle that the base, indicated by a dotted line, represents the imputed relation which obtains between a Symbol and the thing it refers to, its Referent as the Authors name it. In developed functions of speech, such as are, or at least should be, used in philosophical speculation or scientific language (and it is chiefly with these functions that the Authors are concerned in this book) the gulf of Meaning, as it could be called, is bridged over only by the Act of Thought—the bent line of the two shoulders of the triangle.

Let us try to represent by analogous diagrams the earlier stages of Meaning. At the first stage, when the utterance is a mere sound-reaction, expressive, significant and correlated with the situation, but not involving any act of thought, the triangle is reduced to its base, which stands for a real connection—that

[1] *Argonauts of the Western Pacific.*

between SOUND-REACTION and SITUATION. The first cannot yet be termed a Symbol nor the latter a Referent.

FIRST STAGE

SOUND-REACTION (*connected directly with*) SITUATION

SECOND STAGE

ACTIVE SOUND (Semi-articulated or articulated) (*correlated with*) REFERENT

The beginnings of articulate speech, when, parallel with its appearance Referents begin to emerge out of the Situation, are still to be represented by a single solid line of actual correlation (second stage). The sound is not a real symbol yet, for it is not used detached from its Referent.

THIRD STAGE

(A)
Speech in Action.

ACTIVE SYMBOL (*Used to handle*) REFERENT

(B)
Narrative Speech.

ACT OF IMAGERY.

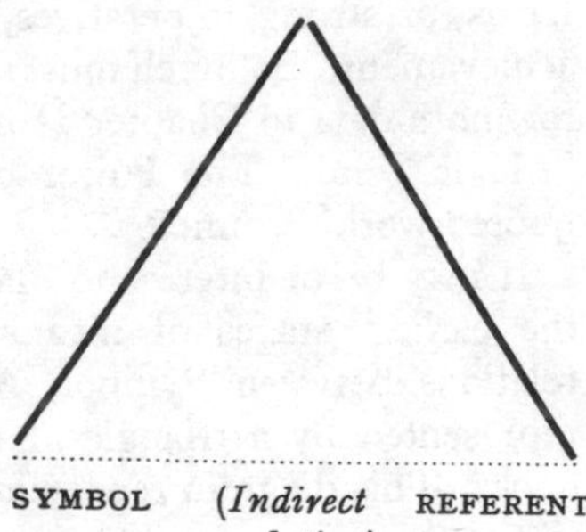

SYMBOL (*Indirect relation*) REFERENT

(C)
Language of Ritual Magic.

RITUAL ACT
(*based on traditional belief*).

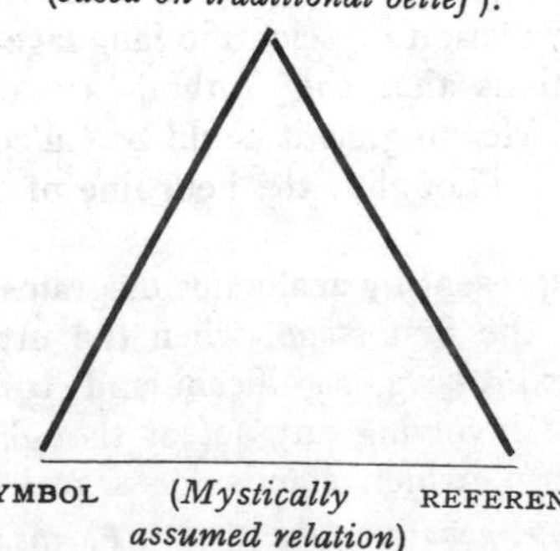

SYMBOL (*Mystically assumed relation*) REFERENT

In the third stage we have to distinguish between the three fundamental uses of language, active, narrative and ritual. Each of them is made sufficiently clear by the diagram here given, which must be taken in conjunction with our previous analysis. The final stage of developed language is represented by the triangle of Ogden and Richards, and its genetic relation to its humble predecessors may explain some of its anatomy. First of all : the possibility of extending the Authors' diagram or pushing it backwards into primitive speech-uses affords an additional proof of its validity and adequacy. Further the solid nature of almost all the bases of our triangles explains why the dotted line in the final figure shows such tenacity and why it is capable of so much mischief. The extreme vitality of the magical attitude to words is explained in our foot-note to this, the theory of the book, not only by a reference to the primitive uses of language by savage and no doubt by prehistoric man, but also by its perpetual confirmation in infantile uses of language and in the very mechanism by which meaning is acquired in every individual life.

Some other corollaries might be drawn from our theory of primitive meaning. Thus we might find in it an additional confirmation of the Authors' analysis of definition. It is clear that they are right when they maintain that 'verbal' and 'real' definition must in the end come to the same thing, and that the making of this artificial distinction into a fundamental one has created a false problem. Meaning, as we have seen, does not come to Primitive Man from contemplation of things, or analysis of occurrences, but in practical and active acquaintance with relevant situations. The real knowledge of a word comes through the practice of appropriately using it within a certain situation. The word, like any man-made implement, becomes significant only after it has been used and properly used under all sorts of conditions. Thus, there can be no definition of a word without the reality which it *means* being present. And again, since a significant symbol is necessary for man to isolate and grasp an item of reality, there is no defining of a thing without defining a word at the same time. Definition in its most primitive and fundamental form is nothing but a sound-reaction, or an articulate word joined to some relevant aspect of a situation by means of an appropriate human action. This definition of definition does not, of course, refer to the same type of linguistic use as the one discussed by the Authors of this book. It is interesting to see, however, that their conclusions, which are arrived at by the study of higher types of speech, hold good in the domain of primitive uses of words.

VI

In the course of this essay I have tried to narrow down the scope of each linguistic problem discussed. At first it was the principle that the study of language needs an ethnographic background of general culture, that linguistics must be a section, indeed the most important one, of a general science of culture. Then an attempt was made to show that this general conclusion leads us to certain more definite views about the nature of language, in which we conceived human speech as a mode of action, rather than as a countersign of thought. We proceeded then to a discussion of the origins and early forms of Meaning, as it must have been experienced by Primitive Man. This gave us the explanation and showed us the roots of the magical attitude of man to words. Thus we moved by a series of conclusions, each more concrete and definite than the previous one.

I wish now to touch upon one more problem, still more definite and concrete than the others, that namely of the structure of Language.

Every human tongue has a definite structure of its own. We have types of isolating, agglutinative, polysynthetic, incorporating and inflectional languages, In every one of them, the means of linguistic action and expression can be brought under certain rules, classified according to certain categories. This body of structural rules with their exceptions and irregularities, the various classes into which the elements of the language can be ranged, is what we call ' the grammatical structure ' of a language.

Language is usually, though, as we have seen, incorrectly, regarded as ' the expression of thought by means of Speech Sounds.' The obvious idea, therefore, is that linguistic structure is the result of the rules of human thought, that ' every grammatical category is—or ought to be—the expression of some logical category.' But it does not require much mental effort to realize that to hope for such perfect conjugal harmony between Language and Logic, is far too optimistic : that in actuality ' they often diverge from one another,' in fact that they are constantly at loggerheads and that Language often ill-treats Logic, till it is deserted by her.[1]

[1] I quote from H. Sweet (*Introduction to the History of Language*), because this author is one of the cleverest thinkers on language. Yet even he sees no alternative but Rule of Logic or Anarchy in language.

Thus we are faced by a dilemma: either the grammatical categories are derived from the laws of thought, and we are at a loss to explain why the two are so ill adapted to each other. Why, if Language has grown up in the services of Thought, has it been so little influenced or impressed by its pattern? Or we can, to escape these difficulties, run on to the other horn of the dilemma as most grammarians do. They haughtily turn away from the sour grapes of any deeper probing or philosophy of Language, and simply affirm that Grammar rules in its own right, by a sort of divine grace, no doubt; that the empire of Grammar must continue in its splendid isolation, as a power hostile to Thought, order, system and common sense.

Both views—the one appealing to Logic for help and the other indicating an autonomous rule for Grammar—are equally in disagreement with facts and to be rejected. It is nothing short of absurd to assume, with the rigid grammarian, that grammar has grown up as a sort of wild weed of human faculties for no purpose whatever except its own existence. The spontaneous generation of meaningless monstrosities in the brain of Man will not be easily admitted by psychology—unless of course the brain is that of a rigid scientific specialist. And, general principles or predilections apart, all human languages show, in spite of great divergences, a certain fundamental agreement in structure and means of grammatical expression. It would be both preposterous and intellectually pusillanimous to give up at the outset any search for deeper forces which must have produced these common, universally human features of Language. In our Theory of Meaning, we have seen that Language serves for definite purposes, that it functions as an instrument used for and adapted to a definite aim. This adaptation, this correlation between language and the uses to which it is put, has left its traces in linguistic structure. But of course it is clear that we must not look in the domain of logical thinking and philosophical speculation for light on the aim and purposes of early human speech, and so this purely logical view of language is as useless as the purely grammatical one.

Real categories there are, on which the grammatical divisions are based and moulded. But these real categories are not derived from any primitive philosophic system, built up by contemplation of the surrounding world and by crude speculations, such as have been imputed to primitive man by certain anthropologists. Language in its structure mirrors the real categories derived from practical attitudes of the child and of primitive or natural man to the surrounding world. The grammatical categories with all their peculiarities, exceptions, and refractory insubordination to rule, are the reflection of the makeshift, unsystematic, practical outlook imposed by man's struggle for existence in the widest sense of this word. It would be futile to hope that we might be able to reconstruct exactly this pragmatic world vision of the primitive, the savage or the child, or to trace in detail its correlation to grammar. But a broad outline and a general correspondence can be found ; and the realization of this frees us anyhow from logical shackles and grammatical barrenness.

Of course the more highly developed a language is and the longer its evolutional history, the more structural strata it will embody. The several stages of culture—savage, barbarous, semi-civilized, and civilized ; the various types of use—pragmatic, narrative, ritual, scholastic, theological—will each have left its mark. And even the final, powerful, but by no means omnipotent purification by scientific use, will in no way be able to obliterate the previous imprints. The various structural peculiarities of a modern, civilized language carry, as shown by Ogden and Richards, an enormous dead weight of archaic use, of magical superstition and of mystical vagueness.

If our theory is right, the fundamental outlines of grammar are due mainly to the most primitive uses of language. For these preside over the birth and over the most plastic stages of linguistic development, and leave the strongest mark. The categories derived from the primitive use will also be identical for all human languages, in spite of the many superficial diversities. For man's essential nature is identical and the primitive uses of language are the same. Not only that, but we have seen that the pragmatic function of language is carried on into its highest stages, especially through infantile use and through a backsliding of adults into unsophisticated modes of thinking and speaking. Language is little influenced by thought, but Thought, on the contrary, having to borrow from action its tool—that is, language—is largely influenced thereby. To sum up, we can say that the fundamental grammatical categories, universal to all human languages, can be understood only with reference to the pragmatic Weltanschauung of primitive man, and that, through the use of Language, the barbarous primitive categories must have deeply influenced the later philosophies of mankind.

This must be exemplified by a detailed analysis of one at least of the concrete problems of grammar ; and I shall choose for a brief discussion the problem of the Parts of Speech. We must turn, therefore, to a stage in the development of the individual or of mankind when the human being is not interested in reflection or speculation, when he does not classify phenomena for purposes of knowledge but only in so far as they enter into his direct dealings with his conditions of existence. The child, the primitive man, or the unsophisticated individual has to use Language as an indispensable means of influencing his social surroundings. In all this, a very definite attitude develops, a manner of taking notice of certain items of reality, of singling them out and connecting them—an attitude not framed in any system of thought, but expressed in behaviour and, in the case of primitive communities, embodied in the ensemble of cultural achievements among which Language looms first and foremost.

Let us begin with the relation of a child to its surroundings. At the earliest stage, its actions and behaviour are governed by the wants of the organism. It is moved by hunger and thirst, desire for warmth and a certain cleanliness, proper conditions for rest and sleep, a due amount of freedom for movement, and last, not least, the need of human companionship, and of handling by adults. At a very early stage the child reacts to general situations only, and hardly even singles out the nearest persons who minister to its comfort and supply it with food. But this does not last long. Even within the first couple of weeks, some phenomena, some units begin to stand out from the general surroundings. Human faces are of special interest—the child smiles back and utters sounds of pleasure. The mother or the nurse is gradually recognized, as even before that, are objects or vehicles of food.

Undoubtedly the strongest emotional appeal is exercised over the child by the personality of its mother, and these articles or vehicles of food. Anyone imbued with Freudian principles might feel inclined to look here for a direct connection. In the young of man, as in those of any Mammalian species, the infant associates with its mother all its emotions about food. Primarily she is for him a vessel of nourishment. If therefore nutrition is given by any other means—and it must be remembered that savage infants are fed with chewed vegetable food almost from birth, as well as by the breast—the tender feelings by which an infant responds to maternal cares are probably extended to other ministrations of food. When one sees the loving attitude of a modern bottle-fed baby to its bottle, the tender caresses and fond smiles which it bestows on it, the identity of response to artificial and natural food-conveyers seems to imply an identical mental attitude of the infant. If this be so, we gain an insight into a very early process of personification of objects, by which relevant and important things of the surroundings release the same emotional response as do the revelant persons. However true may be this suggestion of a direct identification, there is no doubt that a great similarity exists between the early attitude towards the nearest persons and objects which satisfy the needs of nutrition.

When the child begins to handle things, play with objects of its surroundings, an interesting feature can be observed in its behaviour, also associated with the fundamental nutritive tendency of an infant. It tries to put everything into its mouth. Hence the child pulls, tries to bend and ply soft or plastic objects, or it tries to detach parts of rigid ones. Very soon isolated, detachable things become of much greater interest and value than such as cannot be handled in their entirety. As the child grows up and can move things more freely, this tendency to isolate, to single out physically, develops further. It lies at the bottom of the well-known destructive tendency of children. This is interesting, in this connection, for it shows how one mental faculty of singling out relevant factors of the surroundings—persons, nutritive objects, things—has its parallel in the bodily behaviour of the child. Here again, in studying this detail of behaviour, we find a confirmation of our pragmatic view of early mental development.

There can also be found a tendency to personify objects of special interest. By the term ' personification ' I do not mean here any theory or view of the child's own. I mean, as in the case of food items, that we can observe in him a type of behaviour which does not discriminate essentially between persons and objects. The child likes and dislikes some of his playthings, gets angry with them should they become unwieldy ; he hugs, kisses and shows signs of attachment towards them. Persons, no doubt, stand out first in time and foremost in importance. But even from this it results that the relation to them is a sort of pattern for the child's attitude towards things.

Another important point is the great interest in animals. From my own observation, I can affirm that children a few months old, who did not take any prolonged interest in inanimate things, would follow a bird in its movements for some time. It was also one of the first words which a child would understand ; that is, it would look for the bird when it was named. The interest shown in animals at later stages of childhood is well known. In this connection, it is of importance to us, because an animal and especially a bird with its spontaneous movements, with its ease of detachment from surroundings, with its unquestionable reminiscence of persons, is just such an object as would arouse the child's interest, according to our theory.

Analysing the present-day savage in his relation to the surroundings, we find a clear parallel to the attitude just described. The outer world interests him in so far as it yields things useful. Utility here of course must be understood in its broadest sense, including not only what man can consume as food, use for shelter and implement, but all that stimulates his activities in play, ritual, war, or artistic production.

All such significant things stand out for the savage as isolated, detached units against an undifferentiated background. When moving with savages through any natural milieu—sailing on the sea, walking on a beach or through the jungle, or glancing across the starlit sky—I was often impressed by their tendency to isolate the few objects important to them, and to treat the rest as mere background. In a forest, a plant or tree would strike me, but on inquiry I would be informed—' Oh, that is just " bush." ' An insect or bird which plays no part in the tradition or the larder would be dismissed ' *Mauna wala* '—' merely a flying animal.' But if, on the contrary, the object happened to be useful in one way or another, it would be named ; detailed reference to its uses and properties would be given, and the thing thus would be distinctly individualized. The same would happen with regard to stars, landscape features, minerals, fishes and shells. Everywhere there is the tendency to isolate that which stands in some connection, traditional, ritual, useful to man, and to bundle all the rest into one indiscriminate heap. But even within this tendency there is visibly a preference for isolated small, easily handled objects. Their interest in animals is relatively greater than in plants ; greater in shells than in minerals, in flying insects than in crawling ones. That which is easily detached is preferred. In the landscape, the small details are often named and treated in tradition, and they arouse interest, while big stretches of land remain without name and individuality.

The great interest taken by primitive man in animals forms a curious parallel to the child's attitude ; and the psychological reasons of both are, I think, similar. In all manifestations of Totemism, Zoolatry, and of the various animal influences in primitive folk-lore, belief and ritual, the interest of the savage in animals finds its expression.

Now let us restate the nature of this general category in which primitive mind places persons, animals and things. This rough, uncouth category is not defined, but strongly felt and well expressed in human behaviour. It is constructed on selective criteria of biological utility as well as further psychological and social uses and values. The prominent position taken up in it by persons colours it in such a way that things and animals enter into it with a personified character. All items of this category are also individualized, isolated, and treated as units. Out of an undifferentiated background, the practical Weltanschauung of primitive man isolates a category of persons and personified things. It is clear at once that this category roughly corresponds to that of substance—especially to the Aristotelian *ousia*. But, of course, it owes nothing whatever to any philosophical speculation, early or late. It is the rough, uncouth matrix out of which the various conceptions of substance could be evolved. It might be called *crude substance*, or *protousia* for those who prefer learned sounds to simple ones.

As we have seen, parallel with the child's early mental attitudes, and presumably also with those of man in the first stages of his development, there comes the evolution of significant, articulate sound. The category of *crude substance* so prominent in the early mental outlook requires and receives articulate sounds to signify its various items. The class of words used for naming persons and personified things forms a primitive grammatical category of noun-substantives. Thus, this part of speech is seen to be rooted in active modes of behaviour and in active uses of speech, observable in child and in savage, and assumable in primitive man.

Let us next treat briefly the second important class of words—the action-words or verbs. The underlying real category appears later in the child's mental outlook, and it is less preponderant in that of the savage. To this corresponds the fact that the grammatical structure of verbs is less developed in savage tongues. Indeed, human action centres round objects. The child is and has to be aware of the food or of the ministering person before it can or need disentangle the act from the agent or become aware of its own acts. The bodily states of a child also stand out much less from the situation than the things which enter into the latter. Thus only at a subsequent stage of the child's development can we see that it disentangles the changes in its surroundings from the objects which change. This happens at a stage when articulate sounds have begun to be used by the infant. Actions such as eating, drinking, resting, walking ; states of the body, such as sleep, hunger, rest ; moods, such as like and dislike begin to be expressed. Of this real category of action, state and mood, we can say that it lends itself to command as well as to indication or description, that it is associated with the element of change, that is, time, and that it stands in a specially close connection with the persons of the speaker and hearer. In the outlook of savages, the same characters could be noticed in this category; great interest in all changes referring to the human being, in phases and types of human action, in states of human body and moods. This brief indication allows us to state that at the primitive stages of human speech there must have existed a real category into which entered all items of change capable of temporal modification, bearing the character of human mood and of human will, and bound up with the personal action of man.

When we look at the class of words used to denote items of this real category, we find a close correspondence between category and part of speech. The action-word, or verb, is capable in all languages of grammatical modifications expressing temporal relation, moods or modes of utterance, and the verb is also closely associated with pronouns, a class of words which corresponds to another real category.

A few words must be said about the pronouns. What is the real category of primitive human behaviour and primitive speech habits corresponding to that small but extremely vital class of words? Speech, as we saw, is one of the principal modes of human action, hence the actor in speech, the speaker, stands to the foreground of the pragmatic vision of the world. Again, as Speech is associated with concerted behaviour, the speaker has constantly to refer to hearer or hearers. Thus, the speaker and hearer occupy, so to speak, the two principal corner-sites in the perspective of linguistic approach. There comes then a very limited, special class of word corresponding to a real category, constantly in use, easily associable with action-words, but similar in its grammatical nature to nouns—the part of speech called pronoun, including a few words only, but constantly in use; as a rule short, easily manageable words, appearing in intimate association with the verb, but functioning almost as nouns. This part of speech, it is obvious, corresponds closely to its real category. The correspondence could be followed into many more interesting details—the special asymmetric position of the third pronominal person, the problem of genders and classificatory particles, shown especially in the third person.[1]

[1] Cf. the writer's article on 'Classificatory Particles' in the *Bulletin of Oriental Studies*, Vol. II.

One point, however, referring to a common characteristic of nouns and pronouns and dealing with the declension of the various cases of the noun, must still be touched upon. The real category of this latter is derived from personified units of the surroundings. In the child, the first attitude towards items of this category is discrimination, based on biological utility and on pleasure in perceiving them. The infant hails them in significant sounds, or names them with articulate words on their appearance, and calls for them in need. Thus these words, the nouns, are submitted to a definite use, that of naming and appeal. To this there corresponds a subclass of noun-substantives which could be called the appellative case, and which is similar to some uses of the vocative and nominative in the Indo-European declension.

In the more developed uses of Language, this becomes a more efficient adjunct of action. The thing-word comes into a nearer association with the action-word. Persons are named, by their names or by pronominal designations in association with what they do: 'I go,' 'thou comest,' 'so-and-so drinks,' 'animal runs,' etc. The name of a person or personified thing is thus used in a different manner, with a different mode of meaning as an actor, or technically as the subject of action. This is the use corresponding to the subjective case in which a noun is always put as the subject of a predication. It may be said that to this case in nouns corresponds a class of pronouns, the personal pronouns, I, thou, he.

Action is carried out with relation to certain objects. Things and persons are handled. Their names, when associated with an action-word in that manner, stand in the objective case, and pronouns are used in a special form, viz., that called objective or reflexive.

Since language is rooted in man's practical interest in things and persons there is another relationship of fundamental importance, that namely in which a person can lay a definite claim to relation with or possession of, another person or thing. With regard to the surroundings nearest people, there are the ties of kinship and friendship. With regard to things, there comes the economic sentiment of possession. The relation of two nouns, standing to each other as a thing or person related to or possessed by another thing or person, can be called the genitival or possessive relation; and it is found as a distinct mode of connecting two nouns in all human languages. To this corresponds also the genitive case of European languages in its most characteristic uses. In pronouns again, there is a special class of possessive pronouns which expresses relationship.

Finally, one mode of action towards outer things or people stands out from the others, namely that determined by spatial conditions. Without going more into detail on this subject, I suggest that a definite subclass of substantival uses can be assumed in all languages—that corresponding to a prepositional case.

There are still obviously further categories resulting from man's utilitarian attitude, those of the attributes or qualities of a thing, characteristics of an action, relations between things, relations between situations, and it would be possible to show that adjective, adverb, preposition, conjunction are based on these real categories. One could proceed also, still dealing on the one hand with the Semantic Matter-to-be-expressed and on the other with structural features of Language, to explain these latter by a reference to real facts of primitive human nature.

This short sketch, however, is sufficient to indicate the method and the argument, by which such a genetic, primitive Semantics could be established—a science which, referring to the primitive attitude of Man towards Reality, would show what is the real nature of grammatical categories. The results of such primitive Semantics even in so far as we have indicated them, stand, I think, in close connection with the results of Ogden and Richards. Their contention is that a false attitude towards Language and its functions is one of the main obstacles in the advance of philosophical thought and scientific investigation, and in the ever-growing practical uses of language in the press, pamphlet and novel. Now in this and the previous section, I have tried to show that such a crude and unsound attitude towards Language and Meaning must exist. I have tried to demonstrate how it has arisen and why it had to persist; and I try to trace it even into details of grammatical structure.

There is one more thing to add. Through later processes of linguistic use and of thinking, there took place an indiscriminate and wholesale shifting of roots and meanings from one grammatical category to another. For according to our view of primitive Semantics, each significant root originally must have had its place, and one place only, in its proper verbal category. Thus, the roots meaning 'man,' 'animal,' 'tree,' 'stone,' 'water,' are essentially nominal roots. The meanings 'sleep,' 'eat,' 'go,' 'come,' 'fall,' are verbal. But as language and thought develop, the constant action of metaphor, of generalization, analogy and abstraction, and of similar linguistic uses build up links between the categories and obliterate the boundary lines, thus allowing words and roots to move freely over the whole field of Language. In analytic languages, like Chinese and English, this ubiquitous nature of roots is most conspicuous, but it can be found even in very primitive languages.

Now Mr Ogden and Mr Richards have brought out in a most convincing manner the extreme persistence of the old realist fallacy that a word vouches for, or contains, the reality of its own meaning. A peep behind the scenes of primitive root-formation, of the reality of primitive categories and of their subsequent, insidious collapse, adds an important document to the Authors' views. The migration of roots into improper places has given to the imaginary reality of hypostatized meaning a special solidity of its own. For, since early experience warrants the substantival existence of anything found within the category of Crude Substance or Protousia, and subsequent linguistic shifts introduce there such roots as ' going,' ' rest,' ' motion,' etc., the obvious inference is that such abstract entities or ideas live in a real world of their own. Such harmless adjectives as ' good ' or ' bad,' expressing the savage's half-animal satisfaction or dissatisfaction in a situation, subsequently intrude into the enclosure reserved for the clumsy, rough-hewn blocks of primitive substance, are sublimated into ' Goodness ' and ' Badness ' and create whole theological worlds, and systems of Thought and Religion. It must, of course, be remembered that the theory of Ogden and Richards, and the view here expressed, maintain most emphatically that Language, and all Linguistic processes derive their power only from real processes taking place in man's relation to his surroundings. I have merely touched upon the question of linguistic shiftings, and it would be necessary to account for them by the psychological and sociological processes of barbarous and semi-civilized communities; exactly as we accounted for Primitive Linguistics by analysing the mind of Primitive Man—and as the Authors of this book account for the virtues and imperfections of the present-day language by their masterly analysis of the human mind in general.

SUPPLEMENT II

THE IMPORTANCE OF A THEORY OF SIGNS AND A CRITIQUE OF LANGUAGE IN THE STUDY OF MEDICINE

By F. G. Crookshank, M.D., F.R.C.P.

Although the Art of Medicine has been greatly advanced, in many respects, during the last century : although the Practitioners of that Art do freely draw upon the vast storehouse of facts called scientific, to the great benefit of suffering humanity ; and although all medical men have some acquaintance with certain sciences of which the province is in part coterminous with that of the Art of Medicine, there is to-day no longer any Science of Medicine, in the formal sense.

It is true that observation and thought have led medical men to form generalizations which have obtained acceptance ; but there is no longer any organized or systematized *corpus*, or formulated Theory, which can be held to constitute the Science of Medicine, and (in a now obsolete terminology) to form an integral part of Natural Philosophy.

I say ' no longer ' for, in other days, such a Science of Medicine (or, of Physic) did exist, however much and justly we may contemn the ' facts,' the generalizations, and the Theory, by which, at different times, it was built up. To-day, however, notwithstanding the abundance of what are called our accurately observed facts, and the perfection of our scientific methods, writers and lecturers on Medicine find it needful to protest loudly that Medicine is not, and never will be one of the exact sciences.

Perhaps Professors and Practitioners do not always pause to consider what an exact science is, and which are the exact sciences, and why. But the protestation seems a plea for the exemption of medical writers from the duties of defining their terms, and stating their premises ; while, by implication, we are left to accept the inference that the accumulated facts and accepted generalizations with which doctors are concerned are without interrelation or interdependence, and so cannot be arranged in any orderly fashion, or linked together by any general Theory, as can be those dealt with by astronomers, chemists, and biologists.

The province of Medicine seems, indeed, thus to constitute a kind of Alsatia, an *enclave* in the Universe, of which the exploitation is only permitted to the licensed few.

Here for the most part interest is arrested, and it excites neither resentment nor curiosity that Medicine should not be amongst the subjects whose pursuit may lead to the Doctorate of Science, and that there should be a great gulf fixed between the ' scientific ' and the ' medical ' studies of the young physician and surgeon.

The explanation of this indifference is obscure, and to search it out were perhaps irrelevant, but the present position of Medicine requires examination.

It may be said, in general terms, that some statement and attempted definition of fundamentals is necessary to the successful pursuit of any of the recognized sciences, and no systematic exposition of any of these sciences is ever made without the adoption of some *point de départ* which, as it is implied, agreed, or perhaps stated, has been determined by earlier examination, discussion, and decision concerning the nature of things and knowledge, and our methods of thought and communication.

Certainly, I am in the fullest agreement with the Authors of this book if they suggest that lately men of science have too often failed to appreciate that importance of agreement concerning signs and symbols which was so present to the minds of the Scholastics ; and certainly it cannot be said that the *points de départ* adopted by our men of science are always well chosen. But, after all, it is better to set out boldly and with intention rather than to wander round declaring there is neither road nor signpost : and, however defective in form and content many of the first principles and definitions in our scientific text-books, systematic expositors do at least admit the necessity for, and the propriety of some discussion of fundamentals. The case of the doctors is more parlous.

Medicine is to-day an Art or Calling, to whose exercise certain Sciences are no doubt ancilliary ; but she had forfeited pretension to be deemed a Science, *because* her Professors and Doctors decline to define fundamentals or to state first principles, and refuse to consider, in express terms, the relations between Things, Thoughts and Words involved in their communications to others.

So true is this that, although our text-books are occupied with accounts of ‘ diseases,’ and how to recognize, treat and stamp out such ‘ things,’ the late Dr Mercier was perfectly justified when, in not the least incisive of his valuable papers, he declared that “ doctors have formulated no definition of what is meant by ‘ a disease ’,” and went on to say that the time is now arrived in the history of Medicine when a definition of her fundamental concepts is required (*Science Progress*, 1916-17).

Dr Mercier was perfectly justified in his statements, because he was writing of the Medicine of to-day. Had he been acquainted with such ‘ introductory chapters ’ as those of Fernel (1485-1557) entitled respectively “ Quo doctrinæ atque demonstrationis ordine ars medica constituenda sit ” and “ Morbi definitio, quid affectus, quid affectio,” he would not have failed to insist that, when Medicine was a Science, even though less ‘ scientific ’ than to-day, some definitions were attempted, some principles were asserted and some distinction was admitted between Names, Notions, and Happenings.

Nowadays, however, though we accumulate what we call ‘ facts ’ or records of facts without number, in no current text-book is any attempt made to define what is meant by ‘ a disease,’ though some kind of definition is sometimes attempted of ‘ disease’ and of particular diseases. In a word, no attempt is made to distinguish between what we observe in persons who are ill, on the one hand, and the general notions we form in respect of like illnesses in different persons, together with the ‘ linguistic accessories ’ made use of by us for purposes of communication concerning the same, on the other.

It is true that Sir Clifford Allbutt did never cease to tilt, though in a somewhat lonely field, at the ‘ morbid entities ’ which some people tell us diseases are, and not the least pungent of his criticisms may be found in the *British Medical Journal*, for 2nd September 1922, on p. 401.

But the hardy and rare few who have sought (though in language less picked and perhaps less peregrinate) to express the same truths as Sir Clifford, have had hard measure dealt them.

They have been contemned as traffickers, not in the ‘ concrete facts ’ and indifferent reasoning proper to Medicine of the Twentieth Century, but in wordy *nugæ* and in something contemptuously called Metaphysics. For only ‘ mad doctors ’ may in these scientific times dabble in Philosophy without loss of their reputation as practitioners !

And it is perhaps a sign of the times that the admirable essay contributed by Sir Clifford Allbutt to the first edition of his *System of Medicine* in 1896, in which were discussed, in inimitable style, such topics as Diagnosis, Diseases, Causes, Types, Nomenclature and Terminology, should have disappeared from subsequent issues. This essay is now seldom mentioned : perhaps it is even less frequently read. But, to the present writer, in 1896 a raw diplomate, it came as something of a revelation for which he has ever since been humbly grateful.

Now it is true that all teachers and professors of Medicine—save those who, though ' qualified ' are empirics, or ' unqualified ' are quacks—are dependent in the communication of their researches to their fellows and of instruction to their pupils, upon the use they make of Symbols, and upon their understanding of the difference between Thoughts and Things : if, that is, they are not to set up Idols in the Market Place. But, one result of the desuetude into which has fallen the custom of prefacing our text-books with such preliminary discussion as may stimulate, if not satisfy, the thoughtful and intelligent, is that few now comprehend the distinctions between Words, Thoughts, and Things, or the relations engaged between them when statements are communicated.

Common sense, it is true, saves from detection and gross error those who practise their art empirically : so long, that is, as they do not seek or obtain publication of their occasional addresses in our medical Journals, for it is precisely in our most orthodox periodicals and in the Transactions of our most stately Societies that the most melancholy examples of confusion and error arising from a neglect of fundamentals may be seen.

Particularly is this so when any ' new ' experience or idea comes up for discussion, and consequent assimilation or rejection ; and it was a very special case of this nature that, in 1918, turned the thoughts of the present writer back to what he had learned from Sir Clifford Allbutt in 1896, and that has since led him to very sincere appreciation of the purpose and accomplishment of the Authors of this book.

It is thought that some useful purpose may be served if some exposition of this special case is here attempted, and that particular attention may thereby be drawn toward the present difficulties in medical discussion and statement : but, before any such exposition is commenced, it is necessary to say something, in general terms, concerning the confusion that now attends debate owing to persistent failure to distinguish between what I have elsewhere called Names, Notions and Happenings (*Influenza : Essays by Several Authors*, Heinemann, 1922), and the Authors of this book, Words, Thoughts and Things.

Medical men, in the daily practice of their Art, are, in the first place, concerned with the disorders of health that they observe, and are called upon to remedy, in respect of different persons.

Disorder of health is recognized by certain manifestations, usually called symptoms, which are at once appreciated by the sufferer and often by the observer. There are also others : of these, some, called ' physical signs,' require to be deliberately sought by the clinician, and the rest (of inferential or indirect importance only) involve recourse to the methods and appurtenances of the laboratory.

As, however, experience has outrun the limits of individual opportunity, it has long been convenient, for the purpose of ready reference and communication, to recognize the fact that, in different persons, like groups of manifestations of disorder of health occur and recur, by constructing certain *general references* in respect of these like groups. These *general references* constitute disease-concepts ; or, more simply, *diseases*, and are symbolized by *Names* which are, of course, the *Names of Diseases*. But, as time goes on, and the range and complexity of our experiences (or *referents*) extend, we find it necessary to revise our *references* and rearrange our groups of *referents*. Our symbolization is then necessarily involved and we have sometimes to devise a new symbol for a revised reference, while sometimes we retain an old symbol for what is really a new reference.

These processes are usually described as the discovery of a new disease, or the elucidation of the true nature of an old one, and when accurately, adequately, and correctly carried out are of very great advantage in practice, rendering available to all the increments in the personal experience of the few. But when, as so often happens, a *name* is illegitimately transferred from the *reference* it symbolizes to particular *referents*, confusion in thought and perhaps in practice is unavoidable.

Lately, it was reported that a distinguished medical man had declared bacteriologists to have recently shown influenza to be typhoid fever. What was said was, without doubt, that certain cases thought to be properly diagnosed as influenza have been shown, by bacteriological investigation, to be more correctly diagnosed as typhoid fever. But, in journalistic circles the pronouncement was at once taken to imply that the disease " influenza " is really the disease " typhoid fever," and an appropriate paragraph was prepared, trumpeting the discovery much in the way that it might have been announced that Mr Vincent Crummles really was a Prussian.

This anecdote illustrates, it is true, confusion prevailing in the lay mind; but it is a vulgar medical error to speak, write, and ultimately to think, as if these *diseases* we name, these *general references* we *symbolize*, were single things with external existences.

It is not to be thought that any educated medical man really believes ' a disease ' to be a material thing, although the phraseology in current use lends colour to such supposition.

Nevertheless, in hospital jargon, ' diseases ' are ' morbid entities,' and medical students fondly believe that these ' entities ' somehow exist *in rebus Naturæ* and were discovered by their teachers much as was America by Columbus.

Teachers of Medicine, on the other hand, seem to share the implied belief that all known, or knowable, clinical phenomena are resumable, and to be resumed, under a certain number of categories or general references, as so many ' diseases ': the true number of these categories, references, or ' diseases ' being predetermined by the constitution of the universe at any given moment.

In fact, for these gentlemen, ' diseases ' are Platonic realities: universals *ante rem*. This unavowed belief, which might be condoned were it frankly admitted, is an inheritance from Galen, and carries with it the corollary that our notions concerning this, that, or the other ' disease ' are either absolutely right or absolutely wrong, and are not merely matters of mental convenience. In this way, the diseases supposed to be extant at any one moment are capable—so it is thought—of such categorical exhaustion as are the indigenous fauna of the British Isles and the population of London. That our grouping of like cases as cases of the same disease is purely a matter of justification and convenience, liable at any moment to supersession or adjustment, is nowhere admitted; and the hope is held out that one day we shall know all the diseases that there ' are,' and all about them that is to be known.

In the meantime, so prevalent has become the vice or habit of considering ' diseases ' as realities in the vulgar sense of the word, that no adverse comment was excited when, lately, in an official document (*Forty-eighth Ann. Rep. Local Govt. Board*, 1918-19, Med. Supplement, p. 76) it was said that " in the short experience of encephalitis lethargica in this country it is already apparent that its biological properties are altering . . ."

That this attribution of " biological properties " to a disease was no mere *lapsus calami* is attested by the fact that the phrase was somewhat complacently repeated, by the author himself, in the *Annual Report of the Chief Medical Officer of the Ministry of Health*, 1919-20, on p. 366.

To elaborate any warning against the use, in official publications, of such absurdly ' realist ' forms of expression as this would seem, in view of what has been so cogently said by Sir Clifford Allbutt, to be superfluous, at least. Yet warning is necessary when we find one who has done such yeoman service as Sir James Mackenzie declaring that " disease is only revealed by the symptoms it produces." Disease, and diseases, say the realists, must be ' realities ' if they are agents that produce symptoms. So, Sir James Mackenzie, who has so powerfully insisted on the importance of investigating *symptoms*, and who has so strongly protested against our subordination to the tyranny of mere *names*, becomes the unconscious ally of those who engage in a hunt for a mysterious *substantia* that has ' biological properties ' and ' produces ' symptoms.

In modern Medicine this tyranny of names is no less pernicious than is the modern form of scholastic realism. Diagnosis, which, as Mr Bernard Shaw has somewhere declared, should mean the finding out of all there is wrong with a particular patient and why, too often means in practice the formal and unctuous pronunciation of a Name that is deemed appropriate and absolves from the necessity of further investigation. And, in the long run, an accurate appreciation of a patient's " present state " is often treated as ignorant *because* it is incompatible with the sincere use of one of the few verbal symbols available to us as Proper Names for Special Diseases.

In this connection allusion may be made to the enforced use of certain verbal symbols by the Army during the late War.

By the judicious use, under compulsion, and at proper times, of such linguistic accessories as P.U.O. (pyrexia of unknown origin) and N.Y.D. (not yet diagnosed) the inconvenient appearance in official reports of unwelcome diagnoses could always be avoided, and a desirable belief in the absence of certain kinds of illness could easily be propagated. No doubt, for official purposes, some uniformity of practice in the use of symbols is necessary ; but it should not be forgotten that official statistics, which, in theory, should reveal to us what happens, or has happened in the field of clinical experience are, in fact, little more than analyses of the frequency with which certain forms or usages in

symbolization have occurred. And this criticism has even more force when it is remembered that official statistics often bear reference to symbolization for which no official practice—correct or arbitrary—has been defined. Thus, the Ministry of Health has, during the last few years, published statistical tables hailed as showing the different kinds of prevalence in successive years and at different seasons, of what is called *encephalitis lethargica*, and the difference between these prevalences and those of certain 'analogous diseases.'

Now the true lesson to be drawn from these statistics is not that the 'biological properties' of any of these 'diseases' is changing, but that medical men are symbolizing various clinical happenings, in different way at sundry times, and in divers places, and that the practice of the same doctor, in this respect, has changed since 1918 in response to change in his notions concerning the group of 'analogous diseases' in question.

In a word, medical statistics relate to the usage of symbols for general references, whether or no the symbolization is correct and the references adequate, rather than to things, occurrences, or happenings. They have no necessary value, other than as analyses of symbol-frequency, unless the relation of the symbols to the reference and of the reference to the referents be agreed *after* that process of discussion, so abhorrent to the medical mind, and so generally stigmatized as unprofitable word-chopping. Yet surely, if we desire analyses of notifications of disease to be accepted as evidence *of what has happened* in the clinical field, we must act as good accountants, and compare the records in the books with the cash in hand and the evidences of actual transactions.

Related to the question of statistical values is that of Research, when paid for or subsidized by the State, and controlled or directed by Official Bodies. In principle, such research nearly always takes the ostensible form of Investigation into Diseases.

Now without doubt, sincere official investigation into the nature and relation of the general references we call 'diseases' would be productive of some good, but what the public imagine and desire is inquiry into what *happens*. It is not suggested that, in practice, such inquiry is entirely omitted : yet, too often what takes place, and what reflects the greatest official lustre upon the investigators, is neither inquiry into *diseases* nor into *happenings*, but something as little useful as would be an investigation into the Causes of Warfare, by a Committee of Intelligence Officers devoting themselves to an Examination of Prisoners captured in the Trenches and a Description of their Arms and Accoutrements.

Something visible, like a bullet, is what brings conviction to the minds of ' practical men ' ; and so, when epidemiologists discuss certain general references, that they call ' epidemic constitutions,' hard-headed and practical investigators call for the production of one such, on a plate or charger, like the head of a John the Baptist (cf. Sir Thomas Horder : *Brit. Med. Journal*, 1920, i., p. 235).

Over and above all this, the emotive use of language so sways the intellect that phrases suggesting the ' real ' existence of diseases as single objects of perception lead doctors to think as if these diseases were to be kept away by barbed-wire entanglements, or ' stamped out ' by physical agencies ruthlessly employed. And we not merely hypostatize, but personify these abstractions, going on to speak of the " fell enemy of the human race which is attacking our shores " whenever a change in meteorological conditions lowers the resistance of the population to their normal parasites, and coughs and colds abound in consequence.

Then there is inevitable reaction, and some perverse sceptic, without thinking what he means, declares ' Influenza ' to be but a label, whilst another, thinking confusedly, maintains ' it ' to be, not a disease, but a syndrome, or symptom-group.

It thus happens that, in the course of debate (on, for example, Influenza) by one the *name* will be treated as a mere *flatus vocis*, by another as the *name* of some *general reference*, vague or defined, and by a third as the *name* of some object with external and ' real,' if not material, existence.

None of the disputants will discuss the correctness of the symbolization involved, or the adequacy of the reference, whilst someone is sure to imply that positive or negative facts alleged in respect of ' Influenza ' can be proved or disproved by examination of two or three ' cases ' known to be ' cases ' of Influenza, a disease which, *ex hypothesi*, has properties and qualities as definite as the height of Mount Everest or the weight of a pound of lead, and only requiring discovery and mensuration by properly accredited experts.

Any call for definition is met by citation of John Hunter's dictum that definitions are of all things the most damnable : any demand for precision in language or in thought, by the asseveration that Medicine is ***not*** an exact science.

On this point at least, there is general agreement.

But, are we content to leave the matter thus ? Ought we to be content so to leave it ? Are we to acquiesce in the implication that thoughtfulness need be no part of the equipment of the physician ? Surely, to the thinker, the right use of words is as essential a part of his technique as is, to the bacteriologist, the right use of the platinum loop or the pipette ; and there should be no need for shame in acknowledging that thought, and the expression of thought, require an apprenticeship no less severe than do the cutting of sections and the manipulation of a capillary tube. Yet, while there are not a few manuals of laboratory technique, for the use of medical students, there is none devoted to the elucidation of the fundamental principles of Medicine, and of fundamental errors in thought and communication.

Under these circumstances it seemed to the present writer a year or two ago that some useful end might be served if he attempted to clear up some of the sources of confusion, already indicated, by writing in terms of the great scholastic controversy, pointing out how to-day the Scholastic Nominalist is represented by the sceptic who says ' Influenza ' is only a name, and the Scholastic Realist by him who teaches Influenza to be a ' morbid entity.'

One or two essays were therefore written, which have been since reprinted, wherein it was suggested that safety lay in the adoption of the Conceptualist position ascribed to William of Occam in the *Encyclopædia Britannica* (11th ed., arts. ' Occam ' and ' Scholasticism.') There (Vol. 24, p. 355) we are told that " the hypostatizing of abstractions is the error against which Occam is continually fighting ": that for him " the universal is no more than a mental concept signifying univocally several singulars " and " has no reality beyond that of the mental act by which it is produced, and that of the singulars of which it is predicated."

Now, for us who are doctors, the universals with which we are most concerned are those *general references* that we call special diseases, and our frequent singulars are the symptoms and ' cases ' that we observe, so that this hypostatizing of abstractions is the very error against which Sir Clifford Allbutt has ever fought, while the spirit that inspired Occam—" a spirit which distrusts abstractions, which makes for direct observation, for inductive research '—is the spirit that still informs the work of all true clinical physicians. This spirit is the spirit of Hippocrates himself, who " described symptoms in persons and not symptoms drawn to correspond with certain ideal forms of disease" (Adams). But our modern ' researchers ' far outstrip in their unconscious realism the philosophy of their unavowed Master,

Galen the great Neoplatonist, and describe entities at which even he would have jibbed, without scruple or misgiving.

However, even if we avoid the fallacies of the realists, we must none the less avoid contenting ourselves with the mere collecting of singulars on the one hand, and assenting idly, on the other, to some of those inconveniences of conceptualist expression that have been pointed out in this book (vide supra, pp. 99-100). It may be that some of these latter arise from the lack of expertness of amateur expositors (amongst whom the present writer would include himself) rather than from any weakness inherent in Conceptualism ; but they may be acknowledged, and common cause may be made with the Authors in their attempt to provide a more excellent way.

Now, although it is not proposed, in what follows, to express in the terms of these Authors the difficulties which (to write emotively) beset the path of the thinking physician, it is hoped, by the exposition of a special case, to reinforce, from the point of view of a physician, what has been said by them in their plea for the general adoption of a Theory of Symbols.

The special case which will now be stated is that which has been already mentioned as having definitely directed the attention of the present writer, a few years ago, to the questions discussed in this book ; and it is felt that, whether or no the views held by him as to the true solution of the difficulties are valid, the difficulties themselves will not disappear unless the basic issues are first made plain in the light of a Theory of Signs and a Critique of the Use of Language.

Some eighty years ago, an orthopædic surgeon named Heine, practising near Stuttgart, observed the affliction of a number of young children by a form of palsy of one or more limbs, that came on more or less acutely and that was followed by wasting and marked disability. This kind of illness had been earlier recognized by others, but had never been so well described as by Heine. Heine's account attracting general attention, and his observations being generally confirmed, a definite general reference, or ' disease,' became acknowledged, to which, in England, the name ' Infantile Spinal Paralysis ' was attached, it being admitted that the palsy and wasting were dependent upon lesion of the spinal cord. Further experience, and the examination of the spinal cord in cases that died some time after the onset of the palsy, extended our knowledge of the cases, and the symptoms were definitely connoted with lesions of what are called the anterior horns of the grey matter of the cord. The lesions were regarded as, in the beginning, of the nature of an acute inflammation, and the extended clinico-pathological concept was symbolized by the expression ' Acute Anterior Poliomyelitis.'

Many years later, Medin, a Swede who had made extensive observations in practice, showed conclusively that cases of the kind thus indicated occurred in association with each other, or, epidemically, and also in epidemic association with other cases whereof the symptoms were cerebral and due to lesions situate in the brain.

Medin's pupil, Wickman, carried observation still further. He recognized the epidemic association of cases of the nature described by Heine and Medin with cases of yet other clinical types, all manifesting disordered function of some part of the central nervous system. More than this, he showed that in different years, or in different epidemics, different types of case prevailed, though all cases agreed in *the general nature* of the lesions found at post-mortem examination.

To the broad general reference that his clinical genius allowed him to construct, resuming a wide range of cases of different clinical aspect depending on the different localization of the acute process in the nervous system, he gave the name of Heine-Medin Disease.

In later work he broadened the base of even this great synthetic concept, pointing out that, at the onset cases of Heine-Medin Disease (as conceived by him) frequently manifested acute catarrhal (or influenza-like) symptoms and occurred in close association with other cases of acute catarrhal nature that did not manifest any signs of nervous disorder. These cases he regarded as 'abortive' cases of Heine-Medin Disease.

But Wickman proceeded too fast: for, in England, where even yet his work, and that of Medin, have been insufficiently studied, it was said that a case of nervous disorder due to inflammation of the brain could not possibly be one of Acute Anterior Poliomyelitis, which, as all the world knows, is a Disease affecting a limited portion only of the spinal cord!

Talk about a new disease, called Heine-Medin's, was regarded as a rather unworthy attempt on the part of some foreigners to detract from the prestige of English observers who had adopted the views current before Medin and Wickman began their researches. Clearly, it was said, their cerebral cases must be cases of quite another disease, one which attacks the brain, and *not* the spinal cord. The name Acute Polio-encephalitis was then devised, to meet the situation, in spite of Strümpell's earlier warnings against any such unnecessary multiplication of diseases. The maintenance of this purely artificial distinction between what may be called the two ends of the Heine-Medin spectrum was later urged when it was found that the experimental reproduction of symptoms and lesions in monkeys (as a result of inoculation of those animals with portions of diseased tissues from man) was less successful when the inoculated matter was taken from brains than when from spinal cords. Later still, the separate notification by practitioners of cases of 'Acute Poliomyelitis' and 'Acute Polio-encephalitis' was required, and so little was the work of Wickman appreciated even in 1918, that Sir Arthur Newsholme, then Chief Medical Officer to the Local Government Board, wrote of "the many forms of the disease—or group of diseases—to which nosologists at present attach the indiscriminate label 'Heine-Medinische Krankheit.'"

(*Report of an Inquiry into an Obscure Disease, Encephalitis Lethargica :* Reports to the Local Government Board on Public Health and Medical Subjects, New Series, No. 121.)

Even now separate notification of these two 'entities' is required, though no guidance is afforded to the practitioner as to his course of action when, as so frequently happens, symptoms of involvement of both spinal cord and brain are present at the same time.

But to turn back. Before the Great War physicians in the United States began to recognize whole series of cases and epidemics of the nature so faithfully described by Wickman, and so ill understood in England. These epidemics culminated in the vast prevalence in and about New York known as the great epidemic of 1916.

All the characteristics resumed by Wickman in his great general reference, and symbolized by him as Heine-Medin Disease, were at this time recognized and studied by the American physicians, but, unfortunately, the name 'Acute Poliomyelitis' was retained, apparently on the *lucus a non lucendo* principle, since lesions were described, not only in the grey but in the white matter of the brain and spinal cord.

Happily the ridiculous attempt to discriminate between Poliomyelitis' and 'Polio-encephalitis' was not made.

The American physicians, however, except in symbolization, went even further than did Wickman ; and Dr Draper, perhaps the ablest of the commentators, in *Acute Poliomyelitis* defined his concept as one of a general infectious disease in the course of which paralysis is an accidental and incidental occurrence, adding that, though the nervous system is not always involved, when it is the lesions may affect almost any part thereof (cf. Ruhräh and Mayer, *Poliomyelitis in all its Aspects*, 1917).

Draper's conception, far wider than even that of Wickman, is, so far as it goes, absolutely justified when the assembled experiences are considered.

The only doubt (and it is one which I know Dr Draper himself shares with me) is whether a still wider reference, or synthetic concept, is not required if certain observations in the clinical field, more recent than those of 1916, are to be adequately dealt with.

However this may be (and the point will be discussed) the retention by the American physicians of a quite incorrect *symbolization* was- very unfortunate. For we Englishry were, in 1916-17, too busy to think accurately, and, hearing that, in New York, there was a certain epidemic called poliomyelitis, with manifestations quite other than those we were accustomed to identify by that name, we put down many of the accounts received as due to New World phantasies.

Indeed, in 1918, one of our most eminent authorities told me that, from personal experience in New York in 1916, he could vouch that most of the cases put down as poliomyelitis (in Draper's sense, that is) were nothing but influenza ! This statement was made as a sort of *reductio ad absurdum*, but my informant did not know that for years Brorström abroad, and Hamer at home, had been maintaining poliomyelitis (in the old sense) to be a manifestation of the incidence of influenza on the nervous system.

Now, late in 1917, and early in 1918, the present writer (who at that moment was enjoying rather unusual opportunity for the study of disease *en masse*) began to notice the occurrence of peculiar cases of nervous and influenza-like nature which led him to make first the forecast that 1918 was to be a year of pestilence, and then that we were about to experience an epidemic of Heine-Medin Disease of the cerebral, or 'polio-encephalitic' type.

As a matter of fact, shortly afterwards, nearly all the 'types' of Heine-Medin Disease described by Wickman were to be identified in London, although the cerebral forms prevailed (Crookshank, *Lancet*, 1918, i., pp. 653, 699, 751).

But, unfortunately, this prevalence *as a whole* was overlooked, and attention was focussed upon a relatively small number of cases with intense symptoms of unfamiliar type, which were at first thought to be cases of what is called 'botulism' and (it was hinted) due to poisoning by food-stuffs sent from Germany with evil intent. Now the history of the concept symbolized as 'botulism' is, in itself, fantastic beyond belief, and deserves examination.

It is possible that it is valid, and adequate, for a certain number of experiences, or referents : but that is another story. What is known is that the name 'botulism' has been repeatedly applied to cases which, although corresponding *clinically* to the description given of cases of botulism, yet have nothing to do with poisoning by the products of the kind of bacillus called *B. botulinus*—the conceptual cause of botulism.

Whether or no such a form of poisoning is ever met with in the field of experience is here neither affirmed nor denied, but it is now everywhere admitted that the peculiar cerebral cases of the spring of 1918 already alluded to had nothing in the world to do with this famous bacillus and its products, mythical or existent. Before, however, the false diagnosis of botulism had been abandoned, I had expressed the view that these cases fell within the ambit of the Heine-Medin Disease, or *general reference*, and represented as it were an extreme 'type' of that 'disease.' This view was adopted by the late Sir William Osler, and also (though with some degree of reticence) by Dr Draper, who, on service in France at the time, was asked to report on the subject. My own ideas, elaborated later in 1918, when in the Chadwick lectures I traced the growth of the Heine-Medin concept and showed its applicability with but little extension to the cases in question, met with little public support, for the Local Government Board, rapidly abandoning the attribution to botulism, found out that one Von Economo, an Austrian alienist, had described cases of the same nature a year earlier as cases of a 'new disease': *encephalitis lethargica.* This name had been chosen because lethargy was a prominent symptom, and an inflammation of parts of the brain a prominent lesion.

Since the English cases at first called 'botulism' corresponded closely to those seen by Von Economo, it was felt that they *were* cases of the disease he had described ; in accordance with the maxim of Pangloss that things cannot be otherwise than as they are. It was also felt that they could not be cases of poliomyelitis —for reasons already indicated. Sir Arthur Newsholme's slighting references to Heine-Medin Disease were balanced by the suggestion of one of his assistants that many cases thought in the past to be cases of that malady were really cases of encephalitis lethargica, although Sir Arthur had also said that the cases in question *did* " come within the wide limits of the commonly accepted definition of the Heine-Medin disease " (*Report of an Inquiry into an Obscure Disease*, etc., pp. 2, 36).

Encephalitis lethargica it had to be then, and so that entity was created, and *another* notifiable disease added to the list of ' analogous diseases ' headed by Acute Poliomyelitis and Polio-encephalitis.

It was wickedly hinted, however, that the only way in which these ' Protean ' diseases, that so annoyingly mimicked each other, could be definitely distinguished was by the different official forms on which they were to be notified !

Perhaps this gibe was hardly fair, for the official authorities certainly said that poliomyelitis occurs in the summer, attacks children, and implicates the spinal cord, while encephalitis lethargica occurs in the winter, attacks adults, and involves a certain portion of the brain ; and this attempt at distinction seems still to be maintained, though it has been said that " the arbitrary differentiation of *polio-encephalitis* as a notifiable disease has proved a useful measure and has provided a sort of half-way house for borderland cases " (*Report C.M.O. to the Minister of Health*, 1920, p. 64).

It would appear that the general reference ' polio-encephalitis ' is then maintained to provide a half-way house for cases that will not fit into other categories—surely, an admission of their inadequacy—in spite of the earlier admission that ' its cause ' is the same as that of poliomyelitis (*Annual Report of C.M.O. to the Minister of Health*, 1919-20, p. 260).

But the practical difficulty that, in spite of official rulings, it is often quite impossible logically to assign a case to either of the two categories—poliomyelitis and encephalitis lethargica—for some spinal cases occur in the winter and sometimes in adults, while some cerebral cases occur in the summer and not infrequently in children—has been resolved with great acceptance by Dr Netter of Paris, an ardent upholder of belief in separate ' entities.'

Netter explains away the fact that the cases are less easily differentiated than are the official descriptions, by averring that the two diseases mimic each other and that there is a poliomyelitic form of encephalitis and an encephalitic form of poliomyelitis ; thus honouring once more the philosophy of Pangloss. But Netter's solution seems as truly helpful as the classification of a heap of playing-cards into ' red court ' and ' black plain.'

On finding the king of spades, instead of admitting that an untenable classification had been set up, one could easily say that a ' red court ' of the ' black ' type had been found, and would claim the position to be strengthened by the finding of the two of diamonds—clearly a ' black plain ' of the ' red ' type. This is the logic of Medicine to-day.

It is not to be wondered at that, under the circumstances, confusion is becoming worse confounded ; that doctors notify cases in whatever terms they please, and that the officials of the Ministry of Health are reduced to explaining the disconcerting uncertainty of their statistics by alleging a change in the biological properties of a disease!

More troublesome still, there is the unwelcome task of disposing, statistically, the cases of 'encephalitis lethargica' which refuse to display lethargy!

The really serious aspect, however, of the present state of uncertainty and confusion arising from the reluctance to face fundamental questions and to discuss what is meant by 'a disease,' is this, that observation is hampered, communication is difficult, discussion useless, and generalization impossible. And, in a large measure, the blame attaches to official investigators who, taking charge of affairs in 1918, did not properly set out to investigate *the whole* of the relevant circumstances, *the whole pack of cards*, but confined their attention to the cases attracting most attention, *the cards that lay uppermost*. They should have *first* discussed all available referents; but, as the title of the official report shows—*An Inquiry into an Obscure Disease, Encephalitis Lethargica*—the real question at issue was begged from the first. It was *assumed* that there were two existent entities—Poliomyelitis and Encephalitis Lethargica—and the investigators then proceeded to inquire whether or no these entities were 'the same,' finally concluding that they were not. No one, of course, disputes the difference between the two *references*, but the official investigators did not discuss the adequacy of the two references in respect of the referents, or the advantages of maintaining (as some of us proposed) the single reference symbolized as Heine-Medin Disease. Had the latter course been followed, we should have been spared the melancholy spectacle of men of science distinguishing specifically between three 'entities' by regarding each as characterized by a special feature sometimes present to all (Crookshank, *British Medical Journal*, 1920, ii., 916). Yet so it was: and, by a report on the designs of the queen of clubs and two of hearts we were called upon to know the characters of the two groups: the 'red court' and the 'black plain'!

And so, those of us who, casting the eye as it were over *all* the cases in a prevalence, see order, gradation, and continuity, as well as the need for *cross-referencing* amongst all the members of a series, are treated with as much disdain as if we declared one end of the spectrum to be the same as the other! We desire to bring our experiences under as few general references as are possible and are compatible with practical working in communication: we are told that we are confusing separate entities, diseases that are analogous but *sui generis*, and *not* the same! Moreover, our offence is the more heinous in that we have come to see that the physicians of the 16th century were right in maintaining with Brorström and Hamer of to-day, that the nervous cases brought by Wickman under the Heine-Medin reference, together with those called 'Encephalitis Lethargica' by the Ministry of Health, *occur epidemically at the times when the respiratory and gastro-intestinal catarrhs that we call Influenza abound* (Cf. *op. cit.*, *Influenza: Essays by Several Authors*).

It is unthinkable, say in effect the officials, that Influenza, Poliomyelitis, Polio-encephalitis and Encephalitis Lethargica, should all be " the same "! The cases *we* call influenza are *not* those we call by any of the other names, and we can trace no relation between the cases we call by these different names except those of time and space! (Cf. *Rep. C.M.O. to Min. of Health*, 1919-20, p. 48.)

It is, however, only fair to state that, in a more recent document (*Min. of Health: Reps. on Pub. Health, etc.*, *No.* 11, *Encephalitis Lethargica*) it is no longer suggested that, in 1918, we were present at the birth of a new disease; that of a new conception is spoken of instead. But, is there a difference? And after all, scholastic realism comes to the front again, for Prof. MacIntosh's dictum that " encephalitis lethargica is a disease . . . *distinct from analogous affections* " is quoted with approval (*loc. cit.*, p. 126), while the *British Medical Journal* (1922, ii., p. 654) declares the report in question to show that encephalitis lethargica and poliomyelitis have *separate identity!*

It may be asked, does anyone who writes thus mean *only* that the concepts are *different?* We admit so much: but we question their validity, or adequacy. Their validity and adequacy appear even more gravely perilled than before, when the official apologist goes on to write of certain cases and epidemics in Australia in 1917-18, which some of us would bring under the Heine-Medin umbrella, but which do not correspond to any one of the favoured official references. The Ministry of Health's representative, abandoning for the nonce all talk of Protean characteristics, changing biological properties, and half-way houses, declares that the Australian " condition appears to be quite distinct from " encephalitis lethargica, and (presumably) from all other entities, separate identities, analogous affections and diseases *sui generis*. So that, again unafraid of Occam's razor, once more are entities multiplied without necessity.

Moreover, the retention of the symbol ' Encephalitis Lethargica ' for a reference which, whatever its constitution for the moment, has to serve for referents which are frequently not lethargic and are usually more than encephalitic, is itself admitted to require justification. The retention of this name, we are told, is justified by right of primogeniture and the " fortune of illustrious parentage ": by its " clothing the concept in the language which is common to scientists of all countries "; and " partly, perhaps, for euphonious reasons " (*Ibid.*, p. 1).

Perhaps, when Medicine is again a Science, we shall require something more than ' euphonious reasons ' from our officials when discussing the accuracy of symbolizations, but one excellent example of ' euphonious reasoning ' must here be given. It is this: that " no reliable evidence is forthcoming in favour of the identity of influenza and encephalitis lethargica."

Here, though we have not the faintest indication of the sense in which the official writer uses the words ' influenza ' and encephalitis lethargica '—though we know not whether he has in mind the names (symbols) or the concepts (references)—we may be in agreement with him. It is unthinkable that there should be reliable evidence in favour of the *identity* of *different* names, concepts, or happenings.

I would as soon believe in the identity of the two ends of a stick. Nevertheless, though I fully and frankly admit that one end of the stick is not the other ; is in fact distinct from it (even though 'analogous' thereto) ; has separate identity, and is an end *sui generis*, I know that I shall fail to advance appreciation, in official quarters, of a point of view which, though possibly impolitic, is at any rate not intrinsically irrational.

It seems clear then that, under the conditions of discussion imposed by present habits of thought and expression, debate is little profitable : at any rate, in Medicine.

Ultimately, no doubt, the pressure of collective experience will lead to the formation of fairly sound and workable, though unscientifically constructed and chosen, references and symbols concerning all the clinical and epidemiological happenings here alluded to : that is, if common sense be not, as usual, overborne by pseudo-science and mere jargon.

But there should be, and is, a better and more speedy way :—namely, to make up our minds *at the beginning* concerning the questions treated of in the present volume.

It was with some such purpose as that of the Authors of this Theory of Signs that, six or seven years ago, the present writer, at a meeting of the Epidemiological Section of the Royal Society of Medicine, attempted to expound the distinction between Names, Notions and Happenings, or (as may otherwise be said) between Words, Thoughts and Things. He met with but scant applause, and was told by one of our most distinguished medical administrators that only a Christian Scientist could doubt the reality of Toothache, for example. He had it at the time of speaking, he said, and so was quite sure about it. After this, the debate came to an end, but the paper then read has been reprinted in the book of essays on *Influenza* to which reference has been already made, together with some further attempted elucidation of the questions at issue.

There can be no doubt of the importance to Medicine, if Medicine is to resume her place amongst the Sciences, of the further exploration of these issues by some such way of approach as that sought by the present writer, and far more ably considered by Mr Ogden and Mr Richards.

The object of this note will have been attained if, by the presentation of a living problem of to-day, the necessity to Medicine of a Theory of Signs, is brought home to her Professors and Practitioners, but it is hoped that, in a future volume in this Library, it may be possible to include a study of the whole subject under the title of *The Theory of Medical Diagnosis*.

In the meantime, however, Dr Simon Flexner, the celebrated investigator and authority, of the Rockefeller Institute, nailing his labels to the mast, declares himself, in the *American Journal of the Medical Sciences* for April 1926, " as one holding the view that epidemic influenza and epidemic encephalitis are *distinct entities*."

INDEX OF SUBJECTS

INDEX OF NAMES